About Island Press

Island Press is the only nonprofit organization in the United States whose principal purpose is the publication of books on environmental issues and natural resource management. We provide solutions-oriented information to professionals, public officials, business and community leaders, and concerned citizens who are shaping responses to environmental problems.

In 2002, Island Press celebrates its eighteenth anniversary as the leading provider of timely and practical books that take a multidisciplinary approach to critical environmental concerns. Our growing list of titles reflects our commitment to bringing the best of an expanding body of literature to the environmental community throughout North America and the world.

Support for Island Press is provided by The Nathan Cummings Foundation, Geraldine R. Dodge Foundation, Doris Duke Charitable Foundation, Educational Foundation of America, The Charles Engelhard Foundation, The Ford Foundation, The George Gund Foundation, The Vira I. Heinz Endowment, The William and Flora Hewlett Foundation, Henry Luce Foundation, The John D. and Catherine T. MacArthur Foundation, The Andrew W. Mellon Foundation, The Moriah Fund, The Curtis and Edith Munson Foundation, National Fish and Wildlife Foundation, The New-Land Foundation, Oak Foundation, The Overbrook Foundation, The David and Lucile Packard Foundation, The Pew Charitable Trusts, The Rockefeller Foundation, The Winslow Foundation, and other generous donors.

The opinions expressed in this book are those of the author(s) and do not necessarily reflect the views of these foundations.

Rocky Mountain
FUTURES

Rocky Mountain
FUTURES

▲

An Ecological Perspective

Edited by Jill S. Baron

Foreword by Paul R. Ehrlich

ISLAND PRESS

Washington • Covelo • London

Library of Congress Cataloguing-in-Publication Data
Rocky Mountain futures : an ecological perspective / edited by
Jill S. Baron.
    p. cm.
Includes bibliographical references and index.
ISBN 1-55963-953-9 (acid-free paper)—ISBN
1-55963-954-7 (pbk. : acid-free paper) 1. Rocky Mountains—Envi-
ronmental conditions. 2. Nature—Effect of human beings on—Rocky
Mountains.
I. Baron, Jill.
    GE160.R58 R63 2002
    333.73'0978—dc21   2002007978

British Cataloguing-in-Publication Data available

Printed on recycled, acid-free paper ✵
Manufactured in the United States of America
09 08 07 06 05 04 03 02   8 7 6 5 4 3 2 1

For Claire and Kyle:

may they have the vision to take the broad and historic view,

to see the whole as well as all the parts;

and for Dennis, who already does.

Contents

▲

List of Figures

▲

List of Plates

▲

List of Tables

▲

List of Boxes

▲

Rocky Mountain High

Paul R. Ehrlich

▲

This wide-ranging assessment of the Rocky Mountain region, from its landforms and climate to the history of human influence on its ecosystems, does justice to the area's extraordinary diversity, richness, and beauty. Reading *Rocky Mountain Futures* took me back to one of my first romances. I fell in love with the Rockies when I first saw them in 1947. I was fifteen, and I well remember the thrill of catching my first *Parnassius* butterfly on a slope above Alamosa and then being caught in a thunderstorm and seeing a tree explode in a flash and puff of steam less than 100 yards from me. But my real love affair started in the summer of 1959 at the Rocky Mountain Biological Laboratory (RMBL), in the former ghost town of Gothic, where my wife, Anne, and I have done research every summer but two since. The area is not just incredibly beautiful but also a marvelous place for our group's research. Butterflies are the test system my colleagues and I use to unravel the mysteries of ecology and evolution, and the area around Gothic has the richest butterfly fauna in the United States. Above treeline it hosts representatives of the arctic-alpine species I worked with as a kid in the far Arctic, and on the valley floor species can be found with semi-tropical affinities. Besides butterflies, I have fond memories of RMBL-based studies on the keystone role in mountain ecosystems of sapsuckers (woodpeckers that create and maintain sap wells in trees, from which they harvest a sugary diet supplement); the ecology of monument

Paul R. Ehrlich is Bing Professor of Population Studies and president of the Center for Conservation Biology, Department of Biological Science, Stanford University.

plants; and the use of fly communities in conservation planning. And, of course, the area is a wonderful outdoor laboratory for many other kinds of biological research as well a picture book of geologic information.

RMBL, with its community of fine researchers, is emotionally our home. Anne and I built a cabin there at 9,600 feet on an aspen-covered slope above the lab, and many scientific friends have lived at the lab and collaborated with us over the years. The cabin has wonderful views of Gothic Mountain from one set of windows and Mount Crested Butte from another. From our cozy retreat we have watched with interest, and horror, as our "backyard" has metamorphosed over the past half-century in just the ways this book documents and seeks to address.

RMBL is six miles north, up the East River valley, from the town of Crested Butte. When we arrived, CB had a few hundred residents, a small grocery, a hamburger joint, a shit-kicking bar, a dirt main street, and Tony's Conoco station. It had once been a coal-mining town, but the mine had closed a decade earlier and the railroad had pulled out. The nearest supermarket and laundry were in Gunnison, twenty-eight miles farther south. "Development" seemed the last thing on anyone's mind. Tourists were few and butterflies were abundant—it was a researcher's paradise. True wilderness, of course, was scarce. Cow pies already littered the landscape, making the lab stink to high heaven in fall (the cows and rains often arrived at that altitude about the same time). But the area almost *felt* like wilderness—on the good side of the middle ground between the familiar messes of Philadelphia, Lawrence, Kansas, and Stanford and the magnificence of the Canadian Arctic and Alaska.

Tony turned out to be a wonderful man from the coal-mining era. He became a friend, and he died only recently, having worked at his gas station–hardware store well into his nineties. When, in the early 1960s, a halfway decent restaurant opened up as well as a booze-free night spot that welcomed "the Brothers Four," most people at the lab were happy, and many of us began to make more friends in the growing town. We could go into CB after a hard day in the field, have a cup of fancy coffee, and listen to (sometimes) good music. Little did we realize what was to follow.

First came the ski area, built on the road to Gothic. "Civilization" was starting to creep toward the lab in the form of ugly and badly built development (rumor has it that one of the worst-looking condo units had the same architect as Hitler's West Wall). The view of Mount Crested Butte from our rustic cabin was polluted with reflections from the shiny metal of ski lifts. People fleeing the summer hells of Texas and Oklahoma were soon trying to drive their mobile homes—locally called "rolling sties"—up the Gothic road past the lab. We were torn between hatred for our decreased isolation and pleasure in knowing that Texans and Oklahomans valued what the Rockies could offer.

The ski area went bankrupt a time or two, but Crested Butte was gradually transformed as more and more easterners, many of them hippies, sought refuge in the mountains. More restaurants and a funky movie theater opened, a small camera-and-book store was established, and streets were paved. Gradually our need to travel to Gunnison to find amenities disappeared. It was a pleasant, if worrying, trend for people who liked isolation and wilderness but did not want to camp out for months at a time. And it provided one great conservation benefit as people from the town and the lab united to defeat an attempt to destroy the entire area with a giant molybdenum mining complex. A more sophisticated local population has also added strength to Gunnison County's attempt to fend off water grabs to service runaway urbanization on the slopes of Colorado's Front Range.

Gradually, though, the worries replaced the pleasures. More and more sleazy souvenir shops opened. A multiplex replaced the funky theater. Restaurants proliferated. Tourists in thousand-dollar ersatz cowboy outfits drove around in shiny, overequipped off-road vehicles that had never so much as departed from the asphalt. CB evolved into Carmel in the Cordillera, in a more beautiful spot than Aspen but exuding the same fake western atmosphere. And as CB became a summer-and-winter tourist attraction, the suburbs began to sprawl. In the ski area, enormously expensive and enormously ugly trophy homes sprouted everywhere, on small lots and each with a panoramic view of the other atrocities. The same happened south of CB on the road to Gunnison. Meadows where our research group had marked and released butterflies to build an understanding of the population biology of herbivorous insects (perhaps humanity's biggest competitors for food), and aspen groves that had been central to our studies of the intricacy of the ecological relationships of red-naped sapsuckers with swallows, willows, and a fungus that attacks aspens, disappeared under fancy subdivisions. RMBL and the local ranchers, previously sometimes on different sides of environmental issues, began to make common cause against the rampant development that threatened to destroy the things ranchers and researchers most valued in the area.

With the increase of development and tourist interest, attempts by the USDA Forest Service to control activities escalated, sometimes with the agency's classic "Land of Many Abuses" policies, later with more reasoned efforts to deal with conflicting goals, directives, and needs. The results for our research were mixed—we were forbidden to write small numbers on rocks to help plot butterfly movements because the meadow was part of a wilderness area. Fair enough. But because of significant underfunding of the Forest Service on the western slope (not enough voters!), there was not sufficient patrolling to prevent unleashed dogs from disrupting the work or to keep a bulldozer from widening a road, at the expense of the meadow, to provide better access to a gold-mine claim. And more subtle changes connected with ever-escalating human activities decreased the quality of our lives. When in the field, we could no longer drink from any stream we wished as the nasty parasite *Giardia* became ubiquitous even in snowmelt. Whirling disease removed the joy of fishing after a long day of research. And chronic wasting disease of deer and elk lessened our interest in eating the meat served to us by hunting friends.

Of course, we were viewing in a microcosm what is so well described in this excellent book, which could well serve as a model for projecting the future of other regions. In our vastly overpopulated and overconsuming country, one of the last areas where people might seek beauty and solitude, the wonderful Rocky Mountain region, is being overoccupied. In the process, people are destroying what many go there to find. And, not surprisingly, people have not even tackled the very difficult task of building a consensus on exactly what they should be seeking. Even conservation biologists aren't sure of the goals. The entire biosphere has been altered by human activities, and it is technically impossible to return it to any "pristine," pre-industrial–*Homo sapiens* condition. There is not even agreement as to whether, for example, the goal in the Yellowstone ecosystem should be to restore it to some semblance of its 1950 condition, its 1850 condition, or its pre-Columbian condition.

There are brave attempts to put caps on development and try to preserve or reestablish some sort of wilderness in the Rocky Mountain West. I hope those attempts will succeed, but I have severe doubts about their long-term prospects as long as the U.S. population continues to grow, rather than shrink to a sustainable size, and the creed of "ever more" is the guiding philosophy of our civilization. Many people have not yet realized that sooner or later growth must stop, nor have they wondered *how* it will stop, and what the Rockies—and the world—will be like when it does stop.

But, for the time being, at RMBL things are still pretty good. True, on the trail to Copper Lake where I often hike in summer, one frequently runs into tourists with illegally unleashed dogs. Overweight optimists in shorts and sandals strolling in late afternoon toward the lake, at almost 12,000 feet and with a stiff two-hour climb ahead, will ask how much farther it is. They are generally oblivious of the thunderheads already obscuring the pass below which the lake lies, and stunned to hear they could get caught in a nasty hailstorm and icy rain. But if I take another trail or climb one of the higher peaks nearby, I generally see no one. So those other trails and peaks still beckon, and I can hardly wait until I once more round the bend on the Gothic road and see the wonderful buttressed peak on the left and the aspen-covered slope that conceals our cabin on the right. Then I'll know I'm home.

Preface

▲

This book is an attempt to look objectively at the cumulative ecological effects of human activity in the Rocky Mountain region. We ask how ecosystems have changed as a result of past human use and project how they might look in the future, given current uses of natural resources in the region. Historian William J. Cronon exhorts ecologists to recognize that ecology is a genuinely *historical* science. What he means is that there is an important time dimension within which ecosystems change and adapt to external forces, including human intervention. The Rocky Mountain West provides prima facie evidence that this is so because it is arid and steep, and therefore scars from past use are visible for hundreds of years. In this book, we explore a number of questions about human influence, past and present, in the Rocky Mountain region: Just how damaging were past exploitations of land, water, and animals? How do current disturbances compare with past mining, grazing, and water diversion activities? In the face of constant change, what constitutes a "natural" ecosystem; are some places more natural than others? And can a high quality of life be achieved for both humans and ecosystems in this region? Sustainability, the ability to meet the needs of the current generation without compromising the needs of future generations, is predicated on the idea of coexistence of humans and nature. In the pages that follow, we attempt to quantify the ecological consequences of human activities in the Rocky Mountains.

The Rocky Mountain West is the fastest-growing region of the United States and Canada, with population increases of more than 23% between 1990 and 1999 for Colorado, Utah, and Idaho. More modest growth rates were reported for Montana, New Mexico, British Columbia, Alberta, and Yukon Territory, with annual population growth rates of 10%–15%, and Wyoming's population grew by 6%. Although much of the population influx is to cities, rural areas and small communities are increasing as well. The population of Whistler, British Columbia, for instance, rose by 61% between 1991 and 1996. People come to the

West because of its superior livability, says Bill Hornby of the *Denver Post*. This influx of people is what prompted, in part, the writing of this book.

Migration to the Rockies is certainly not without drawbacks, especially to native ecosystems. Wallace Stegner, in *Wolf Willow* (1973), his memoir of growing up in Saskatchewan, commented, "Anyone who has lived on a frontier knows the inescapable ambivalence of the old-fashioned American conscience, for he has first renewed himself in Eden and set about converting it into the lamentable modern world" (p. 282). A dichotomy has sprung up between Old and New Westerners based largely on how each group views use of the region's landscapes and natural resources, many of which are in public ownership. "Long-time residents are especially disturbed at New Westerners' enthusiasm to preserve, or 'museumnize,' the region's natural and working landscapes," notes William Riebsame in his *Atlas of the New West* (1997). "They crave wilderness and like the look of cattle country, though they demand well-marked trails in the backcountry and call for animal rights when ranchers shoot coyotes or prairie dogs" (pp. 56–57). Riebsame describes current settlement as being fundamentally different from earlier shantytowns and trailer parks that characterized the short-lived mining and energy development booms. Immigrants are buying into cookie-cutter subdivisions and mammoth houses spread across the landscape, often on thirty-five-acre ranchettes. "Subdivisions are considered such a serious threat by some," observes Dan Dagget, author of *Beyond the Rangeland Conflict: Toward a West That Works* (1995), "that ranchers use them as a kind of bogeyman when the debate over public lands grazing gets really hot. 'If you chase us off, we'll sell our private lands to the subdividers,'" they menace. (p. 59). In an affluent and mobile society, Americans and Canadians are moving to the West for aesthetic reasons, often on the basis of perceptions that have little to do with regional roots or family ties. In an article about Robert Redford, Richard Raynor points out "unexpected side effects" Redford's movies have had on American behavior: "*A River Runs Through It* dangerously swelled the banks of American rivers with novice fishermen. It seems likely that Redford's loving rendition of ranch life in *The Horse Whisperer* . . . will have a similar effect on western Montana, filling it with even more people in a nostalgic search for American rapture and simplicity" (Raynor 1998, 75).

People have been attracted to the beauty and grandeur of the Rocky Mountains for a long time. The mountains were sacred to Native Americans of the region long before the arrival of Europeans. Early visitor Pierre de La Vérendrye in 1743 called the northern Rockies the "Land of Shining Mountains," and explorer John Williams Gunnison in 1853 described his vista when surrounded by Pikes Peak, the Spanish Peaks, and the Sierra Mojada (now the Wet Mountains) as "the finest prospect it has ever fallen my lot to have seen" (Mumey 1955, 42). Until very recently, however, the Rocky Mountain region has been sparsely populated. Its use by Americans and Canadians has been mostly exploitive: first beavers; then precious metals, timber, and water; and finally energy. Wallace Stegner described the West into the 1980s as a colony for the rest of the nation: "It seems to be almost like a continuous repetitive act of God that the western resources should be mined . . . , that populations should rush in and have to rush out again, or trickle out again. . . . Get in, get rich, get out. . . . Every boom and bust leaves the West physically a little poorer, a little worse damaged" (Stegner and Etulain 1996, ix, xvii, xxiii).

Exploitation of natural resources was not an exclusive habit of immigrants, of course, but Euro-American immigrants had or developed far more effective tools for extraction than Native Americans. A fundamental change in the relation Euro-American immigrants held with the land occurred during the early settlement of North America. The new Americans were not bound by European feudalism, with its rigid laws of property ownership that predetermined a person's lot in life. Freedom of self-determination and the almost limitless natural resources of the continent offered endless opportunities for getting rich. American land law, notes James Howard Kuntsler in *The Geography of Nowhere* (1993), was predicated on the principle that land was first and foremost a commodity for capital gain. Speculators and boosters of western expansion sold land in 160-square-acre parcels in spite of warnings from prescient men such as John Wesley Powell, who realized that most western land could not be redeemed for agriculture because of the scarcity of water (Rabbitt 1969).

Not all changes to Rocky Mountain landscapes have been destructive. Society has grown somewhat wiser with time, and farsighted legislation prevents wanton destruction of many resources. In some cases, environmental regulations and agencies help to restore resources that have been degraded. Environmental laws since the 1970s have dramatically improved water and air quality, reduced both the production and disposal of toxic wastes, and increased overall awareness that destruction of the environment is also harmful to people and their economies. The Endangered Species Act of 1973, though flawed, provides a mechanism for protecting plants and animals from total extinction. And recent attempts to gauge the value of nature's goods and services have spawned an awareness of the need for sustainable use of renewable natural resources.

We are not treading new ground in writing about the Rocky Mountains. A visit to the historical section of any western library reveals hundreds of accounts, from pioneer journals and biographies to reports of explorations and the Great Surveys. Dozens more camping guides, scenic descriptions, and photographic journals line other aisles. Excellent state-specific ecological descriptions, such as *Mountains and Plains: The Ecology of Wyoming Landscapes,* by Dennis H. Knight, and *From Grassland to Glacier: The Natural History of Colorado and the Surrounding*

Region, by Cornelia Fleischer Mutel and John C. Emerick, are available for students of natural history. Of course, the literature also abounds with professional manuscripts and agency reports. We aspired to synthesize from this great body of information an assessment of ecological integrity for the Rocky Mountain region as a whole.

This book deconstructs the natural and human influences on the region in various ways. It builds a picture of natural ecosystem function and the many layers of human activities and their consequences in the brief period since Euro-American and Euro-Canadian occupation. Like the layers of an onion, present activities overlay past manipulations. The combination of past and present reveals where Rocky Mountain ecosystems are heading, and the authors project what the future holds on the basis of the patterns that emerge. The book has four parts, in addition to chapter 1, which describes historical and present settlement patterns in the Rocky Mountain region, and the conclusion, which addresses the future. Part I describes the region's biogeography, paleoenvironmental setting, and historical climate, which define an expected range of variability and provide a context for interpreting ecological change. Part II traces the region's history of use and manipulation, from Euro-American settlement through the present, from an ecological perspective. Each chapter in this part projects future use on the basis of economic and social trends. Part III explores the cumulative effects of past, present, and projected future human activities on tundra, subalpine and montane forests, valleys, and grasslands. Part IV then uses case studies to illustrate specific examples of human influence, such as cumulative effects of agriculture and settlement on watersheds and current efforts to restore the environment in northern New Mexico; exurban development and one example of wildlife habitat protection in Summit County, Colorado; inadvertent experiments with aquatic ecosystems in the Flathead River valley, Montana; and combined human effects on the natural resources of Alberta. Some of these case studies are cautiously optimistic that resources can be conserved and preserved, and others suggest approaches for meeting both human and environmental requirements; collectively they present a trajectory of natural resource use that tilts, unbalanced, toward continued exploitation. Finally, in exploring the future of the Rocky Mountain region, the conclusion raises some critical questions: Have we learned anything? Can the projected level of human activities coexist with natural ecosystems of the Rockies without degrading them beyond sustainability? If so, what levels and types of activities inflict the greatest harm to species, communities, and ecosystem processes? Where is development appropriate, and where are natural processes least influenced by human activity?

There are two options in considering the future of the Rocky Mountain region: begin the very difficult task of planning and working toward an environmental future we as a society want, or ignore the trends described in this book and face the future that will happen by default, to the detriment of Rocky Mountain ecosystems. Although the first option may seem almost insurmountably difficult, the second one is unacceptable.

As illustrated by the map facing the preface, the authors take a relaxed approach to defining boundaries in the Rocky Mountain region. For the most part, the boundaries begin in the Yukon and end in northern New Mexico. Some chapters include discussions of the Black Hills of South Dakota; others include a large part of the mountainous area of British Columbia or Arizona. Unfortunately, access to Canadian data was often limited. The emphasis is on physical, ecological, and societal processes that have shaped and will continue to shape the Rocky Mountain environment. Many, if not all, of these processes are the same ones that affect mountain ecosystems worldwide. A region that spans thirty degrees of Earth's latitude is hardly a microcosm, but what we report for the Rocky Mountains has already occurred or will occur in mountain regions worldwide. Recognizing that degradation of mountain ecosystems affects nearly half the world's population, the United Nations declared 2002 the International Year of Mountains.

The impetus for this book came from the realization that changes to Rocky Mountain ecosystems are caused by a complex mixture of natural variability and direct human actions in addition to indirect human activity, such as greenhouse gas–caused global warming and long-range air pollution transport. Further, there is not an overall understanding of, let alone a consensus about, threats to the ecological integrity of the Rocky Mountain region. We held a workshop in 1997 evaluating the extent of past and present human-driven change in order to develop a context for evaluating human-caused alterations to the Rocky Mountains. Forty-two scientific experts attended what was a very exciting gathering.

Our audience for the book is an educated public, including college students, resource managers, planners, and others interested in the state of the Rocky Mountains. We hope the book will influence readers to think more deeply about the cumulative effects of human activities on Rocky Mountain landscapes and will motivate them to slow or reverse the trends that have become apparent to us. Albert Einstein said, "Those who have the privilege to know have the duty to act." Make it so.

Many people devoted countless hours to the preparation of this book, and we are grateful for their help. Some are mentioned in specific chapters, but I especially want to thank Sanjay Advani, Tammy Fancher, Terry Giles, Laurie Richards, Diane Schneider, and Jennifer Shoemaker. The U.S. Geological Survey sponsored the workshop and offered unlimited support and encouragement throughout this project.

References

Dagget, D. 1995. *Beyond the rangeland conflict: Toward a West that works.* Layton, Utah: Gibbs-Smith, in cooperation with the Grand Canyon Trust.

Knight, D. H. 1994. *Mountains and plains: The ecology of Wyoming landscapes.* New Haven, Conn.: Yale University Press.

Kuntsler, J. H. 1993. *The geography of nowhere: The rise and decline of America's man-made landscape.* New York: Simon & Schuster.

Mumey, N. 1955. *John Williams Gunnison (1812–1853), the last of the western explorers: A history of the survey through Colorado and Utah, with a biography and details of his massacre.* Denver, Colo.: Artcraft Press.

Mutel, C. F., and J. C. Emerick. 1992. *From grassland to glacier: The natural history of Colorado and the surrounding region.* Boulder, Colo.: Johnson Books.

Rabbitt, M. C. 1969. John Wesley Powell: Pioneer statesman of federal science. In *The Colorado River region and John Wesley Powell,* 1–23. U.S. Geological Survey Professional Paper 669-A. Washington, D.C.: U.S. Government Printing Office.

Raynor, R. 1998. Existential cowboy: A profile of Robert Redford. *New Yorker,* 18 May.

Riebsame, W. E., ed. 1997. *Atlas of the New West: Portrait of a changing region.* New York: Norton.

Stegner, W. 1973. *Wolf willow.* New York: Viking Press.

Stegner, W., and R. W. Etulain. 1996. *Stegner: Conversations on history and literature.* Las Vegas: University of Nevada Press.

Rocky Mountain
FUTURES

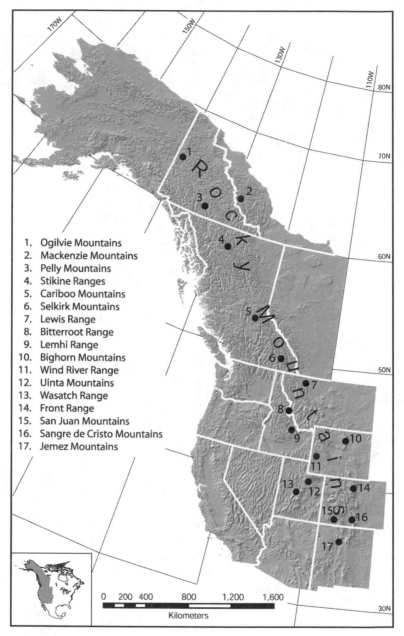

1. Ogilvie Mountains
2. Mackenzie Mountains
3. Pelly Mountains
4. Stikine Ranges
5. Cariboo Mountains
6. Selkirk Mountains
7. Lewis Range
8. Bitterroot Range
9. Lemhi Range
10. Bighorn Mountains
11. Wind River Range
12. Uinta Mountains
13. Wasatch Range
14. Front Range
15. San Juan Mountains
16. Sangre de Cristo Mountains
17. Jemez Mountains

The Rocky Mountains. Map by David M. Cairns

CHAPTER 1

Transforming the Rockies: Human Forces, Settlement Patterns, and Ecosystem Effects

William R. Travis, David M. Theobald, and Daniel B. Fagre

▲

The current ecological condition of the Rocky Mountains can be viewed from two somewhat opposing perspectives. The first is that human occupation has had relatively little effect on the Rockies: large natural, if not pristine, areas remain, and the region's open spaces provide wildlife habitat, majestic scenery, and a sense of wildness. Unlike the situation in, say, the Swiss Alps, where even high-elevation meadows have been mown and grazed intensively for as long as 500 years and many large mammals have been extirpated, most elements of Rocky Mountain landscapes and biota are reasonably unaltered. Even the presumption that Native Americans changed regional landscapes with deliberately set fires has been challenged by Baker and Ehle (2001) and others who think that most fires were lightning-caused or accidental ignitions.

The second view is that humans have dramatically transformed the Rockies, at least since Euro-American settlement in the mid- to late 1800s. The slaughter of vast buffalo herds, the clearing of timber for railroad ties, and even the removal of whole hillsides in hydraulic placer mining represented substantial transformation. Ranch, resort, and residential development marks the latest incarnation of this transformation. Numerous, complex layers of land use have left landscape legacies, some of which may be unrecognized or underappreciated in modern assessments (Wohl 2001).

Here we consider both perspectives because we are impressed with both the many effects of human use of the Rockies and the region's remaining wild landscapes. Ironically, much of the recent population growth and development in

1

the Rockies is driven by the region's wild landscapes, which make the present widespread transformation seem all the more significant. It is, of course, the rapid clip of current human transformation—high population growth rates, pervasive rural residential development, and landscape fragmentation (Baron, Theobald, and Fagre 2000)—that worries ecologists and others concerned with Rocky Mountain ecosystems. So although we offer an overview of historical changes in the Rockies, especially since the 1800s, much of our attention here is on land uses, economies, and settlement patterns since the 1970s and on their future trends.

Making and Remaking the Rockies: Changing Human Geographies

The Rocky Mountain region is booming at the turn of the millennium, exhibiting some of highest population growth rates in the United States and Canada (figure 1.1). Two Rocky Mountain counties, Douglas in Colorado and Summit in Utah, grew faster than any others in the United States during the 1990s. The Rocky Mountain sections of even slower-growing states such as Montana and Wyoming grew at two to three times the national average in the 1990s. Population growth and land development go hand in hand, but the landscape effects of a given human population can vary tremendously, depending on how development is structured and which ecological settings are most affected.

The region has boomed before. Humans probably first found their way into the Rockies some 15,000 years ago; by 5,000 years ago essentially all the region's habitats were used at least seasonally by humans. Regional ecosystems were altered by early settlement, hunting, setting of fires, and even rudimentary irrigation, in at least subtle but poorly documented ways. Human populations within the Rockies themselves were low compared with populations supported by bison herds on the nearby Great Plains or in the extensive settlements of the American Southwest, where Anasazi and Chacoan cultures cultivated stable food supplies, irrigated land, and created urban-like settlements (Lekson 1999). Certainly the lower intermontane valleys, such as the Rocky Mountain Trench and major river corridors, were used extensively, many year-round, and teepee rings and discarded arrowheads are found at treeline and vision quest sites on the summits of many peaks, indicating frequent use of alpine areas (Reeves 2000).

The first Europeans, entering the southern Rockies during the 1500s, found some permanent native settlements and wide seasonal transhumance (populations that migrated seasonally). The settlers quickly filled the Rio Grande valley with farms, villages, and military posts (Hornbeck 1990). Waves of development began

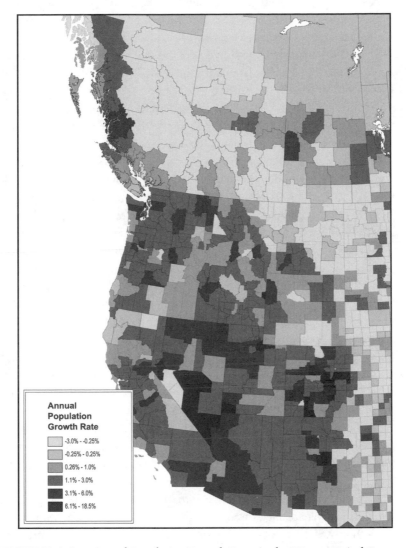

FIGURE 1.1 *Annual Population Growth Rates in the Western United States and Canada, 1990–2000.* Rates for the United States are from U.S. Bureau of the Census county data for 1990 and 2000. Rates for Canada are from Statistics Canada regional division data for 1991 and 1996.

washing over the middle and northern Rockies in the 1800s during a series of natural resource booms. Trappers pioneered commercial resource extraction in the Rockies. Following Meriwether Lewis and William Clark, whose 1804–1806 expedition was undertaken partly to assert American control over the rich beaver regions of the northern Rockies (Beck and Haase 1989), they created a thriving trapping economy that, although thin on the ground, managed to deplete most Rocky Mountain beaver populations by the 1840s (chapter 6; White 1991, Wishart 1992). Still, trails established by the trappers opened the Rockies to further development. Those trails (and trapper guides) helped, for example, the Mormons to pass through the Rockies in 1847 and settle on the shore of the Great Salt Lake, at the western foot of the Wasatch Range. Salt Lake City would become one of the major cities edging against the Rockies.

Rocky Mountain development shifted into high gear during the gold and silver rushes of the mid-1800s (chapter 5). The West's first gold rush, at Sutter's Mill in the Sierra Nevada foothills, affected the Rockies by attracting prospectors who, unable to afford the ocean journey around South America, passed through the region on their way to California. In Canada, the first major Rocky Mountain rush occurred on the western slopes of the Cariboo Range and in the Fraser River valley in 1858, a region settled not from the east but from the Pacific Coast cities of Vancouver and Victoria. A year later, some of the prospectors who were headed across the Rockies for California found gold in what is now Colorado, and by the summer of 1860, more than 5,000 miners a week inundated the southern Rockies. Many mountain towns owe their start to gold and silver: Colorado Springs, Canon City, and Cripple Creek emerged from Colorado's rush; Montana's Virginia City and Helena started with the 1864 gold (and then copper) boom; and silver and gold got Coeur d'Alene, Idaho, off to a start in 1883. Successful mineral mining and milling required better wagon roads and railroads—much of the mineral belt of the southern Rockies was roaded by the 1870s and laced with rails by the 1880s (Wyckoff 1999). These roads and rails then began to serve ranching and logging—industries that also fed the mines and miners—which were operating pretty much along the entire length of the Rockies by 1900.

Military forts were planted throughout the Rockies to safeguard settlers and project authority, and they often formed the nucleus of a future town. Fort Missoula, established in 1877, became present-day Missoula, the largest city in western Montana. The need to supply and maintain better communication with such outposts provided impetus for better roads. A network began to form in Montana in the 1860s. Booming mining camps attracted settlers, who followed rough and dangerous roads, such as the Bozeman Trail to Montana Territory or the Cariboo Road from the coast to the interior of British Columbia. Although mainly associated with resource extraction, the transportation network also moved passengers, mail, consumer goods, and, quite soon, even tourists. The first tourists made their way into Yellowstone in 1871, a year before it was designated a national park (Bartlett 1985); by 1873 they enjoyed well-worn wagon roads.

Commodities and "seeing the sights" weren't the only attraction: land itself lured settlers to the Rockies. Survey parties mapped the interior of the Rockies in detail during the 1860s and 1870s as a prelude to homesteading. In policies to foster western settlement, both the United States and Canada encouraged homesteading in the Rockies. The first transcontinental railroad was pushed across the Laramie Mountains in 1868 and dropped down through the Wasatch Range to the Great Salt Lake in 1869, thus bisecting the Rockies. By 1883, the Burlington Northern Railroad had crisscrossed the northern Rockies with rails. The Great Northern Railway actively enticed settlers to establish farming communities along its route from Minneapolis to Seattle to create a market for its services. From their start, the transcontinental railroads also encouraged tourism in the Rockies as a way to increase ridership. Banff, Yellowstone, and Glacier National Parks were heavily advertised as tourist destinations by the railroads.

The homesteaders brought new land uses and technologies, transforming the region's ecology and economy in more profound and enduring ways than did their predecessors. Homesteading permanently carved the land into parcels to be developed for the highest value the market would bear. Rocky Mountain terrain imparted a pattern of homesteading different from that on the plains: most homesteads were in valley bottoms along the streams and rivers, whereas most of the higher slopes remained in public ownership.

The land not homesteaded continued to be used for logging, grazing, and mining, often with significant degradation (Coggins, Wilkinson, and Leshy 1993; Wilkinson 1992). By the 1890s, this degradation of public lands was so obvious that the United States Congress began to restrict homesteading and reserve public lands in a series of acts (e.g., the Forest Reserve Act in 1891) that would eventually retain more than half the land area of the Rockies in federal administration. In Canada, control of most public lands and resources was transferred to the provinces in 1930. The federal government, however, had created several national parks in the Canadian Rockies, starting in 1885 with a large area around Banff. Federal reservation of land in the U.S. Rockies began with creation of Yellowstone National Park in 1872 and selected forest reserves in 1891. But large additional public land designations were made in the first three decades of the 1900s—some 65,000 square kilometers (km^2), or 16 million acres, of forest reserves and huge tracts of public land were retained under the 1936 Taylor Grazing Act. Thus, by 1940 the public lands of the Rockies were almost fully in place, establishing a key pattern of land tenure that profoundly affected regional development (plate 1). Public lands would continue to shape regional development, especially as they came to be seen, after World War II, as a valuable fount of habitat and recreational lands.

A more recent regional development boom began in the 1970s, when global oil prices quadrupled and American and Canadian energy policy makers favored domestic sources. The Rockies, especially the overthrust belt in Wyoming and the Rocky Mountain Front in Montana and Alberta, filled with oil rigs, coal mines, and natural gas wells. Eventually, though, oil prices fell in the face of mounting supplies, and the energy boom busted in the early 1980s.

As detailed elsewhere in this book, Rocky Mountain ecosystems were modified by each of these human invasions. Mining in particular resulted in deforestation, water diversions and altered streamflows, and pollution. Placer mining reshaped entire valleys, obliterating wetlands and creating large expanses of gravel tailings (Wohl 2001). Wagons and railroads themselves transformed linear swaths of landscapes and provided access for other development (Kindquist 1995). Grazing intensified to supply the burgeoning mining towns. As a result, the composition of the region's vegetation, from tundra down through montane forests to lower-valley grasslands, was visibly transformed, as documented in several rephotographic surveys (e.g., Amundson 1991, Fielder 1999, Gruell 2001, Veblen and Lorenz 1991).

Each regional boom also set the geographic stage for subsequent development. In particular, roads meant to export resources further opened the Rockies to recreation and settlement, fueled in recent decades by the services and high-technology economy. Improved transportation and communication allow people to live and work farther from cities and still function in the global economy; people and businesses disperse across the landscape, city dwellers move to the mountains, and small-town residents look farther afield for properties to develop and market. Settlement spreads, and valley bottoms are laced with more roads and driveways as land is carved up into subdivisions, mini-estates, and ranchettes (Theobald, Gosnell, and Riebsame 1996).

As natural landscapes, and even isolation, have become desired commodities, road improvement has become controversial in many parts of the Rockies, in part because people know that better highways bring more people and development while reducing habitat and fragmenting the landscape. The small community of Polebridge, in the North Fork area of the Flathead River valley, Montana, has debated whether to pave its washboard gravel main access road, forcing residents to trade off convenience, comfort, and their automobile suspensions against the likely influx of development. At the other extreme, the main highway through Colorado's Roaring Fork Valley (serving Aspen) was recently widened to four lanes, complete with a high-occupancy vehicle (HOV) lane.

New Demographics and Economics

The latest development boom in the Rockies is tied less to extractive commodities and more to environmental amenities. The region's recreational resources have long attracted people, but it was in the 1990s that trends in the economy, the nature of work, communications, and lifestyle preferences converged and the Rockies became the destination of choice for footloose people and businesses. Demographers, economists, and geographers cite a litany of driving forces behind this growth, including the dispersion of businesses and jobs away from the coasts and core cities in a world of mobile capital and information; a natural fit between the services and high-technology economy and the region's newness as an economic development pole; and a quality of life that increasingly attracts businesses and individuals (Power 1996; Cromartie and Wardwell 1999; Riebsame, Gosnell, and Theobald 1997).

And though the boom slowed in the early 2000s, it is too early to pronounce it over or to diagnose its structure in detail. But a few dimensions stand out. First, regional population growth in the 1990s was widespread, from the cities on the periphery of the Rockies to some of the most rural areas; most Rocky Mountain areas grew in the 1990s at double or triple the national rates. Lack of growth in a few places (with some even losing population; see figure 1.1) can be explained as further decline of the traditional economy: a closed lumber mill in Jackson County, Colorado; shut-down mines in northern Idaho; and declining energy income along with a thinning ranch economy in central Wyoming.

Rocky Mountain population and economic growth is now tethered to two major geographic features. First, counties adjacent to metropolitan areas or within an hour's drive of them are the fastest-growing in the West. We discuss the landscape effects of this exurban development later in the chapter. Second, high-amenity areas removed from cities have become new Rocky Mountain growth poles. This includes well-known resorts such as in Banff and Aspen but also less-developed areas now supporting a recreation-based economy and sporting second homes and ranchettes. Resort development is a long-standing, well-known geographic phenomenon in the Rockies (Gill and Hartmann 1992), though the rate of resort growth in the 1990s surprised many regional observers and raised concerns about the resorts' ecological and social effects (Ringholz 1996; Howe, McMahon, and Propst 1997).

This development was spurred by a dramatic change in the regional economy: a significant decline in natural resource jobs and earnings and a rise in service and professional employment and earnings associated with investment, retirement, and other so-called nonlabor sources (Power and Barrett 2001). In the U.S. Rockies, natural resource jobs declined from 11% to 4% of all employment during 1970–1999 while service jobs grew from 20% to 31% of employment. The income effects of this change are shown in figure 1.2 for five Rocky Mountain states. Additionally, significant new income now comes to the region from nonlabor sources, such as retirement income and investments. Many regional analysts believe that this amenity boom, based on the region's natural qualities and enabled by the postindustrial economy, will endure and outlast previous booms (Power and Barrett 2001). But, like previous booms, it too has the potential to remake Rocky Mountain landscapes in profound ways.

The Modern Development Geography of the Rockies

Contemporary economic and demographic changes yield a new development geography that will mark the Rockies in the twenty-first century much as the extractive economy characterized the nineteenth and twentieth centuries. The larger cities on the edges of the mountains (e.g., Calgary, Denver, Albuquerque, Salt Lake, and Boise) are growing and sprawling for a variety of economic and social reasons, and their effects on mountain areas—demand for water and recreation—are increasing apace. These cismontane cities also insinuate a low-density exurban development into the nearby mountains. Development in the heart of the Rockies includes growing small cities such as Missoula and Santa Fe,

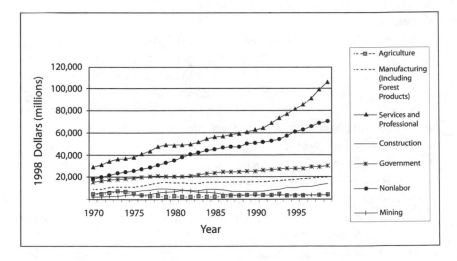

FIGURE 1.2 *Income by Economic Sector in U.S. Rocky Mountain States, 1970–1999.* States included are Colorado, Utah, Wyoming, Montana, and Idaho. Data from BEA 2002 and Sonoran Institute 2002.

resorts such as Vail and Banff, and widely dispersed low-density residential and commercial land use.

The Metropolitan Fringe

From the beginning of Euro-American development of the Rockies right through to recent energy and amenity booms, cities on the periphery of the Rockies have affected the mountain landscape. Calgary, Denver, Salt Lake City, Albuquerque, Boise, Helena, and Spokane prospered on montane resource extraction. They reached into the mountains for water, building reservoirs, ditches, and tunnels that transformed regional hydrology, and their urban populations provided the demand for important contemporary resources such as recreation, wilderness, and wildlife areas (Wyckoff 1999).

But recent changes in the economy and structure of the cities themselves drove new development of their mountain hinterlands. The service and professional economy granted greater workplace and residential freedom, and jobs within the cities shifted out to the urban edge, often to large "edge city" developments. Residents found that they could live in a rural, montane setting and still enjoy urban amenities and participate in the urban economy, and the open spaces between Calgary and the foothills became a more popular residential setting, as did the mountains west of Denver (in Douglas, Teller, and Park Counties), east of Salt Lake City (around the resorts of Summit County), and in the foothills above Boise.

Indeed, such nonmetropolitan counties adjacent to metropolitan areas are the fastest-growing places in the western United States (Cromartie and Wardwell 1999). Such exurbs gained jobs faster (44.5%) than did metropolitan (26.6%) or more rural counties (32.5%) during 1985–1995 in the West (Byers 1999). Rural sections grew faster than the urban areas of nearly two-thirds of the counties in the U.S. Rockies. In a sense, these adjacent nonmetropolitan places are now part of the urban geography of the West. Their populations rely on the nearby cities if not for daily jobs, then at least for their urban services: hub airports, entertainment, venture capital, banking, professional services, and so forth.

Resort Development

The Rockies are home to the largest ski resorts on the continent. Resorts are a special case of micro-urban development, often deploying very high development densities (including high-rise condominium and hotel complexes) into and adjacent to wild and semi-wild lands (figure 1.3). They also affect montane habitats with ski runs cut from valley bottom to ridge top, thus placing facilities (e.g., ski lifts and restaurants with increasing year-round activity) and people in higher-elevation forest and tundra settings.

FIGURE 1.3 *Copper Mountain Ski Resort, Colorado Rocky Mountains.* Photograph by William R. Travis.

Several aspects of resorts make their imprint on the land unique among settlement patterns. First, most mountain resort towns are associated with thousands of acres of ski slopes marked by deforested ski runs, semi-natural areas between the runs, dispersed skiing above timberline, and the relatively small structures of on-slope facilities such as lift and gondola houses and towers, restaurants, and other buildings. Still, compared with the cities, even the largest resort towns have relatively small footprints. The townsite of Vail, Colorado, covers about 1,166 hectares (ha), or 4.5 square miles (mi.^{2}), of an elongated swath along Gore Creek, including a four-lane divided interstate highway that runs the length of the valley. The Vail ski resort, the largest in the Rockies, encompasses some 2,140 ha (8.2 mi.^{2}) of "skiable terrain." Thus, about 12% of the 26,400 ha (102 mi.^{2}) Gore Creek watershed is developed.

Resorts also exhibit larger development footprints, or areas developed to some extent, than do nonresort towns of similar population. Typically, more than half the residential units in resorts are owned by nonresidents (so-called second homes). In extreme cases, as in Eagle County, Colorado (home to Vail), as much as 80% of residential units are second homes. Resorts represent the most quickly expanding residential and commercial land use in the Rocky Mountain bioregion.

Low-Density Development

A third pattern of Rocky Mountain settlement covers much more area: low-density residential and commercial development spreading through rural areas (Theobald 2000). It is driven by preferences for rural living and enabled by the locational freedoms of the postindustrial economy. Medium- to low-density development can quickly fill the strip of privately owned lands that marks most Rocky Mountain valley bottoms (figure 1.4). The Roaring Fork Valley, below Aspen, is rapidly becoming a strip development roughly 60 km (40 mi.) by 9 km (5 mi.) (Odell, Theobald, and Knight 2002). The Bitterroot River valley, outside Missoula, is experiencing both small-town and leapfrog exurban development of agricultural lands (Grandstaff 2001). The valley grew by more than 11,000 people in the 1990s, from 25,010 in 1990 to 36,070 in 2000, for a 44.3% growth rate, making Ravalli County the fastest-growing in Montana. Development occurs both on the edges of existing small towns and cities—Hamilton, Florence, Sula—and farther out in rural subdivisions arrayed along the river and pushed up into the forested slopes of the Bitterroot Range and Sapphire Mountains, a pattern that exacerbated wildfire problems in the summer of 2000. Demographer John Cromartie, analyzing 2000 U.S. census data, found that most small towns in the American West were not growing as fast as

FIGURE 1.4 *Low-Density Residential Development outside Mount Crested Butte, Colorado.* Photograph by David M. Theobald.

the counties in which they are located; much of the new growth was occur-ring beyond the annexed edges of towns (plate 2; Cromartie 2001).

Low-density development also spreads out from Rocky Mountain resorts. We studied a valley below Crested Butte in the central Colorado mountains and found agricultural properties being subdivided into thirty-five-acre ranchettes and home construction working its way over time up from the valley floor and into the higher-elevation forests (Theobald, Gosnell, and Riebsame 1996). Jack-son and Wall (1995) found new home construction also dispersing in western Montana; residents were attracted by federal lands and other amenities. They plotted the location of rural real estate development in western Montana for 1990–1995 and discovered that the area's two large national parks, Glacier and Yellowstone, both attracted rural development like magnets, as did wilderness areas and water bodies. Rural areas well served by roads developed faster, as did rural areas not too far from towns. They concluded that from the buyers' point of view, the "optimum new rural residential location in Western Montana allows ready access to the wild and the civilized" (p. 16).

Overall, some 36,000 km² (8.9 million acres) of land had been developed at exurban densities (1 dwelling unit per 0.04–0.16 km², or 1 per 10–40 acres) in the seven Rocky Mountain states by 2000 (plate 2). We project that this will increase to 80,000 km², or 19.7 million acres (121% growth), by 2050, on the basis of a projected population doubling (104%), which many analysts think will occur before 2050. The key point is that low-density development con-sumes land at a faster rate than population growth, indicating further sprawl-ing of settlement.

Extraction and Infrastructure Land Uses

Two other major land uses affect the Rockies: extractive land uses, such as min-ing, timber cutting, water diversions, and grazing; and infrastructure, such as roads and highways. Although we have focused on private land development, Rocky Mountain ecosystems remain affected by past and present economic activities such as logging and grazing, most of it on public land. Forests cover about one-quarter of the Rocky Mountain states, and about half of those forests support species, such as Douglas-fir, traditionally used for commercial timber products (USDA Forest Service 1989). Three-fourths of this forested land is in public ownership, and one-third of that is restricted from timber extraction in some way. All but a small percentage of the remainder has been cut at least once, and official statistics claim that essentially all this is regrowing timber (though there is some controversy about how much is regrowing). Logging rates have declined dramatically in the Rockies from highs reached in the late 1980s. In 1997, total timber harvested from national forests in the southern Rockies was just 10% of the 1989 volume (SREP 2000). U.S. Department of Agriculture projections to 2040 suggest that timber cutting will further decline in the Rocky Mountains and that forested area will stabilize at current levels (Haynes 1990).

Essentially all large open spaces in the U.S. Rockies outside the national parks and a few other nature preserves are grazed by domestic livestock (chapter 5; Mitchell 2000). Some 70% of the 72,000 km^2 (17.9 million acres) of national forest land in the southern Rockies is currently grazed (SREP 2000), and 93% of the Bureau of Land Management lands in Colorado (33,600 km^2, or 8.3 million acres) is grazed. Much of the montane grazing is relatively low-intensity and seasonal, and the net ecological effect is hotly debated. Many, probably most, range professionals view widespread grazing, especially in the wetter, more productive montane settings of the Rockies, as a relatively benign, even positive, land use (Vavra, Laycock, and Pieper 1994). Grazing critics disagree, especially with regard to effects on riparian, or stream corridor, areas (Belsky, Matzke, and Uselman 1999). One grazing critic has even argued that the region would be better off if all grazing were removed from public lands, even if the private ranchlands it supports were subdivided (Wuerthner 1994). Because of the inscrutability of the consequences of grazing and the widely recognized difficulty of assessing short- or long-term effects of livestock grazing (Committee on Rangeland Classification 1994), the debate is not likely to be resolved anytime soon. Nevertheless, it is worthwhile to note two side effects of grazing. First, livestock grazing supports an agricultural economy that maintains large units of open land, much of which provides wildlife habitat. Second, it must be recognized that ranchers generally oppose species protection, wilderness designation, and other preservation policies (Donahue 1999).

Infrastructural land uses, particularly roads and highways, also dissect the region. Road densities in the mountains proper are relatively low. By one rough estimate, the southern Rockies ecoregion has an average density of 2 road km per 2.6 km^2 of land, or 1.2 road mi. per mi.^{2} (SREP 2000). On the 40% of land in the southern Rockies that is privately owned, road densities range from 160–320 or more road km per 2.6 km^2 (100–200 or more road mi. per mi.^{2}) in most developed areas to roughly 16 road km per 2.6 km^2 (10 road mi. per mi.^{2}) in rural areas. The Greater Yellowstone Coalition (1991) estimates that some 12,000 km (7,500 mi.) of roads exist on the 56,000 km^2 (13.9 million acres) of federal lands in the Greater Yellowstone Ecosystem (GYE), or about 0.4 road km per 2.6 km^2 (0.4 road mi. per mi.^{2}). This relatively low density is associated with the GYE's large designated wilderness areas and the generally less-roaded nature of the northern Rockies in comparison with the southern Rockies. Roads, like other development features, are unevenly distributed across landscapes. Alberta's foothills have a road density of 3.2 km/km^2, consistent with oil and gas exploration and drilling (chapter 15). Two key determinants of this distribution are interrelated: altitude and landownership (private vs. public). Most roads and other developments reside in lower-elevation zones, as does most of the region's private land. This means that some habitat types are more affected by roads than others, as illustrated in table 1.1 for the San Juan and Sangre de Cristo Mountains.

Land Development and Ecosystem Effects

Growth and expansion of developed areas affects ecosystems both directly and indirectly. Although specific ecological responses are covered in more detail elsewhere in this book, we briefly discuss a few cases here. Just outside Banff National Park in Alberta, Canada, the long-term survival of wildlife populations is threatened by fragmentation of habitat in the Bow River valley (chapter 15). The Trans-Canada Highway disrupts natural movement patterns and is a major source of mortality for the fauna of Banff National Park, and land uses adjacent to the highway decrease the efficacy of mitigation efforts such as wildlife under- and overpasses (Clevenger and Waltho 2000). Bird abundance and richness in the GYE are highest in deciduous forests in riparian areas, such as cottonwood, aspen, and willow (Hansen, Rotella, and Kraska 1999), but these hot spots also have more nest predators and brood parasites when they exist within a rural residential matrix (Saab 1999). In the southern Rockies, Odell and Knight (2001) found that relative bird density of human-sensitive species declined within 180 meters (m), or 590 feet (ft.), of exurban housing. Roads have been shown to nearly double the edge habitat in forests (Reed, Johnson-Barnard, and Baker 1996). McGarigal and colleagues (2001) found that

TABLE 1.1. Road Densities in Selected Vegetation Communities, Arrayed Roughly from Higher to Lower Elevation

Vegetation Community	Road Density (road mi./mi.^{2})
Tundra	0.14
Spruce-fir	0.50
Aspen	0.72
Lodgepole pine	0.35
Foothill and mountain grassland	1.51
Piñon-juniper woodland	1.39
Riparian	2.38

Source: Forest Guardians 1998.

the tripling of road density in the San Juan Mountains of Colorado from the 1950s had a greater influence on landscape fragmentation than logging, particularly in mature forests. Maestas, Knight, and Gilgert (2001) compared exurban, ranch, and protected areas and found marked declines of native communities associated with exurban land use.

Two aspects of the settlement pattern have particularly important indirect effects on Rocky Mountain ecosystems. First, although the Rockies are fortunate to have large areas set aside in national parks and other protected areas, these protected areas tend to occur at high elevations. Much of the private land, not subject to such protection, is at lower elevations. As a result, alpine and high montane ecosystems are fairly well protected, whereas lower-elevation ecosystems, plants, and animals are poorly protected (Shands and Healy 1977, Scott et al. 2001). Future efforts to protect biodiversity will need to involve ecosystems on privately held lands. Second, landownership is highly fragmented, so protected areas are often intertwined with private land, typically at lower elevations and in the highly productive valley bottoms. As a result, although more than one-third of the land in the seven Rocky Mountain states is publicly held, less than one-quarter is more than 2 km (1.2 mi.) removed from private land (table 1.2). And the arrival of more than a quarter million new residents in the forest fringe in the 1990s (table 1.3) makes maintenance of ecological processes such as fire increasingly problematic. Growth rates along the forest fringe now outpace statewide growth rates.

TABLE 1.2. Proportion of Public Land as a Function of Distance from Private Land, Showing the Fragmented Landownership Pattern of the U.S. Rocky Mountains

	% Public Land	*% Public Land 1 km from Private Land*	*% Public Land 2 km from Private Land*	*% Public Land 5 km from Private Land*
Arizona	41.58	31.12	23.87	12.43
Colorado	29.44	18.12	11.79	3.45
Idaho	57.91	45.08	36.07	19.54
Montana	32.76	24.23	19.61	12.22
New Mexico	32.29	19.52	12.81	5.55
Utah	68.94	56.48	47.02	29.96
Wyoming	39.51	28.63	22.90	14.42
Rocky Mountain region	41.30	30.18	23.41	13.06

TABLE 1.3. Population in the Forest Fringe Compared with Statewide Population, U.S. Rocky Mountains

	Statewide			Forest Fringe[1]		
	1990 (thousands)	2000 (thousands)	Annual Growth Rate (%)	1990 (thousands)	2000 (thousands)	Annual Growth Rate (%)
Arizona	3,664	5,130	4.0	184	235	2.8
Colorado	3,293	4,301	3.1	249	364	4.6
Idaho	1,006	1,293	2.9	42	52	2.4
Montana	799	902	1.3	81	107	3.2
New Mexico	1,514	1,819	2.0	1	2	3.9
Utah	1,723	2,233	3.0	94	138	4.7
Wyoming	403	439	0.9	9	12	4.2
Rocky Mountain region	12,402	16,117	3.0	660	910	3.8

[1] Forest fringe is within 1 km of forested land cover.

Planning for the Future

Rural in-filling of the Rocky Mountains is driven both by tourism and recreational development and by changes in the late-twentieth-century economy that encouraged rural residential development. Amenity-based population growth creates a New West irony. Immigrants are drawn by natural areas and recreational opportunities, but their arrival changes these very landscape attributes by reducing agricultural land, mottling valley slopes with roads and houses, limiting access to public lands, and increasing conflict between people and nature. In many ways, this neo-homesteading of the Rocky Mountains is similar to past immigrations: a rush is on to settle a charismatic landscape. Economic and social mobility in the United States and Canada would seem to ensure continued population growth in the Rocky Mountains, and the landscape transformations described here are likely to intensify as development further invades rural areas.

Planning theory holds that proper land use regulation can mitigate the ecological effects of development and create desirable and sustainable communities. Many planning tools, both regulatory and market-based, are available for just this purpose (Duerksen et al. 1997, Dale and Haeuber 2001). But land use planning in practice falls well short of its potential in the Rockies. None of the Rocky Mountain states practices statewide land use planning; indeed, comprehensive growth management initiatives in Colorado and Arizona were defeated in the 2000 elections. Also in theory, federal, provincial, and state law on wetlands, endangered species, and air and water pollution would seem to provide the basis for ecological protection, but such laws are applied piecemeal and have not coalesced into landscape- or ecosystem-level protection. Indeed, strong adherence to property rights and a general economic preference for development over preservation in the Rocky Mountains means that government, from federal to local, can have only limited influence on the way land use patterns evolve. Most property owners can be expected to pursue maximum economic return, which in this rapidly developing region means more intense development.

Federal lands, constituting one-third of the land area of the seven Rocky Mountain states and more than half of the land in the Rocky Mountain bioregion, provide most of the natural habitat in the region. Except for the national parks and some wilderness areas, these lands have been mined, logged, and grazed for a century and a half. Laws protecting the ecological value of public lands have been in place since the 1970s, but they have not much altered utilitarian public land policies (Wilkinson 1992). Overall, there is little reason to expect land use planning that will protect ecological values in the future. Even something as obvious as building regulations in the worst wildfire hazard zones is notably absent, and the potential for widespread planning for something as subtle as, say, wildlife migration corridors seems remote.

The most salient and interesting features of the region's planning landscape are those cases in which something approaching ecologically based land use planning is practiced. We classify ecologically based land use and development in three categories: bioregional, local, and private. Although most of the cases we can cite have weaknesses, we highlight their positive qualities to provide examples that could be followed elsewhere.

Bioregional Efforts

Planning efforts at the broad ecoregional scale in the Rockies are mostly put forward by nongovernmental organizations. The federal land agencies have embarked on a few "ecosystem assessments" in the region, most notably the Columbia River basin assessment, which incorporates a large part of the northern Rockies, but these are just that, assessments, with little effect on actual public or private land use. The agencies also cooperate on a few single-purpose efforts, such as grizzly bear recovery or fire management at the bioregional scale, but nongovernmental groups are responsible for most bioregional initiatives in the Rockies.

For sheer scale and bioregional ambitiousness, the Yellowstone to Yukon (Y2Y) conservation initiative tops the list. Y2Y, now coordinated by the nonprofit Sonoran Institute, embraces a "community conservation" approach to a 2,800 km (4,500 mi.) corridor of the Rocky Mountains straddling the U.S.-Canadian border. The main thrust is to improve planning, land use, and development decisions by individual communities along the corridor. In theory, and with the cooperation of the public land agencies, this effort could result in different landscape outcomes with the goal of maintaining a viable migration route for wildlife. Y2Y's first step is to convince communities that their economic well-being is linked less to resource extraction and more to environmental quality (Rasker and Alexander 2000).

Only slightly less ambitious are the efforts of the Greater Yellowstone Coalition (GYC) to conserve ecological values in a 73,000 km^2 (17.9 million acre) area covering twenty-two counties in three states centered on Yellowstone National Park (Greater Yellowstone Coalition 1991). This Greater Yellowstone Ecosystem (GYE) is 80% public land—a mixture of wilderness and multiple-use lands, some heavily used for lumber, energy, minerals, grazing, and recreation. Thus, much of the GYC's effort is aimed at changing land management by federal agencies. But many critical habitats in the ecosystem are on private lands, and rapid growth and development, especially sprawling rural development, is also of concern. The GYC deploys a mixture of classic challenges to federal actions: conservation alternatives, collaboration, grassroots pressure, lawsuits, and local watchdogging. It has also begun a series of integrated programs based on ecological principles and assessments, including a focus on major rivers, a conservation biology assessment of the entire ecosystem, and sustainable design of the GYE's human communities. To reduce the effects of land development, the GYC created guidelines for community development, stressing compact development, and it supports grassroots planning groups to push local governments toward more ecological planning. It has also used litigation when necessary to block what it sees as the worst cases of habitat loss. For example, the GYC successfully blocked a large residential development in a wildlife migration corridor on the western boundary of Yellowstone National Park (Greater Yellowstone Coalition 2001).

Not every bioregion of the Rockies has such an effective conservation group working in it, though the Southern Rockies Ecosystem Project (SREP) has begun to take up this effort in the south, and some of the larger, more advanced watershed coalitions (e.g., the Henry's Fork Foundation) are acting to alter land use decisions at the landscape scale.

Local Government

In both the United States and Canada, growth and land use are managed mostly by local government. Of course, state and provincial policies on transportation, land, and water development all affect local land use, but decisions on virtually all private land uses, from residential subdivision to major commercial and industrial development, reside with local government.

For the most part, local planning is effected through two main tools—comprehensive plans and detailed land use zoning. Wildlife habitat, water quality, open space, agricultural land preservation, and other elements of ecological planning are now recognized in many county and community plans in the Rockies, from Kamloops, British Columbia, to Santa Fe, New Mexico. But such comprehensive plans are notoriously ineffective, their positive sentiments and goals quite removed from the regulatory zoning and permitting procedures that actually determine land use. In only a very few cases do development regulations formally incorporate ecological values, and anecdotal evidence suggests that even these policies are frequently violated in local development decisions. Rather than restriction of development through regulations, which is politically quite difficult, simple land acquisition has become the most widespread local planning tool with significant ecological benefits (Deurksen et al. 1997). By purchasing land or at least the development rights associated with it, towns and counties can preserve habitat with less real or perceived infringement of property rights. Open space systems, such as those in Boulder and Jefferson Counties, Colorado, and Park City, Utah, account for hundreds of square kilometers (e.g., 240 km^2, or 60,000 acres, in Boulder County alone). New open space programs emerged from the 2000 elections in several Rocky Mountain areas threatened with spreading development, including Gallatin County, Montana, and Larimer County, Colorado.

Size limitation and the need to meet nonecological goals, especially on land purchased with local tax revenues, mean that local open space programs will amount to only a small contribution to the conservation of Rocky Mountain biodiversity. Moreover, few of the programs with which we are familiar use systematic ecological guidelines. Ecological screening tools are now available (see, e.g., Theobald and Hobbs 2002, White et al. 1997), but price, recreational access, and visual effect often matter more to local officials and taxpaying residents. It is also too early to tell whether ecological guidelines established in places such as Summit County, Colorado, described in chapter 13, will result in net ecological benefits.

After open space acquisition, tools for local land use planning that exhibit some promise for ecological conservation include growth boundaries and emerging regulations such as conservation design for subdivisions (instituted, for example, in 1996 by voters in Routt County, Colorado). Growth boundaries are not catching on very rapidly in the Rockies, but they are at least being discussed, and some have found their way into comprehensive plans, though not into regulations. The Denver Regional Council of Governments created a voluntary urban growth boundary that would keep urban development from lapping into the mountains, and most of the member counties have agreed to consider it in their planning, though they are not bound to do so. Even a few smaller towns and rural counties have considered such boundaries, mostly on the basis of their need to preserve agricultural land—Gunnison, Colorado, drew up a boundary for its future growth but did not adopt it formally. Flathead County, Montana, considered neighborhood growth plans but also failed to adopt county-wide zoning or growth limits.

Land Trusts and Private Conservation

Most of the private land in the Rocky Mountains is still undeveloped, and some unknown proportion of it can be considered to be under preservation. This is certainly true for lands owned by The Nature Conservancy (TNC), such as Red Canyon Ranch in the Wind River Range and the 405 km^2 (100,000 acre) Medano-Zapata Ranches in the San Luis Valley. Although most TNC properties were acquired for specific, often local, reasons, the organization now has in place the most sophisticated bioregional planning and land conservation process ever developed (Nature Conservancy 2001). For example, the Southern Rocky Mountains Ecoregional Plan calls for some form of conservation action on 188 conservation sites covering roughly 50% of the ecoregion (Neely et al. 2001). Through acquisition, community conservation, and simply leadership by example, TNC has taken on the breathtaking goal of conserving the nation's extant biodiversity in perpetuity (Stein, Kutner, and Adams 2000). TNC's current projects in the Rocky Mountains include dozens of landscape-scale efforts, such as on the upper Green River, that complement public lands and other privately conserved lands.

More than 100 active land trusts in the Rocky Mountains now hold at least 6,000 km^2 (1.5 million acres) in the United States and some 2,000 km^2 (0.5 million acres) in Canada (in British Columbia) in some level of preservation, ranging from intense agricultural use to something approaching untrammeled wildness (Land Trust Alliance 2001; Land Trust Alliance of British Columbia, pers. comm., 17 November 2001). As with local open space programs, the ecological effectiveness of land trusts is compromised by idiosyncratic approaches and varied goals (e.g., preserving agriculture or scenic views). We know little of the net ecological condition of land trust holdings. Finally, of course, some private land not typically thought of as preserved is protected by its owners for various reasons. Many ranchers manage their land in ways that provide important ecological services, and some large residential parcels are managed for as much naturalness as can characterize smaller land units. But we do not know the scale of this kind of land conservation, its net ecological effects, its permanency, or its potential in the Rockies.

Conclusions

Human activity has pervasively altered natural dynamics and landscape structure in the Rocky Mountains. Yet the region retains some of the most natural landscapes and fullest complement of biodiversity in the United States and Canada: the ecological glass is both half empty and half full in the Rockies. Sustaining regional ecosystems requires ecologically thoughtful planning, planning that must be informed by a deepening scientific understanding of the effects of human activities on ecological systems and a growing realization that historical land use legacies are an important, but poorly understood, component of current landscapes. The Rockies came under increasing development pressure in the 1990s in a new land rush driven by environmental amenities and enabled by the new economy of services and high technology. Ironically, many of the region's new residents perceive it as a pristine, intact landscape and wish to live as close to this wildness as possible. Perhaps this provides an opportunity that has not existed in previous booms: the realization that what is good for the environment is good for the economy. Although we are ambivalent about the efficacy of land use planning, we nevertheless hold out hope that science-based planning and local decision making can help Rocky Mountain communities achieve more sustainable development.

References

Amundson, M. A. 1991. *Wyoming time and again.* Boulder, Colo.: Pruett.

Baker, W. L., and D. Ehle. 2001. Uncertainty in surface-fire history: The case of ponderosa pine forests in the western United States. *Canadian Journal of Forest Research* 31 (7): 1205–1226.

Baron, J. S., D. M. Theobald, and D. B. Fagre. 2000. Management of land use conflicts in the United States Rocky Mountains. *Mountain Research and Development* 20 (1): 24–27.

Bartlett, R. A. 1985. *Yellowstone: A wilderness besieged.* Tucson: University of Arizona Press.

BEA (U.S. Department of Commerce, Bureau of Economic Analysis). 2002. On-line at <http://www.bea.gov>.

Beck, W. A., and Y. D. Haase. 1989. *Historical atlas of the American West.* Norman: University of Oklahoma Press.

Belsky, A. J., A. Matzke, and S. Uselman. 1999. Survey of livestock influences on stream and riparian ecosystems in the western United States. *Journal of Soil and Water Conservation* 54:419–431.

Byers, W. B. 1999. Employment growth in the rural West from 1985 to 1995 outpaced the nation. *Rural Development Perspectives* 14 (2): 38–43.

Clevenger, A. P., and N. Waltho. 2000. Factors influencing the effectiveness of wildlife under-passes in Banff National Park, Alberta, Canada. *Conservation Biology* 14 (1): 47–56.

Coggins, G. C., C. F. Wilkinson, and J. D. Leshy. 1993. *Federal public land and resource law.* 3rd ed. Westbury, N.Y.: Foundation Press.

Committee on Rangeland Classification. 1994. *Rangeland health: New methods to classify, inventory, and monitor rangelands.* Washington, D.C.: National Academy Press.

Cromartie, J. B., and J. N. Wardwell. 1999. Migrants settling far and wide in the rural West. *Rural Development Perspectives* 14 (2): 2–8.

Dale, V. H., and R. A. Haeuber, eds. 2001. *Applying ecological principles to land management.* New York: Springer.

Donahue, D. L. 1999. *The western range revisited: Removing livestock from public lands to conserve native biodiversity.* Norman: University of Oklahoma Press.

Duerksen, C. J., N. T. Hobbs, D. L. Elliott, E. Johnson, and J. R. Miller. 1997. *Managing development for people and wildlife: A handbook for habitat protection by local governments.* PAS No. 470/471. Chicago: American Planning Association.

ESRI (Environmental Systems Research Institute). 2000. *ESRI data and maps 2000.* National and provincial parks of Canada. On-line at <http://www.esri.com/data/datacd00.html>.

Fielder, J. 1999. *Colorado: 1870–2000.* Photography by W. H. Jackson and J. Fielder. Englewood, Colo.: Westcliffe.

Forest Guardians. 1998. *State of the southern Rockies: San Juan–Sangre de Cristo bioregion.* Santa Fe, N.M.: Forest Guardians.

Gill, A., and R. Hartmann, eds. 1992. *Mountain resort development.* Burnaby, British Columbia: Simon Fraser University, Centre for Tourism Policy and Research.

Grandstaff, C. 2001. Planning to fail: Why sprawl in the Bitterroot is out of control and why it will never be fixed. *Missoula Independent* 12 (16).

Greater Yellowstone Coalition. 1991. *An environmental profile of the Greater Yellowstone Ecosystem.* Bozeman, Mont.: Greater Yellowstone Coalition.

———. 2001. Montana Supreme Court sides with GYC at Duck Creek. *Greater Yellowstone Report* (summer): 6.

Gruell, G. E. 2001. *Fire in Sierra Nevada forests: A photographic interpretation of ecological change since 1849.* Missoula, Mont.: Mountain Press.

Hansen, A. J., J. R. Rotella, and M. L. Kraska. 1999. Dynamic habitat and population analysis: A filtering approach to resolve the biodiversity manager's dilemma. *Ecological Applications* 9 (4): 1459–1476.

Haynes, R. W. 1990. *An analysis of the timber situation in the United States, 1989–2040.* General Technical Report RM-1999. Fort Collins, Colo.: U.S. Department of Agriculture, Forest Service, Rocky Mountain Forest and Range Experiment Station.

Hornbeck, D. 1990. Spanish legacy in the borderlands. In *The making of the American landscape,* ed. M. P. Conzen, 51–62. Boston: Unwin Hyman.

Howe, J., E. McMahon, and L. Propst. 1997. *Balancing nature and commerce in gateway communities.* Washington, D.C.: Island Press.

Jackson, D. H., and K. Wall. 1995. *Mapping and modeling real estate development in rural western Montana.* Discussion Paper No. 2. Missoula: University of Montana, Bolle Center for People and Forests.

Kindquist, C. E. 1995. Communication in the Colorado high country. In *The mountainous West: Explorations in historical geography,* ed. W. Wyckoff and L. M. Dilsaver, 114–137. Lincoln: University of Nebraska Press.

Land Trust Alliance. 2001. *National land trust census.* Washington, D.C.: Land Trust Alliance. 12 September.

Lekson, S. H. 1999. *The Chaco meridian: Centers of political power in the ancient Southwest.* Walnut Creek, Calif.: AltaMira Press.

McGarigal, K., W. H. Romme, M. Crist, and E. Roworth. 2001. Cumulative effects of roads and logging on landscape structure in the San Juan Mountains, Colorado (USA). *Landscape Ecology* 16 (4): 327–349.

Maestas, J. D., R. L. Knight, and W. C. Gilgert. 2001. Biodiversity across rural land uses in the mountain West. *Geographical Review.* 91: 509–524.

Mitchell, J. E. 2000. *Rangeland resource trends in the United States: A technical document supporting the 2000 USDA Forest Service RPA assessment.* General Technical Report RMRS-GTR-88. Fort Collins, Colo.: U.S. Department of Agriculture, Forest Service, Rocky Mountain Research Station.

Nature Conservancy. 2001. *Conservation by design: A framework for mission success.* Arlington, Va.: Nature Conservancy.

Neely, B., G. Bell, P. Comer, H. Copeland, J. Humke, M. Lammert, C. Moritz, C. Pague, R. Rondeau, T. Schulz, S. Spackman, D. Theobald, and L. Valutis. 2001. *Southern Rocky Mountains: An ecoregional assessment and conservation blueprint.* Arlington, Va.: Nature Conservancy. September.

Odell, E. A., and R. L. Knight. 2001. Songbird and medium-sized mammal communities associated with exurban development in Pitkin County, Colorado. *Conservation Biology* 15 (4): 1143–1150.

Odell, E. A., D. M. Theobald, and R. L. Knight. 2002. The songbirds' case for clustered development. *Journal of the American Planning Association.*

Power, T. M. 1996. *Lost landscapes and failed economies: The search for a value of place.* Washington, D.C.: Island Press.

Power, T. M., and R. Barrett. 2001. *Post-cowboy economics: Pay and prosperity in the new American West.* Washington, D.C.: Island Press.

Rasker, R., and B. Alexander. 2000. The changing economy of Yellowstone to Yukon: Good news for wild lands? *Wild Earth* (spring): 99–103.

Reed, R. A., J. Johnson-Barnard, and W. L. Baker. 1996. Contribution of roads to forest fragmentation in the Rocky Mountains. *Conservation Biology* 10 (4): 1098–1106.

Reeves, B. O. K. 2000. *Mistakis: The people and their land for the past 10,000 years—Glacier National Park Archeological Inventory and Assessment Program, 1993–1996.* Final Draft Technical Report. Vol. 1. Denver, Colo.: National Park Service, Intermountain Region.

Riebsame, W. E., H. Gosnell, and D. M. Theobald. 1996. Land use and landscape change in the U.S. Rocky Mountains. I. Theory, scale, and pattern. *Mountain Research and Development* 16:395–405.

———, eds. 1997. *Atlas of the New West.* New York: Norton.

Ringholz, R. C. 1996. *Paradise paved: The challenge of growth in the New West.* Salt Lake City: University of Utah Press.

Saab, V. 1999. Importance of spatial scale to habitat use by breeding birds in riparian forests: A hierarchical analysis. *Ecological Applications* 9:135–151.

Scott, J. M., F. W. Davis, R. G. McGhie, R. G. Wright, C. Groves, and J. Estes. 2001. Nature reserves: Do they capture the full range of America's biological diversity? *Ecological Applications* 11 (4): 999–1007.

Shands, W. E., and R. G. Healy. 1977. *The lands nobody wanted*. Washington, D.C.: Conservation Foundation.

Sonoran Institute. 2002. Tucson, Arizona. On-line at <http://www.sonoran.org/si/>.

SREP (Southern Rockies Ecosystem Project). 2000. *The state of the southern Rockies ecoregion*. Nederland, Colo.: Southern Rockies Ecosystem Project. On-line at <http://csf.colorado.edu/srep>.

Stein, B. A., L. S. Kutner, and J. S. Adams. 2000. *Precious heritage: The status of biodiversity in the United States*. New York: Oxford University Press.

Theobald, D. M. 2000. Fragmentation by inholdings and exurban development. In *Forest fragmentation in the central Rocky Mountains,* ed. R. L. Knight, F. W. Smith, S. W. Buskirk, W. H. Romme, and W. L. Baker, 155–174. Boulder: University Press of Colorado.

Theobald, D. M., H. Gosnell, and W. E. Riebsame. 1996. Land use and landscape change in the U.S. Rocky Mountains. II. A case study of the East River valley, Colorado. *Mountain Research and Development* 16:407–418.

Theobald, D. M., and N. T. Hobbs. 2002. A framework for evaluating land use planning alternatives: Protecting biodiversity on private land. *Conservation Ecology* 6 (1): 5. On-line at <http://www.consecol.org/vol6/iss1/art5>.

USDA Forest Service. 1989. *An analysis of the land base situation in the United States, 1989–2040*. General Technical Report RM-181. Fort Collins, Colo.: U.S. Department of Agriculture, Forest Service, Rocky Mountain Forest and Range Experiment Station.

Vavra, M., W. A. Laycock, and R. D. Pieper, eds. 1994. *Ecological implications of livestock herbivory in the West*. Denver, Colo.: Society for Range Management.

Veblen, T. T., and D. C. Lorenz. 1991. *The Colorado Front Range: A century of ecological change*. Salt Lake City: University of Utah Press.

White, D., P. G. Minotti, M. J. Barczak, J. C. Sifneos, K. E. Freemark, M. V. Santelmann, C. F. Steinitz, A. R. Kiester, and E. M. Preston. 1997. Assessing risks to biodiversity from future landscape change. *Conservation Biology* 11:1–13.

White, R. 1991. *"It's your misfortune and none of my own": A new history of the American West*. Norman: University of Oklahoma Press.

Wilkinson, C. F. 1992. *Crossing the next meridian: Land, water, and the future of the West*. Washington, D.C.: Island Press.

Wishart, D. J. 1992. *The fur trade of the American West, 1807–1840: A geographical synthesis*. Lincoln: University of Nebraska Press.

Wohl, E. 2001. *Virtual rivers: Lessons from the mountain rivers of the Colorado Front Range*. New Haven, Conn.: Yale University Press.

Wuerthner, G. 1994. Subdivisions versus agricultu.e. *Conservation Biology* 8:905–908.

Wyckoff, W. 1999. *Creating Colorado: The making of the western American landscape, 1860–1940*. New Haven, Conn.: Yale University Press.

PART I

THE BACKGROUND OF ENVIRONMENTAL CHANGE

▲

Ecology is the study of the interrelationships between living organisms and the physical factors that shape and influence their environment. In the Rocky Mountains, the influence of extremely strong physical gradients on organisms is especially apparent. The mountain massif, evident from far away on the plains, poses a barrier to the movement of wildlife, and it prevented early human migration except where there were accessible mountain passes. Climate is one of the dominant environmental controls on natural mountain systems; on a structure as large as the Rocky Mountains, climate exhibits both latitudinal and elevational gradients (Beniston 2000). A summer trip from east to west over a mountain pass reveals steep changes in climate as one climbs from warm grasslands and shrublands through forests and into cold and windy tundra. Western slopes are more mesic (moist) and often more densely vegetated because of the greater precipitation they receive. Even paleohistory is apparent to casual visitors in the presence of glacial features such as moraines and cirques. The subject of part I is how past and present climate and geologic factors shape Rocky Mountain ecosystems.

Chapter 2 addresses the geomorphic and biogeographic setting of the Rocky Mountains. It shows how large-scale mountain building, intermediate-scale valley-forming factors, and, most of all, small-scale activities such as avalanches, fire, and debris flows have shaped the environment we recognize today. Chapter 3 adds the temporal dimension by describing the past 20,000 years of climate and biogeography. The past is painstakingly reconstructed from lake and bog sediment cores and pack rat middens. Pollen, charcoal, algae, insects, leaves, and wood are all interpreted to tell a story, not only about what happened but also about past rates of change.

Past rates of change are important to our understanding of current climate and possible future climates. Chapter 4 describes the global forces that shape Rocky Mountain climate. It presents a detailed primary data analysis of the past 100 years and postulates potential future climates on the basis of global circulation model projections.

It is the combination of past and present physical and biological forces that shapes current Rocky Mountain ecosystems, and the most important force today is human transformation of the landscape. Part I provides the baseline from which the history and magnitude of human societal actions now influence the environment.

References

Beniston, M. 2000. *Environmental change in mountains and uplands.* New York: Oxford University Press.

CHAPTER 2

Geomorphic and Biogeographic Setting of the Rocky Mountains

David M. Cairns, David R. Butler, and George P. Malanson

▲

When people think of the Rocky Mountains, they often think of either the entire spine of mountains running through North America, specific ranges within the greater Rocky Mountains region, or, probably most commonly, specific basins or slopes with which they have had personal experience. This division of the Rocky Mountains into a series of nested hierarchical levels has a basis in scientific theory as well as in the general perception of the public. Hierarchy theory holds that processes and patterns at different scales have typical relations: those at a given scale are created by the combinations of processes at the next lower scale and are constrained by the patterns of the next higher scale (Allen and Hoekstra 1992). Our discussion of the Rocky Mountains examines patterns and processes at three scales. At the continental scale, we focus on the general processes responsible for the creation of the Rocky Mountains. We then discuss the Rockies at the scale of individual ranges, emphasizing valley heterogeneity. Finally, we highlight some geomorphic and biogeographic patterns and processes that operate within individual drainage basins and on slopes.

Continental Scale

The north–south axis of the Rocky Mountains forms a fundamental constraint on the physical geography of North America because it lies along the global latitudinal gradient of received solar radiation and is transverse to the prevailing westerly winds. Within the Rockies, there is evidence of both of the major

27

mountain-building mechanisms ascribed to plate tectonics: collision and subduction. Subduction, the process that results when two continental plates collide and the denser oceanic crust dives below the less dense continental crust, has been responsible for creating the majority of the Rocky Mountain mass, but collision of island arcs resulting in the accretion of terranes (small migrating pieces of Earth's crust) on the North American continent has also played a role.

Major Rock Types

The southern Rocky Mountains are primarily granitic intrusions with associated metamorphic rocks such as gneisses and schists, forming anticlinal (uplifted) domes of fractured sedimentary rocks in roughly elliptical or circular patterns surrounding the central igneous and metamorphic core. The Black Hills of South Dakota, an outlier of the Rocky Mountains, are a classic example of this type of mountain. Other examples include the Colorado Front Range, the Bighorn Mountains and Wind River Range of Wyoming, and the Uinta Mountains of Utah.

Igneous extrusive rocks are associated with many of the mountain ranges in the greater Yellowstone National Park region as well as in the San Juan Mountains of southwestern Colorado. Sedimentary units heavily deformed by faulting, local intense folding, and overthrusting characterize areas of the northern Rocky Mountains such as along the mountain front west of Calgary, Alberta, and southward into the Rocky Mountain Front, stretching from Glacier National Park, Montana, to west of Great Falls and Helena.

Faulting is prevalent in the northern U.S. Rockies and in the Canadian Rockies as well as in part of the Middle Rocky Mountains physiographic province. Two types of faulting are evident: overthrust and block. Great tilted blocks form the Teton Range, the Wasatch Range, and the Lost River and Lemhi Ranges and Beaverhead Mountains of east-central Idaho and western Montana. Farther north in Montana and along the eastern cordilleran front in Canada, overthrust faults are more prevalent. The Lewis Overthrust in northern Montana is perhaps the best example, showing Precambrian mudstones thrust over weaker Cretaceous rocks (Yin and Kelty 1991).

Climatic Gradients

The physical structure of the Rocky Mountains results in marked transverse and longitudinal climatic gradients across the component ranges. Differences in latitude along the Rocky Mountain Cordillera result in a north–south gradient in solar radiation, temperature, and length of growing season. Although the energy gradient is generally smooth from south to north, the climatic gradient is not. Because the Rockies are oriented perpendicular to the prevailing westerly winds, there is an extreme climatic gradient extending from the western flanks of the mountains to the eastern side. The major east–west climatic gradient is not continuous because of the alternating importance of orographic uplift (air being forced higher in altitude as a result of the mountainous terrain) and rain shadow effects from west to east across a series of ranges (Changnon, McKee, and Doesken 1991).

A variety of processes and patterns are constrained by these macro-scale patterns. These include the distribution and intensity of snow, glaciation, and snow avalanches and the distribution of vegetation types and their patterns.

Glacial Activity

Glacial activity has influenced the development of slopes and valleys and their associated ecosystems in the Rockies (chapter 3). Currently active glaciers in the Rockies are small and limited in their geographic extent. Locations in the northern Rockies receive less precipitation and so have less potential to retain a glacier. Col-fed, or gully, glaciers persist in Colorado, fed by windblown snow that replenished Little Ice Age ice bodies (Outcalt and MacPhail 1980), but in general, warm temperatures in the southern Rockies preclude the presence of glaciers. Many currently active glaciers in the Rockies are retreating rapidly subsequent to the Little Ice Age (McCarthy and Smith 1994). In Glacier National Park, Montana, however, we have observed that near fast-retreating glaciers, some small glaciers and summer snow patches remain unchanged since the 1930s. It is possible that these smaller features responded quickly in the mid-nineteenth century and the larger glaciers are still racing toward equilibrium with current climatic conditions.

Vegetation Patterns

The Rocky Mountains are divided into four floristic zones (Peet 1988). The boreal mountain zone of the far northern region extends north of Jasper National Park, Alberta, Canada, into Alaska. In this zone, subalpine fir (*Abies lasiocarpa*) and lodgepole pine (*Pinus contorta*) share dominance with the typically boreal species white spruce (*Picea glauca*). The northern Rocky Mountain floristic zone extends southeast of Jasper to Yellowstone National Park in southern Montana and northern Wyoming. In this zone, subalpine fir and lodgepole pine remain dominant, but white spruce is replaced by Engelmann spruce (*Picea engelmannii*) and Douglas-fir (*Pseudotsuga menziesii*). Many species indicative of the western slope of the Cascade Range are also present here, such as western hemlock (*Tsuga heterophylla*) and western red cedar (*Thuja plicata*). In the southern Rockies floristic zone, southeast of Yellowstone to the Sangre de Cristo Mountains of New Mexico and the San Francisco Peaks in northern Arizona, Gambel oak (*Quercus gambelii*), one-seed juniper (*Juniperus monosperma*), blue spruce (*Picea pungens*), and single-leaf pine (*Pinus monophylla*) join subalpine fir, Engelmann spruce, and ponderosa pine (*Pinus ponderosa*) as locally important canopy dominants. Bristlecone pine (*Pinus aristata*) also occurs in the southern Rockies. The southernmost floristic region of the Rockies has been called the Madrean zone, and it has many distinctive species. The forest of this region is made up of oaks and pines, including species common in Central America and Mexico. These include Mexican white pine (*Pinus strobiformis*), Mexican piñon (*Pinus cembroides*), and Emory oak (*Quercus emoryi*).

Climate determines the boundaries of the four floristic zones and is described in more detail in chapter 4. The southern limit of the boreal mountain zone is controlled by a major storm track that carries Pacific air inland. The southern boundary of this storm track runs from northeastern California to western Montana (Mitchell 1976). South of the storm track, drier continental air limits the southward expansion of the Cascadian species indicative of the northern Rockies floristic zone. Similarly, the Arizona monsoon and its summer precipitation patterns influence the southern floristic zone. A combination of winter cold and summer drought controls the northern limit of the Madrean zone.

There are common zones, or bands, of vegetation from the bases of mountains to their peaks along the entire Rocky Mountain chain. Low elevations near the Rocky Mountains are typically composed of grasslands that grade into a series of forest types with increasing elevation (chapter 11). Although the dominance of particular species varies from north to south, some common qualities of elevational transects are found. Daubenmire (1943) identified five forested vegetation zones distinguishable by species. The five zones, from lowest to highest elevation, are (1) the oak–mountain mahogany (*Quercus-Cercocarpus*) zone, (2) the juniper–piñon (*Juniperus–Pinus edulis*) zone, (3) the ponderosa pine (*Pinus ponderosa*) zone, (4) the Douglas-fir (*Pseudotsuga menziesii*) zone, and (5) the spruce-fir (*Picea engelmannii Abies lasiocarpa*) zone. Above the spruce-fir zone are areas of fell-field vegetation (sparse patches of vegetation in a mostly rocky landscape) and alpine tundra (see chapter 9). Not all zones are present at every location along the cordillera, and the elevation at which the zones occur varies from north to south and with patterns of moisture availability. Furthermore, the species composition of the zones changes along the cordillera. For example, the spruce-fir elevation zone in the northern Rockies is dominated by subalpine fir (*Abies lasiocarpa*), with some Engelmann spruce (*Picea engelmannii*). In contrast, in the southern Rockies, Engelmann spruce dominates in the spruce-fir zone. There are similar differences in tundra species composition from south to north. In Rocky Mountain National Park, tundra communities are characterized by vast expanses of kobresia (*Kobresia myosuroides*), whereas in Glacier National Park kobresia is uncommon and tundra communities are primarily composed of alpine avens (*Dryas octopetala*).

Alpine treeline marks the transition from closed-canopy subalpine forest to the uppermost vegetation zone dominated by alpine tundra. This vegetation transition occurs at higher elevations farther south than it does in the northern part of the cordillera (chapter 9) because of the gradient in solar radiation and temperature. Note, however, that the treeline in the Montana Rockies is considerably lower than would be predicted on the basis of gradients in solar radiation and temperature because of the effects of disturbance (Brown 1994). The other major vegetation zones also show corresponding reductions in elevation with increased latitude. At a given latitude, many of the major vegetation zones occur at a higher elevation on the western slopes of the Rockies than on the eastern slopes because more precipitation falls on the windward side (Walsh, Malanson, and Butler 1993).

Although there are controlling gradients in temperature, moisture, and solar radiation along both the north–south and east–west axes of the Rocky Mountains, a corresponding gradient in annual plant production (net primary productivity, or NPP) is not readily apparent (Peet 1988). Heterogeneity along the Rocky Mountains in successional stage, disturbance history, climatic conditions, stand age, and vegetation type produce a complex relationship between NPP and location. In general, NPP increases with elevation (Whittaker and Niering 1975) up to a point and then decreases as treeline and ultimately tundra communities are encountered. Average aboveground alpine tundra NPP is near 0.2 kilogram of carbon per square meter of land per year (Körner 1999), which is comparable to the NPP of low-elevation desert scrub vegetation in the southern Rocky Mountains (Whittaker and Niering 1975).

Ranges

Ridge and valley ecosystems within individual mountain ranges display considerable environmental heterogeneity. All such ecosystems are constrained in their composition and structure by the larger regional-scale controls of climate, glaciation, and geology. Variability in lithology (the physical characteristics of rock), topography, and disturbance histories (such as fire and mass movement) results in the environmental heterogeneity seen within the ranges.

Lithology and Topography

Geologic structure determines the spatial arrangement of ridges and valleys within a range, which in turn determines the heterogeneity of climate within the range. In Glacier National Park, the Lewis and Livingston Ranges were formed by folding and faulting and have a generally north–south axis. The result is that the glacial troughs run primarily east–west and create a strong gradient in solar radiation and wind exposure between slopes. The Uinta Mountains in Utah are the exception. Great contrasts in solar radiation and moisture availability are common across ridges because of the predominance of north- and south-facing slopes.

Constraints of lithology on geomorphic processes are common (see, e.g., Oelfke and Butler 1985, Butler and Walsh 1990). Rock substrate is also an important factor in determining vegetation composition and structure. For example, avalanche path locations are linked to lithology and bedrock structure (Butler and Walsh 1990). Snow avalanches influence the local vegetation type, so lithology indirectly affects the pattern of vegetation on a landscape. Similar effects can be inferred for debris flows (Malanson and Butler 1984).

Fire History

Fire history differentiates landscapes in the same way as lithology and topography. In general, fire histories are related to synoptic-scale climatology (Johnson and Wowchuk 1993, Bessie and Johnson 1995). At this scale, there are frequency patterns among rather than within ranges (Johnson and Larsen 1991, Fowler and Asleson 1982). In the Bitterroot Range, valleys are geologically similar but have very different vegetation communities because of the unique fire history in each valley (McCune and Allen 1985a, b). In general, these types of differences in history may result from chance and the vagaries of ignition or may also reflect patterns of topography, local climate, and vegetation within the valleys (Goldblum and Veblen 1992). There is a consistent pattern of decreasing fire frequency with increasing elevation and with more northerly aspect, and there is an indirect relation between frequency of fires and their size and intensity.

Basins and Slopes

Basins and slopes are heterogeneous with regard to hydrology, geomorphology, biogeography, and soils. This heterogeneity is constrained by higher-level processes such as the lithologic, climatological, and historical conditions of valleys within ranges, but it is in turn structured by more fine-scale processes such as water movement, weathering and erosion, plant and animal dynamics, and soil development (Barry 1973, Greenland 1989, Saunders and Bailey 1994).

Slope Processes

The study of slope processes in the Rocky Mountains has focused on periglacial processes including solifluction (soil creep), movement of rock glaciers (a form of glacier with many rocks embedded in the surface), debris flows (Butler et al. 1998), and fluvial processes that produce alluvial fan and deltaic deposits

(Nicholas and Butler 1996, Church and Ryder 1972). For example, the presence of periglacial landforms in areas where periglacial processes are not currently active leads us to conclude that colder climatic conditions existed at these locations in the past (see, e.g., Hall and Shroba 1995 for the Wind River Range, Wyoming; Butler 1988 for the Lemhi Range, Idaho; and Benedict 1970 for Colorado).

Soil Development

The development of soils in mountain environments depends on topographic position, climate, parent material, vegetation, and time (Jenny 1941). Topography often is the dominant pedogenic, or soil-forming, factor, simply because of the extremes found in mountain environments. Topography controls snow cover, deposition of loess (windblown fine soil particles), soil creep, and debris flows, which in turn are important determinants of soil development and vegetation community structure (Burns and Tonkin 1982; Seastedt 2001; Stanton, Rejmanek, and Galen 1994).

Environmental Gradients and Vegetation

At the scale of slopes and basins within the Rocky Mountains, elevation is the primary environmental gradient that structures vegetation communities (Habeck 1987). Growth and reproductive ability of plants are influenced by other environmental gradients, including temperature, moisture availability, soil nutrients, and geomorphic surface (Kershaw and Gardner 1986). Although gradients of these essential elements for plants are not necessarily ordered in space, in the case of mountainous environments there is often a high correlation between slope position and temperature and moisture availability. The shape of slopes and historical factors, such as grazing at low elevation and fire at high elevation, structure the fine-scale heterogeneity of the major environmental gradients (Barton 1993).

The vegetation type on mountain slopes is influenced by differences in evapotranspiration. Wind and solar radiation influence the patterns of moisture loss from tundra, for instance, structuring the composition of fell-field and snow patch vegetation in Colorado (Isard 1986).

Disturbance

The fine-scale biogeography of the Rocky Mountains is influenced heavily by disturbance. The primary disturbance type in montane forests is fire, the size and severity of which are hierarchically constrained by regional patterns of temperature and moisture availability. Other disturbance types also are important. Insect pests, blowdown, simple gap dynamics, and human activity all play important roles in structuring the fine-scale heterogeneity of Rocky Mountain vegetation (Romme, Knight, and Yavitt 1986; Price 1985; Veblen and Lorenz 1986; part III of this book). Disturbances do not act singly to influence vegetation. Studies of the interaction of two or more disturbance types provide a clearer understanding of forest type. For instance, fire-caused devastation of forests was shown to preclude beetle infestations, but avalanche paths shaped the overall pattern by structuring the spread of fire across the landscape (Baker and Veblen 1990, Veblen et al. 1994). Repeat photography has served as a data source for documenting the effects of fire suppression, climatic change, and grazing in both the Colorado Front Range (Veblen and Lorenz 1991) and Glacier National Park, Montana (Butler, Malanson, and Cairns 1994).

Riparian Vegetation

Patterns of streamside, or riparian, vegetation are multi-scale, but it is the fine-scale patterns within valleys that are reset most frequently (Baker 1989, Bendix 1994). Establishment events are key elements in differentiating riparian environments and wetlands adjacent to streams and rivers. Establishment events are controlled in large part by high-energy, frequent floods (high flow volumes and velocities), which are common in mountain environments (Baker 1989). Sediment, woody debris, soil, and vegetation act together to affect the episodic transport of sediment in subalpine rivers. They also influence the composition of pioneer vegetation (Malanson 1993, Wohl 2000).

Prior to Euro-American contact, many riparian environments in the Rocky Mountains maintained significant beaver populations. The activities of fur trappers in the nineteenth century nearly drove the beaver to extinction, but isolated populations persisted in the mountains of northwestern Montana and Alberta (chapters 6 and 8). During the twentieth century, beaver populations expanded throughout their former native range, resulting in the reintroduction of beaver dams and ponds along riparian corridors (Meentemeyer and Butler 1995). Beaver ponds elevate local water tables, decrease net flow velocity, and reduce stream erosion. They thereby provide valuable habitat for wetland-dependent plants and animals. The absence of beaver ponds in much of the Rocky Mountains throughout the late nineteenth and early twentieth centuries produced a disequilibrium condition that has yet to be corrected (Wohl 2000).

Avalanche Paths

Avalanche paths are characterized by an upslope starting zone, a track, and a runout zone. Avalanches move large amounts of material across the landscape and consequently can do a great amount of geomorphic work (Luckman 1978).

The current importance of the geomorphic work done by avalanches varies with location. Avalanches near Lake Louise in the Canadian Rockies still move significant quantities of rock materials, but slightly farther south, in Glacier National Park, little geomorphic work is being accomplished (Gardner 1970, Butler 1985).

At the basin and slope level, studies of avalanche paths have concentrated on patterns within the paths. The transverse structure of an avalanche path consists of as many as three zones: an inner zone, a flanking zone, and a drier outer zone. The longitudinal pattern of vegetation in avalanche paths reflects the gradient in elevation and is influenced by disturbance frequency (Butler 1985, Patten and Knight 1994). In addition, avalanche paths may affect the dynamics of nearby vegetation by being a source area for early successional species (Malanson and Butler 1984).

Meadow Creation and Invasion

The biogeographic patterns of the Rocky Mountains are not static; the creation and invasion of alpine meadows is an example of a relatively dynamic vegetation system. Shifts between meadow and forest and back are most commonly attributed to climate change, human influence, or a combination of the two. Human influence on meadows is often the result of livestock introduction (chapter 5). In the Wind River Range of Wyoming, grazing enhanced tree establishment by removing grass cover and allowing the establishment of tree seedlings (Dunwiddie 1977). Meadow invasion has also been attributed to climate change in Idaho and in Yellowstone National Park (Butler 1986, Jakubos and Romme 1993). Human activities, such as hydrologic diversions, can change the composition of meadows and peatlands in the Rocky Mountains. In Rocky Mountain National Park, Colorado, the ditching of Big Meadows Fen lowered the water table, creating aerobic conditions that changed the vegetation (Cooper et al. 1998).

Implications of Geomorphology and Biogeography for Human-Caused Change

Rocky Mountain ecosystems are defined by the template on which they occur. At the coarsest level, climate and mountain structure dictate the location of floristic zones. Glacial history, lithology, and topographic structure add finer-scale characteristics for specific mountain ranges, and at the finest level, specific hillslope and disturbance processes add the final controls on the Rocky Mountain environment (see box 2.1).

BOX 2.1. Integration

To synthesize these concepts and examples, consider one example within the hierarchy established here. The distribution of beavers (*Castor canadensis*) and their associated dams and ponds is controlled by the presence of specific types of riparian vegetation (Malanson 1993). The distribution of riparian vegetation is influenced by stream characteristics, including stream order, which is also important because beavers can dam only between first- and fourth-order streams (Butler 1995). The structure and pattern of riparian vegetation are controlled by the hydrologic characteristics of the waterway along which it grows, which is in turn controlled by higher-level characteristics of the system, such as the valley form and the paraglacial-fluvioglacial-fluvial sediment regime. At one level above the local hydrology, the valley form and types and amounts of sediment are influenced by the lithologic structure and glacial history of mountain valleys. Ultimately, the presence of mountains and valleys is the result of the most coarse-scale processes: tectonic uplift and the climatic patterns created by the presence of the cordillera.

Human activity may interrupt or augment processes at any level within this hierarchical system. Human activity, as described in the chapters that follow, is certainly notable at the level of basins and slopes as the result of direct land use change. Road and dam building, mining, forest harvest, and home and resort development directly alter the physical and biogeographic structure of the Rocky Mountains. Larger-scale societal influences are affecting even the highest, global, level of the hierarchy through anthropogenic climate change, loss of global stratospheric ozone, and specific regional and local disturbances.

Perhaps fortunately, even local to regional human activities are constrained by the same broad regional definitions that define biogeography. Agriculture, for instance, is confined to valley bottoms, and only where water is available and the climate is suitable. Climate-constrained plant productivity has prevented large-scale silvicultural replacement of native tree species with more economically desirable trees, as has happened in many European mountains where deciduous beech forests were replaced with Norway spruce. Mineral extraction is undertaken where there are valuable ores. Just as our perception of the Rocky Mountains is shaped by whether we think of them as the entire cordillera, specific ranges, or even valleys and slopes, our perception of the influence of human activity is shaped by the scale of our vision.

Dee —

We found these books
in Carbondale
storeroom.
I hope that are
useful for you.

Rob S
Carbondale

References

Allen, T. H. F., and T. Hoekstra. 1992. *Toward a unified ecology.* New York: Columbia University Press.

Baker, W. L. 1989. Macro- and micro-scale influences on riparian vegetation in western Colorado. *Annals of the Association of American Geographers* 79:65–78.

Baker, W. L., and T. T. Veblen. 1990. Spruce beetles and fires in the nineteenth-century subalpine forests of western Colorado, USA. *Arctic and Alpine Research* 22:65–80.

Barry, R. G. 1973. A climatological transect on the east slope of the Front Range, Colorado. *Arctic and Alpine Research* 5:89–110.

Barton, A. M. 1993. Factors controlling plant distributions: Drought, competition, and fire in montane pines in Arizona. *Ecological Monographs* 63:367–397.

Bendix, J. 1994. Scale, direction, and pattern in riparian vegetation-environment relationships. *Annals of the Association of American Geographers* 84:652–665.

Benedict, J. B. 1970. Downslope soil movement in a Colorado alpine region: Rates, processes, and climatic significance. *Arctic and Alpine Research* 2:165–226.

Bessie, W. C., and E. A. Johnson. 1995. The relative importance of fuels and weather on fire behavior in subalpine forests. *Ecology* 76:747–762.

Brown, D. G. 1994. Comparison of vegetation-topography relationships at the alpine treeline ecotone. *Physical Geography* 15:125–145.

Burns, S. F., and P. J. Tonkin. 1982. Soil-geomorphic models and the spatial distribution and development of alpine soils. In *Space and time in geomorphology,* ed. C. E. Thorn, 25–43. London: Allen and Unwin.

Butler, D. R. 1985. Vegetational and geomorphic change on snow avalanche paths, Glacier National Park, Montana, USA. *Great Basin Naturalist* 45:313–317.

———. 1986. Conifer invasion of subalpine meadows, central Lemhi Mountains, Idaho. *Northwest Science* 60:166–173.

———. 1988. Neoglacial climatic inferences from rock glaciers and protalus ramparts, southern Lemhi Mountains, Idaho. *Physical Geography* 9:71–80.

———. 1995. *Zoogeomorphology: Animals as geomorphic agents.* Cambridge: Cambridge University Press.

Butler, D. R., G. P. Malanson, and D. M. Cairns. 1994. Stability of alpine treeline in northern Montana, USA. *Phytocoenologia* 22:485–500.

Butler, D. R., G. P. Malanson, F. D. Wilkerson, and G. L. Schmid. 1998. Late Holocene sturzstroms in Glacier National Park, Montana, U.S.A. In *Geomorphological hazards in high mountain areas,* ed. J. Kalvoda and C. Rosenfeld, 149–166. Dordrecht, Netherlands: Kluwer Academic, Geojournal Library.

Butler, D. R., and S. J. Walsh. 1990. Lithologic, structural, and topographic influences on snow-avalanche path location, eastern Glacier National Park, Montana. *Annals of the Association of American Geographers* 80:362–378.

Changnon, D., T. B. McKee, and N. J. Doesken. 1991. Hydroclimatic variability in the Rocky Mountains. *Water Resources Bulletin* 27:733–743.

Church, M., and J. M. Ryder. 1972. Periglacial sedimentation: A consideration of fluvial processes conditioned by glaciation. *Bulletin of the Geological Society of America* 83:3059–3072.

Cooper, D. J., L. H. MacDonald, S. K. Wenger, and S. W. Woods. 1998. Hydrologic restoration of a fen in Rocky Mountain National Park, Colorado, USA. *Wetlands* 18:335–345.

Daubenmire, R. 1943. Vegetation zonation in the Rocky Mountains. *Botanical Review* 9:325–393.

Dunwiddie, P. W. 1977. Recent tree invasion of subalpine meadows in the Wind River Mountains, Wyoming. *Arctic and Alpine Research* 9:393–399.

Fowler, P. M., and D. O. Asleson. 1982. Spatial properties of lightning-caused forest fires. *Physical Geography* 3:180–189.

Gardner, J. 1970. Geomorphic significance of avalanches in the Lake Louise area, Alberta, Canada. *Arctic and Alpine Research* 2:135–144.

Goldblum, D., and T. T. Veblen. 1992. Fire history of a ponderosa pine/Douglas fir forest in the Colorado Front Range. *Physical Geography* 13:133–148.

Greenland, D. 1989. The climate of Niwot Ridge, Front Range, Colorado, USA. *Arctic and Alpine Research* 21:380–391.

Habeck, J. R. 1987. Present-day vegetation in the northern Rocky Mountains. *Annals of the Missouri Botanical Garden* 74:804–840.

Hall, R. D., and R. R. Shroba. 1995. Soil evidence for a glaciation intermediate between the Bull Lake and Pinedale glaciations at Fremont Lake, Wind River Range, Wyoming, USA. *Arctic and Alpine Research* 27:89–98.

Isard, S. A. 1986. Factors influencing soil moisture and plant community distribution on Niwot Ridge, Front Range, Colorado, USA. *Arctic and Alpine Research* 18:83–96.

Jakubos, B., and W. H. Romme. 1993. Invasion of subalpine meadows by lodgepole pine in Yellowstone National Park, Wyoming, USA. *Arctic and Alpine Research* 25:382–390.

Jenny, H. 1941. *Factors of soil formation.* New York: McGraw-Hill.

Johnson, E. A., and C. P. S. Larsen. 1991. Climatically induced change in fire frequency in the southern Canadian Rockies. *Ecology* 72:194–201.

Johnson, E. A., and D. R. Wowchuk. 1993. Wildfires in the southern Canadian Rocky Mountains and their relationship to mid-tropospheric anomalies. *Canadian Journal of Forest Research* 23:1213–1222.

Kershaw, L. J., and J. S. Gardner. 1986. Vascular plants of mountain talus slopes, Mt. Rae area, Alberta, Canada. *Physical Geography* 7:218–230.

Körner, C. 1999. *Alpine plant life: Functional plant ecology of high mountain ecosystems.* Berlin: Springer-Verlag.

Luckman, B. H. 1978. Geomorphic work of snow avalanches in the Canadian Rocky Mountains. *Arctic and Alpine Research* 10:261–276.

McCarthy, D. P., and D. J. Smith. 1994. Historical glacier activity in the vicinity of Peter Lougheed Provincial Park, Canadian Rocky Mountains. *Western Geography* 4:94–109.

McCune, B., and T. F. H. Allen. 1985a. Forest dynamics in the Bitterroot Canyons, Montana. *Canadian Journal of Botany* 63:377–383.

McCune, B., and T. F. H. Allen. 1985b. Will similar forests develop on similar sites? *Canadian Journal of Botany* 63:367–376.

Malanson, G. P. 1993. *Riparian landscapes.* Cambridge: Cambridge University Press.

Malanson, G. P., and D. R. Butler. 1984. Transverse pattern of vegetation on avalanche paths in the northern Rocky Mountains, Montana. *Great Basin Naturalist* 44:453–458.

Meentemeyer, R. K., and D. R. Butler. 1995. Temporal and spatial changes in beaver pond locations, eastern Glacier National Park, Montana, USA. *Geographical Bulletin* 37:97–104.

Mitchell, V. L. 1976. The regionalization of climate in the western United States. *Journal of Applied Meteorology* 15:920–927.

Nicholas, J. W., and D. R. Butler. 1996. Application of relative age-dating techniques on rock glaciers of the LaSal Mountains, Utah: An interpretation of Holocene paleoclimates. *Geografiska Annaler* 78:1–18.

Oelfke, J. G., and D. R. Butler. 1985. Landslides along the Lewis Overthrust Fault, Glacier National Park, Montana. *Geographical Bulletin* 27:7–15.

Outcalt, S. I., and D. D. MacPhail. 1980. A survey of neoglaciation in the Front Range of Colorado. In *Geoecology of the Colorado Front Range: A study of alpine and subalpine environments,* ed. J. D. Ives, 203–208. Boulder, Colo.: Westview Press.

Patten, R. S., and D. H. Knight. 1994. Snow avalanches and vegetation pattern in Cascade Canyon, Grand Teton National Park, Wyoming, USA. *Arctic and Alpine Research* 26:35–41.

Peet, R. K. 1988. Forests of the Rocky Mountains. In *North American terrestrial vegetation,* ed. M. G. Barbour and W. D. Billings, 63–101. Cambridge: Cambridge University Press.

Price, M. F. 1985. Impacts of recreational activities on alpine vegetation in western North America. *Mountain Research and Development* 5:263–277.

Romme, W. H., D. H. Knight, and J. B. Yavitt. 1986. Mountain pine beetle outbreaks in the Rocky Mountains: Regulators of primary productivity? *American Naturalist* 127:484–494.

Saunders, I. R., and W. G. Bailey. 1994. Radiation and energy budgets of alpine tundra environments of North America. *Progress in Physical Geography* 18:517–538.

Seastedt, T. R. 2001. Soils. In *Structure and function of an alpine ecosystem: Niwot Ridge, Colorado,* ed. W. D. Bowman and T. R. Seastedt, 157–173. New York: Oxford University Press.

Stanton, M. L., M. Rejmanek, and C. Galen. 1994. Changes in vegetation and soil fertility along a predictable snowmelt gradient in the Mosquito Range, Colorado, USA. *Arctic and Alpine Research* 26:364–374.

Veblen, T. T., K. S. Hadley, E. M. Nel, T. Kitzberger, M. Reid, and R. Villalba. 1994. Disturbance regime and disturbance interactions in a Rocky Mountain subalpine forest. *Journal of Ecology* 82:125–135.

Veblen, T. T., and D. C. Lorenz. 1986. Anthropogenic disturbance and recovery patterns in montane forests, Colorado Front Range. *Physical Geography* 7:1–24.

———. 1991. *The Colorado Front Range: A century of ecological change.* Salt Lake City: University of Utah Press.

Walsh, S. J., G. P. Malanson, and D. R. Butler. 1993. Alpine treeline in Glacier National Park, Montana. In *Geographical snapshots of North America,* ed. D. G. Janelle, 167–171. New York: Guilford Press.

Whittaker, R. H., and W. A. Niering. 1975. Vegetation of the Santa Catalina mountains, Arizona. V. Biomass, production, and diversity along the elevation gradient. *Ecology* 56:771–790.

Wohl, E. 2000. *Mountain rivers.* Washington, D.C.: American Geophysical Union.

Yin, A., and J. T. Kelty. 1991. Development of normal faults during emplacement of a thrust sheet: An example from the Lewis Allochton, Glacier National Park, Montana (USA). *Structural Geology* 13:37–47.

CHAPTER 3

Paleoenvironmental History of the Rocky Mountain Region during the Past 20,000 Years

Cathy Whitlock, Mel A. Reasoner, and Carl H. Key

▲

In the past 20,000 years the Earth system has undergone a shift from glacial conditions to the present interglacial period, the Holocene epoch. In the course of the transition, the vast ice sheets disappeared, sea level rose by 100 meters (m), or 328 feet (ft.), and levels of carbon dioxide in the atmosphere increased. This climatic change profoundly affected ecosystems as species adjusted their ranges and abundance and in the process created new communities. In the Rocky Mountain region, subalpine forests and tundra were widespread during full-glacial time but were replaced by closed forests in the Holocene. Low elevations that previously supported montane forest became steppe and desert. The frequency and intensity of natural disturbances varied with climatic change, and it is likely that fire was an important trigger of the vegetation response. The magnitude and rate of environmental change in the past have been compared to those that may occur in the future with projected increases in greenhouse gases in the atmosphere. What can we learn from history that is relevant to understanding modern Rocky Mountain ecosystems? What does the biotic response to past environmental change portend for the future?

Paleoecology, the study of past ecological interactions, provides an opportunity to answer these questions. The paleoecologic record offers a chronology of past changes in climate, vegetation, and disturbance regime as well as insights into the cause of such changes. Moreover, paleoecology offers an opportunity to compare environmental changes due to climate and human activity in prehistoric times with those resulting from Euro-American activity in recent centuries.

Our information on past ecological conditions comes primarily from the sediments of lakes and natural wetlands (see figure 3.1 for site locations). Lake sediments are excellent repositories of paleoenvironmental information, containing material introduced into the site from airborne fallout, stream and surface processes, and the lake itself. Sediment cores from Rocky Mountain lakes commonly are several meters (yards) in length and span the past 10,000 years or more. Fossil pollen records provide information about the watershed vegetation as well as the aquatic plants that grew within the lake. Leaves, seeds, and other plant macrofossils found in sediment cores often supplement the pollen interpretation by providing species identification and confirmation of local occurrence. In semi-arid regions, where natural wetlands are scarce, middens of pack rats (*Neotoma*) contain well-preserved plant macrofossil assemblages (Betancourt, Van Devender, and Martin 1990). The plant assemblages represent a snapshot from a particular time of local vegetation collected by ancient rodents for their nests in outcrops and caves. Intervals of abundant charcoal are used to establish the long-term frequency of fires and to examine the role of fire in major biotic reorganizations. Charcoal-based fire reconstructions span thousands of years and provide information about fire conditions during a wide range of climate and vegetation conditions (Whitlock and Anderson 2002).

The information in this chapter is expressed in terms of radiocarbon years before present (^{14}C yr. B.P.), but it is important to keep in mind that radiocarbon years depart from calendar years in the early Holocene and the late-glacial period (Stuiver et al. 1998). By convention, the late-glacial period refers to the period 14,000–10,000 ^{14}C yr. B.P., and the Holocene epoch represents the past 10,000 radiocarbon years. In many western lakes, volcanic ash layers from eruptions of Cascade Range volcanoes offer another dating method. For example, ash from the eruption of Mount Mazama in southwestern Oregon, dated at 6,750 ^{14}C yr. B.P. (Hallett, Hills, and Clague 1997), is found in most lakes from the northern Rocky Mountains.

Long-Term Changes in Climate

During the glacial maximum, the Cordilleran Ice Sheet covered the Canadian Rockies and extended east to the western margin of the Great Plains and south into northern Montana. Isolated glacier complexes also covered the high mountain ranges farther south (Porter, Pierce, and Hamilton 1983). Snowline elevation during the glacial maximum was 600–1,000 m (1,970–3,280 ft.) lower than at present. The most important influence on climate in the Rocky Mountains, however, was not these local glaciers but the Laurentide Ice Sheet, which at its maximum covered northeastern North America. The western United States was affected by the North American ice sheets in three ways (Thompson et al. 1993, Bartlein et al. 1998). First, the presence of the ice sheets depressed temperatures and steepened the latitudinal temperature gradient at lower latitudes. Areas immediately south of the ice sheet experienced extreme cold, with temperatures at least 10°C lower than at present. Farther south, the temperatures may have been less than 5°C lower. Second, the presence of the ice sheet shifted the jet stream south of its present position. Storm tracks that today bring winter moisture to the Pacific Northwest were centered at latitude (lat.) 35° N in full-glacial time. This southward shift accounts for the relatively dry full-glacial conditions in the Pacific Northwest and northern Rocky Mountains and wet conditions in the American Southwest, which allowed for high lake levels and expanded forest zones. The third effect was the presence of stronger-than-present surface easterlies south of the ice sheet as a result of a persistent glacial anticyclone. This circulation pattern further intensified aridity along the ice margin in both the Pacific Northwest and the northern Rocky Mountains.

During the full-glacial period, lowlands were covered by cold steppe dominated by sagebrush (*Artemisia*) (Beiswenger 1991). The vertebrate fauna included northern bog lemmings and other boreal taxa mixed with sagebrush voles, marmots, and pikas (Graham and Mead 1987). Permafrost features in southern Wyoming and fossil beetle data collected from the High Plains indicate that similar conditions extended east of the mountains as well (Elias and Toolin 1990). Upper treeline was lower by 600 m (1,970 ft.) of elevation in full-glacial time (Legg and Baker 1980). In the central and southern Rocky Mountains, pines and other conifers probably grew at middle and lower elevations during the glacial period. Farther south, pack rat midden data and pollen records from the Colorado Plateau suggest that species ranges were shifted downslope into areas now occupied by open conifer woodland. The glacial assemblages, however, combine mixtures of taxa that do not occur together today and suggest that taxa were responding individualistically to climate change (Thompson et al. 1993).

The large-scale controls of climate in the Rocky Mountains started to change as the ice sheets receded in late-glacial time. The position of the jet stream shifted northward, and as a result winter precipitation decreased in the south and increased in the north. Pollen and glacial records suggest warming throughout the Rocky Mountains by 14,000 ^{14}C yr. B.P., although the trend was interrupted in some regions by a return to cool conditions between 11,000 and 10,000 ^{14}C yr. B.P. (see the discussion later in the chapter of the Younger Dryas cooling event). By the beginning of the Holocene, glaciers had disappeared

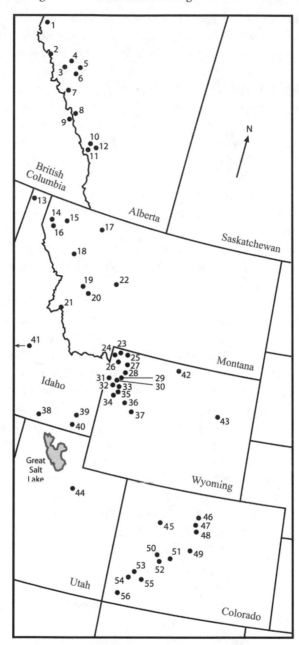

FIGURE 3.1 *Sites of Published Pollen Records, Rocky Mountain Region.* Chronologies were established by radiocarbon dating and span the past 10,000 years or more. (1) Boone Lake and Spring Lake (White and Mathewes 1986, Hickman and White 1989). (2) Tonquin Pass (Kearney and Luckman 1983). (3) Maligne Lake (Kearney and Luckman 1987). (4) Excelsior and Watchtower Basins (Luckman and Kear-

from all but the highest elevations of the Rocky Mountains and temperate plant taxa were widespread.

The late-glacial period marks a time of great biotic reorganization. Plant taxa colonized regions vacated by glaciers, creating new pioneer communities. Areas of tundra and steppe were replaced by forest. As the climate continued to warm, subalpine taxa became restricted to higher-elevation regions and the vegetation became zonally arranged by latitude and elevation.

The Holocene climate history is dominated by variations in the seasonal cycle of insolation (incoming solar radiation) that occurred as a result of changes in the timing of perihelion (when Earth is closest to the sun during its annual orbit)

---

ney 1986). (5) Fairfax Lake (Hickman and Schweger 1981). (6) Muskiki Lake (Kubiw, Hickman, and Vitt 1989). (7) Wilcox Pass (Beaudoin and King 1990). (8) Crowfoot Lake (Reasoner and Huber 1999). (9) Lake O'Hara and Opabin Lake (Reasoner and Hickman 1989, Beaudoin and Reasoner 1992). (10) Yamnuska Bog (MacDonald 1982). (11) Wedge Lake (MacDonald 1982). (12) Toboggan Lake (MacDonald 1989). (13) Hager Pond (Mack et al. 1978). (14) Teepee Lake (Mack, Rutter, and Valastro 1983). (15) McKillop Creek Pond (Mack, Rutter, and Valastro 1983). (16) Johns Lake (Whitlock 1995). (17) Guardipee Lake (Barnosky 1989). (18) Sheep Mountain Bog (Mehringer 1985). (19) Telegraph Creek site (Brant 1980). (20) Forest Lake (Brant 1980). (21) Lost Trail Pass Bog (Mehringer, Arno, and Petersen 1977). (22) Lost Lake (Barnosky 1989). (23) Blacktail Pond (Gennett and Baker 1986). (24) Gardiners Hole (Baker 1983). (25) Slough Creek Pond (Whitlock and Bartlein 1993). (26) Cygnet Lake (Whitlock 1993). (27) Cub Creek Pond (Waddington and Wright 1974). (28) Buckbean Fen (Baker 1976). (29) Trail Lake (Whitlock and Sherriff, unpublished data). (30) Mariposa Lake (Whitlock 1993). (31) Loon Lake (Whitlock, Bartlein, and Van Norman 1995). (32) Emerald Lake (Whitlock 1993). (33) Divide Lake (Whitlock 1993). (34) Hedrick Pond (Whitlock 1993). (35) Lily Lake (Whitlock 1993). (36) Fish Creek Park (Lynch 1998). (37) Rapid Lake (Fall, Davis, and Zielinski 1995). (38) Lake Cleveland (Davis, Sheppard, and Robertson 1986). (39) Grays Lake (Beiswenger 1991). (40) Swan Lake (Bright 1966). (41) McCall Fen (Doerner and Carrara 2001). (42) Sherd Lake (Baker 1983). (43) Antelope Playa (Markgraf and Lennon 1986). (44) Snowbird Bog (Madsen and Currey 1979). (45) White River Plateau (Feiler, Anderson, and Koehler 1997). (46) Sky Pond (Reasoner and Jodry 2000). (47) Redrock Lake (Maher 1972). (48) Devlins Park (Legg and Baker 1980). (49) Lost Park (Vierling 1998). (50) Crested Butte area (Fall 1997). (51) Cottonwood Pass (Fall 1997). (52) Alkali Lake (Markgraf and Scott 1981). (53) Hurricane Basin (Andrews et al. 1975). (54) Lake Emma (Carrara et al. 1984; Carrara, Trimble, and Rubin 1991). (55) Black Mountain Lake (Reasoner and Jodry 2000). (56) Twin Lakes (Petersen and Mehringer 1976).

and the extent of Earth's tilt. Summer insolation was higher than present between 12,000 and 6,000 14^C yr. B.P. and was greatest at about 9,000 ^{14}C yr. B.P. This orbital configuration led to an 8.5% increase in summer insolation at lat. 45° N, whereas winter insolation was 10% less than at present. Greater-than-present summer insolation directly increased summer temperatures by a few degrees over much of the Rocky Mountains and increased summer drought. Indirectly, the summer insolation maximum affected atmospheric circulation patterns. The northeastern Pacific subtropical high became stronger, and as a result the Pacific Northwest and northern Rocky Mountains became drier than at present. The summer monsoon of the southwestern United States also intensified as a result of greater heating of the continental interior. The southern Rocky Mountains experienced summers that were warmer and wetter in the early Holocene than they are today as a result of the strengthened monsoonal circulation (Thompson et al. 1993).

After 9,000 ^{14}C yr. B.P., summer insolation decreased while winter insolation increased to present levels. The cool, wet conditions that characterize the present northern Rocky Mountains climate were established between 4,000 and 3,000 ^{14}C yr. B.P. In the southern Rocky Mountains, higher-than-present summer insolation and reduced summer precipitation led to warm, dry conditions during the middle Holocene. As the effects of summer insolation and monsoonal circulation waned in the late Holocene, the climate became steadily cooler and drier until modern conditions, addressed in chapter 4, were established about 3,000 ^{14}C yr. B.P.

Short-Term Climate Changes

The transition from glacial to interglacial conditions 14,000 to 9,000 years ago was characterized by a series of short-term variations in climate. Understanding the expression of these variations in the Rocky Mountains can help us understand how the region adjusts to rapid climate change. The data suggest that short-term climate changes, occurring on time scales of decades to centuries, represent a flickering of the global climate system between glacial and interglacial modes caused by shifts in the balance between temperature, salinity, and circulation in the North Atlantic Ocean (Taylor et al. 1993).

The Late-Glacial Period
The Younger Dryas (YD) cooling event (ca. 11,000–10,000 ^{14}C yr. B.P.) was a return to near full-glacial conditions following an initial postglacial warming. The onset of cooling in most places took place over several hundred years, and the YD event lasted approximately 1,400 calendar years. Termination of the YD

event was more abrupt than its onset, with mean annual temperatures rising from 7°C to 10°C in less than twenty years. This rate of warming is comparable to or faster than current projections of global warming associated with anthropogenic input of greenhouse gases into the atmosphere.

YD cooling may have led to renewed glacier activity (Reasoner, Osborn, and Rutter 1994; Gosse et al. 1995; Menounos and Reasoner 1997). Records from Colorado suggest that alpine timberline advanced upslope prior to YD time and declined to lower elevations during YD time (Reasoner and Jodry 2000). The predominance of dry-adapted taxa during the YD period implies that glacier advances and vegetation changes, at least in Colorado, were caused by lower-than-present temperatures rather than increased precipitation. At the end of the YD, warmer temperatures allowed alpine treeline to shift to higher elevations and glaciers to recede and disappear. Well-dated pollen records throughout the Rocky Mountains document a shift from tundra or subalpine parkland (open forest) to more temperate forest at the beginning of the Holocene, circa 10,100 ^{14}C yr. B.P., marking the beginning of widespread warming.

The Past 1,000 Years

Climate changes of the past 1,000 years provide an important basis for assessing conditions of the current century. Long-lived organisms (e.g., trees) survived many of these climatic fluctuations, so current forests are, to some extent, a legacy of these events. In the Rocky Mountains, the history of the past 1,000 years is disclosed with near-annual resolution in tree-ring growth chronologies, oxygen isotope profiles from ice and trees, and annually laminated lake sediments.

Medieval Warm Period

The warmest interval of the past 1,000 years, recognized as the Medieval Warm Period (MWP), lasted from approximately 900 to 1300 B.P. (Grove and Switsur 1994). Warm episodes are reported for many areas of the world, with responses exhibited by glacier recession, increased tree growth, and immigration of native peoples and plants into formerly inhospitable lands (Villalba 1994, Deer 1994, Baroni and Orombelli 1994).

Glaciers stagnated or retreated during the MWP in glaciated areas from Canada to Colorado (Osborn and Luckman 1988, Leonard 1997, Richmond 1986, Benedict 1985). Highest treelines occurred during 950–1100 B.P., when alpine larch occupied areas 90 kilometers (km), or 56 miles (mi.), north of current geographic ranges and forests near treeline contained symmetrical arborescent trees, compared with the stunted krummholz forests that developed later. Cooling from the twelfth to fourteenth centuries allowed glaciers to override mature forest. This was followed by a second warming in about 1350–1700 B.P., when glaciers receded and treelines rose once again.

In the southern Rockies, regional climate during 900–1300 B.P. involved complex precipitation and inconsistent patterns of warming. In some areas, increased drought frequency and severity during that period are indicated by variations in groundwater, reduced sedimentation, and little variation in tree growth (Dean 1994). In others, increased precipitation during the MWP, particularly in summer, brought rising lake levels, decreased water salinity, increased freshwater algae and pollen diversity, and enhanced monsoons (Petersen 1988, Davis 1994). Elevated summer precipitation is compatible with expanded forest and human occupation of the Colorado Plateau and central Rockies (Petersen 1994). Anasazi, Hohokam, and Mogollon cultures expanded after 600 B.P. and farmed as far north as northern Utah and southwestern Wyoming. Populations reached peak densities by 1100 B.P. After about 1200, cultures declined and eventually disappeared, coincident with a shift to aridity.

The Little Ice Age

The Little Ice Age (LIA) followed the MWP when glaciers expanded throughout many regions of the world, including the Rocky Mountains, during the fourteenth to nineteenth centuries (Desloges 1994, Grove 1988). Cooling lowered treelines, reduced tree growth, increased sedimentation, and shifted human populations, basically reversing trends established during the MWP. Overall, the LIA in western North America appeared as a series of cold intervals, with century-long averages about 1°C below preceding or subsequent time (figure 3.2). Oscillations within the LIA, however, were only approximately synchronous among regions.

In the Canadian Rockies, modest cooling began in the late fourteenth century, with pronounced cooling during 1690–1705 B.P. The most severe phase of the LIA began about 1800–1838 (Colenutt and Luckman 1995, Luckman et al. 1997). Dates of tree mortality correspond with or immediately follow the coldest periods, and some forests were overtaken by advancing glaciers (Kearney and Luckman 1987). Tree-ring data from the central and southern Rockies indicate similar cooling episodes (Fritts and Shao 1992, Naftz 1993). Summer cooling of 1.5°C–2.0°C is implied in alpine regions, and severe winters are suggested by historical records from the Great Plains and Great Salt Lake basin (Brunstein 1996).

Nowhere in the Rocky Mountains are effects of the LIA more evident than in glacial cirques from northern Canada to central Colorado, where moraines (glacial deposits) are prominent, sharp-crested, and easily recognized (Osborn and

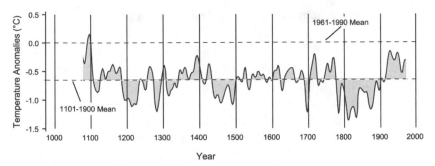

FIGURE 3.2 *Reconstructed April–August Temperature Anomalies at the Columbia Icefield, 1073–1983 B.P.* The temperature reconstruction is based on a calibration of tree-ring density and width with the regional instrumental climate record for the period 1891–1994. The anomalies are compared with the 1961–1990 mean. Note that the reconstructed record terminates in 1983 and half of the fourteen positive years of the 1961–1990 interval occurred during 1981–1990. From Luckman et al. 1997.

Luckman 1988, Davis 1988). Glaciers extended farther down-valley in the north (more than 1,000 m, or 3,280 ft., elevation below present) than in the south (100–300 m, or 328–984 ft., elevation below present), whereas late Pleistocene snowline depressions were fairly uniform over the region (Richmond 1986, Davis 1988, Menounos and Reasoner 1997). In Canada and Montana, LIA advances frequently exceed those of the late Pleistocene, whereas they terminate 1–3 km (1.6–4.8 mi.) up-valley from late Pleistocene moraines in the central Rockies and are absent from the southern Rockies (Clark and Gillespie 1997). Data suggest that LIA climate approached late Pleistocene conditions in the north, but severity diminished steadily with decreasing latitude, at least in alpine regions.

Temperature oscillations at the end of the LIA are inferred from a 300-year oxygen isotope record from the Fremont Glacier of Wyoming (Naftz et al. 1996). Relatively warm climate prevailed from 1716 B.P. (the glacier's basal age) until the mid-1700s, when an abrupt transition to colder climate occurred. The episode lasted until the mid-1800s, characterized by cool summers and perhaps enhanced seasonality. A shift back to warming followed the end of the LIA, evidently within a span of only two to three years. Since then, Rocky Mountain glaciers have shrunk in area by 30%–70% (Key, Fagre, and Menicke 1998) and treeline has advanced in alpine environments of Canada and Colorado, where increases in subalpine forest density are evident (Lavoie and Payette 1994, Hessl and Baker 1997).

Implications of the Past for the Future

The paleoecologic record has important implications for the way we view and manage Rocky Mountain ecosystems today. First, data indicate that the composition and dynamics of Rocky Mountain vegetation have changed on multiple time scales. Understanding environmental history requires disentangling these superimposed signals. Changes on millennial time scales were caused by shifts in the timing and intensity of summer drought, in turn driven by changes in the seasonal amplitude of insolation and the position of winter storm tracks. Climate has also changed on centennial and decadal time scales, with less dramatic consequences in the vegetation, but these changes are evident in glacier margins, shifts in the position of ecotones (vegetation boundaries), especially treeline, and changes in fire regime. The paleoecologic and geologic evidence confirms that climate is continually changing, and so too is the physical and biotic environment.

Paleoecologic records reveal the relatively ephemeral nature of modern plant communities. Species apparently respond individualistically to environmental changes. During the past 20,000 years, plant associations in the Rocky Mountains have been dismantled and reformed several times. Combinations of taxa have existed that have no modern analog and very likely represent climate conditions with no modern counterpart.

How fast can Rocky Mountain forests adjust to climate change? In mountainous regions where strong temperature and precipitation gradients are established by the topography, distinct vegetation communities are closely spaced and are separated by narrow ecotones (see part III of this book). Because the environmental gradients are foreshortened, lags between climate change and vegetation response may be negligible. Consequently, vegetation in mountainous regions is, and has been, very responsive to climate change. The response of montane and subalpine forests to past climate change, sometimes within decades, is a reminder of how sensitive present-day communities will be to anticipated climate changes associated with human activity.

Charcoal data from the Rocky Mountains indicate that fire frequency is closely tied to climate and it has changed continuously over the Holocene as the climate has varied. Fire occurrence was greatest during times of drought, for example, in the early Holocene and the MWP and less frequent during the LIA. Because there is no evidence of a long-term fire cycle, forest management plans that rely on mean return intervals ignore the variability or nonstationarity of the fire signal. Superimposed on the long-term patterns, fire regimes were also influenced by Native American practices at the local scale (Barrett and Arno 1999, Baker 2002). Human-set fires, for example, may have contributed to the open character of low-elevation pine forests at the time of Euro-American settlement.

Because of the changing nature of climate, vegetation, and fire occurrence, it is impossible to recreate the Rocky Mountain forests that existed at any time in the past. Efforts to return forests to the way they looked at the time of Euro-American contact will inevitably fail because the present-day climate is unique on both centennial and millennial time scales. We cannot reconstruct the forests of the LIA, the MWP, or the early Holocene because the climate and disturbance regime are different now. The paleoecologic record argues against this type of "snapshot" approach to restoration and instead suggests that natural ecosystems are best managed as dynamic systems, capable of change beyond that witnessed in the past few centuries.

A study of changes that might occur in the distribution of tree species in Yellowstone National Park with future climate change suggests surprising alterations in species distribution (Bartlein, Whitlock, and Shafer 1997). In computer model simulations, ranges of high-elevation species decreased, and some species, such as whitebark pine, were exterminated from the region completely. New communities combined taxa that grow today in the Yellowstone region, such as lodgepole pine and Douglas-fir, with northern and central Rocky Mountain taxa, including western larch, ponderosa pine, and scrub oak. The combination of widespread extirpations and biogeographic displacements projected for the future has no precedence in the paleoecologic record.

Decisions about proper management of Rocky Mountain forests will become ever more complex in light of projected changes in regional climate. Conservation efforts that emphasize the preservation of communities or vegetation types will quite likely be unsuccessful because such associations will probably dissolve (Overpeck, Bartlein, and Webb 1991; Davis and Shaw 2001). Similarly, as the climate continues to change, many present-day reserves will no longer protect the species for which they were intended. Rather than focusing on the preservation of communities, conservation plans should identify and protect areas with enough environmental diversity to permit connectivity among habitats (Hunter, Jacobson, and Webb 1988). An emphasis on environmental variability, rather than species richness, as the criterion for protection means that reserves should encompass the broad environmental gradients of the Rocky Mountains. Within north–south-trending mountain ranges, for example, reserves should allow species to shift to higher elevations and higher latitudes during periods of warming and drought. On a broader scale, reserves should be connected by corridors to enable species to shift their range without depending on long-distance dispersal. Unusual habitats should also be set aside for species that are limited by soil or other physical conditions. Protecting diversity in the Rocky Mountains will require a comprehensive approach that includes federal, state, and private lands.

Acknowledgment

Support for the work presented in this chapter was provided in part by a grant from the National Science Foundation to Cathy Whitlock (SBR-9615961, EAR-99006100).

References

Andrews, J. T., P. E. Carrara, F. B. King, and R. Stuckenrath. 1975. Holocene environmental changes in the alpine zone, northern San Juan Mountains, Colorado: Evidence from bog stratigraphy and palynology. *Quaternary Research* 5:173–197.

Baker, R. G. 1976. *Late Quaternary vegetation history of the Yellowstone Lake basin.* U.S. Geological Survey Professional Paper 729-E. Washington, D.C.: U.S. Geological Survey.

———. 1983. Holocene vegetational history of the western United States. In *Late-Quaternary environments of the United States*, ed. H. E. Wright Jr., 109–127. Minneapolis: University of Minnesota Press.

Baker, W. L. 2002. Indians and fire in the U.S. Rocky Mountains: The wilderness hypothesis renewed. In *Fire, native peoples, and the natural landscape*, ed. T. R. Vale, 41–76. Washington, D.C.: Island Press.

Barnosky, C. W. 1989. Postglacial vegetation and climate in the northwestern Great Plains of Montana. *Quaternary Research* 31:57–73.

Baroni, C., and G. Orombelli. 1994. Holocene glacier variations in the Terra Nova Bay area (Victoria Land, Antarctica). *Antarctic Science* 6:497–506.

Barrett, S. W., and S. F. Arno. 1999. Indian fires in the northern Rockies: Ethnohistory and ecology. In *Indians, fire, and the land in the Pacific Northwest,* ed. R. Boyd, 50–64. Corvallis: Oregon State University Press.

Bartlein, P. J., K. H. Anderson, P. M. Anderson, M. E. Edwards, C. J. Mock, R. S. Thompson, R. S. Webb, and C. Whitlock. 1998. Paleoclimate simulations for North America over the past 21,000 years: Features of simulated climate and comparisons with paleoenvironmental data. *Quaternary Science Reviews* 17:549–585.

Bartlein, P. J., C. Whitlock, and S. L. Shafer. 1997. Future climate in the Yellowstone National Park region and its potential impact on vegetation. *Conservation Biology* 11:782–792.

Beaudoin, A. B., and R. H. King. 1990. Late Quaternary vegetation history of Wilcox Pass, Jasper National Park, Alberta. *Palaeogeography, Palaeoclimatology, Palaeoecology* 80:129–144.

Beaudoin, A. B., and M. A. Reasoner. 1992. Evaluation of differential pollen deposition and pollen focusing from three Holocene intervals in sediments from Lake O'Hara, Yoho National Park, British Columbia, Canada: Inter-lake variability in pollen percentages, concentration, and influx. *Review of Palaeobotany and Palynology* 75:103–131.

Beiswenger, J. M. 1991. Late Quaternary vegetational history of Grays Lake, Idaho. *Ecological Monographs* 61:165–182.

Benedict, J. B. 1985. *Arapaho Pass: Glacial geology and archeology at the crest of the Colorado Front Range.* Research Report No. 3. Ward, Colo.: Center for Mountain Archeology.

Betancourt, J. L., T. R. Van Devender, and P. S. Martin. 1990. *Packrat middens: The last 40,000 years of biotic change.* Tucson: University of Arizona Press.

Brant, L. A. 1980. A palynological investigation of postglacial sediments at two locations along the Continental Divide near Helena, Montana. Ph.D. diss., Pennsylvania State University.

Bright, R. C. 1966. Pollen and seed stratigraphy of Swan Lake, southeastern Idaho: Its relation to regional vegetation history and to Lake Bonneville history. *Tebiwa* 9:1–47.

Brunstein, F. C. 1996. Climatic significance of the bristlecone pine latewood frost-ring record at Almagre Mountain, Colorado, USA. *Arctic and Alpine Research* 28:65–76.

Carrara, P. E., W. N. Mode, M. Ruben, and S. W. Robinson. 1984. Deglaciation and postglacial timberline in the San Juan Mountains, Colorado. *Quaternary Research* 21:42–55.

Carrara, P. E., D. A. Trimble, and M. Rubin. 1991. Holocene treeline fluctuations in the northern San Juan Mountains, Colorado, U.S.A., as indicated by radiocarbon-dated conifer wood. *Arctic and Alpine Research* 23:233–246.

Clark, D. H., and A. R. Gillespie. 1997. Timing and significance of late-glacial and Holocene cirque glaciation in the Sierra Nevada, California. *Quaternary International* 38/39:21–38.

Colenutt, M. E., and B. H. Luckman. 1995. Dendrochronological studies of *Larix lyallii* at Larch Valley, Alberta. *Canadian Journal of Forest Research* 21:1222–1233.

Davis, M. B., and R. G. Shaw. 2001. Range shifts and adaptive response to Quaternary climate change. *Science* 292:667–673.

Davis, O. K. 1994. The correlation of summer precipitation in the southwestern USA with isotopic records of solar activity during the Medieval Warm Period. *Climatic Change* 26:271–287.

Davis, O. K., J. C. Sheppard, and S. Robertson. 1986. Contrasting climate histories for the Snake River Plain, Idaho, resulting from multiple thermal maxima. *Quaternary Research* 26:321–339.

Davis, P. T. 1988. Holocene glacier fluctuations in the American cordillera. *Quaternary Science Reviews* 7:129–157.

Dean, J. S. 1994. The Medieval Warm Period on the southern Colorado Plateau. *Climatic Change* 26:225–241.

Deer, Z. 1994. Evidence for the existence of the Medieval Warm Period in China. *Climatic Change* 26:289–297.

Desloges, J. R. 1994. Varve deposition and the sediment yield record at three small lakes of the southern Canadian cordillera. *Arctic and Alpine Research* 26:130–140.

Doerner, J. P., and P. E. Carrara. 2001. Late-Quaternary vegetation and climate history of the Long Valley area, west-central Idaho, U.S.A. *Quaternary Research* 56:103–111.

Elias, S. A., and L. J. Toolin. 1990. Accelerator dating of a mixed assemblage of late Pleistocene insect fossils from the Lamb Spring site, Colorado. *Quaternary Research* 33:122–126.

Fall, P. L. 1997. Timberline fluctuations and late Quaternary paleoclimates in the southern Rocky Mountains, Colorado. *Geological Society of America Bulletin* 109:1306–1320.

Fall, P. L., P. T. Davis, and G. A. Zielinski. 1995. Late Quaternary vegetation and climate of the Wind River Range, Wyoming. *Quaternary Research* 43:393–404.

Feiler, E. J., R. S. Anderson, and P. A. Koehler. 1997. Late Quaternary paleoenvironments of the White River plateau, Colorado, USA. *Arctic and Alpine Research* 29:53–62.

Fritts, H. C., and X. M. Shao. 1992. Mapping climate using tree-rings from western North

America. In *Climate since A.D. 1500,* ed. R. S. Bradley and P. D. Jones, 269–295. London: Routledge.

Gennett, J. A., and R. G. Baker. 1986. A late-Quaternary pollen sequence from Blacktail Pond, Yellowstone National Park, Wyoming. *Quaternary Research* 43:393–404.

Gosse, J. C., E. B. Evenson, J. Klein, B. Lawn, and R. Middleton. 1995. Precise cosmogenic [10]Be measurements in western North America: Support for a global Younger Dryas cooling event. *Geology* 23:877–880.

Graham, R. W., and J. I. Mead. 1987. Environmental fluctuations and evolution of mammalian faunas during the last deglaciation in North America. In *North America and adjacent oceans during the last deglaciation,* ed. W. F. Ruddiman and H. E. Wright Jr., 371–402. Vol. K-3 of *The geology of North America.* Boulder, Colo.: Geological Society of America.

Grove, J. 1988. *The Little Ice Age.* London: Methuen.

Grove, J. M., and R. Switsur. 1994. Glacial evidence for the Medieval Warm Period. *Climatic Change* 6:143–169.

Hallett, D. J., L. V. Hills, and J. J. Clague. 1997. New accelerator mass spectrometry radiocarbon ages for the Mazama tephra layer from Kootenay National Park, British Columbia, Canada. *Canadian Journal of Earth Sciences* 34:1202–1209.

Hessl, A. E., and W. L. Baker. 1997. Spruce-fir growth form changes in the forest-tundra ecotone of Rocky Mountain National Park, Colorado, USA. *Ecography* 20:356–367.

Hickman, M., and C. A. Schweger. 1981. A palaeoenvironmental study of Fairfax Lake, a small lake situated in the Rocky Mountain foothills of west-central Alberta. *Journal of Paleolimnology* 6:1–15.

Hickman, M., and J. M. White. 1989. Late Quaternary paleoenvironments of Spring Lake, Alberta, Canada. *Journal of Paleolimnology* 2:305–317.

Hunter, M. L., G. L. Jacobson, and T. Webb III. 1988. Paleontology and the coarse-filter approach to maintaining biological diversity. *Conservation Biology* 2:375–385.

Kearney, M. S., and B. H. Luckman. 1983. Postglacial vegetational history of Tonquin Pass, British Columbia. *Canadian Journal of Earth Sciences* 20:776–786.

———. 1987. A mid-Holocene vegetational and climatic record of the subalpine zone of the Maligne Valley, Jasper National Park, Alberta (Canada). *Palaeogeography, Palaeoclimatology, Palaeoecology* 59:227–242.

Key, C. H., D. B. Fagre, and R. K. Menicke. 1998. Glacier recession in Glacier National Park, Montana. In *Satellite image atlas of glaciers of the world,* ed. R. S. Williams Jr. and J. G. Ferrigno, Chapter J, Glaciers of North America. U.S. Geological Survey Professional Paper 1386-J. Washington, D.C.: U.S. Geological Survey.

Kubiw, H., M. Hickman, and D. H. Vitt. 1989. The development of peatlands at Muskiki and Marguerite Lakes, Alberta. *Canadian Journal of Botany* 76:3534–3544.

Lavoie, C., and S. Payette. 1994. Recent fluctuations of the lichen spruce forest limit in subarctic Quebec. *Journal of Ecology* 82:725–734.

Legg, T. E., and R. G. Baker. 1980. Palynology of Pinedale sediments, Devlins Park, Boulder County, Colorado. *Arctic and Alpine Research* 12:319–333.

Leonard, E. M. 1997. The relationship between glacial activity and sediment production: Evidence from a 4450-year varve record of neoglacial sedimentation in Hector Lake, Alberta, Canada. *Journal of Paleolimnology* 17:319–330.

Luckman, B. H., K. R. Briffa, J. D. Jones, and F. H. Schweingruber. 1997. Tree-ring based reconstruction of summer temperatures at the Columbia Icefield, Alberta, Canada, A.D. 1073–1983. *Holocene* 7:375–389.

Luckman, B. H., and M. S. Kearney. 1986. Reconstruction of Holocene changes in alpine vegetation and climate in the Maligne Range, Jasper National Park, Alberta. *Quaternary Research* 26:244–261.

Lynch, E. A. 1998. Origin of a park-forest vegetation mosaic in the Wind River Range, Wyoming. *Ecology* 79:1320–1338.

MacDonald, G. M. 1982. Late Quaternary paleoenvironments of the Morley Flats and Kananaskis Valley of southwestern Alberta. *Canadian Journal of Earth Sciences* 18:23–35.

———. 1989. Postglacial palaeoecology of the subalpine forest-grassland ecotone of southwestern Alberta: New insights on vegetation and climate change in the Canadian Rocky Mountains and adjacent foothills. *Palaeogeography, Palaeoclimatology, Palaeoecology* 73:155–173.

Mack, R. N., N. W. Rutter, V. M. Bryant Jr., and S. Valastro. 1978. Reexamination of postglacial history in northern Idaho: Hager Pond, Bonner County. *Quaternary Research* 12:212–225.

Mack, R. N., N. W. Rutter, and S. Valastro. 1983. Holocene vegetation of the Kootenai River Valley, Montana. *Quaternary Research* 20:177–193.

Madsen, D. B., and D. R. Currey. 1979. Late Quaternary glacial and vegetation changes, Little Cottonwood Canyon area, Wasatch Mountains. *Quaternary Research* 12:254–270.

Maher, L. J. Jr. 1972. Absolute pollen diagram of Redrock Lake, Boulder County, Colorado. *Quaternary Research* 2:531–553.

Markgraf, V., and T. Lennon. 1986. Paleoenvironmental history of the last 13,000 years of the eastern Powder River basin, Wyoming, and its implication for prehistoric cultural patterns. *Plains Anthropologist* 31:1–12.

Markgraf, V., and L. Scott. 1981. Lower timberline in central Colorado during the past 15,000 years. *Geology* 9:231–234.

Mehringer, P. J. 1985. Late-Quaternary pollen records from the interior Pacific Northwest and northern Great Basin of the United States. In *Pollen records of late-Quaternary North American sediments,* ed. V. M. Bryant Jr. and R. G. Holloway, 167–189. Austin, Tex.: American Association of Stratigraphic Palynologists.

Mehringer, P. J. Jr., S. F. Arno, and K. L. Petersen. 1977. Postglacial history of Lost Trail Pass Bog, Bitterroot Mountains, Montana. *Arctic and Alpine Research* 9:345–368.

Menounos, B., and M. A. Reasoner. 1997. Evidence for cirque glaciation in the Colorado Front Range during the Younger Dryas chronozone. *Quaternary Research* 48:38–47.

Naftz, D. L. 1993. Ice-core records of the chemical quality of atmospheric deposition and climate from mid-latitude glaciers, Wind River Range, Wyoming. Ph.D. diss., Colorado School of Mines.

Naftz, D. L., R. W. Klusman, R. L. Michel, P. F. Schuster, M. M. Reddy, H. E. Taylor, T. M. Yanosky, and E. A. McConnaughey. 1996. Little Ice Age evidence from a south-central North American ice core, U.S.A. *Arctic and Alpine Research* 28:35–41.

Osborn, G., and B. H. Luckman. 1988. Holocene glacier fluctuations in the Canadian cordillera (Alberta and British Columbia). *Quaternary Science Reviews* 7:115–128.

Overpeck, J. T., P. J. Bartlein, and T. Webb III. 1991. Potential magnitude of future vegetation change in eastern North America: Comparisons with the past. *Science* 254:692–695.

Petersen, K. L. 1988. *Climate and the Dolores River Anasazi.* University of Utah Anthropological Papers No. 113. Salt Lake City: University of Utah Press.

———. 1994. A warm and wet Little Climatic Optimum and a cold and dry Little Ice Age in the southern Rocky Mountains, USA. *Climatic Change* 26:243–269.

Petersen, K. L., and P. J. Mehringer. 1976. Postglacial timberline fluctuations, La Plata Mountains, southwestern Colorado. *Arctic and Alpine Research* 8:275–288.

Porter, S. C., K. L. Pierce, and T. D. Hamilton. 1983. Late Wisconsin mountain glaciation in the western United States. In *Late-Quaternary environments of the United States,* ed. S. C. Porter, vol. 1, 71–111. Minneapolis: University of Minnesota Press.

Reasoner, M. A., and M. Hickman. 1989. Late Quaternary environmental change in the Lake O'Hara region, Yoho National Park, British Columbia. *Palaeogeography, Palaeoclimatology, Palaeoecology* 72:291–316.

Reasoner, M. A., and U. M. Huber. 1999. Postglacial palaeoenvironments of the upper Bow Valley, Banff National Park, Alberta, Canada. *Quaternary Science Reviews* 18:475–492.

Reasoner, M. A., and M. A. Jodry. 2000. Rapid response of alpine timberline vegetation to the Younger Dryas climate oscillation in the Colorado Rocky Mountains, USA. *Geology* 28:51–54.

Reasoner, M. A., G. Osborn, and N. W. Rutter. 1994. Age of the Crowfoot advance in the Canadian Rocky Mountains: A glacial event coeval with the Younger Dryas oscillation. *Geology* 22:439–442.

Richmond, G. M. 1986. Stratigraphy and correlation of glacial deposits of the Rocky Mountains, the Colorado Plateau, and the ranges of the Great Basin. *Quaternary Science Reviews* 5:99–127.

Stuiver, M., P. J. Reimer, E. Bard, J. W. Beck, G. S. Burr, K. A. Hughen, B. Kromer, G. McCormac, J. Van der Plicht, and M. Spurk. 1998. INTCAL89 radiocarbon age calibration, 24,000–0 cal. B.P. *Radiocarbon* 40:1041–1083.

Taylor, K. C., G. W. Lamorey, G. A. Doyle, R. B. Alley, P. M. Grootes, P. A. Mayeski, J. W. C. White, and L. K. Barlow. 1993. The "flickering switch" of late Pleistocene climate change. *Nature* 361:549–552.

Thompson, R. S., C. Whitlock, P. J. Bartlein, S. P. Harrison, and W. G. Spaulding. 1993. Climate changes in the western United States since 18,000 years B.P. In *Global climates since the last glacial maximum,* ed. H. E. Wright Jr., J. E. Kutzbach, T. Webb III, W. F. Ruddiman, F. A. Street-Perrott, and P. J. Bartlein, 468–513. Minneapolis: University of Minnesota Press.

Vierling, L. A. 1998. Palynological evidence for late- and postglacial environmental change in central Colorado. *Quaternary Research* 49:222–232.

Villalba, R. 1994. Tree-ring and glacial evidence for the Medieval Warm Epoch and the Little Ice Age in southern South America. *Climatic Change* 26:1183–1197.

Waddington, J. C. B., and H. E. Wright Jr. 1974. Late Quaternary vegetational changes on the east side of Yellowstone Park, Wyoming. *Quaternary Research* 4:175–184.

White, J. M., and R. W. Mathewes. 1986. Postglacial vegetation and climate change in the Peace River District, Canada. *Canadian Journal of Botany* 64:2305–2318.

Whitlock, C. 1993. Postglacial vegetation and climate of Grand Teton and southern Yellowstone National Parks. *Ecological Monographs* 63:173–198.

————. 1995. The history of *Larix occidentalis* during the last 20,000 years of environmental change. In *Ecology and management of Larix forests,* ed. W. C. Schmidt and K. J. McDonald, 83–90. General Technical Report GTR-INT-319. Ogden, Utah: U.S. Department of Agriculture, Forest Service, Intermountain Research Station.

Whitlock, C., and R. S. Anderson. 2002. Fire history reconstructions based on sediment records from lakes and wetlands. In *Fire and climatic change in the Americas,* ed. T. T. Veblen, W. L. Baker, G. Montenegro, and T. W. Swetnam. New York: Springer.

Whitlock, C., and P. J. Bartlein. 1993. Spatial variations of Holocene climatic change in the Yellowstone region. *Quaternary Research* 39:231–238.

Whitlock, C., P. J. Bartlein, and K. J. Van Norman. 1995. Stability of Holocene climate regimes in the Yellowstone region. *Quaternary Research* 43:433–436.

CHAPTER 4

Climates of the Rocky Mountains: Historical and Future Patterns

*Timothy G. F. Kittel, Peter E. Thornton, J. Andy Royle,
and Thomas N. Chase*

▲

The Rocky Mountains encompass a wide range of climates, from the boreal set-ting of the Mackenzie River to warm temperate domains of the American South-west. These climates set the context for ecological, hydrologic, and societal processes in this mountain region. In this chapter, we describe the geography and recent history (the past 100 years) of climate in the Rocky Mountains. We then explore the sensitivity of these climates to ongoing changes in regional and global factors that control climate throughout the Rockies.

This chapter discusses five Rocky Mountain regions divided along physio-graphic lines and political boundaries; two are in Canada and three are in the United States. The Canadian regions are the northern (Yukon and adjacent Northwest Territories) and southern (British Columbia and Alberta) Canadian Rockies (see the map facing the preface). The U.S. regions are distinguished phys-iographically as the northern, central, and southern U.S. Rockies (figure 4.1).

Continental Context

The Rocky Mountains have a north–south axis that spans the Northern Hemi-sphere's middle latitudes (roughly lat. 35°–65° N). In this location, the moun-tains form a significant 2,000–4,000 meter (m), or 7,000–14,000 feet (ft.), high barrier to the general westerly midlatitude flow of the atmosphere. The arrange-ment of mountains and atmospheric flow carrying moisture from the Pacific

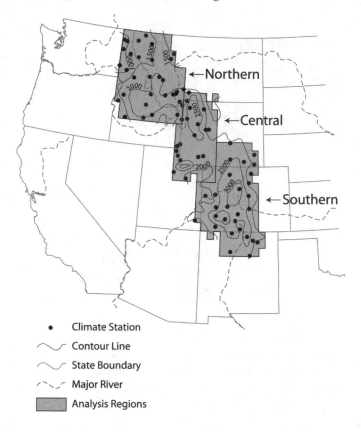

FIGURE 4.1 *Northern, Central, and Southern Rocky Mountains of the United States.* Open circles mark locations of stations used in historical analyses; contour lines indicate elevation above sea level in meters (500 m contour interval).

Ocean generates a classic orographic precipitation pattern, with enhanced precipitation on the windward side and a rain shadow on the lee (figure 4.2).

Actual regional patterns are, of course, more complicated. Winter storms approaching the southern Canadian and northern U.S. Rockies from the Pacific Ocean are laden with moisture, whereas those arriving in the southern U.S. Rockies have lost much of their moisture in crossing the Sierra Nevada and the intermountain West (figure 4.2). On the eastern side of the Rockies, both polar continental cold air from boreal regions and warmer maritime tropical moist air from the Gulf of Mexico are blocked by the mountain front from Alberta to New Mexico. As these winter air masses collide with the mountain front, they move upslope and generate precipitation along the eastern ranges of the Rockies.

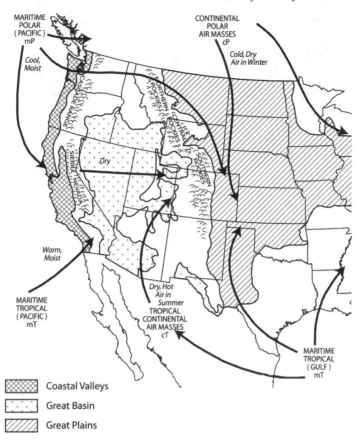

MARITIME POLAR (PACIFIC) mP

Cool, Moist

CONTINENTAL POLAR AIR MASSES cP

Cold, Dry Air in Winter

CASCADE RANGE

NORTHERN ROCKIES

CENTRAL ROCKIES

SIERRA NEVADA

Dry

SOUTHERN ROCKIES

Warm, Moist

MARITIME TROPICAL (PACIFIC) mT

Dry, Hot Air in Summer

TROPICAL CONTINENTAL AIR MASSES cT

MARITIME TROPICAL (GULF) mT

Coastal Valleys

Great Basin

Great Plains

FIGURE 4.2 *Air Mass Source Areas and Flow Patterns Influencing Climates of the U.S. Rocky Mountains.* From *A Sierra Club Naturalist's Guide to the Southern Rockies* by Audrey Benedict and Barbara Bash, 1991. Used by permission.

In summer, the southern Canadian Rockies continue to receive moist Pacific air. To the south, however, much of the interior western United States is under the influence of either dry continental air or monsoonal flows from the Gulfs of Mexico and California. In the U.S. Rockies, the boundary between these air masses depends on incursion of gulf air into the southern Rockies driven by circulation from the Bermuda subtropical high-pressure center (figure 4.2) (Mitchell 1976).

An understanding of source regions for air masses that give rise to climates of the Rockies helps to identify causes of interannual, decadal, and longer-term variability. Regions receiving flows from the Pacific (the Canadian and northern U.S.

Rockies) are strongly influenced by variability in North Pacific Ocean surface temperatures and atmospheric circulation patterns, such as reflected by the strength of the Aleutian low-pressure center. In contrast, the southern U.S. Rockies are more influenced by subtropical and tropical sea surface temperatures and circulation patterns, such as El Niño and the Southern Oscillation (ENSO).

Geography of Climate

Climate is spatially highly variable in mountainous regions. Variability is determined largely by the effects of topography (elevation, slope, and aspect) on precipitation, temperature, solar radiation, and humidity. There are few records of temperature and precipitation in complex terrain compared with adjacent flatlands, and fewer still of solar radiation and humidity. It is usually necessary to infer topographic effects in order to quantify the climate of a region of complex terrain. This is accomplished by generating high-resolution maps of climate (e.g., grid interval less than 5 kilometers [km], or 3 miles [mi.]) with uniform data density over complex terrain using both horizontal interpolation of observations and vertical extrapolation to estimate climate at elevations higher than local observations (Thornton, Running, and White 1997; Daly, Neilson, and Phillips 1994). There are typically not enough observations of solar radiation and humidity to perform direct and accurate interpolations and extrapolations, but reasonable proxies can be derived from the more common observations of temperature and precipitation (Thornton, Hasenauer, and White 2000). Plates 3 and 4 present high-resolution climatologies for the U.S. and Canadian Rockies.

Climatology of the U.S. Rockies

We analyzed regional differences in the mean climatology of the U.S. Rocky Mountains based on a 1 km gridded eighteen-year database of daily surface weather parameters (the U.S. Daymet data set) (Thornton, Running, and White 1997); see plate 3 and table 4.1. Within each region, we also evaluated other climatological statistics, including interannual standard deviation and regressions with elevation (table 4.1).

Spatial Patterns. All regions show substantial spatial variation in mean climate reflecting roles of latitude, elevation, and continental position (plate 3). From south to north, the Rockies broadly become cooler (at the same elevation), receive more moisture (with the increasing influence of Pacific air), and have less solar radiation (table 4.1, plate 3). In the context of the entire western United States, the Rockies differ markedly from mountains to the west. The Coast Ranges, Cascade Range, and Sierra Nevada are more strongly influenced

TABLE 4.1. U.S. Rocky Mountain Climatological Analysis

	Regional Statistics: Mean, (Interannual SD), [Interannual CV]				Elevation Regression: Slope (R²)			
Analysis Period	All Regions	Northern	Central	Southern	All Regions	Northern	Central	Southern
TOTAL PRECIPITATION (cm)								
Annual	55.7 (11.5) [0.21]	75.5 (15.4) [0.20]	46.2 (9.7) [0.21]	45.8 (9.5) [0.21]	9.5 (0.54)	13.1 (0.99)	23.7 (0.91)	30.7 (0.98)
January	4.6 (2.9) [0.63]	7.6 (4.1) [0.54]	3.2 (2.2) [0.69]	3.2 (2.4) [0.75]	0.5 (0.25)	1.1 (0.99)	3.2 (0.96)	2.5 (0.95)
July	3.9 (2.9) [0.74]	3.9 (3.1) [0.79]	3.6 (2.8) [0.78]	4.3 (2.7) [0.63]	1.1 (0.81)	0.8 (0.90)	0.5 (0.34)	2.3 (0.99)
PRECIPITATION FREQUENCY (% wet days)								
Annual	21.6 (3.8)	27.3 (4.4)	19.1 (3.7)	18.4 (3.3)	0.2 (0.00)	−2.3 (0.98)	5.1 (0.92)	6.8 (0.99)
January	21.8 (11.2)	31.5 (13.8)	17.7 (10.1)	16.3 (9.7)	−1.4 (0.12)	−4.5 (0.95)	9.3 (0.88)	5.7 (0.99)
July	17.8 (11.0)	16.8 (12.0)	16.4 (10.5)	20.4 (10.5)	3.0 (0.86)	−0.1 (0.00)	0.2 (0.04)	7.1 (0.94)
PRECIPITATION AVERAGE EVENT SIZE (cm/wet day)								
Annual	0.68 (0.08)	0.73 (0.08)	0.64 (0.08)	0.67 (0.08)	0.12 (0.91)	0.20 (0.98)	0.14 (0.82)	0.20 (0.97)
January	0.56 (0.21)	0.68 (0.20)	0.47 (0.20)	0.54 (0.23)	0.13 (0.85)	0.18 (0.95)	0.25 (0.97)	0.23 (0.96)
July	0.64 (0.30)	0.67 (0.35)	0.63 (0.30)	0.62 (0.25)	0.10 (0.93)	0.16 (0.99)	0.11 (0.70)	0.15 (0.99)

(continued)

TABLE 4.1. (continued)

Analysis Period	Regional Statistics: Mean, [Interannual SD], [Interannual CV]				Elevation Regression: Slope (R^2)			
	All Regions	Northern	Central	Southern	All Regions	Northern	Central	Southern
MAXIMUM TEMPERATURE (°C)								
Annual	12.8 (0.9)	11.4 (1.0)	12.5 (1.0)	14.6 (0.8)	-3.6 (0.94)	-4.7 (0.99)	-5.0 (0.97)	-6.9 (0.99)
January	0.4 (2.4)	-1.1 (2.2)	-0.4 (2.8)	-2.6 (2.2)	-1.9 (0.94)	-3.2 (0.99)	-3.1 (0.96)	-4.5 (0.99)
July	26.1 (1.9)	24.9 (2.6)	26.3 (2.0)	27.2 (1.2)	-4.6 (0.92)	-5.0 (0.99)	-5.9 (0.96)	-8.4 (0.99)
MINIMUM TEMPERATURE (°C)								
Annual	-2.2 (1.0)	-2.6 (1.2)	-2.7 (1.0)	-1.3 (0.7)	-3.8 (0.99)	-5.1 (0.99)	-4.0 (0.97)	-6.3 (0.99)
January	-12.2 (2.7)	-11.3 (3.0)	-13.5 (2.9)	-11.7 (2.2)	-3.8 (0.99)	-5.6 (0.99)	-2.6 (0.95)	-5.4 (0.99)
July	8.3 (1.3)	6.8 (1.6)	8.5 (1.4)	9.6 (1.0)	-3.7 (0.95)	-4.5 (0.99)	-4.9 (0.98)	-7.3 (0.98)

	Regional Statistics: Mean, (Interannual SD), [Interannual CV]				Elevation Regression: Slope (R²)			
Analysis Period	All Regions	Northern	Central	Southern	All Regions	Northern	Central	Southern
DAILY TOTAL SOLAR RADIATION (MJ m⁻² day⁻¹)								
Annual	15.7	14.3	15.7	17.1	1.0	0.6	0.5	−0.2
	(0.3)	(0.3)	(0.3)	(0.3)	(0.85)	(0.99)	(0.45)	(0.75)
January	7.0	5.2	6.8	8.9	1.4	0.7	0.6	0.0
	(0.3)	(0.3)	(0.2)	(0.3)	(0.92)	(0.99)	(0.63)	(0.08)
July	24.4	24.2	24.5	24.4	0.4	0.7	0.5	−0.1
	(1.2)	(1.4)	(1.2)	(1.2)	(0.51)	(0.98)	(0.47)	(0.18)
DAILY AVERAGE WATER VAPOR PRESSURE (Pa)								
Annual	479	511	455	470	−98	−144	−89	−86
	(56)	(52)	(59)	(56)	(0.94)	(0.98)	(0.95)	(0.99)
January	259	293	234	252	−78	−120	−45	−82
	(53)	(58)	(48)	(52)	(0.95)	(0.96)	(0.98)	(0.98)
July	792	842	802	731	−167	−168	−215	−116
	(152)	(133)	(166)	(156)	(0.94)	(0.99)	(0.87)	(0.96)

Source: Analyses are based on U.S. Daymet data set for the period 1980–1997 (Thornton, Running, and White 1997).

Note: Analysis includes regional mean, interannual standard deviation (SD), interannual coefficient of variation (CV; as fraction, for total precipitation only), and elevation regressions slope and R^2 statistic. Elevation regressions were performed on climate parameters averaged over five elevation classes in each region.

by maritime air masses and are generally warmer and wetter and receive less solar radiation than the Rocky Mountains at similar latitudes.

The climatology of daily precipitation is complex because precipitation is not a temporally continuous process. The same long-term average of total annual precipitation could be obtained by either a high frequency of small events or a low frequency of large events. Precipitation frequency at low elevations is highest in the northern U.S. Rockies (35% wet days), reflecting the influence of relatively warm, moist air masses from the Pacific, compared with the central and southern regions (less than 12% wet days during winter). The average precipitation per event ranges substantially, from 1.2 centimeters (cm) per day, or approximately 0.5 inch (in.) per day, in winter at high elevations in the north to 0.25 cm/day (0.1 in./day) in winter at low elevations in the central Rockies.

Shortwave (solar) radiation received at the surface increases from north to south in winter but is nearly constant across regions in summer, when longer day length in the north compensates for lower sun angles. Winter solar radiation as a percentage of summer values ranges from 21% in the north to 36% in the south. Absolute humidity is highest in the northern region and lowest in the central region for all seasons, reflecting the maritime influence in the north. Humidity is slightly higher in the southern region than in the central region because of incursions of moist air from the Gulf of Mexico and the Pacific.

Elevation Relationships. Precipitation increases significantly with elevation in all three regions of the U.S. Rockies, with peak precipitation occurring near mountaintops, a pattern characteristic of midlatitude mountainous regions (table 4.1). The northern region has higher annual and January total precipitation for a given elevation than either the central or the southern region. In July, however, the southern U.S. Rockies receive more total precipitation at high elevations than the regions to the north because of the southwestern summer monsoon. Differences in annual totals among regions are greatest at low elevations.

The frequency at which it rains or snows decreases with elevation in the northern region but increases with elevation in the central and southern regions, a pattern that is stronger in January than in July. Higher elevations get more precipitation per event (defined as a wet day) in all regions and all seasons. In contrast to annual total precipitation and precipitation frequency, the largest differences in annual average event size among regions are at the highest elevations.

Temperatures can be colder at the lowest elevations in the central region than at similar elevations in the northern region. This is because of stronger influence from continental air masses in the central Rockies and maritime air masses in the north. Relationships with elevation for both maximum and minimum temperature (i.e., temperature lapse rates) are strong and linear in all regions and all seasons (table 4.1). Lapse rates for maximum and minimum temperature are in general stronger (larger decrease in temperature with increasing elevation) in summer than in winter, with summer lapse rates for maximum temperature stronger than for minimum temperature. Lapse rates for all seasons are stronger in the southern region than in the northern and central regions. As a result, there is a convergence in temperatures across regions at higher elevation. For all regions, interannual variability of maximum temperature decreases with elevation in winter, whereas that for minimum temperature increases in summer.

Winter solar radiation increases with elevation in the northern U.S. Rockies, but in the southern region it peaks at mid-elevations and then decreases slightly with elevation. This regional difference is in part a result of lower sun angles in winter in the north, which cause lower and mid-elevation sites to be shaded by adjacent mountains. Another contributing factor is the tendency for low-level clouds and fog to form as a result of temperature inversions during winter in valleys of the northern and central regions. In all three regions, peak summer solar radiation occurs at mid-elevations, around 2,500 m (8,000 ft.). Interannual variability of solar radiation increases strongly with elevation in all regions in winter and in the northern and southern regions in summer.

Water vapor pressure (absolute humidity) decreases with elevation in all regions and all seasons, consistent with decreasing temperature and surface air pressure. Decreases in absolute humidity with elevation are largest in summer, whereas those for relative humidity are largest in winter. Interannual variability in absolute humidity decreases with elevation in all regions in winter.

Climatology of the Canadian Rockies

A high-resolution gridded analysis for western Canada reveals the distribution of mean annual precipitation and mean January temperature (plate 4; Daly et al. 2001, 2002). These maps show the same pattern as in the United States of wetter and warmer climate in coastal ranges than in the Canadian Rocky Mountains. The southern region is wetter and warmer than the northern Canadian Rockies. This precipitation gradient is the reverse of that in the U.S. Rockies and is caused by the stronger presence of Pacific maritime air (and higher elevations) in the southern Canadian Rockies. The influence of the wintertime arctic front (southern limit of arctic continental air) is clearly defined as a strong gradient in mean January maximum temperature along the border between British Columbia and Yukon Territory (plate 4, right panel).

Recent Climate History

We evaluated centennial trends and interannual variability in annual and seasonal precipitation, mean minimum and maximum temperature, and mean diurnal temperature range for the U.S. and Canadian Rockies. Trends in minimum and maximum temperatures reflect different climatic processes and have different effects on ecological dynamics and surface hydrology, so they are considered separately. Diurnal temperature range is a useful index that summarizes their different dynamics.

Historical Climate Trends

We evaluated centennial climate trends for the U.S. Rockies on the basis of longest-running station records selected from the United States Historical Climatology Network (HCN) data set (Kittel and Royle, unpublished analysis). The HCN monthly precipitation and mean minimum and maximum temperature data set includes stations that are long-term with relatively complete records that were corrected for time-of-observation differences, instrument changes, instrument moves, station relocations, and urbanization effects (Quinlan, Karl, and Williams 1987). Although there is a natural bias in longer records toward lower elevations (because early settlement was in mountain valleys and foothills), the stations span a wide range of elevations in each of the three U.S. regions (figure 4.1).

Annual and seasonal precipitation and mean minimum temperature increased significantly during the twentieth century. The magnitude and statistical significance of these trends varied by region and season. The strongest precipitation trends occurred in the northern and central U.S. Rockies in summer: 30% and 33% per century, respectively ($P < 0.05$) (figure 4.3a, b). Trends in annual mean minimum temperature were +0.7°C and +0.9°C per century, respectively ($P < 0.005$), for these regions. Annual and seasonal trends were not significant in the southern U.S. Rockies for all variables (figure 4.3c, f).

Mean diurnal temperature range decreased significantly. Trends were strongest in the northern and central U.S. Rockies (−0.6°C and −1.2°C/century, respectively, for summer; figure 4.3d, e). The decrease in mean diurnal temperature range came primarily from increasing minimum temperatures rather than from changes in maximum temperature. This pattern of decreasing diurnal range is consistent with trends observed throughout the United States, which are attributed to increased cloud cover. Greater cloud cover increases nighttime temperatures and decreases daytime temperatures (or at least causes smaller increases if there is a background increase in surface air temperatures) (Plantico et al. 1990; Dai, Trenberth, and Karl 1999). Observed increases in precipitation (with concurrent increases in cloud cover) are consistent with this explanation (figure 4.3a, b).

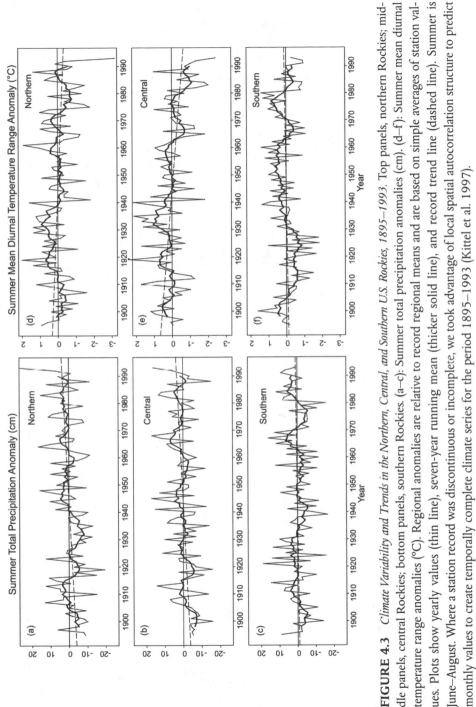

FIGURE 4.3 *Climate Variability and Trends in the Northern, Central, and Southern U.S. Rockies, 1895–1993.* Top panels, northern Rockies; middle panels, central Rockies; bottom panels, southern Rockies. (a–c): Summer total precipitation anomalies (cm). (d–f): Summer mean diurnal temperature range anomalies (°C). Regional anomalies are relative to record regional means and are based on simple averages of station values. Plots show yearly values (thin line), seven-year running mean (thicker solid line), and record trend line (dashed line). Summer is June–August. Where a station record was discontinuous or incomplete, we took advantage of local spatial autocorrelation structure to predict monthly values to create temporally complete climate series for the period 1895–1993 (Kittel et al. 1997).

In the southern Canadian Rockies, annual and seasonal mean minimum temperature increased significantly from 1900 to 1998 (+1.0°C to +2.5°C/century), and diurnal temperature range decreased (–0.5°C to –2.0°C/century; Zhang et al. 2000). For midlatitude Canada in general, the negative trend in diurnal temperature range was strongly correlated with increasing cloud cover, precipitation, and streamflow for this same period (Dai, Trenberth, and Karl 1999). In the southern Canadian Rockies, precipitation increased both annually and seasonally by +5% to +40% since 1900 (Zhang et al. 2000).

There were significant and comparable increases in maximum and minimum temperature (trends in annual means +1.5°C to +2.0°C per 50 years [yr.]) from 1950 to 1998 for both the southern and northern Canadian Rockies, with generally larger changes in the north (Zhang et al. 2000). This continues the positive poleward gradient in trends we found in the U.S. Rockies, with temperature changes for the second half of the twentieth century in the northern Canadian Rockies on the order of four times those farther south in the U.S. Rockies (Nicholls et al. 1996).

Elevation Dependence in Trends

The noted ability of mountains to "generate their own climate" comes from the strong modification of circulation, precipitation, and solar radiation regimes by mountain massifs. Although this is evident in long-term climatologies, how these processes affect climate variability and trends in mountains is not as well understood. Previous studies in the Rocky Mountains and elsewhere have pointed out significant differences in century-scale trends and interannual variability between mountain environments and adjacent lowlands (Greenland and Kittel 2002; Inouye et al. 2000; Beniston, Diaz, and Bradley 1997; Diaz and Bradley 1997). These differences can reflect an amplification of lower-elevation signals with elevation (Beniston and Rebetez 1996) or can reflect divergent signals, suggesting that lowland and highland climates are decoupled (Diaz and Bradley 1997, Greenland and Losleben 2001).

There are several explanations for an elevation effect. Higher reaches of mountain systems are in closer contact with the free troposphere and so respond rapidly to upper-air circulation changes. Higher mountains may also be less affected by ameliorating surface processes (e.g., irrigation, large lake effects, urbanization) (Greenland and Losleben 2001, Giorgi et al. 1997). In addition, upper air can override lower air (especially in the presence of inversions), decoupling high-elevation climates from convective mixing of the lower troposphere and development of valley fogs (Greenland and Losleben 2001, Diaz and Bradley 1997). A feedback between snow cover and surface albedo (fraction of solar radiation reflected at the surface) can also amplify a regional temperature signal with elevation (Giorgi et al. 1997). Regional higher temperatures result in less snow cover, more absorption of solar radiation, and therefore greater local warming, enhancing the regional signal. The opposite is true in colder years.

Dependence of long-term temperature changes on elevation results in changes in lapse rate with consequences for atmospheric stability and generation of local circulation and precipitation. We found that changes in lapse rate varied by region and season. In the northern U.S. Rockies, daytime warming trends tended to be stronger with elevation, so lapse rates were generally reduced, resulting in a more stable atmosphere during the day. We found little elevation dependence in nighttime temperature trends or a weakening of these trends with elevation. These results contrast with those of Diaz and Bradley (1997), who found stronger warming at higher elevations due largely to increases in minimum temperature for midlatitude Northern Hemisphere mountains. However, their result depended on what elevation span was used and what time period was assessed (Diaz and Bradley 1997, Pepin 2000).

Interannual and Interdecadal Climate Variability

There is strong variation in monthly precipitation, monthly mean minimum and maximum temperature, and monthly mean diurnal temperature range at interannual and decadal scales (figure 4.3). Some of the variability is shared across the three regions, and some is distinct. Adjacent regions were more similar to one another than those farther apart. Correlation between adjacent regions in precipitation variability diminishes at time scales longer than five to ten years but is generally high for temperature at both shorter and longer time scales.

There were strong droughts in the late 1910s and early 1920s in the northern and central U.S. Rockies. The 1930s drought was strongest in the north, and the 1950s drought was most pronounced in the central and southern regions (figure 4.3a–c). Late-twentieth-century precipitation extremes associated with the midcontinental 1988 drought and 1993 floods extended into the northern and central U.S. Rockies.

Temperature minima and maxima had a general pattern of cooling until 1915, warming through the late 1930s, cooling or little trend into the 1970s, and then warming. This pattern agrees with the overall decadal pattern for the contiguous United States (Karl et al. 1996) and is reflected in the twentieth-century record for southern Canada (Zhang et al. 2000). The signal is related to shifts in Northern Hemisphere circulation patterns (Wallace, Zhang, and Bajuk 1996) and is possibly related to combined effects of solar output variation, volcanic eruptions, and enhanced greenhouse gas forcing (Houghton et al. 2001).

Although there is a hemispheric component of decadal variability in the Rocky Mountain signal, there is also a regional, elevation-dependent element.

There was a series of cold years in the early 1980s for high-elevation stations (higher than 3,000 m, or 9,800 ft.) in Colorado and Wyoming, but not for lower-elevation stations (Losleben 1997). We saw the same pattern in regional annual mean maximum temperature for all three regions of the U.S. Rockies. Although this is in some ways a local signal, isolated to higher elevations, regional consistency suggests broader-scale processes acting on the Rocky Mountains. The cold anomaly was related to extreme, near-synchronous events: particulates from volcanic eruptions reduced solar inputs, and a strong El Niño and changes in North Pacific atmospheric circulation patterns caused greater high-elevation increases in precipitation and cloud cover (Greenland and Losleben 2001).

Diurnal temperature range in the northern and central U.S. Rockies generally decreased until around 1910, increased through the mid-1930s, and decreased markedly since then (e.g., for summer; figure 4.3d, e). The midcentury shift from weakly increasing to strongly decreasing trends is similar to that for the conterminous United States as a whole, with some variation in timing of this break (Plantico et al. 1990). The shift in trends is in contrast to that in the southern Canadian Rockies, where there was a strong decline prior to the 1950s and weak trends since (Zhang et al. 2000). Increasing total cloud amounts in the Canadian midlatitudes in the first half of the twentieth century are the probable cause (Zhang et al. 2000).

Hemispheric and Global Teleconnections

Interannual climate variability in the U.S. Rockies is linked to global and hemispheric circulation patterns. An analysis of such teleconnections (long-distance climate links) showed that a significant portion of interannual variation in temperature and precipitation can be explained by (1) the intensity of the Aleutian low-pressure center, which is inversely represented by the North Pacific Index (NPI) (Trenberth and Hurrell 1994), and (2) reversals in eastern Pacific sea surface temperature anomalies (with warm anomalies, or deviations from the average, identified as El Niño) and tropical Pacific atmospheric pressure anomalies (reflecting the Southern Oscillation) (Kittel and Royle, unpublished analysis).

Winter temperatures are negatively correlated with the NPI throughout the U.S. Rockies, with the relationship strongest in the central and northern regions ($P < 0.005$). A negative correlation indicates that warm winter temperatures occur when the Aleutian Low is most intense (deep low-pressure center) so that flow around the Low is more from the south, bringing warm air northward into the Rockies.

Winter precipitation is significantly positively correlated with the NPI in the central U.S. Rockies. This suggests that when the Aleutian Low is weaker, the resulting westerly flow brings Pacific storms directly into the central Rockies. Winter precipitation and snow cover are also positively correlated with the occurrence of El Niño in the southern Rockies and are anticorrelated in the northern and central U.S. Rockies and the southern Canadian Rockies (Kittel and Royle, unpublished analysis; Groisman et al. 1994).

We found that summer precipitation in the northern U.S. Rockies was negatively correlated with the NPI and therefore positively linked to a deeper Aleutian Low. A stronger Low in summer directs storm tracks farther south than normal. Summer precipitation in the southern and central U.S. Rockies was not correlated with the NPI but was, on the other hand, strongly positively correlated with El Niño (Kittel and Royle, unpublished analysis; Dai and Wigley 2000).

Groisman et al. (1994) showed elevation dependence in the sign of snowpack response to El Niño across the Northern Hemisphere, including the Canadian and U.S. Rockies, supported by a regional analysis for the southern U.S. Rockies (M. Losleben, pers. comm.). Elevation-dependent teleconnections are found elsewhere, such as the Swiss Alps, where winter temperature responses to hemispheric circulation patterns are strongest at higher elevations (Giorgi et al. 1997).

Sensitivity of Mountain Climates to Altered Forcing

Terrestrial environments are experiencing a range of anthropogenic forcings that affect their current and future status. Some of these forcings act on climate; some are global in scope, and others are regionally generated. We consider two that directly influence climates of the Rocky Mountains: (1) changing character of the land surface at both regional and global scales and (2) changing composition of the atmosphere, especially with respect to radiatively active (greenhouse) gases. The potential effect of the resulting changes in climate will influence the function and structure of ecological and surface hydrologic systems and the human economies that depend on them.

Changing Land Use—Regional to Global Forcing

Although the Rockies deprive adjacent regions of precipitation by blocking and capturing moisture from maritime air masses, the cordillera is at the same time the source of great river systems on the Arctic, Pacific, and Gulf of Mexico sides of the Continental Divide—the Saskatchewan, Columbia, Peace-Slave-Athabaska, Colorado, Missouri, Arkansas, and Rio Grande, among others. Many of these rivers give rise to ribbons of moisture well out into the semi-arid Great Plains and the arid West, supplying irrigation flows throughout these regions. Development of irrigation systems and other land use changes in the Great

Plains have influenced local and regional climate (Pielke and Avissar 1990, Segal et al. 1998). Land use change in the Great Plains and in regions well removed (e.g., the Tropics) very likely has altered, and potentially can alter, climates of the Rocky Mountains.

Changing land cover has been demonstrated to affect regional and global climate significantly in modeling and observational studies at a variety of spatial scales (e.g., Betts et al. 1996). A change in land cover can have profound effects on the total energy absorbed by the land surface by altering surface albedo and on how that absorbed energy is returned to the atmosphere via latent and sensible heat fluxes. For example, energy in a densely vegetated region is returned to the atmosphere mostly by means of transpiration and evaporation (i.e., latent fluxes). This limits the direct (sensible) heating of the air, causing cooler, moister conditions. The opposite occurs in sparsely vegetated regions, where sensible heating dominates. Land cover–mediated changes in the surface energy budget affect surface hydrology, storm formation, regional circulations, and other quantities of meteorological and ecological interest.

Climate model simulations are used (almost exclusively) to address the influence of land cover changes on regional climate. Modeling studies of the effects of observed land cover changes across Canada and the conterminous United States found winter warming in the northern Canadian Rockies of as much as 2°C, significant springtime warming of more than 1°C and little July temperature response in the U.S. Rockies, and a significant increase in July precipitation in the southern and central U.S. Rockies (Copeland, Pielke, and Kittel 1996; Bonan 1997).

A high-resolution modeling study of the effect of change in agricultural land cover adjacent to the Colorado Front Range found that irrigated lands had a significant effect on the mountain-plains breeze circulation in summer and therefore affected weather patterns in the mountain regions as well as on the plains (Chase et al. 1999). The study suggested that land use change has resulted in reduced daytime upslope winds and cooling in the mountains in summer. Changes in summer upslope circulation patterns, as suggested by these simulations, would also significantly affect advection of pollution from nearby urban areas (e.g., Denver), altering nitrogen deposition rates in the Rocky Mountain alpine zone (chapter 9; Sievering 2001).

The potential effect of land cover change on the Rocky Mountains is not limited to local land cover changes. Climate model studies indicate that land cover changes across the globe, particularly in the Tropics, affect global-scale circulations and have the potential to affect areas far removed from the source of change (Chase et al. 1996, 2000; Zhao, Pitman, and Chase 2001). The exact nature of the effects is a function of model configuration and interacting environmental influences and is therefore uncertain. However, the suggested climatic changes are of similar magnitude to those simulated for elevated greenhouse gases and therefore represent potentially significant factors in regional climate change (Chase et al. 2001, Pitman and Zhao 2000). Land cover–climate model simulations are incomplete for many reasons, but they do serve to illustrate processes and interactions at work. They emphasize that the atmosphere communicates environmental changes over large distances. No compilation of potential regional effects can focus solely on local and regional processes.

Changing Atmospheric Composition

Greenhouse gas concentrations and tropospheric aerosols (very fine suspended particles) have been increasing since the mid-nineteenth century, largely as a result of human activities. These increases have raised the concern that they have altered and will continue to alter surface climates (Houghton et al. 2001). We address the potential magnitude of the effects of rising greenhouse gases and aerosols on Rocky Mountain climates and how mountain regional processes might modify these global- to continental-scale forced changes. The effects must be considered in the context of other sources of climatic change, including land use change, natural internal oscillations in atmosphere-ocean-cryosphere (sea and land ice) dynamics, variation in solar output, and volcanic eruptions. Reports by the Intergovernmental Panel on Climate Change (Houghton et al. 2001, McCarthy et al. 2001) and the U.S. National Assessment Synthesis Team (NAST 2001, Wagner and Baron 1999) review scientific issues and assessments of these effects and their potential consequences for environmental and human systems.

For the U.S. Rockies, we evaluated climate sensitivity of coupled global climate model (GCM) experiments from (1) the Canadian Centre for Climate Modelling and Analysis and (2) the Hadley Centre for Climate Prediction and Research, United Kingdom, run under future emission-forcing scenarios of approximately 1%/yr. increases in greenhouse gases and sulfate aerosols through the twenty-first century (Boer, Flato, and Ramsden 2000; Mitchell et al. 1995). These simulations, referred to here as CCC and HAD, respectively, have a coarse resolution (grid intervals approximately 200–375 km, or 120–225 mi.), which was rescaled to a 0.5° latitude/longitude grid for the conterminous United States (Kittel et al. 2000). We looked at annual and seasonal changes in precipitation, mean minimum and maximum temperature, and two integrative variables: (1) Palmer Drought Severity Index (PDSI) and (2) length of the snow-free season (Kittel et al. 2000, Kittel and Thornton, unpublished analysis).

There was greater temperature sensitivity in the CCC experiment than in the HAD scenario (+5.6°C vs. +3.6°C/century for mean temperature) and minimally higher precipitation sensitivity (+20% vs. +18%/century; e.g., figure 4.4a) in response to rising greenhouse gases and sulfate aerosols. These responses were larger than observed historical trends and varied by season. Both experiments showed generally greater changes in minimum temperature than in maximum temperature, resulting in a decrease in diurnal temperature range for most seasons (e.g., figure 4.4b; plate 5a, b).

Changes in PDSI were small in HAD compared with those in CCC (figure 4.4c; plate 5c, d). This was because the drying effect of increased temperatures (higher potential evapotranspiration) was roughly countered by increases in precipitation, whereas in CCC higher temperature sensitivity overwhelmed increased moisture inputs. The snow-free period increased in both scenarios, more strongly in CCC (by one or more months; see plate 5b). This change was largely in response to higher spring and early summer temperatures but possibly also because of less winter precipitation falling as snow in spite of strong increases in winter precipitation (30%–65%/century).

The CCC experiment showed temperature increases from 1971–1990 to the 2030s of 1°C–2°C in the southern Canadian Rockies, increasing to +2°C–3°C poleward in the northern Canadian Rockies (Boer, Flato, and Ramsden 2000). Modeled trends in precipitation in the Canadian Rockies were small and mostly positive; the signal was weaker than that simulated farther south in the U.S. Rockies (figure 4.4a).

Elevation dependence in climate change response to increasing greenhouse gases has been little explored but is suggested by elevation dependence in historical climatic trends, interannual variability, and teleconnections and by simulated dynamic interactions between mountain and adjacent lowland climates. In the CCC experiment, surface temperature response intensified with elevation over the Rockies (Fyfe and Flato 1999). The effect was restricted to winter and spring and was related to the snow-albedo feedback, wherein reduction of snowpack at mid- and higher elevations due to higher temperatures under elevated greenhouse gases resulted in greater absorption of solar radiation, further elevating surface air temperatures. Finer-resolution model simulations for the Swiss Alps found similar results and also showed more precipitation at higher elevations from winter through summer (Giorgi et al. 1997). With respect to hydrologic effects, changes in precipitation timing and type (e.g., snow vs. rain) and snowmelt timing strongly altered seasonal runoff patterns with elevation.

Although CCC results demonstrate elevation dependence in climate sensitivity at the broad scale across the Rocky Mountains, there is also a strong locally forced component that comes through in finer-resolution PDSI and snowpack dynamics (plate 5c–f). Responses in PDSI and snow-free period to the broad-scale GCM

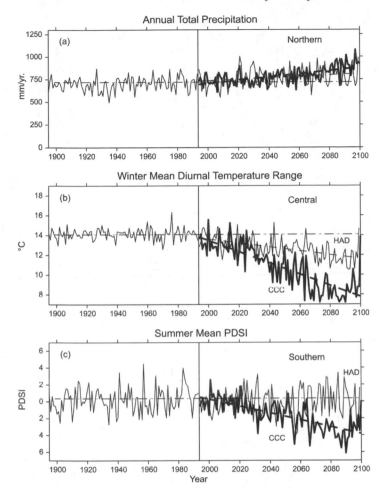

FIGURE 4.4 *Sensitivity of U.S. Rocky Mountain Climates to Transient Greenhouse Gases and Sulfate Aerosol Forcing.* Values for 1994–2100 are based on two coupled global climate model experiments (HAD and CCC; see text). Historical observed record (1895–1993) is also shown for reference. (a) Annual total precipitation (mm/yr.), northern U.S. Rockies. (b) Winter mean diurnal temperature range (°C), central U.S. Rockies. (c) Summer mean Palmer Drought Severity Index (PDSI), southern U.S. Rockies. Climate series are plotted as a thin solid line for historical period and HAD future climate scenario and a thick solid line for CCC scenario. Horizontal line is the 1960–1991 baseline climate mean. Regression (long-dash) lines are plotted if significant ($P < 0.05$); slopes for annual precipitation in (a) were +11% and +25%/century for HAD and CCC scenarios, respectively; for winter mean diurnal temperature range in (b), −2.0 °C and −5.7°C/century for HAD and CCC; and for summer mean PDSI in (c), −4.1 units/century for CCC.

forcing are patchy by comparison, with much of this pattern correlated with finer-grid (0.5° lat.) elevations. Correlations were similar under the two climate scenarios but differed by region. Under CCC forcing, negative changes in PDSI were intensified at higher elevations in the northern U.S. Rockies but diminished with elevation in the central and southern regions (plate 5c). These patterns come from nonlinear relationships among elevation, climate, and snowpack, soil moisture dynamics, and interactions with vegetation and soil distribution. These results suggest that, as in the historical record, future climate sensitivity of the three U.S. Rocky Mountain regions will have distinct responses and that fine-scale processes will operate to enhance or diminish larger-scale changes within each of the regions.

Uncertainties and Approaches in Assessing Climate Sensitivity

Climate model results must be viewed with caution, especially when applied to mountainous terrain. They are limited by our understanding and model representation of key processes and forcings (Wigley and Raper 2001). A major limitation of GCMs is their coarse model resolution, which cannot adequately address regional processes such as convection or sufficiently resolve topography. Poor representation of land surface features and processes results in a high level of uncertainty associated with regional scenarios of climate change. In spite of these limitations, GCM experiments reveal general sensitivity of climate and potential magnitude of change. Regional climate models also have their limitations but are better suited to evaluate the sensitivity of mountain climates across highly heterogeneous terrain (Giorgi and Mearns 1991).

Although climate model results for the U.S. and Canadian Rocky Mountains do not constitute forecasts or even realistic projections of climate change that can be used as a basis for policy or land management decisions, they are a foundation for understanding potential magnitude for climatic shifts and for identifying potential vulnerability of social and environmental processes to anthropogenic climate change. Climate model output can be used to identify potential vulnerability of social and environmental processes to anthropogenic climate change. In spite of high uncertainty about the exact nature of possible future climate outcomes, regional and global climate modeling sensitivity studies serve as one component in the development of "least regrets" strategies for reducing vulnerability of human systems to rapid climate change, independent of any particular climate change scenario and in the context of multiple stressors (Sulzman, Poiani, and Kittel 1995; Pielke 2001).

Once and Future Climates

The Rocky Mountains are home to a wide variety of climates. Across their span, these climates exhibit behavior at interannual through centennial scales that responds to hemispheric and global forcing but also is distinguished by region and elevation. These relationships carry through to our current insights as to the sensitivity of Rocky Mountain climates to land use change and altered radiative forcing from increasing levels of greenhouse gases and aerosols. Although we cannot foretell what future climate changes will bring to the region, we have a clear understanding that the Rocky Mountains will experience change in climates, ecosystems, and hydrology that reflects not only global forcing but also a substantial reworking of this forcing by the mountain system itself.

Acknowledgments

This work was supported by grants from NASA Mission to Planet Earth, the USDA Forest Service, and the Electric Power Research Institute (EPRI) though sponsorship of the Vegetation/Ecosystem Modeling and Analysis Project (VEMAP); the Geophysical Statistics Project at the National Center for Atmospheric Research (NCAR); and the U.S. Geological Survey, Biological Resources Division, Global Change Research Program. NCAR is sponsored by the National Science Foundation. The authors are indebted to Nan Rosenbloom, Steve Aulenbach, Hank Fisher, Mark Berliner, and Doug Nychka for their role in data set development and analysis. Many thanks to David Yates for developing and providing the VEMAP2 PDSI data set and to Chris Daly and the Spatial Climate Analysis Service, Oregon State University, for making available high-resolution maps of Canadian climatology; these maps were created with funding and station data provided primarily by Environment Canada, Pacific and Yukon Region and Prairie and Northern Region. We thank Jill Baron, Chris Daly, David Greenland, Jim Hurrell, Mark Losleben, Roger Pielke Sr., and Bill Reiners for valued comments and discussion. Thanks go to NCAR's Data Support Section and the National Oceanic and Atmospheric Administration's National Climatic Data Center for access to and assistance with HCN and other meteorological data sets.

References

Benedict, A. D. and B. Bash. 1991. *A Sierra Club naturalist's guide to the southern Rockies: The Rocky Mountain regions of southern Wyoming, Colorado, and northern New Mexico.* San Francisco: Sierra Club Books.

Beniston, M., H. F. Diaz, and R. S. Bradley. 1997. Climatic change at high elevation sites: An overview. *Climatic Change* 36:233–251.

Beniston, M., and M. Rebetez. 1996. Regional behavior of minimum temperatures in Switzerland for the period 1979–1993. *Theoretical and Applied Climatology* 53:231–243.

Betts, A. K., J. H. Ball, A. C. M. Beljaars, M. J. Miller, and P. A. Viterbo. 1996. The land surface-atmosphere interaction: A review based on observational and global modeling perspectives. *Journal of Geophysical Research* 101:7209–7225.

Boer, G. J., G. Flato, and D. Ramsden. 2000. A transient climate change simulation with greenhouse gas and aerosol forcing: Projected climate to the twenty-first century. *Climate Dynamics* 16:427–450.

Bonan, G. B. 1997. Effects of land use on the climate of the United States. *Climatic Change* 37:449–486.

Chase, T. N., R. A. Pielke, T. G. F. Kittel, J. S. Baron, and T. J. Stohlgren. 1999. Potential impacts on Colorado Rocky Mountain weather due to land use changes on the adjacent Great Plains. *Journal of Geophysical Research* 104:16673–16690.

Chase, T. N., R. A. Pielke, T. G. F. Kittel, R. Nemani, and S. W. Running. 1996. The sensitivity of a general circulation model to large scale changes in Leaf Area Index. *Journal of Geophysical Research* 101:7393–7408.

———. 2000. Simulated impacts of historical land cover changes on global climate in northern winter. *Climate Dynamics* 16:93–105.

Chase, T. N., R. A. Pielke Sr., T. G. F. Kittel, M. Zhao, A. J. Pitman, S. W. Running, and R. R. Nemani. 2001. Relative climatic effects of landcover change and elevated carbon dioxide combined with aerosols: A comparison of model results and observations. *Journal of Geophysical Research* 106:31685–31691.

Copeland, J. H., R. A. Pielke, and T. G. F. Kittel. 1996. Potential climatic impacts of vegetation change: A regional modeling study. *Journal of Geophysical Research* 101:7409–7418.

Dai, A., K. E. Trenberth, and T. R. Karl. 1999. Effects of clouds, soil moisture, precipitation, and water vapor on diurnal temperature range. *Journal of Climate* 12:2451–2473.

Dai, A. G., and T. M. L. Wigley. 2000. Global patterns of ENSO-induced precipitation. *Geophysical Research Letters* 27:1283–1286.

Daly, C., W. P. Gibson, G. H. Taylor, G. L. Johnson, and P. Pasteris. 2002. A knowledge-based approach to the statistical mapping of climate. *Climate Research,* 2002.

Daly, C., R. P. Neilson, and D. L. Phillips. 1994. A statistical-topographic model for mapping climatological precipitation over mountainous terrain. *Journal of Applied Meteorology* 33:140–158.

Daly, C., G. H. Taylor, W. P. Gibson, T. W. Parzybok, G. L. Johnson, and P. Pasteris. 2001. High-quality spatial climate data sets for the United States and beyond. *Transactions of the American Society of Agricultural Engineers* 43:1957–1962.

Diaz, H. F., and R. S. Bradley. 1997. Temperature variations during the last century at high elevation sites. *Climatic Change* 36:253–279.

Fyfe, J. C., and G. M. Flato. 1999. Enhanced climate change and its detection over the Rocky Mountains. *Journal of Climate* 12:230–243.

Giorgi, F., J. W. Hurrell, M. R. Marinucci, and M. Beniston. 1997. Elevation dependency of the surface climate change signal: A model study. *Journal of Climate* 10:288–296.

Giorgi, F., and L. O. Mearns. 1991. Approaches to the simulation of regional climate change: A review. *Geophysical Reviews* 29:191–216.

Greenland, D., and T. G. F. Kittel. 2002. Temporal variability of climate at the U.S. Long-Term Ecological Research (LTER) sites. *Climate Research* 19:213–231.

Greenland, D., and M. Losleben. 2001. Climate. In *Structure and function of an alpine ecosystem: Niwot Ridge, Colorado,* ed. W. D. Bowman and T. R. Seastedt, 15–31. New York: Oxford University Press.

Groisman, P. Y., T. R. Karl, R. W. Knight, and G. L. Stenchikov. 1994. Changes of snow cover, temperature, and radiative heat-balance over the Northern Hemisphere. *Journal of Climate* 7:1633–1656.

Houghton, J. T., Y. Ding, D. J. Griggs, M. Noguer, P. J. van der Linden, X. Dai, K. Maskell, and C. A. Johnson, eds. 2001. *Climate change: The scientific basis. Contribution of Working Group I to the Third Assessment Report of the Intergovernmental Panel on Climate Change.* Cambridge: Cambridge University Press. On-line at <http://www.ipcc.ch/pub/tar/index.htm>.

Inouye, D. W., B. Barr, K. B. Armitage, and B. D. Inouye. 2000. Climate change is affecting altitudinal migrants and hibernating species. *Proceedings of the National Academy of Sciences USA* 97:1630–1633.

Karl, T. R., R. W. Knight, D. R. Easterling, and R. G. Quayle. 1996. Indices of climate change for the United States. *Bulletin of the American Meteorological Society* 77:279–292.

Kittel, T. G. F., N. A. Rosenbloom, C. Kaufman, J. A. Royle, C. Daly, H. H. Fisher, W. P. Gibson, S. Aulenbach, D. Yates, R. McKeown, D. S. Schimel, and VEMAP2 Participants. 2000. *VEMAP phase 2 historical and future scenario climate database.* Oak Ridge, Tenn.: Oak Ridge National Laboratory, ORNL Distributed Active Archive Center. On-line at <http://www-eosdis.ornl.gov/>.

Kittel, T. G. F., J. A. Royle, C. Daly, N. A. Rosenbloom, W. P. Gibson, H. H. Fisher, D. S. Schimel, L. M. Berliner, and VEMAP2 Participants. 1997. A gridded historical (1895–1993) bioclimate dataset for the conterminous United States. In *Proceedings of the 10th Conference on Applied Climatology* (20–24 October 1997, Reno, Nev.), 219–222. Boston: American Meteorological Society.

Losleben, M. 1997. An uncommon period of cold and change of lapse rate in the Rocky Mountains of Colorado and Wyoming. In *Proceedings of the Thirteenth Annual Pacific Climate (PACLIM) Workshop,* ed. C. M. Isaacs and V. L. Tharp, 33–38. Technical Report No. 53. Sacramento: California Department of Water Resources.

McCarthy, J. J., O. F. Canziani, N. A. Leary, D. J. Dokken, and K. S. White, eds. 2001. *Climate change 2001: Impacts, adaptation, and vulnerability. Contribution of Working Group II to the Third Assessment Report of the Intergovernmental Panel on Climate Change (IPCC).* Cambridge: Cambridge University Press. On-line at <http://www.ipcc.ch/pub/tar/index.htm>.

Mitchell, J. F. B., T. C. Johns, J. M. Gregory, and S. Tett. 1995. Climate response to increasing levels of greenhouse gases and sulphate aerosols. *Nature* 376:501–504.

Mitchell, V. L. 1976. The regionalization of climate in the western United States. *Journal of Applied Meteorology* 15:920–927.

NAST (National Assessment Synthesis Team). 2001. *Climate change impacts for the United States: The potential consequences of climate variability and change.* Foundation Document. Cambridge: Cambridge University Press.

Nicholls, N., G. V. Gruza, J. Jouzel, T. R. Karl, L. A. Ogallo, and D. E. Parker. 1996. Observed climate variability and change. In *Climate change 1995: The science of climate change,* ed. J. T. Houghton, L. G. Meira Filho, B. A. Callander, N. Harris, A. Kattenberg, and K. Maskell, chap. 3, 133–192. Cambridge: Cambridge University Press.

Pepin, N. 2000. Twentieth-century change in the climate record for the Front Range, Colorado, USA. *Arctic, Antarctic, and Alpine Research* 32:135–146.

Pielke, R. A. 2001. Earth system modeling: An integrated assessment tool for environmental studies. In *Present and future of modeling global environmental change: Toward integrated mod-*

eling, ed. T. Matsuno and H. Kida, 311–337. Tokyo: Terrapub.

Pielke, R. A., and R. Avissar. 1990. Influence of landscape structure on local and regional climate. *Landscape Ecology* 4:133–155.

Pitman, A. J., and M. Zhao. 2000. The relative impact of observed change in landcover and carbon dioxide as simulated by a climate model. *Geophysical Research Letters* 27:1267–1270.

Plantico, M. S., T. R. Karl, G. Kukla, and J. Gavin. 1990. Is recent climate change across the United States related to rising levels of anthropogenic greenhouse gases? *Journal of Geophysical Research* 95 (D10): 16617–16637.

Quinlan, F. T., T. R. Karl, and C. N. Williams Jr. 1987. United States Historical Climatology Network (HCN) serial temperature and precipitation data. NDP-019. Oak Ridge, Tenn.: Oak Ridge National Laboratory, Carbon Dioxide Information Analysis Center.

Running, S. W., and J. C. Coughlan. 1988. A general model of forest ecosystem processes for regional applications. I. Hydrological balance, canopy gas exchange, and primary production processes. *Ecological Modeling* 42:125–154.

Segal, M., Z. Pan, R. W. Turner, and E. S. Takle. 1998. On the potential impact of irrigated areas in North America on summer rainfall caused by large-scale systems. *Journal of Applied Meteorology* 37:325–331.

Sievering, H. 2001. Atmospheric chemistry and deposition. In *Structure and function of an alpine ecosystem: Niwot Ridge, Colorado,* ed. W. D. Bowman and T. R. Seastedt, 32–44. New York: Oxford University Press.

Sulzman, E. W., K. A. Poiani, and T. G. F. Kittel. 1995. Modeling human-induced climatic change: A summary for environmental managers. *Environmental Management* 19:197–224.

Thornton, P. E., H. Hasenauer, and M. A. White. 2000. Simultaneous estimation of daily solar radiation and humidity from observed temperature and precipitation: An application of complex terrain in Austria. *Agricultural and Forest Meteorology* 104:255–271.

Thornton, P. E., S. W. Running, and M. A. White. 1997. Generating surfaces of daily meteorologic variables over large regions of complex terrain. *Journal of Hydrology* 190:214–251. Data set on-line at <http://www.daymet.org>.

Trenberth, K. E., and J. W. Hurrell. 1994. Decadal atmosphere-ocean variations in the Pacific. *Climate Dynamics* 9:303–319.

Wagner, F. H., and J. Baron, eds. 1999. *Proceedings of the Rocky Mountain/Great Basin Regional Climate-Change Workshop: U.S. National Assessment of the Consequences of Climate Change.* U.S. Global Change Research Program. On-line at <http://www.usgcrp.gov/usgcrp/nacc/rockies workshop.pdf>.

Wallace, J. M., Y. Zhang, and L. Bajuk. 1996. Interpretation of interdecadal trends in Northern Hemisphere surface air temperature. *Journal of Climate* 9:249–259.

Wigley, T. M. L., and S. C. B. Raper. 2001. Interpretation of high projections for global-mean warming. *Science* 293:451–454.

Zhang, X., L. A. Vincent, W. D. Hogg, and A. Niitsoo. 2000. Temperature and precipitation trends in Canada during the twentieth century. *Atmosphere-Ocean* 38:395–429.

Zhao, M., A. J. Pitman, and T. N. Chase. 2001. Influence of landcover change on the atmospheric circulation. *Climate Dynamics* 17:467–477.

PART II

HUMAN-DRIVEN CHANGES TO ROCKY MOUNTAIN LANDSCAPES

▲

John Wesley Powell believed strongly that western resources were meant to be "redeemed" from a state of idleness for societal use (Powell 1878, deBuys 2001). He wrote of his vision for development of the Rocky Mountain region in his great 1878 work, *Report on the Lands of the Arid Region of the United States:* "Three great classes are recognized—the irrigable lands below, the forest lands above, and the pasturage lands between" (deBuys 2001, 162). Today, the Rocky Mountain environment shows the legacy of water diversion, forest harvest, and grazing as well as mineral extraction. Hunting and stocking of game and fish, fire suppression activities, and increased settlement rates and recreation round out the list of human activities on Rocky Mountain landscapes. One hundred fifty years of human enterprise have left permanent marks on Rocky Mountain landscapes and have altered ecosystem structure and function. We address these direct human influences in the chapters that follow.

Societal values play a central role in constraining or encouraging activities that influence landscape condition. As values change over time, so does the acceptability of activities (Rapport et al. 1998). Extensive logging of old-growth forests was acceptable, for instance, when wood was the primary building material and forest resources were perceived as infinite. Old-growth forests are rare today, and public opinion favors protection over exploitation.

We like to think that societal values change in response to increased understanding of human influences on natural resources and ecosystem processes. Our understanding of human effects on the environment has increased greatly over the past hundred years, yet it remains to be seen whether ecological understanding will translate into adoption of sustainable—or, in the case of mining, at least environmentally benign—use of natural resources.

The ecological effects of what are commonly thought of as traditional industries are examined in chapter 5, which traces the story of mining, logging, and grazing in the Rocky Mountains. Chapter 6 addresses the other major commodity of the Rocky Mountains—water. The Rockies serve as the water supply for much of the western United States, but at a great ecological price. The consequences of fire suppression to western fire-adapted forests and grasslands are covered in chapter 7, which concludes with the sobering thought that restoration of essential fire processes will take decades to centuries. Chapter 8 addresses the biodiversity of the Rockies and the complex web of threats to species, food webs, and assemblages.

References

deBuys, W., ed. 2001. *Seeing things whole: The essential John Wesley Powell.* Washington, D.C.: Island Press.

Powell, J. W. 1878. *Report on the lands of the arid region of the United States, with a more detailed account of the lands of Utah.* 45th Cong., 2nd sess. H.R. Exec. Doc. 73.

Rapport, D. J., C. Gaudet, J. R. Karr, J. S. Baron, C. Bohlen, W. Jackson, B. Jones, R. J. Naiman, B. Norton, and M. M. Pollock. 1998. Evaluating landscape health: Integrating societal goals and biophysical processes. *Journal of Environmental Management* 53:1–15.

CHAPTER 5

Natural Resource Extraction:
Past, Present, and Future

Heather M. Rueth, Jill S. Baron, and Linda A. Joyce

▲

The discovery of gold paved the way for settlement in the Rocky Mountains. Thus, although this chapter addresses the environmental effects of natural resource extraction in the Rocky Mountains, the reader should bear in mind the pivotal role mining played in settlement history, particularly in the mineralized regions of Colorado, Idaho, and southwestern Montana (Rohe 1995). Mining vastly accelerated western migration, adding tens of thousands of people to the region, often in the period of a few months (Wyckoff and Dilsaver 1995). Merchants, farmers, ranchers, and lumbermen rushed to fill the needs of miners, and though mining settlements came and went, many people stayed. The actual mining boom in most locales lasted for at most thirty years, but there remains a lasting legacy of towns, second-growth forests, abandoned mine lands, and highly altered waterways that has shaped the regional environment.

Mining

Today, there are more than 7,000 abandoned mines in Colorado, more than in any other state or province (Ferderer 1996; Mackasey 2000; table 5.1). Alberta, Montana, and Utah each have about 2,000. More than 2,600 kilometers (km), or 1,616 miles (mi.), of streams have been affected by mine drainage in Colorado alone.

It is difficult to underestimate the role of mining in the human history of the Rocky Mountains. In 1923, 99% of the assessed value of the state of Colorado came from the gross value of gold, silver, copper, lead, and zinc (Henderson

TABLE 5.1. Number of Hardrock Mines and Extent of Streams Affected by Mine Drainage in the U.S. and Canadian Rocky Mountains

State/Province	Inactive Mines	Active Mines (as of 1994)	Mining-Related Superfund Sites	Stream km (mi.) Impaired by Mining	Total Perennial Stream km (mi.)	% Total Stream km Impaired
Colorado	7,302	16	10	2,539 (1,578)	50,635 (31,470)	5
Idaho	1,638	29	5	—[1]	88,411 (54,948)	—
Montana	1,980	17	9	8,463 (5,260)	85,632 (53,221)	10
New Mexico	1,284	16	6	1,971 (1,225)	13,969 (8,682)	14
South Dakota	648	10	2	801 (498)	31,105 (1,932)	26
Utah	2,144	7	11	476 (296)	26,479 (16,457)	15
Wyoming	919	0	0	1,280 (796)	52,325 (32,520)	2
Alberta	~ 2,100	—	N/A	—	—	—
British Columbia	247	20	N/A	—	—	—
Yukon Territory	~ 120	2	N/A	—	—	—

Source: Numbers of inactive mines (based approximately on 1:200,000 scale resolution) from Ferderer 1996 and Mackasey 2000. Current mine and Superfund site data from EPA 1995a, EPA 2002, and Environmental Mining Council of British Columbia 2001. Stream miles from EPA 1996, where number of stream miles impaired is the sum of metals, pH, and oil as the leading pollutants and processes as reported by EPA 2002.

[1] Dashes denote data not found.

1926). The almost unimaginable wealth extracted from the West catapulted the United States into a world power, spurred the development of transportation networks, and fostered a tremendous amount of research in industrial sciences and engineering.

Environmental concerns were rarely voiced in the nineteenth century. Mining was characterized by a "get rich quick" mentality, and it was assumed that denuded landscapes, fouled streams, and polluted air were the necessary prices to be paid (Smith 1983, Eggert 1994). Then, as now, interest in conservation and the adverse effects of mining waxed and waned with the political climate.

The great Colorado gold rush began in 1859. Within ten years, major deposits had been found in Idaho, Montana, Wyoming, and New Mexico, and by 1877 all major gold and silver lodes had been discovered in these states, Utah, and South Dakota (figure 5.1a). Uranium began to be mined in the 1940s and 1950s in Colorado, Utah, Wyoming, and Montana. Later, deposits of copper, lead, zinc, and molybdenum were exploited as more efficient technologies were developed. Today, there are few active hardrock mines in the Rocky Mountain region, largely as a result of lower-priced international sources of metals and somewhat as a result of the cost of environmental mitigation (Smith 1993).

The Rockies and their flanks still hold major deposits of oil and natural gas (figure 5.1b) and of coal (figure 5.1c) that will continue to be developed through the middle of the twenty-first century (Higley, Pollastro, and Clayton 1995; Flores and Nichols 1999; Bustin and Smith 1993). Sand and gravel excavations are expected to supply building materials for an ever-increasing population of newcomers (Langer et al. 1997).

Environmental Consequences of Past Mining Activities

Mining is destructive by definition. In the Rockies, as elsewhere, ore is extracted from underground mines by removing large quantities of rock. Because raw ore is worthless, mills and smelters are built to refine and retrieve precious metals. Heap or dump leaching practices are used in mills wherein cyanide, mercury, or acid solution is allowed to percolate through crushed ore, or tailings. Metals are collected from the leachate below. Prior to environmental regulations, heap and dump leaching was simply carried out on the ground where the ore lay, and excess fluids drained into the ground or nearby streams.

Smelters further refine ores. If uncontrolled, smelters emit tons of sulfurous gas and heavy metals (Smith 1983). Sulfur oxides kill vegetation, often for miles around (Lauenroth and Preston 1984). Lead emitted from smelters travels long distances through the atmosphere; paleolimnological reconstructions of lake histories show that lead deposition in remote alpine lakes of Colorado and Wyoming began as early as 1850 (Baron et al. 1986, Norton and Kahl 1985).

(a)

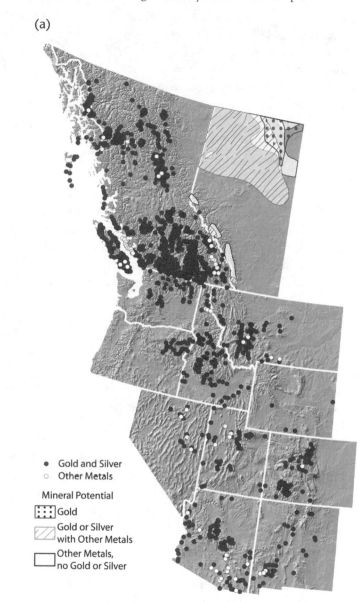

FIGURE 5.1 *Minerals of the Rocky Mountain West.* (a) Precious metals. (b) Oil and gas fields. (c) Major coal deposits. Data compiled from U.S. Geological Survey 1995, 1998; Wyckoff and Dilsaver 1995; Environmental Mining Council of British Columbia 2001.

(b)

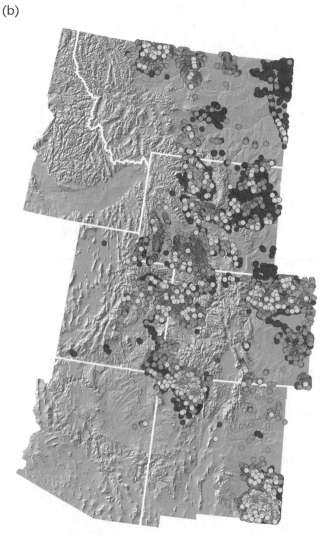

- ● > 1 Productive Oil Well
- ● > 1 Productive Gas Well
- ○ > 1 Productive Oil Well and/or Gas Well

(c)

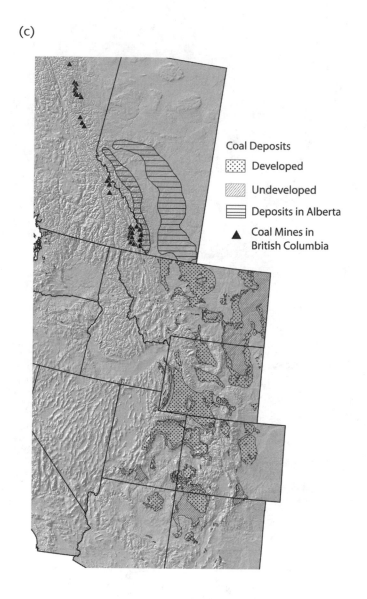

Placer mining, the removal of metals from stream gravel and riparian areas, was dominated by sluicing, hydraulic mining, "booming," and dredging (Smith 1983). Sluicing forced the gravel of entire streambeds down long wooden channels with water pressure from upstream dams, concentrating the gold and creating extensive waste heaps. Hydraulic mining shot pressurized water through hoses to blast gravel banks, leaving behind large tracts of gravel waste in areas that were once riparian benches and streams. Dams and ditches were required to divert the water for this practice, which evolved into booming, the sudden release of a large amount of impounded water in order to wash entire hillslopes into a flume for gold recovery. Large-scale dredging came into practice in Montana in the 1860s and later in Colorado, enabling sediments as deep as 6–9 meters (m), or 20–30 feet (ft.), to be overturned and mined (Smith 1993). Entire basins were thus affected by complete reworking of the streambed and adjacent hillslopes (figure 5.2).

Placer mining destroyed thousands of miles of streambed structure in the Rocky Mountains. Vast amounts of fine sediment were washed downstream, coating surfaces and reducing water clarity (Reetz 1998). What remained were unvegetated coarse gravel beds across the entire riparian areas of affected streams (Wohl 2001).

By far the most serious long-term environmental consequence of hardrock mining has been acid mine drainage. Precious metals are associated with min-

FIGURE 5.2 *Dredge Operation in Grasshopper Creek near Bannock, Montana, circa 1890–1900.* Photograph courtesy of Montana Historical Society; photographer unknown.

erals that form sulfuric acid when exposed to air and water. Zinc, iron, cadmium, copper, lead, and aluminum are soluble in acidic waters and are highly toxic to aquatic organisms. Snowmelt and rain drain through waste piles and underground tunnels of old mines, collecting sulfuric acid and metals and contaminating groundwater and streams for miles. Remediation is difficult, if not impossible, because of the many point and nonpoint (localized and more diffuse) sources of leach water from a single mine and the persistence of acid generation (Reetz 1998, EPA 1995b).

The ecological effects of acid mine drainage are profound. Acute concentrations of acid from nearby leaching sites are lethal to fish, invertebrates, and algae. Algal metabolism is depressed in the presence of high metal concentrations (Hill et al. 1997, 2000). Metals affect invertebrate density and species distributions; for instance, mayflies and stone flies are especially sensitive to even moderate levels of pollution (Clements and Kiffney 1995). Aquatic community structure is altered; communities become characterized by low diversity and acid-tolerant species. Metals accumulate in the livers and gills of fish, and bioaccumulation of copper from contaminated food webs leads to reduced survivorship and reproductive fitness, limiting the distribution and abundance of fish populations (Taylor et al. 2000, Farag et al. 1999, Besser et al. 2001). Cadmium, which is extremely toxic, appears to work its way up the food chain and has been found in measurable quantities in white-tailed ptarmigans in Colorado (Larison et al. 2000).

Mine regulation history reflects the populating of a once-empty landscape, as well as national sentiment. As more people moved west, the industry began to affect its neighbors. Debates over the rights of hydraulic mining companies to bury downstream farms and towns with tailings and to ruin fisheries were first brought into courts in the 1860s. Fumes from stamp mills and smelters that were injurious to human health, livestock, and vegetation were challenged in the 1870s and 1880s. Gifford Pinchot in 1898 advocated establishment of forest preserves partly in response to the complete denudation of forests for mining activities. In the 1920s, concerns were raised over acid mine drainage that reached streams and rivers. Not until the 1960s, however, did environmental legislation begin to change mining practices across the country, and by then, most hardrock mining activities in the Rocky Mountains were over (Smith 1993).

Current Mining Activities in the Rocky Mountains

Mineral extraction continues to be important to the economies and landscapes of the Rocky Mountains. Although gold and silver mining is greatly reduced from times past, other metals are still mined. Drilling for energy minerals, including coal, oil, and natural gas, is increasing. And an ever-increasing population requires a continued supply of sand, gravel, and other building materials.

Metals and Industrial Minerals. Today, the United States is the world's second largest producer of gold, which comes from all Rocky Mountain states except Wyoming. Gold is also mined in Yukon Territory and British Columbia (table 5.1; EPA 1995a; Mackasey 2000). A large number of other metals and industrial minerals, such as silica, gypsum, magnesite, and barite, are also mined. Mining is important to the economies of Canada's western provinces and supplies raw materials to the industrial and affluent societies of both the United States and Canada.

The long-term effectiveness of current pollution prevention regulations remains to be seen in both Canada and the United States. The Summitville mine, an open-pit cyanide heap-leach gold mine at 3,500 m (11,500 ft.) elevation in the San Juan Mountains of Colorado, received all appropriate permits in 1986 yet still leaked significant quantities of acidic, metal-rich drainage and cyanide into a tributary of the Alamosa River. The drainage destroyed all aquatic life for 27 km (17 mi.) downstream. Irrigators in the San Luis Valley using Alamosa River water discovered metal accumulation in soils and livestock. In 1992, the mining corporation declared bankruptcy, and cleanup was left to the federal and state governments. Summitville is now one of forty-three mining-related Superfund sites in the Rocky Mountain region (table 5.1).

Energy Minerals. Alberta, Montana, Wyoming, Yukon Territory, and British Columbia contain considerable coal resources. Open-pit coal mining produces large quantities of waste material, which is often dumped into adjacent valleys, causing significant habitat fragmentation and damage to riparian and stream ecosystems. Selenium leaches into waterways, where it harms fish and waterfowl. Blasting with explosives releases nitrates into groundwater and surface water in concentrations well beyond safe drinking water standards. There is also significant air pollution in the form of dust. Western coal production increased fifteenfold between 1973 and 1998 (Flores and Nichols 1999).

Oil, coal-bed methane, and natural gas fields are found throughout the Rockies, and their development will increase during the first three decades of the twenty-first century. Nitrogen oxides and hydrocarbons are air pollutants produced from natural gas wells. Nitrogen oxides contribute to excess nitrogen deposition, often at some distance from the source. High mountain ecosystems downwind of nitrogen oxide sources are vulnerable first to nitrogen fertilization and eventually to acidification and loss of soil fertility (chapter 9; Baron et al. 2000).

Escaped methane from coal-bed methane production adds a potent greenhouse gas to Earth's atmosphere. Coal-bed methane production also produces water from the coal seams as a by-product. The water, which can be highly saline, is injected back into the rock formations but sometimes is allowed to flow overland and into waterways. Local to regional effects on wildlife, native plants, and water quality are as yet unexplored.

Aggregates. Sand, gravel, and stone are required in large quantities for construction and are mined from regions near growing urban and exurban development. They are used to produce cement and to pave roads and lots and are thus a vital resource for societal development (Langer et al. 1997). Quarries are usually located near rivers and create holes in the ground. Although these can be "remediated" by being made into artificial wetlands and reservoirs, they nonetheless cause significant and permanent alteration of river valley riparian reaches.

Future Mining Activities in the Rocky Mountains

The abundance of economically important minerals in the Rocky Mountains means that mining activities will continue in the region until supplies are exhausted. Active exploration is occurring currently in all states and provinces (Environmental Mining Council of British Columbia 2001). Although the rate of development may depend on national economies and perceived urgency, continued extraction of metals, minerals, and energy is certain.

The challenge is to mine while causing as little environmental harm as possible. Although a preoccupation with short-term economic profits is still rampant in the mining community, mining corporations have been forced to address environmental effects as a result of legislation in the twentieth century (Smith 1983). Enforcement, however, can be lax; egregious failures still occur, as evidenced by the Summitville disaster, and hope springs eternal within the industry that environmental regulations will be eased (Mackasey 2000, Eggert 1994, DOE 2001).

Rocky Mountain Forest Resources

Rapid settlement of the West after 1860 initiated deforestation in a widening radius away from mines and townsites (Veblen and Lorenz 1991). Wood was in high demand for mine timbers, sluices, housing materials, charcoal, firewood, and especially railroad ties. The Union Pacific Railroad reached Cheyenne, Wyoming, in 1867 and Denver by 1870, and thereafter rail service to mountain mining towns proliferated (Wohl 2001). Prior to 1880, forests were viewed as inexhaustible resources to be harvested. The perception did not last long, however. Early conservationists wrote of the "wanton destruction of timber" that occurred simultaneously with mine development and of the resulting "wilderness of stumps" (Wohl 2001, 89).

By 1879, there were seventy sawmills in Colorado's South Platte River valley. Sawmills ranged in capacity from 5,000 to 50,000 board feet per day, so even the smallest mill could process 3 hectares (ha), or 7.5 acres, of trees per day (Wohl 2001). An army of loggers, including tie and timber choppers, teamsters, and sawmillers, supplied wood products to graders, bridge builders, tracklayers, and miners. Lumbermen concentrated on large trees, but charcoal burners cut everything, even digging stumps out of the ground. Timber was skidded down mountains with mules and horses or floated downriver in tie drives. Tie drives, common in the South Platte, Arkansas, Medicine Bow, and Absaroka River drainages, entailed stacking ties in the river during fall and winter and floating them to a collection point during spring snowmelt (chapter 6). Although the great tie drives were mostly over by 1880, cutting for ties continued. Wohl (2001) noted that more ties were probably cut from 1880 to 1900 than before, but they were hauled by ox or mule teams.

Most low-elevation forests in the Rocky Mountains were cut over by 1900, and by 1920 little old-growth Rocky Mountain forest remained (figure 5.3). American conservationists, witnessing almost complete deforestation of the extensive eastern forests and rapid removal of Rocky Mountain trees, identified three major concerns that led to the development of national forest preserves: (1) destruction of eastern forests was thorough and complete; (2) lumbering reduced forests to wastelands or unproductive second- and third-growth forests; and (3) loss of old-growth forest would produce a "timber famine" (Whitney 1994). These arguments were instrumental in helping to establish the National Forest System (NFS) in 1891. The first national forest in the United States was Shoshone National Forest, in Wyoming. Systematic forest research began in 1909 at Manitou Springs, Colorado, followed shortly by more research in experimental forests and watersheds in Colorado, Idaho, and Utah. Research investigations were not confined to increasing forest yield but also addressed the influence of harvest on streamflow, erosion from overgrazing, and the effects of fire (RMRS 2000).

Early forest management policy limited natural resource extraction, and by the 1930s a framework was in place protecting forests, water quality, and watershed resources (Kennedy and Quigley 1994, Powell et al. 1994). The conservation philosophy held until the 1950s, when a shift took place emphasizing timber production to support population and economic growth (Kennedy and Quigley 1994). The environmental movement of the 1960s and 1970s forced land stewards to acknowledge public desires for forest conservation. Managing for multiple use initiated a dilemma that continues to this day of how to harvest forest resources while simultaneously providing for public recreation and environmental protection (Shepard 1994).

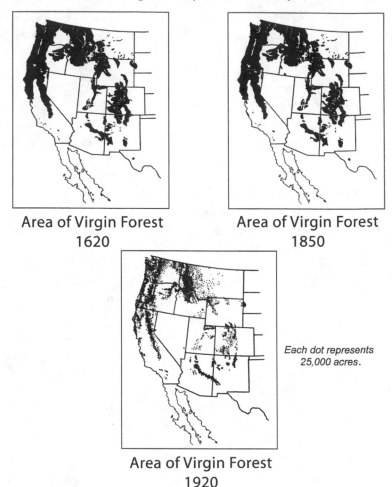

Area of Virgin Forest
1620

Area of Virgin Forest
1850

Area of Virgin Forest
1920

Each dot represents
25,000 acres.

FIGURE 5.3 *Distribution of Old-Growth Forest in the Western United States, 1620, 1850, and 1920.* Reprinted with permission of Clark University from W. B. Greeley, "The Relation of Geography to the Timber Supply," *Economic Geography* 1, no. 1 (1925): 4–5.

Effects of Timber Harvesting

Extensive logging, accompanied by fire suppression, has modified forest structure, function, and species composition throughout the Rockies. Forest fragmentation, the division of a relatively homogeneous forest landscape into progressively smaller sections, has greatly decreased habitat for wildlife and encouraged the encroachment of non-native organisms into native habitats. Forest harvest alters soil, water, and nutrient cycling properties, with potentially significant consequences to stream water quality and quantity. A discussion of these follows.

Vegetation usually grows back after harvest, although not always of the original species or proportions that were harvested. Although the basic forest types and amount of forested area in the Rocky Mountains are similar today to conditions prior to European settlement, the forest structure is very different. Open stands of ponderosa pine, for instance, have been replaced with dense even-aged stands of Douglas-fir and lodgepole pine (Long 1995). Fire suppression practices have encouraged dense stands of young trees where historically frequent fires created more open, park-like stands (chapter 7). Dense stands are more prone to insect outbreaks, and because of their high fuel content, they burn intensely if ignited (Samman and Logan 2000). Boise National Forest experienced mortality of more than 650,000 trees from infestation by western pine beetles, Douglas-fir beetles, fir engraver beetles, and other bark beetles in the 1990s, the result of fire suppression in second-growth stands (USDA Forest Service 2001a).

Wildlife habitat is directly affected by timber harvest and associated road-building activities (Fahrig et al. 1995, Trombulak and Frissell 2000). Wildlife that requires old-growth forests is displaced or extirpated. "Doghair" replacement stands of densely packed trees are not good wildlife habitat because they hinder animal movement and their shade prevents understory browse plants from thriving. Roads become corridors for encroachment by non-native species (Tyser and Worley 1992). Clear-cutting and road building fragment forest landscapes and create distinctive edges between contrasting harvested, road, and intact forest environments (Forman and Alexander 1998).

Roads cause greater forest fragmentation than clear-cuts (Reed, Johnson-Barnard, and Barker 1996a, b). Road edges are fundamentally different from clear-cut edges in that clear-cuts gradually become less distinct over time, whereas road edges remain dramatic. Fragmentation increases the quantity of forest edge within a landscape, with strong consequences for wildlife (chapter 8). Many native bird species are negatively affected by edge habitat, for example, because nest predators tend to concentrate at edges.

Timber harvest increases the light and moisture that reach forest soils, influencing nutrient cycling properties. Nutrients may leach out, decreasing soil fertility and increasing stream nutrients (Reuss, Stottlemyer, and Troendle 1997). The disturbance to soils directly increases soil erosion into streams, affecting sediment transport, channel morphology, and aquatic habitat (MacDonald, Smart, and Wissmar 1991; Troendle and Olsen 1994; Wohl 2001). Direct effects such as these have been documented to persist for at least thirty years (Troendle and King 1985, Binkley and Brown 1993).

Much of the Rocky Mountain region's water comes from high-elevation forests, which occupy 10%–15% of the land areas (Troendle 1983). Timber harvesting reduces forest-canopy transpiration, interception, and evaporation, resulting in more water for streamflow. Forest harvests can thus increase total streamflow, alter the magnitude of peak discharge, and influence the duration and frequency of storm flow events. Forest clear-cutting experiments in western Colorado increased average and peak streamflow by 40% and 23%, respectively, and the effect lasted for decades (Troendle and King 1985).

Rocky Mountain Forests Today and Tomorrow

There are approximately 40 million ha (200 million acres) of forest in the Rocky Mountains, split evenly between Canada and the United States. Most of this land is government-owned. Forest management practices are similar in both countries in that clear-cutting is the major harvest method, and attempts to meet multi-use resource demands are expanding (Smith and Lee 2000). The major difference lies in Canada's dependence on natural resource extraction. Six percent of the 1996 Canadian gross domestic product (GDP) came from forest products, compared with 2% of U.S. GDP (inclusive of paper and allied products) in 1997 (Smith and Lee 2000, USDA Forest Service 2001b). Sixty-eight percent of subalpine forests and 88% of montane forests in Canada are allocated to what are called logging tenures. Although this does not mean harvest is inevitable, the companies with leases are not prevented from cutting. The rate of logging in Canadian forests has steadily increased since 1820, and harvest rates for subalpine forests grew by 60% between 1975 and 1988 (Smith and Lee 2000).

Compared with forests in warmer and wetter regions of the Pacific Northwest and the southeastern United States, Rocky Mountain forests are slow-growing and produce limited timber. In 1991, only 5% of total U.S. timber harvests came from the Rocky Mountains, and that proportion is expected to decline as recreation becomes more important (SREP 2000). Biomass growth of U.S. Rocky Mountain forests in 1991 surpassed removal by 163% (Powell et al. 1994). Timber harvest is still important in northern Idaho and western Montana, where 58% of the entire U.S. Rocky Mountain region's growing stock volume resides (Adams 1995). Idaho and Montana rank fifth and sixth, respectively, among U.S. sawtimber-producing states (figure 5.4). Northern Idaho and western Montana are exceptional among Rocky Mountain states in that they contain the largest unfragmented tracts of forested land in the contiguous United States.

According to the World Resources Institute, only 1% of remaining North American temperate forests are in undisturbed condition. These are found in four intact natural forest ecosystems large enough to maintain all their biodiversity (Bryant, Nelson, and Tangley 1997). Two of the four are in the northern Rocky Mountains: the Greater Yellowstone Ecosystem, and Glacier National

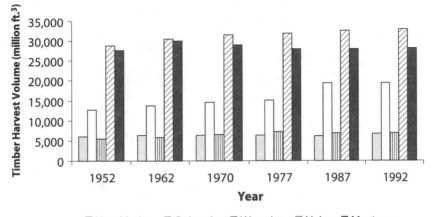

FIGURE 5.4 *Timber Harvest Volume in Five Western States, 1952–1992.* Data from Smith et al. 1997; Waddell, Oswald, and Powell 1987.

Park and surrounding parks and wildernesses of Montana, British Columbia, and Alberta (Bryant, Nelson, and Tangley 1997). The size of the remaining unfragmented forest is biologically significant; large predators such as grizzly bears, wolves, lynx, and wolverines require large tracts of undisturbed habitat for survival.

Within the U.S. Rocky Mountains, 23 million ha (25 million acres) of roadless area remains, but only 34% of that area is protected from development (table 5.2). Low-elevation forests today are in sad shape as a result of a combination of factors. Past logging practices, fire suppression, housing encroachment, and fragmentation of stands have left very little quality old-growth or healthy second-growth montane forests. In Canada, approximately 50% of high-elevation spruce-fir forests and close to 80% of lower-elevation mixed conifer forests have been fragmented by road-building and clear-cutting activities (Smith and Lee 2000).

Historical and Current Domestic Livestock Grazing

The introduction of domestic livestock into the West is a complex story of ill-formed government settlement policies; settlers unaware of the harshness of western environments; competing demands among sheep grazers, cattle barons, and crop farmers; and the environmental consequences of overgrazing in an unforgiving environment. The Spanish brought domestic livestock from Mexico into the southern Rocky Mountains as early as the 1600s. The Homestead

TABLE 5.2. Roadless Areas within the National Forest System (NFS) Lands of the Western United States

	NFS Land (thousands of acres)	Portion of NFS Land in Protected Areas[1] (thousands of acres)	Inventoried Roadless Area (thousands of acres) [% total NFS land]	Roadless Area That Does Not Allow Road Construction (thousands of acres)	Roadless Area That Allows Road Construction (thousands of acres) [% total roadless area]
New Mexico	9,327	1,617	1,597 [17%]	1,167	430 [27%]
Colorado	14,509	3,368	4,433 [31%]	936	3,498 [79%]
Wyoming	9,238	3,364	3,257 [35%]	171	3,085 [95%]
Idaho	20,458	4,818	9,322 [46%]	3,656	5,666 [61%]
Montana	16,893	4,124	6,397 [38%]	2,553	3,844 [60%]
Total	70,425	17,291	25,006	8,483	16,523

Source: USDA Forest Service 2000b.

[1] Protected areas are wilderness areas protected from development.

Act of 1862 and subsequent legislation brought settlers and their livestock to many parts of the Rocky Mountains (figure 5.5). As homesteads intermingled with public land, land use patterns were initiated that still influence grazing land management in the Rocky Mountains today.

Homesteading policies, developed in ignorance of western climates and ecosystems, did not address the need for seasonal grazing areas or the limited water resources of the West (Clawson 1950). The grazing capacity of much of the Rocky Mountains ranges from 1.6 ha (4 acres) to 4 ha (10 acres) per animal unit month (AUM), which is equivalent to one month of forage for a mature cow. A ranch with 100 head of cattle needs approximately 1,940–4,860 ha (4,800–12,000 acres) of grazing land; thus, homestead allotments of 65, 130, and 260 ha (160, 320, and 640 acres) were simply too small to be economically viable agricultural operations. Homesteading policies therefore fostered uncontrolled grazing on adjacent public land and a process of ranch consolidation.

Expansion of livestock operations proceeded slowly from 1860 to 1880 (figure 5.5), but economic conditions of the 1880s produced the open-range cattle boom. Eastern publications told of large profits from cattle ranching, drawing interest and capital from as far away as England (Mitchell and Hart 1987). Longhorns driven overland from Texas could not meet the great demand for livestock, and eastern cattle, less suited to harsh western conditions, were shipped west. Companies worth more than $12 million incorporated within the territory of Wyoming in 1883 alone.

Rangelands from Montana to Colorado quickly became overstocked. A catastrophic crash in the cattle market in 1885, followed by a severe winter and hot, dry spring in 1885–1886, resulted in the loss of tens of thousands of cattle. Even then, ranchers did not reduce livestock numbers on rangelands, leading to complete dessication of many creeks and water holes. The extreme cold and heavy snows of the winter of 1886–1887 killed off even more cattle. By some estimates, at least 60% of all cattle within the northern region starved to death (Mitchell and Hart 1987).

Finally, after these heavy livestock losses, ranchers recognized that hay production was essential to ensure sufficient forage for livestock during the long winter months. In practice, this meant fencing off sections of land to exclude grazing, and planting forage crops. Land grant universities throughout the West were established around this time to provide technical information for managing western rangelands.

After large cattle losses in the late 1890s, some operators switched to sheep. Sheep numbers in Montana rose from 279,000 in 1880 to 4.2 million in 1900, and cattle numbers declined from 1.5 million in 1890 to 735,000 in 1900 (Mitchell and Hart 1987). Expansion of sheep ranching across the West followed

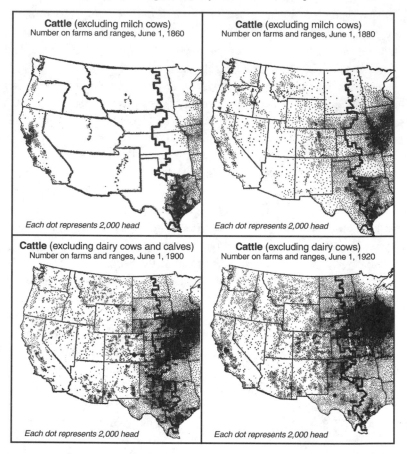

FIGURE 5.5 *Distribution of Beef Cattle in the Western United States by Census Period, 1860, 1880, 1900, and 1920.* Beef cattle spread into and throughout the range region, chiefly from southeastern Texas. Reprinted with permission from Clawson 1950.

a much different pattern from that of cattle ranching. In 1850, the sheep industry was concentrated in the eastern United States; only small numbers of sheep were raised in New Mexico and Utah. By 1920, three-fifths of the sheep in the United States were found west of the Mississippi River (Clawson 1950). Sheep were seen as better adapted to the mountainous West than cattle (Clawson 1950, Thilenius 1975).

New Mexico's sheep herds expanded to supply nearly half a million sheep to the gold country of California in the 1850s and thousands of sheep to Colorado, Kansas, Utah, Wyoming, and Nebraska between 1870 and 1880. Summer grazing of alpine ecosystems in the Rocky Mountains started in the mid-1800s.

Conflicts arose between small ranch owners who grazed their flocks partly on public domain and "tramp bands" who owned no property and grazed only the public domain. The conflicts led to attempts by operators to get to the spring forage first, and they often arrived too early. New forage was destroyed, less palatable species became the dominant plant cover, erosion increased, and overall range carrying capacity was reduced (Rowley 1985). By the early 1900s, overgrazing in the mountain ranges in central Utah resulted in devastating floods coming out of the canyons along the Wasatch Plateau and Wasatch Front. The floods caused great and repeated damage to communities located in the valleys and at mouths of canyons (RMRS 2000).

Federal Grazing Management Policies

Federal land management policies were initiated in the late 1800s. Previously, during the homestead years, there had been no policy for managing grazing on public land. The period from 1865 to the 1890s was marked by violence among herders and depletion of rangeland through overgrazing (Rowley 1985). In 1891, lands that would become the national forests were removed from the public domain to protect timber and water. It was not until 1910, however, nearly 50 years after the first Homestead Act and more than 300 years after introduction of the first cattle and sheep into the West, that grazing on forested federal lands was regulated. Unclaimed lower-elevation lands, today managed by the Bureau of Land Management (BLM), came under federal management through the 1936 Taylor Grazing Act.

Public lands offered seasonal forage that complemented the seasonal availability of forage on private lands. A fee and permit system was first organized for national forests. The initial permit system required a rancher to own the livestock to be grazed and to have sufficient forage to support the livestock when not grazed in the national forest. Both of these requirements were established to shift grazing to privately owned land near the forests and to discourage transient grazers with no local interest in rangeland protection (Robinson 1975). Although their ten-year permits were not supposed to be transferable, in practice they were assigned to the new owners when ranches changed ownership. Permits have been and are adjusted to reflect changes in forage resources.

Today, cattle, sheep, and horses graze on public lands. The level of livestock grazing on NFS and BLM lands has held steady since the 1960s or 1970s (Mitchell 2000). In the northern parts of the Rocky Mountain region, grazing use is currently at 3.1 million AUMs on NFS lands. Water development for livestock across the landscape has had the unintended result of contributing to wildlife habitat. Elk are now found in areas of the Rocky Mountains where water scarcity once limited their range.

Effects of Domestic Livestock Grazing

The legacy of overgrazing on western rangelands represented a challenge to range managers in the early 1900s. Characterizing the original native plant community was difficult because grazing and overgrazing had occurred for so long. The first national assessment of the rangelands, *The Western Range,* cautioned that at least 75% of western rangeland showed excessive erosion and reduced soil productivity and watershed function (U.S. Senate 1936). Although the report may have been accurate, it is not clear that overgrazing was the sole cause of range deterioration; severe drought in the 1930s also contributed to poor conditions (Clawson 1950).

A lack of appropriate methods for assessing rangeland condition has led to heated disagreement on the status of rangelands in the United States (Committee on Rangeland Classification 1994). Early rangeland inventories relied on a metric called range condition to assess the health of rangelands. Range condition compares plant species with the composition of species theoretically found in the native vegetation (present before Euro-American settlement) for that location. Excellent condition implied that the vegetation at a site was similar to the presettlement vegetation; poor condition meant it was similar to early successional stages.

Although rangeland condition has improved since the 1930s, pre-Euro-American conditions remain unknown, and evaluating rangeland ecosystem status with only one variable, plant species composition, is misleading (Box 1990, Joyce 1989, Lauenroth and Laycock 1989). The climate, fire regime, and number and distribution of livestock and wildlife also influence the effect of grazers on vegetation. A more holistic approach to evaluating effects of grazing has been suggested (Committee on Rangeland Classification 1994). It addresses multiple scales of grazing influence on rangelands, including plant-level traits (plant physiology, morphology, and genetics), ecosystem-level characteristics (vegetation productivity, plant and animal species composition, nutrient cycling, changes in erosion, and soil compaction), and landscape-level changes in the disturbance regimes of fire and the introduction of nonindigenous species (Trlica and Rittenhouse 1993).

Although the effects of grazing have been studied at specific locations within the Rocky Mountains, a comprehensive assessment across the Rocky Mountain region has not been accomplished (Committee on Rangeland Classification 1994). Some rangeland inventories suggest that rangelands are static or improving in terms of their vegetation condition or management, but others identify new disturbances, often not associated strictly with grazing, that increasingly affect western rangelands. The ability to comprehensively assess the health of rangeland ecosystems remains a critical research need.

The direct effects of grazing depend on where it occurs, although any land can be overgrazed to its detriment. In shortgrass steppe and some mountain grasslands east of the Continental Divide, plant communities coevolved with herbivory by bison, elk, and deer. Here, the absence of grazing is a disturbance, and moderate grazing probably has little effect on native species richness and may enhance productivity of native grasses (Milchunas and Lauenroth 1993; Stohlgren, Schell, and Vanden Heuvel 1999). Large grazers were much less common on rangelands of the Great Basin, where cattle broke up long-established soil crusts, enhanced erosion, and contributed to the spread of nonindigenous plants such as cheatgrass (chapters 8, 11; Stohlgren, Schell, and Vanden Heuvel 1999).

Ecosystem-level damage from overgrazing is apparent in riparian plant communities and adjacent aquatic systems (Flenniken et al. 2001). Cattle concentrate in riparian zones, so overgrazing and trampling are more prevalent along streamsides than in other places (NRC 1992). They eat virtually all grassy and woody vegetation and use the stream for drinking water (CEQ 1996). A report by the U.S. General Accounting Office (GAO) concluded that riparian conditions throughout the West remained largely in a degraded condition as of 1996 (CEQ 1996).

Overgrazing by domestic livestock has left a legacy still notable in some western ecosystems, particularly in very dry regions and riparian areas. Fortunately, restoration technologies are improving. Improved livestock management, including a combination of restricted access through herding, fencing, shorter grazing rotations, and different grazing seasons, successfully restored twenty-two riparian areas on public lands in western states (GAO 1988). Ten innovative ranchers, who define success in terms of increased biodiversity and healthy riparian areas as well as healthy livestock, have shown it is possible to achieve these goals and increase economic productivity (Dagget 1995).

An important agent for improving range condition may be political rather than physical. The GAO (1988) reports that western grazing on federal lands is heavily subsidized. The National Research Council recommends that grazing practices on federal lands be reexamined and changed to minimize damage to river-riparian ecosystems (NRC 1992).

Current Grazing Trends

Current private ranch patterns are contradictory: there is both consolidation and subdivision (Mitchell 2000). Farm size is increasing across the United States; however, the number of small ranches is increasing in the West. The boom in Rocky Mountain population growth has led to a proliferation of ranchettes, wherein large ranches are subdivided into smaller parcels limited in size by local land use regulations, such as 14 ha (35 acres) in Colorado (chapter 1). In addition to ranch fragmentation, 0.6 million ha (1.4 million acres) of farm- and ranchland was converted to other uses in 1987–1997 (Sherrod 2001). The effect of land conversion is difficult to establish because national inventories do not recognize fragmented ranches as built-up land, but these parcels are clearly too small for livestock production (Mitchell 2000).

Livestock numbers in the Rocky Mountain region increased during the twentieth century in all western states. Peak numbers were seen in the 1970s, and changes since then reflect fluctuations of the cattle market in response to climate and meat prices. The size of livestock operations within the Rocky Mountain region is much different from that in any other region of the United States; nearly 40% of operations in the Rocky Mountain region have more than 100 head of cattle, compared with less than 20% in all other parts of the United States (Mitchell 2000). Ranch operations in the Rocky Mountains have diversified to increase their economic base. Nontraditional livestock such as llamas and emus have been added to some, and recreation and tourism opportunities include bed-and-breakfast operations, hay wagon tours, and facilities for small meetings and social gatherings such as weddings.

Some authors predict that the amount of grazing land is likely to continue a slow decline, both nationally and in the Rocky Mountain region (Van Tassell, Bartlett, and Mitchell 2001; Mitchell 2000). Shifts in land use away from grazing will be much greater in areas of more rapid population increases and concomitant appreciation in land values. Huntsinger (2000) described rangeland grazing in California as having been reinvented many times, most recently as a cultural and ecological force for land conservation. Managers of Rocky Mountain rangelands will very likely explore this possibility as states grapple with increased populations, cultural values, and economic viability of rural communities.

Summary: The Future of the Extractive Industries

Today, extraction accounts for only a small proportion of state revenues in the Rocky Mountain region, having been overtaken by tourism and a postindustrial economy (chapter 1). The question remains of how to foster sensible discussions about where mining, timber harvest, and livestock grazing can be done with minimal disturbance, and especially about where these activities may be inappropriate.

Collaborative efforts such as the Sustainable Rangeland Roundtable and the Policy Analysis Center for Western Public Lands are attempting to address rangeland sustainability with a diverse set of stakeholders (Tanaka 2001). British Columbia requires mining permit applicants to address sustainability issues under its Environmental Assessment Act. In at least one instance, a permit was not approved because the small amount of ore projected to be mined was not worth the long-term damage that would have been caused by building a road through wilderness and the potential for acid mine drainage (Green 2001). Ecosystem management, an attempt to balance social, economic, and ecological demands of forest resources to develop an optimal land use plan, is meant to guide revisions to national forest plans (Jensen and Bourgeron 2001).

These examples are hopeful, but are they common? Apparently not. Voices for compromise tend to be drowned out by extreme views, as exemplified by the summary of public comments on the White River (Colorado) forest plan. More than 14,000 individual comments, the summary noted, could be divided into sharply contrasting camps: "One group sees the revision as an overdue step toward protecting the Forest's natural ecosystems, ultimately improving human well being and preserving the health of the forest. The other group sees it as a recipe for declining forest health, a threat to human freedom, and a further attack on their (extraction-based) way of life" (USDA Forest Service 2000a, 8). How we will move beyond this divided state remains to be seen.

References

Adams, D. L. 1995. The northern Rocky Mountain region. In *Regional silviculture of the United States,* ed. J. W. Barrett, 387–440. New York: Wiley.

Baron, J. S., S. A. Norton, D. R. Beeson, and R. Herrmann. 1986. Sediment diatom and metal stratigraphy from Rocky Mountain lakes, with special reference to atmospheric deposition. *Canadian Journal of Fisheries and Aquatic Sciences* 43:1350–1362.

Baron, J. S., H. M. Rueth, A. M. Wolfe, K. R. Nydick, E. J. Allstott, J. T. Minear, and B. Moraska. 2000. Ecosystem responses to nitrogen deposition in the Colorado Front Range. *Ecosystems* 3:352–368.

Besser, J. M., W. G. Brumbaugh, T. W. May, S. E. Church, and B. A. Kimball. 2001. Bioavailability of metals in stream food webs and hazards to brook trout (*Salvelinus fontinalis*) in the upper Animas River watershed, Colorado. *Archives of Environmental Contamination and Toxicology* 40:48–59.

Binkley, D., and T. C. Brown. 1993. *Management impacts on water quality of forests and rangelands.* General Technical Report RM-239. Fort Collins, Colo.: U.S. Department of Agriculture, Forest Service, Rocky Mountain Forest and Range Experiment Station.

Box, T. W. 1990. Rangelands. In *Natural resources for the 21st century,* ed. R. N. Sampson and D. Hair, 101–120. Washington, D.C.: Island Press.

Bryant, D., D. Nelson, and L. Tangley. 1997. *Last frontier forests: Ecosystems and economies on the edge.* Washington, D.C.: World Resources Institute.

Bustin, R. M., and G. G. Smith. 1993. Coal deposits in the Front Ranges and foothills of the Canadian Rocky Mountains, southern Canadian cordillera. *International Journal of Coal Geology* 23:1–27.

CEQ (Council on Environmental Quality). 1996. *Environmental quality: Along the American River. The 1996 annual report of the Council on Environmental Quality.* Washington, D.C.: Council on Environmental Quality.

Clawson, M. 1950. *The western range livestock industry.* New York: McGraw-Hill.

Clements, W. H., and P. M. Kiffney. 1995. The influence of elevation on benthic community responses to heavy metals in Rocky Mountain streams. *Canadian Journal of Fisheries and Aquatic Science* 52:1966–1977.

Committee on Rangeland Classification. 1994. *Rangeland health: New methods to classify, inventory, and monitor rangelands.* Washington, D.C.: National Academy Press.

Dagget, D. 1995. *Beyond the rangeland conflict: Toward a West that works.* Layton, Utah: Gibbs Smith, in cooperation with the Grand Canyon Trust.

DOE (U.S. Department of Energy). 2001. *Oil and gas R&D: Environmental research and analysis.* On-line at <http://www.fe.doe.gov/oil_gas/environment/>.

Eggert, R. G. 1994. *Mining and the environment: International perspectives on public policy.* Washington, D.C.: Resources for the Future.

Environmental Mining Council of British Columbia. 2001. Interactive maps. On-line at <http://www.miningwatch.org/emcbc/mapping/>.

———. 2001. *Mining in the Pacific Northwest.* On-line at <http://www.miningwatch.org/emcbc/index.htm>.

EPA (U.S. Environmental Protection Agency). 1995a. *EPA Office of Compliance Sector Notebook Project: Profile of the metal mining industry.* EPA/310-R-95-008. Washington, D.C.: U.S. Environmental Protection Agency. On-line at <http://es.epa.gov/oeca/sector/#metal>.

———. 1995b. *Historic hardrock mining: The West's toxic legacy.* EPA/908-F-95-002. Washington, D.C.: U.S. Environmental Protection Agency.

———. 1996. *The quality of our nation's water. National Water Quality Inventory: 1996 report to Congress.* On-line at <http://www.epa.gov/305b/96report/index.html>.

———. 2002. *Superfund sites.* On-line at <http://www.epa.gov/superfund/sites/>.

Fahrig, L., J. H. Pedlar, S. E. Pope, P. D. Taylor, and J. F. Wegner. 1995. Effects of road traffic on amphibian density. *Biological Conservation* 73:177–182.

Farag, A. M., D. W. Woodward, W. Brumbaugh, J. N. Goldstein, E. MacConnell, C. Hogstrand, and F. T. Barrows. 1999. Dietary effects of metals-contaminated invertebrates from Coeur d'Alene River, Idaho, on cutthroat trout. *Transactions of the American Fisheries Society* 128:578–592.

Ferderer, D. A. 1996. National overview of abandoned mine sites utilizing the Minerals Availability System (MAS) and geographic information systems (GIS) technology. U.S. Geological Survey Professional Paper OF 96-0549. Denver, Colo.: U.S. Geological Survey.

Flenniken, M., R. R. McEldowney, W. C. Leininger, G. W. Frasier, and M. J. Trlica. 2001. Hydrologic responses of a montane riparian ecosystem following cattle use. *Journal of Range Management* 54:567–574.

Flores, R. M., and D. J. Nichols. 1999. *Tertiary coal resources in the northern Rocky Mountains and Great Plains region: A clean and compliant fossil fuel beyond 2000.* U.S. Geological Survey Professional Paper 1625-A. Denver, Colo.: U.S. Geological Survey.

Forman, R. T. T., and L. E. Alexander. 1998. Roads and their major ecological effects. *Annual Reviews of Ecology and Systematics* 29:207–231.

GAO (U.S. General Accounting Office). 1988. Public rangelands: Some riparian areas restored, but widespread improvement will be slow. GAO/RCED-99-105. Gaithersburg, Md.: U.S. Government Printing Office.

Green, T. L. 2001. *Mining and sustainability: The case of the Tulsequah Chief Mine.* Environmental Mining Council of British Columbia. On-line at <http://www.miningwatch.org/emcbc/index.htm>.

Henderson, C. W. 1926. *Mining in Colorado: A history of discovery, development, and production.* U.S. Geological Survey Professional Paper 138. Washington, D.C.: U.S. Government Printing Office.

Higley, D. K., R. M. Pollastro, and J. L. Clayton. 1995. Denver Basin Province (039). In *1995 National assessment of United States oil and gas resources.* On-line at <http://certmapper.cr.usgs.gov/data/noga95/prov39/text/prov39.pdf>.

Hill, B. H., J. M. Lazorchak, F. H. McCormick, and W. T. Willingham. 1997. The effects of elevated metals on benthic community metabolism in a Rocky Mountain stream. *Environmental Pollution* 95:183–190.

Hill, B. H., W. T. Willingham, L. P. Parrish, and B. H. McFarland. 2000. Periphyton community responses to elevated metal concentrations in a Rocky Mountain stream. *Hydrobiologia* 428:161–169.

Huntsinger, L. 2000. The end of the trail: Latter-day ranching transformation on the Pacific slope. Presentation at conference, The Culture, Ecology, and Economics of Ranching West of the 100th Meridian, 4–6 May, Fort Collins, Colo.

Jensen, M. T., and P. S. Bourgeron, eds. 2001. *A guidebook for integrated ecological assessments.* New York: Springer.

Joyce, L. A. 1989. An analysis of the range forage situation in the United States: 1989–2040. General Technical Report RM-180. Fort Collins, Colo.: U.S. Department of Agriculture, Forest Service, Rocky Mountain Forest and Range Experiment Station.

Kennedy, W. B., and T. M. Quigley. 1994. Evolution of Forest Service organization and culture and adaptation issues in embracing ecosystem management. In *Ecosystem management: Principles and applications,* ed. M. E. Jensen and P. S. Bourgeron, 16–26. General Technical Report PNW-318. Portland, Oreg.: U.S. Department of Agriculture, Forest Service.

Langer, W. H., G. N. Green, D. H. Knepper Jr., D. A. Lindsey, D. W. Moore, L. D. Nealey, and J. C. Reed Jr. 1997. *Distribution and quality of potential sources of aggregate, Infrastructure Resources Project Area, Colorado and Wyoming.* U.S. Geological Survey Open-File Report 97-477. Denver, Colo.: U.S. Geological Survey.

Larison, J. R., G. E. Likens, J. W. Fitzpatrick, and J. G. Crock. 2000. Cadmium toxicity among wildlife in the Colorado Rocky Mountains. *Nature* 406:181–183.

Lauenroth, W. K., and W. A. Laycock. 1989. *Secondary succession and the evaluation of rangeland condition.* Westview Special Studies in Agriculture Science and Policy. Boulder, Colo.: Westview Press.

Lauenroth, W. K., and E. M. Preston, eds. 1984. *The effects of SO$_2$ on a grassland: A case study in the northern Great Plains of the United States.* New York: Springer-Verlag.

Long, J. N. 1995. The middle and southern Rocky Mountain region. In *Regional silviculture of the United States,* ed. J. W. Barrett, 335–386. New York: Wiley.

MacDonald, L. H., A. W. Smart, and R. C. Wissmar. 1991. *Monitoring guidelines to evaluate effects of forestry activities on streams in the Pacific Northwest and Alaska.* USEPA/910/9-91-001. Seattle: U.S. Environmental Protection Agency, Pacific Northwest Region.

Mackasey, W. O. 2000. *Abandoned mines in Canada.* Report prepared for Miningwatch Canada. On-line at <http://www.miningwatch.ca>.

Milchunas, D. G., and W. K. Lauenroth. 1993. Quantitative effects of grazing on vegetation and soils over a global range of environments. *Ecological Monographs* 63:327–366.

Mitchell, J. E. 2000. *Rangeland resource trends in the United States: A technical document supporting the 2000 USDA Forest Service RPA assessment.* General Technical Report RMRS-GTR-68. Fort Collins, Colo.: U.S. Department of Agriculture, Forest Service, Rocky Mountain Research Station.

Mitchell, J. E., and R. H. Hart. 1987. Winter of 1886–1887: The death knell of open range. *Rangelands* 9:3–8.

Norton, S. A., and J. S. Kahl. 1985. Geochemical analysis of sediment cores, Wind River Mountains, Wyoming. Unpublished report submitted to USDA Forest Service, Jackson, Wyoming.

NRC (National Research Council). 1992. *Restoration of aquatic ecosystems.* Washington, D.C.: National Academy Press.

Powell, D. S., J. L. Faulkner, D. R. Darr, Z. Zhu, and D. W. MacCleery. 1994. *Forest resources of the United States, 1992.* General Technical Report RM-234. Fort Collins, Colo.: U.S. Department of Agriculture, Forest Service, Rocky Mountain Forest and Range Experiment Station.

Reed, R. A., J. Johnson-Barnard, and W. L. Barker. 1996a. Contribution of roads to forest fragmentation in the Rocky Mountains. *Conservation Biology* 10:1098–1106.

———. 1996b. Fragmentation of a forested Rocky Mountain landscape, 1950–1993. *Biological Conservation* 75:267–277.

Reetz, G. R. 1998. *Water quality in the West: Report to the Western Water Policy Review Advisory Commission.* On-line at <http://www.waterinthewest.org/reading/readingfiles/fedreportfiles/quality.pdf>.

Reuss, J., R. Stottlemyer, and C. Troendle. 1997. Effect of clear cutting on nutrient fluxes in a subalpine forest at Fraser, Colorado. *Hydrology and Earth System Sciences* 1.333–344.

RMRS (Rocky Mountain Research Station). 2000. *A retrospective look at the Rocky Mountain Research Station.* On-line at <http://www.fs.fed.us/rm/main/rmrs_reports/history.html>.

Robinson, G. O. 1975. *The Forest Service.* Baltimore, Md.: Johns Hopkins University Press.

Rohe, R. 1995. Environment and mining in the mountainous West. In *The mountainous West: Explorations in historical geography,* ed. W. Wyckoff and L. M. Dilsaver, 169–193. Lincoln: University of Nebraska Press.

Rowley, W. D. 1985. *U.S. forest grazing and rangelands.* College Station: Texas A&M University Press.

Samman, S., and J. Logan. 2000. *Assessment and response to bark beetle outbreaks in the Rocky Mountain area. Report to Congress from Forest Health Protection, Washington Office, Forest Service, USDA.* General Technical Report RMRS-GTR-62. Ogden, Utah: U.S. Department of Agriculture, Forest Service, Rocky Mountain Research Station.

Shepard, W. B. 1994. Ecosystem management in the Forest Service: Political implications, impediments, and imperatives. In *Ecosystem management: Principles and applications,* ed. M.

E. Jensen and P. S. Bourgeron, 31–37. General Technical Report PNW-318. Portland, Oreg.: U.S. Department of Agriculture, Forest Service.

Sherrod, L. 2001. A history of beauty, going, going, gone? Presentation at conference, The Culture, Ecology, and Economics of Ranching West of the 100th Meridian, 4–6 May, Fort Collins, Colo.

Smith, D. A. 1993. *Mining America: The industry and the environment, 1800–1980.* Niwot: University Press of Colorado.

————, ed. 1983. *A taste of the West: Essays in honor of Robert G. Athearn.* Boulder, Colo.: Pruett.

Smith, W., and P. Lee, eds. 2000. *Canada's forests at a crossroads: An assessment in the year 2000.* Global Forest Watch Canada Report. Washington, D.C.: World Resources Institute. On-line at <http://www.globalforestwatch.org>.

Smith, W. B., J. S. Vissage, D. R. Darr, and R. M. Sheffield. 1997. *Forest resources of the United States, 1997.* St. Paul, Minn.: U.S. Department of Agriculture, Forest Service, North Central Research Station. On-line at <http://www.ncrs.fs.fed.us>.

SREP (Southern Rockies Ecosystem Project). 2000. *The state of the southern Rockies ecoregion.* Nederland, Colo.: Southern Rockies Ecosystem Project. On-line at <http://csf.colorado.edu/srep>.

Stohlgren, T. J., L. D. Schell, and B. Vanden Heuvel. 1999. How grazing and soil quality affect native and exotic plant diversity in Rocky Mountain grasslands. *Ecological Applications* 9:45–64.

Tanaka, J. A. 2001. Rangelands and sustainability. *Trail Boss News,* November 2001, 1–2.

Taylor, L. N., J. C. McGeer, C. M. Wood, and D. G. McDonald. 2000. Physiological effects of chronic copper exposure to rainbow trout (*Onchorhynchus mykiss*) in hard and soft water: Evaluation of chronic indicators. *Environmental Toxicology and Chemistry* 19:2298–2308.

Thilenius, J. F. 1975. *Alpine range management in the west United States—principles, practices, and problems: The status of our knowledge.* Research Paper RM-157. Fort Collins, Colo.: U.S. Department of Agriculture, Forest Service, Rocky Mountain Forest and Range Experiment Station.

Trlica, J. J., and L. R. Rittenhouse. 1993. Grazing and plant performance. *Ecological Applications* 3:21–23.

Troendle, C. A. 1983. The potential for water yield augmentation from forest management in the Rocky Mountains. *Water Resources Bulletin* 19:359–373.

Troendle, C. A., and R. M. King. 1985. The Fool Creek watershed—thirty years later. *Water Resources Research* 21:1915–1922.

Troendle, C. A., and W. K. Olsen. 1994. Potential effects of timber harvest and water management on stream flow dynamics and sediment transport. In *Sustainable ecological systems: Implementing an ecological approach to land management,* coord. W. W. Covington and L. F. DeBano, 34–41. General Technical Report RM-247. Flagstaff, Ariz.: U.S. Department of Agriculture, Forest Service, Rocky Mountain Forest and Range Experiment Station.

Trombulak, S. C., and C. A. Frissell. 2000. Review of ecological effects of roads on terrestrial and aquatic communities. *Conservation Biology* 14:18–30.

Tyser, R. W., and C. A. Worley. 1992. Alien flora in grasslands adjacent to road and trail corridors in Glacier National Park, Montana (USA). *Conservation Biology* 6:253–262.

USDA Forest Service. 2000a. *Executive summary, analysis of public content (draft): White River*

National Forest Plan revision and draft EIS. On-line at <http://www.fs.fed.us/r2/whiteriver/planning/exec_sum_content_analysis.pdf>.

————. 2000b. *Roadless area conservation.* On-line at <http://www.roadless.fs.fed.us>.

————. 2001a. *Forest Health on the Boise National Forest.* On-line at <http://www.fs.fed.us/r4/boise/timber/forhealth.html>.

————. 2001b. *2000 RPA assessment of forests and rangelands.* Washington D.C.: U.S. Department of Agriculture, Forest Service.

U.S. Geological Survey. 1995. *Digital map data, text, and graphical images in support of the 1995 National Assessment of United States Oil and Gas Resources Oil and Gas Assessment; Coal Fields of the United States.* Digital Data Series 35. On-line at <http://energy.cr.usgs.gov/oilgas/noga/nogaindex.htm>.

————. 1998. *Minerals information.* Nonferrous metal mines digital data set. On-line at <http://minerals.er.usgs.gov/minerals/>.

U.S. Senate. 1936. *The western range.* 74th Cong., 2nd sess. S. Doc. 199. Washington, D.C.: U.S. Government Printing Office.

Van Tassell, L. W., E. T. Bartlett, and J. E. Mitchell. 2001. *Projected use of grazed forages in the United States: 2000 to 2050.* General Technical Report RMRS-GTR-82. Fort Collins, Colo.: U.S. Department of Agriculture, Forest Service, Rocky Mountain Research Station.

Veblen, T. T., and D. C. Lorenz. 1991. *The Colorado Front Range: A century of ecological change.* Salt Lake City: University of Utah Press.

Waddell, K. L., D. D. Oswald, and D. S. Powell. 1987. *Forest statistics of the United States.* Resource Bulletin PNW-RB-168. Portland, Oreg.: U.S. Department of Agriculture.

Whitney, G. G. 1994. *From coastal wilderness to fruited plain: A history of environmental change in temperate North America, 1500 to the present.* Cambridge: Cambridge University Press.

Wohl, E. 2001. *Virtual rivers: Lessons from the mountain rivers of the Colorado Front Range.* New Haven, Conn.: Yale University Press.

Wyckoff, W., and L. M. Dilsaver. 1995. Defining the mountainous West. In *The mountainous West: Explorations in historical geography,* ed. W. Wyckoff and L. M. Dilsaver, 1–60. Lincoln: University of Nebraska Press.

CHAPTER 6

Ecological Effects of Resource Development in Running Waters

David M. Pepin, N. LeRoy Poff, and Jill S. Baron

▲

On John Wesley Powell's first exploratory trip to the West in 1867, he predicted that "in a very few decades all the waters of the arid region of the United States would be used in irrigation for agricultural purposes" (deBuys 2001, 142). Powell's predictions were correct, and more than 130 years later western rivers are controlled by immense engineering projects that store, channel, and divert Rocky Mountain waters. In 1990, fully 95% of the 78.8 billion cubic meters (m^3), or 63.8 million acre-feet (acre-ft.), of water in the Rocky Mountain states was used in agriculture (Solley, Pierce, and Perlman 1998). The production of western crops and the vitality of western cities in the past, present, and future depend on water that originates high in the Rocky Mountains.

The major Rocky Mountain river systems—the Colorado, Rio Grande, Arkansas, Missouri, Columbia, Saskatchewan, Fraser, and Peace-Athabasca—are the sources of freshwater that sustain western life and livelihood. However, transformation of these wild and variable rivers into pipelines has come at a large cost to aquatic and riparian ecosystems throughout the Rocky Mountain region. Sandra Postel of the Worldwatch Institute observed: "Many rivers now resemble elaborate plumbing works, with the timing and amount of flow completely controlled, like water from a faucet, so as to maximize the rivers' benefits for humans. But while modern engineering has been remarkably successful at getting water to people and farms when and where they need it, it has failed to protect the fundamental ecological function of rivers and aquatic systems" (Postel 1996, 45). The story of water development and its ecological effects is the subject of this chapter.

Natural River Conditions

Rocky Mountain rivers are characterized by a steep average channel gradient, turbulent flow and sediment movement, many rocks and boulders, and high spatial variability because of elevational differences in rock type, vegetation, and sediment supply. The flow regime is distinctive—there is a strong seasonal peak discharge driven by snowmelt each year, and periodically there are large floods from storm events or debris flows that have the potential to move tremendous amounts of sediment (Wohl 2000).

Annually, peak flows typically occur over the course of one to two months in late spring as warm overnight temperatures initiate high-elevation snowmelt and groundwater aquifers become saturated. For the remaining ten to eleven months, groundwater-influenced base flow conditions dominate the hydrograph. Glacial melt contributes significantly to base flow where glaciers persist (Fountain and Tangborn 1985). The magnitude of peak discharge for a given year is highly variable. High- and low-flow years have been positively correlated with the El Niño and the Southern Oscillation (ENSO) in the southern Rocky Mountain region and negatively correlated with El Niño northward (chapter 4; Molles and Dahm 1990, Dai and Wigley 2000). And though the timing and magnitude of snowmelt drive annual variation in river discharge almost entirely in these systems, severe summer storm events are often associated with major economic, geomorphic, and ecological effects (see, e.g., the description of the 1976 Big Thompson flood in Wohl 2001).

Historically, one of the most important biological modifiers of river ecosystems throughout the Rocky Mountain region was the North American beaver (*Castor canadensis*) (Naiman, Johnston, and Kelley 1988). The beavers' current ecological importance to river systems derives not from their presence but from the consequences of their extirpation by early Euro-American fur trappers (chapter 8; Wohl 2001). Beaver dams and the activities associated with their construction modify stream channel form and habitat structure. Ponds resulting from beaver dams enhance nutrient cycling, store fine sediments, and dissipate the energy associated with flood events. Consequently, a high level of aquatic habitat and biological diversity are associated with river systems that have resident beaver populations (Naiman, Johnston, and Kelley 1988; Naiman and Rogers 1997). Before the arrival of Euro-Americans, rivers in the region probably existed as a series of stepped ponds delineated by beaver dams, rather than the steep and rapidly flowing ribbon of water that characterizes today's rivers (Naiman, Johnston, and Kelley 1988; Wohl 2001).

Natural Rocky Mountain rivers are clear and cold at high elevations. Bedrock materials influence their chemical composition, but above elevations where beavers were common in presettlement times, concentrations of nutrients and dissolved organic carbon would have been very low. At lower elevations, waters influenced by beaver activity would have become richer in organic carbon and possibly colored. Sediment inputs were low in presettlement times except after debris flows, avalanches, or fires. An unknown number of streams in the mineralized regions of Colorado and possibly Montana would have had naturally acidic waters draining from sulfur-bearing ores that were later mined for metals.

Aquatic species in high-elevation rivers are slow-growing because of low water temperatures and low available food base. Native cutthroat and bull trout survived on a diet of stone flies and mayflies. Other fish, such as pikeminnows and suckers, some of which are endemic to the region, live at lower elevations and in bigger rivers. Riparian areas adjacent to rivers and streams were disproportionately rich in numbers of species compared with the rest of the Rocky Mountain landscape (SREP 2000). Tiger salamanders, boreal toads, and many mammals, such as river otters, beavers, grizzly bears, and rodents, require aquatic and riparian habitats and were present in larger numbers than today along riverine corridors.

Water Use and Development in the Rocky Mountain Region

Exploitation of water resources began with the arrival of fur trappers at small to mid-sized mountain streams in the early nineteenth century. Extirpation of beaver populations occurred by approximately 1830, with severe repercussions. It is likely that the gradient of these rivers changed; the stepped profiles associated with the presence of many small beaver dams along a river's length became more uniform as dams deteriorated and eventually failed. When the dams were breached, sediments and stored nutrients were liberated and transported downstream, altering the trophic, or nutrient, status of those reaches. Because breached dams were not rebuilt, sediment transport and nutrient cycling rates were permanently altered, which in turn altered the geomorphology, habitat structure, and biotic communities (Wohl 2001).

Manipulation of Rocky Mountain rivers took a great leap forward with the discovery of gold in Front Range river valleys in the middle of the nineteenth century (chapter 5). Settlement began around 1860, and immediately populations began developing water resources for human and livestock consumption, irrigation, waste disposal, and precious metal and timber extraction.

Many of the activities associated with settlement directly affected river structure. In as little as thirty-five to forty years, the centuries-long dynamic equilibrium between habitat and biota of presettlement rivers was radically altered (Wohl 2001). Placer and dredge mining reworked the streambed and liberated fine sediments stored beneath a coarse, armored layer (figure 5.2). As sediment loads increased as a result of mining activities, stable, slowly meandering channels shifted to mobile or braided channels (Wohl 2001). Water quality deteriorated, and habitat availability was reduced.

Simultaneously, timber was harvested from forested hillslopes (chapter 5). Timber was used to make railroad ties for the transcontinental railroad and to support mining activities. Ties were transported by river from the mountains to sawmills. Tie drives of as far as 80 kilometers (km), or 50 miles (mi.), and consisting of thousands of ties were common (Wohl 2001). There were major direct and indirect geomorphic consequences from the timber harvests of the mid-nineteenth century. Indirectly, erosion brought sediment from hillslopes to stream channels as timber was cleared, affecting the geomorphology in much the same way as did placer and dredge mining (Wohl 2000, 2001). More direct effects resulted from channel straightening. Sections of stream were blasted or dredged to remove irregularities, and valley bottoms were disconnected from the main channel with dikes (Wohl 2001). Rivers subjected to tie drives in the nineteenth century are now as much as 3.6 times wider than similar unaffected streams; they also have less bank development and lower habitat diversity (Wohl 2001).

Today, we are most aware of water development for irrigation, the third great manipulation that has profoundly affected Rocky Mountain rivers. The scope of water resource development throughout the region, measured as the rate of completion of dam construction, has kept pace with population expansion in the 140 years since the arrival of the first Europeans (figure 6.1). Water development occurs in two main ways. Rivers can be impounded (dammed and stored), or they can be diverted. Both impoundments and diversions significantly alter flow regimes, habitat structure, and biological communities of affected rivers. Transbasin diversions (moving of waters through tunnels or ditches across watershed boundaries) are common, with the largest structural diversion, the Colorado–Big Thompson project, located in Colorado.

Some uses of the region's water resources do not alter flow regimes but can dramatically alter water quality. Rivers are used to dilute a variety of pollutants and other biotic stressors in urban and industrial environments. Sediments and waste products contained in municipal wastewater treatment plant effluent, irrigation return flow, and industrial waste sources such as mine drainage all enter recipient streams.

A final insult to the integrity of Rocky Mountain rivers has been the deliberate introduction of non-native fish species, beginning in the late 1800s. Native cutthroat, bull, and lake trout were thought inferior to rainbow, brook, and European brown trout and kokanee salmon. Beginning in the late 1800s, regional fish hatcheries (themselves a large source of polluted water) were estab-

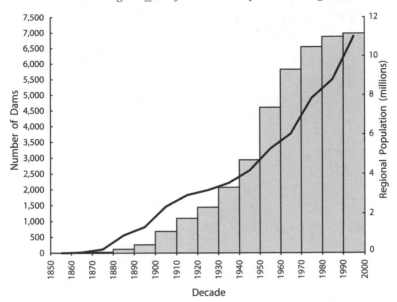

FIGURE 6.1 *Number of Dams and Regional Population in U.S. Rocky Mountain States, 1850–2000.* Data compiled from USACE 2000 and U.S. Bureau of the Census statistics.

lished to grow vast numbers of game fish (chapter 8). Fingerlings historically were transported throughout the Rockies in railroad boxcars and buckets (Pister 2001). Stocking still occurs in most Rocky Mountain rivers, and native fish populations have been severely reduced or extirpated.

Current Storage and Diversion within the Rocky Mountain Region

There are a total of 6,352 dams in the states that make up the U.S. Rocky Mountain region (table 6.1; USACE 2000). There are 2,500 dams in British Columbia, but most of them are small irrigation dams in the interior (Government of British Columbia 2002). There are 26 large dams, defined as greater than 15 meters (m), or 45 feet (ft.), in the Kootenay and Penticton regional hydrologic districts of British Columbia (Will Jolley, British Columbia Ministry of Sustainable Resource Management, pers. comm.). Approximately 20 large dams are located in the Rocky Mountain region of Alberta. Water impounded by dams is used for irrigation, water supply, flood control, and hydroelectric power generation.

Approximately 49,300 square kilometers (km²), or 12.2 million acres, of agricultural land is irrigated in the six states constituting the U.S. portion of the

TABLE 6.1. Density of Dams in the U.S. Rocky Mountains, by Primary Use

State	Control	Supply	Agriculture	Hydropower	Stock Watering
New Mexico	173	29	95	1	4
Colorado	198	245	842	34	49
Utah	101	32	352	11	0
Wyoming	40	60	728	6	309
Idaho	8	24	238	44	18
Montana	42	44	827	27	1,771
Total	562	434	3,082	123	2,151

Source: Data compiled from USACE 2000.

Rocky Mountain region. Colorado and Idaho each irrigate in excess of 12,120 km² (3 million acres). Wyoming, Montana, and Utah each irrigate less than 8,080 km² (2 million acres), and New Mexico irrigates only approximately 3,636 km² (0.9 million acres) of cropland. Alberta irrigates more than 5,050 km² (1.25 million acres) of cropland, whereas British Columbia irrigates only 113.2 km² (28,000 acres). Approximately 44% of the surface water applied for cropland irrigation—790 million m³ per second (cms), or 18 billion gallons per day (gal./day)—is used consumptively, meaning it evaporates or transpires into the atmosphere, making it unavailable downstream (Solley, Pierce, and Perlman 1998). As an anecdote regarding regional irrigation, the water lost to the atmosphere is sufficient to change the local climate by increasing humidity, atmospheric turbulence, and cloud cover and decreasing temperature extremes (chapter 4).

Data gathered regarding surface water diversions in Colorado provide an impressive example of the extent to which water resources have been developed for agriculture in the semi-arid and arid landscapes of the western United States. Within Colorado's national forests and grasslands and as far as 10 km (6 mi.) outside them, there are 67,747 points of surface water diversion. More than 35% of these diversions are used exclusively for irrigation; 55% of the total are used primarily for irrigation, with other secondary or tertiary uses (table 6.2). These diversions have decreed water allotments totaling more than 2.2 trillion m³ (1.8 billion acre-ft.) annually (USDA 1999). This volume of water is more than 150 times the historical mean annual runoff for the entire state of Colorado, which is 13 billion m³ (10.7 million acre-ft.) (Colorado Division of Water Resources 1995). Clearly, Colorado's surface water resources are overappropriated.

TABLE 6.2. Surface Water Withdrawals (million gal./day) for 1995 (United States) and 1989 (Canada), by Region and Purpose

State/Province	Storage	Agriculture	Thermoelectric	Industrial	Mining	Total (million gal./day)	Population (thousands)	Per Capita Water Use (gal./day)
New Mexico	34	1,714	46	2	0.7	1,800	1,686	1,066
Colorado	605	10,736	93	86	27	11,547	3,747	3,081
Utah	204	3,240	48	31	1	3,525	1,951	1,806
Wyoming	52	6,421	219	1.2	25	6,720	480	13,996
Idaho	10	11,940	0	7.9	27	11,985	1,163	10,305
Montana	89	8,495	22	29	4	8,640	870	9,929
Alberta	N/A[1]	N/A	N/A	N/A	N/A	3,400	2,781	1,223
British Columbia	505	489	77	840	54	1,965	3,882	502
Yukon	—[2]	—	—	—	—	—	32	—

Source: Data are from Solley, Pierce, and Perlman 1998 and Environment Canada 2000.

[1] Only total data were available for Alberta.

[2] Dash indicates that Yukon totals were combined with those for British Columbia.

There are 123 dams in the Rocky Mountain region of the United States that impound water for hydroelectric power generation (tables 6.1, 6.2). The amount of water used and the power generated by the states in this region vary widely but are commensurate with the numbers of dams in each. For example, Idaho uses 5 billion cms (115 billion gal./day) to generate 11.3 billion kilowatt-hours (kWh), whereas New Mexico uses only 120 million cms (2.75 billion gal./day) to generate 353 million kWh (Solley, Pierce, and Perlman 1998). Three large dams on the Columbia River in British Columbia store water for hydroelectric power generation at lower elevations (in both Canada and the United States), two are on the Peace River and several more are in Alberta. In 1995, more than 85% of the total power generated in British Columbia and Yukon Territory was from hydroelectric power sources, whereas only approximately 4% of the total power generated in coal-rich Alberta came from hydropower (Environment Canada 2000).

Physical Effects and Ecological Consequences of Development

The presence of dams alters thermal regimes and interrupts the movements of water, sediment, and organisms along the entire longitudinal continuum of the rivers they affect (Baxter 1979, Petts 1984, Stanford et al. 1996). Naiman and colleagues note in *The Freshwater Imperative* that "existing flow regimes, particularly in large rivers and western drainages, largely reflect human demands for water rather than natural cycles" (Naiman et al. 1995, 33). The flow regime is considered to be one of the most important factors influencing the availability and diversity of habitat in riverine ecosystems (Resh et al. 1988, Poff et al. 1997, Hart and Finelli 1999). Aquatic plants and animals have specific physical habitat requirements, and discharge plays a major role in their distribution and abundance by creating and maintaining the necessary physical habitat in river systems (Resh and Rosenberg 1984).

The physical habitat in streams and rivers responds directly to the range and variability of flows (chapter 14). Patterns in sediment size and heterogeneity, coarse woody debris transport and deposition, gravel bar and floodplain development, pool scour (excavation), and lateral channel migration are all regulated directly by spatially discrete and temporally variable discharge events (Knighton 1998). Biological communities develop and persist in response to this flow-defined habitat template (Southwood 1977, Poff and Ward 1990). Species and functional taxonomic groups evolve life history traits and habitat preferences that make them well adapted to the natural flow regime (Poff and Ward 1990).

In highly connected ecosystems, such as river networks, alterations to the physical environment have far-reaching ecological consequences. Thus, it is not surprising that development of Rocky Mountain water resources has led to a state of ecological degradation.

Physical Effects of Development

Despite some general similarities, different types of impoundments and diversions affect downstream flow regimes differently. Dams used for hydroelectric power generation impart some unique changes to the downstream hydrograph that other types of impoundments, such as flood control reservoirs, do not. Municipal, flood control, and irrigation storage impoundments create downstream conditions of long-term flow constancy, whereas hydropower peaking generation impoundments cause rapid short-term flow fluctuations.

The purpose of storage reservoirs is to hold water for later off-stream use. Flood control dams capture and store extreme flow events at an upstream location to minimize flood damage downstream (Petts 1984). Both types of reservoir capture peak flows, reducing or compressing the range of variability and magnitude of discharge (figure 6.2a). The stored water is released in measured increments over the course of the year according to societal needs instead of occurring in the normal pulsed patterns, so peak flows are reduced and base flows are elevated (Petts 1984, Poff et al. 1997, Graf 1999, Rood et al. 1995). Riparian areas are not replenished, and rivers cut into their beds when they are starved of the sediment trapped behind the dam (Wolman and Miller 1960, Wolman and Gerson 1978).

Water releases from hydropower dams are scheduled to match the daily and seasonal energy needs of the populations they serve. Hydroelectric power generation leads to rapid, short-term flow fluctuations in downstream river segments and severe changes to the timing, or seasonality, of annual flows. Under hydropeaking operations, discharge can deviate from stable and smooth (i.e., seasonally predictable) to flashy and uncoupled from any kind of natural flow (figure 6.2b).

Some reservoirs release water through the bottoms of their dams. In large, deep reservoirs, the temperature of lake bottom waters, or hypolimnion, is approximately 4°C year-round, the temperature that corresponds to the maximum density of water. Cold hypolimnetic releases alter the thermal regimes of downstream segments of regulated rivers (Ward 1976, Vinson 2001). Hypolimnetic releases have been shown to cause winter-warm and summer-cool shifts in the thermal regime of regulated relative to free-flowing segments of the same river (e.g., Ward 1976; figure 6.3). In other words, the regulated annual temperature pattern is radically different from natural annual temperature patterns (figure 6.3). Alterations to natural thermal regimes have ecological consequences; changing the period of time during which aquatic organisms are able to grow can impair their development and reproduction (see, e.g., Ward 1976; Magnuson, Crowder, and Medvick 1979; Vannote and Sweeney 1980).

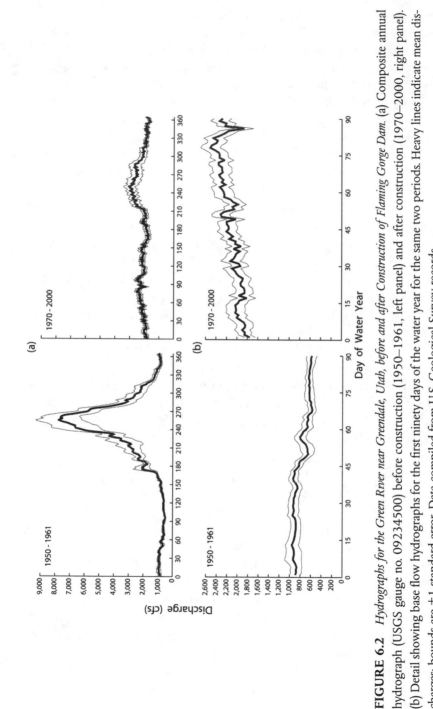

FIGURE 6.2 *Hydrographs for the Green River near Greendale, Utah, before and after Construction of Flaming Gorge Dam.* (a) Composite annual hydrograph (USGS gauge no. 09234500) before construction (1950–1961, left panel) and after construction (1970–2000, right panel). (b) Detail showing base flow hydrographs for the first ninety days of the water year for the same two periods. Heavy lines indicate mean discharges; bounds are ±1 standard error. Data compiled from U.S. Geological Survey records.

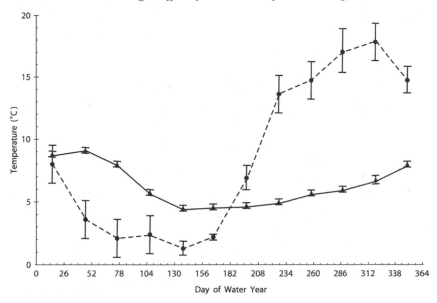

FIGURE 6.3 *Composite Annual Thermographs for the Green River, Utah, before and after Construction of Flaming Gorge Dam.* Dashed line with circles represents period before construction (1956–1962); solid line with triangles represents period after construction (1963–1978). Error bars are ±1 standard error. Modified from Vinson 2001.

Ecological Consequences

Aquatic biodiversity and ecosystem functions have been lost or degraded as a result of fragmentation caused by dams and diversions. Virtually *all* rivers in North America have been dammed or diverted; only 2% are still free-flowing (Benke 1990). In the Rocky Mountain region, algal, invertebrate, and vertebrate biomass and richness (number of taxa) are significantly altered in developed river systems compared with similar undeveloped systems (chapter 14). Although the exact mechanisms for these changes vary by location, they are broadly the result of river modifications that increase either *constancy* or *variability* in flow and temperature (Blinn et al. 1995; Ward, Zimmerman, and Cline 1986; Rader and Belish 1999). Additional changes come from pollutants, including mine drainage, and introduction of non-native species.

Prolonged constancy in the aquatic environment alters development or life history cues for critical life stages, with the consequent loss of sensitive species. Additionally, prolonged constancy may confer a competitive advantage to introduced exotic species. Exotic invaders often dominate fish and riparian communities of regulated river systems. Highly variable flow conditions can wash out or strand organisms not adapted to unpredictable flows. Excessively variable thermal conditions lead to temperature extremes outside many species' normal tolerance ranges, resulting in the loss of sensitive taxa. What remains in regulated streams are species that are tolerant to the highly modified conditions (box 6.1).

Cold, sediment-free water below dams causes invertebrate and fish assemblages to shift so they resemble communities from smaller tributaries upstream that are adapted to cold, clear conditions (Stanford and Ward 1984, 1989; Hauer, Stanford, and Ward 1989; Hauer and Stanford 1982). For example, caddis fly assemblages collected from regulated mainstem rivers in Montana were more similar to those found in upstream tributaries than in similar-sized but unregulated mainstem sites (Hauer and Stanford 1982). Similar discontinuities have been reported in Colorado for Gunnison River assemblages of salmonids, caddis flies, and stone flies (Stanford and Ward 1984, 1989; Hauer, Stanford, and Ward 1989).

Box 6.1. Ecological Responses to Diversion

A fifty-two-year invertebrate record of the Green River in northeastern Utah dramatically shows the response to dam construction (Vinson 2001). Completion of Flaming Gorge Dam in 1962 increased constancy in both discharge and thermal conditions downstream of the dam (see figures 6.2 and 6.3). Invertebrate species richness declined from more than seventy genera before impoundment to fewer than thirty genera after impoundment immediately downstream from the dam. The relative abundance of insects in the community shifted from approximately 80% mayflies (Insecta: Ephemeroptera) under the natural flow regime to 90% midges and blackflies (Insecta: Diptera) following dam closure; fifteen Ephemeroptera genera were extirpated from downstream reaches (Vinson 2001).

A streamflow diversion in the Fraser River basin of central Colorado, where the disturbance was prolonged low flows downstream of the diversion, had much the same result as was found downstream from Flaming Gorge Dam (Rader and Belish 1999). Mayfly and stone fly (Insecta: Plecoptera) richness was lower in diverted reaches than in upstream, undiverted reaches. In fact, ten abundant taxa were locally extirpated from downstream sections of the study streams. In addition, the relative abundance of invertebrates shifted below diversion structures from an even mix of mayflies, stone flies, caddis flies (Insecta: Trichoptera), and midges to a community dominated by midges and noninsect invertebrates (Ostracoda).

The movement and distribution of many native fishes have been disrupted and availability of quality spawning habitat has been severely reduced in fragmented, regulated systems of the Rocky Mountain region. Biodiversity has declined, and introduced non-native species have proliferated (chapter 8). The Colorado River fish fauna historically contained thirty-two native species, including large-bodied razorback suckers and Colorado pikeminnows (Stanford and Ward 1986). Under natural conditions, the Colorado system exhibited a multitude of diverse habitats, including channel pools and riffles, backwaters, and floodplain marshes. Periodic flood flows reworked and redistributed sediments, maintaining the diversity of habitats, which subsidized large fish populations by accumulating detritus and supporting planktonic and invertebrate production (Stanford and Ward 1986). Since regulation, the fish fauna of the Colorado system has become dominated by non-native species; one native fish species is extinct, and fifteen of the original thirty-two occur only in small, fragmented populations (Stanford and Ward 1986).

The primary cause of this decline is habitat loss. Clear water discharged from deep release dams has led to coarsening of stream bottoms because fine sediments no longer travel downstream; the removal of large peak flows (see figure 6.2a) prevents backwaters and floodplain ponds from receiving water in most years. Interactions among native fishes and introduced exotic sport fishes have further contributed to the decline in native fish biodiversity (Stanford and Ward 1986).

Rivers downstream from large dams experience fewer and smaller floods. More water runs down the channel, with less available to support riparian communities. Streamside vegetation is limited directly downstream of a dam because of enhanced erosion. Farther down, the lack of fine sediments and localized drought from low flows can prevent young cottonwood seedlings from becoming established (SREP 2000). The closure of a dam on the St. Mary's River in Alberta in 1951 caused the death of 68% of mature cottonwoods while preventing the establishment of young trees (Rood et al. 1995). Plants that can take advantage of the altered environment invade regulated systems; these are often difficult-to-control invasive species such as tamarisk or Russian olive (Busch and Smith 1995, Merritt and Cooper 2000).

Hydrologic alterations threaten as much as 40% of the species of aquatic fauna in the western United States (Richter et al. 1997). The U.S. Environmental Protection Agency has identified flow regulation or hydrologic alteration of rivers and streams as one of the leading threats to water quality nationwide; 20% of the impaired river miles identified in the 1998 national water quality report to the United States Congress were affected by river regulation or hydrologic alteration (EPA 2000).

Water Pollution

Rivers and streams throughout the Rocky Mountain region have been intentionally and unintentionally used as waste dumps since the early nineteenth century, when the region was first colonized. Today, water quality is variable and the overall status of water quality is not well documented (Reetz 1998). Although Section 305b of the Clean Water Act directs each U.S. state to conduct surveys and report to Congress on the state of water quality every two years, the number of miles surveyed is up to individual states. In 1998 Montana, Idaho, and Utah each surveyed only 10%–11% of their stream miles, and Wyoming and Colorado surveyed 19% and 25%, respectively; New Mexico surveyed the lowest proportion of stream miles, only 4% (EPA 2001).

Even with this little bit of reporting, some of the results are telling. Sixty-seven percent of Idaho's surveyed rivers and streams were deemed impaired by a combination of sediment from agriculture and forestry, mine waste, nutrients from agriculture and urban discharges, and thermal pollution. Wyoming, on the other hand, rated its surface waters as having excellent to good condition, claiming that most current water quality problems were the legacy of past overgrazing, road building, and irrigation practices (EPA 2001). In a study of stream invertebrates in the mineralized region of Colorado, 14% of the seventy-eight randomly selected streams were contaminated with heavy metals from past mining activities (Clements et al. 2000). Certain groups of invertebrates, specifically heptageniid mayflies (Ephemeroptera: Heptageniidae) are intolerant of even moderate metal concentrations, and overall diversity is lower in the presence of heavy metals.

Urbanization causes eutrophication. Long-term research conducted on the Cache la Poudre River where it flows out of the Front Range and through the city of Fort Collins, Colorado, indicates that biological oxygen demand (a surrogate for increased decomposition) doubles and water clarity halves in a distance of less than 15 km (9 mi.) after the water leaves the mountains, where it flows for more than 130 km, or 78 mi. (Voelz et al. 2000). Specific conductivity, a measure of the concentration of dissolved ions in the water, increases by a factor of ten in this same distance. This example serves to remind us that nodes of human population have a disproportionate effect on water quality throughout the Rocky Mountain region.

Five Rocky Mountain river basins have been studied as part of the National Water-Quality Assessment Program of the U.S. Geological Survey. They reveal some of the factors that influence water quality. In the upper Colorado River basin, interbasin water transfers of as much as 12% decrease the dilution capability of low-order streams. Metals and acids from mine drainage contaminate aquatic organisms and reduce biodiversity. Increasing urbanization and recreational facilities, including ski resorts and golf courses, add nutrients to previously oligotrophic streams and rivers. Winter snowmaking activities at ski resorts can dewater streams, creating dangerously low winter streamflows for fish. Water removed for snowmaking can also prevent dilution of nutrients and mine drainage (Apodaca, Stephens, and Driver 1996). Mine waste and agricultural runoff were major influences on the Rocky Mountain reaches of the Rio Grande (Ellis et al. 1993). Past mining activities, agricultural runoff, and increasing urbanization also influence water quality of the South Platte River headwaters (Dennehy et al. 1993). Excessive nutrients, sediment, and pesticides were found in the agricultural portion of the Snake River in south-central Idaho. Concentrations are made worse because of low flows caused by irrigation diversions and five large reservoirs (Clark et al. 1998). In the northern Rockies' intermontane basins of northwestern Montana and northern Idaho, the same concerns exist for water quality as elsewhere: contaminants from mine drainage, sediments and nutrients from agriculture and logging operations, nutrients from urban and recreational activities. For example, in Montana's Clark Fork River basin, mine tailings have been transported more than 240 km (150 mi.), and there have been six major acid-related fish kills since 1984 (Tornes 1997).

The Greater Yellowstone Ecosystem (GYE) contains the headwaters of the Missouri, Yellowstone, Snake, and Green Rivers. A consortium of federal land managers recently assessed watershed integrity for the GYE as part of developing a comprehensive watershed management strategy (Greater Yellowstone Hydrologists Group 2001). An estimated 41% of the GYE has high water quality, with the remaining 59% influenced by bank damage, sediment loading, channel modification, flow disruption, thermal change, chemical contamination, or biological stress. Of these, sediment and bank channel modification caused the majority of damage.

Conclusions

Water resources development in the Rocky Mountain region has been extensive and critical to the region's economic growth. However, the effects on Rocky Mountain aquatic ecosystems have been profound. Rivers that were defined by their upstream-downstream and riparian–stream channel connectivity have been truncated and dewatered by dams and diversion structures. Waters affected by mine drainage are acidic, with high concentrations of heavy metals. Sediment and nutrients come from grazing, logging, agriculture, and urbanization. Water temperatures below dams bear no resemblance to "normal." Non-native species proliferate while native species decline. These adverse effects do not exist in isolation; rather, they interact as multiple stressors on the region's aquatic and riparian ecosystems.

The Fraser River and the Athabasca-Slave-Mackenzie system in Canada are the only large undammed rivers left in all the Rocky Mountains. Some smaller rivers, such as the San Miguel and the Yampa in Colorado, are relatively unaltered. In Wyoming, the Yellowstone, the upper Green above Fontenelle Reservoir, and the Powder are not highly modified. The Salmon, the Selway, and the Clearwater in Idaho are also largely unregulated. Colorado's rivers are the most highly manipulated, but no rivers in Utah or New Mexico are left undeveloped (U.S. Bureau of Reclamation 2002).

Belatedly, water managers are attempting to salvage aquatic and riparian ecosystems with technological solutions. River management plans that incorporate some flow variability to mimic natural flows are at least being discussed for several western rivers (Stibrach and Charles 2000, Stanford et al. 1996). Multi-level water intake capabilities have been installed on Flaming Gorge Dam on the Green River in Utah to partially restore thermal properties below the reservoir (Vinson 2001). Fish ladders help adult fish migrate upstream past many dams, but there have been no salmon in the upper Columbia River for years. Bordering on the absurd, barges and tanker trucks are required to move juvenile salmon back to the ocean. Whether these intensive remedial techniques will work in the long run to restore or maintain aquatic and riparian ecosystems of regulated western rivers is unknown.

A recent assessment of the conservation status and biodiversity of North America's freshwater ecoregions demonstrates that despite these recent management efforts, many of the Rocky Mountain region's freshwater resources are extremely stressed (Abell et al. 2000). Watersheds in the Colorado River basin, the upper Snake River basin in Idaho and Wyoming, the Bonneville Basin within the arid Great Basin, portions of the Columbia River basin that were never glaciated, and the Canadian Rockies ecoregion in Alberta, British Columbia, and northern Montana are considered continentally outstanding with respect to their biological distinctiveness. Of these, the conservation status of the Colorado River ecoregion is considered critical, in large part because of hydrologic alteration and water quality degradation of 90%–100% of the waters, high levels of habitat fragmentation, and exotic species introductions. The Bonneville and Columbia unglaciated ecoregions are endangered by hydrologic alteration, habitat fragmentation, and effects of exotic species. There is the potential for significant loss of biodiversity in these ecoregions if current development and management practices continue.

Most water development in the Rocky Mountains has ended, partly because there are few good remaining dam sites left. Public opinion has also changed, and environmental considerations have become more important (WWPRAC

1998). Agriculture uses all but a small fraction of total water in all Rocky Mountain states, as a by-product of original western water law. Western water law, developed during the heyday of mining and settlement in the late nineteenth century, gives water rights to the senior water user—the one who claimed it first. In Colorado, the poster child for overdevelopment of water resources, 93% of all water is allocated to irrigation. However, agriculture in 2001 accounted for only 1.5% of the gross state product and only 2.0% of total employment (C. W. Howe, pers. comm.). Historical allocations of water clash with federal mandates of the Clean Water Act, the Endangered Species Acts, and public participation in decision making through the National Environmental Policy Act of 1969. Interstate and interbasin conflicts over the finite amount of water are increasing as western states grow in population (Postel 2000, WWPRAC 1998). Perhaps it is time to reevaluate and readjust Rocky Mountain water uses and policies with some consideration for sustaining aquatic and riparian ecosystems.

Acknowledgments

We thank Julian Olden for providing useful comments and Will Jolley of the British Columbia Ministry of Sustainable Resource Management for providing dam numbers.

References

Abell, R. A., D. M. Olson, E. Dinerstein, P. T. Hurley, J. T. Diggs, W. Eichbaum, S. Walters, W. Wettengel, T. Allnutt, C. J. Loucks, and P. Hedao. 2000. *Freshwater ecoregions of North America: A conservation assessment.* Washington, D.C.: Island Press.

Apodaca, L. E., V. C. Stephens, and N. E. Driver. 1996. What affects water quality in the upper Colorado River basin? U.S. Geological Survey Fact Sheet FS-109-96. Washington, D.C.: U.S. Geological Survey.

Baxter, R. M. 1979. Environmental effects of dams and impoundments. *Annual Review of Ecology and Systematics* 8:255–283.

Benke, A. C. 1990. A perspective on America's vanishing streams. *Journal of the North American Benthological Society* 9:77–88.

Blinn, D. W., J. P. Shannon, L. E. Stevens, and J. P. Carder. 1995. Consequences of fluctuating discharge for lotic communities. *Journal of the North American Benthological Society* 14:233–248.

Busch, D. E., and S. D. Smith. 1995. Mechanisms associated with decline of woody species in riparian ecosystems of the southwestern U.S. *Ecological Monographs* 65:347–370.

Clark, G. M., T. R. Maret, M. G. Rupert, M. A. Maupin, W. H. Low, and D. S. Ott. 1998. *Water quality in the upper Snake River basin, Idaho and Wyoming, 1992–1995.* U.S. Geological Survey Circular 1160. On-line at <http://water.usgs.gov/pubs/circ1160>.

Clements, W. H., D. M. Carlisle, J. M. Lazorchak, and P. C. Johnson. 2000. Heavy metals structure benthic communities in Colorado mountain streams. *Ecological Applications* 10:626–638.

Colorado Division of Water Resources. 1995. *Colorado historic average annual streamflows (acre feet)*. Historical averages obtained from USGS Water-Data Report CO-93. Colorado Division of Water Resources, Office of the State Engineer. On-line at <http://water.state.co.us/images/snake.GIF>.

Dai, A. G., and T. M. L. Wigley. 2000. Global patterns of ENSO-induced precipitation. *Geophysical Research Letters* 27:1283–1286.

deBuys, W., ed. 2001. *Seeing things whole: The essential John Wesley Powell*. Washington, D.C.: Island Press.

Dennehy, K. F., D. W. Litke, C. M. Tate, and J. S. Heiny. 1993. South Platte River basin: Colorado, Nebraska, and Wyoming. *Water Resources Bulletin* 29:647–683.

Ellis, S. R., G. W. Levings, L. F. Carter, S. F. Richey, and M. J. Radell. 1993. Rio Grande valley, Colorado, New Mexico, and Texas. In *American Water Resources Monograph Series no. 19*, ed. P. P. Leahy, B. J. Ryan, and A. I. Johnson, 617–646. Middleburg, Va.: American Water Resources Association.

Environment Canada. 2000. *A primer on fresh water: Questions and answers*. 5th ed. Quebec: Environment Canada, Minister of Public Works and Government Services. On-line at <http://www.ec.gc.ca/water/index.htm>.

EPA (U.S. Environmental Protection Agency). 2000. *National Water Quality Inventory: 1998 report to Congress*. Report EPA/841-R-00-001. Washington, D.C.: U.S. Environmental Protection Agency.

Fountain, A. G., and W. V. Tangborn. 1985. The effect of glaciers on streamflow variations. *Water Resources Research* 21:579–586.

Government of British Columbia. 2002. *Dam safety in British Columbia*. On-line at <http://srmwww.gov.bc.ca/wat/dams/dam.html>.

Graf, W. L. 1999. Dam nation: A geographic census of American dams and their large-scale hydrologic impacts. *Water Resources Research* 35:1305–1311.

Greater Yellowstone Hydrologists Group. 2001. Watershed management strategy for the greater Yellowstone area. Unpublished report on file with U.S. Department of Agriculture, Forest Service, Gallatin National Forest, 10 E. Babcock Street, Bozeman, MT 59771.

Hart, D. D., and C. M. Finelli. 1999. Physical-biological coupling in streams: The pervasive effect of flow on benthic organisms. *Annual Review of Ecology and Systematics* 30:363–395.

Hauer, F. R., and J. A. Stanford. 1982. Ecological responses of hydropsychid caddisflies to stream regulation. *Canadian Journal of Fisheries and Aquatic Sciences* 39:1235–1242.

Hauer, F. R., J. A. Stanford, and J. V. Ward. 1989. Serial discontinuities in a Rocky Mountain river. II. Distribution and abundance of trichoptera. *Regulated Rivers: Research and Management* 3:177–182.

Knighton, D. 1998. *Fluvial forms and processes: A new perspective*. New York: Oxford University Press.

Magnuson, J. J., L. B. Crowder, and P. A. Medvick. 1979. Temperature as an ecological resource. *American Zoologist* 19:331–343.

Merritt, D. M., and D. J. Cooper. 2000. Riparian vegetation and channel change in response to river regulation: A comparative study of regulated and unregulated streams in the Green River Basin, USA. *Regulated Rivers: Research and Management* 16:543–564.

Molles, M. C. Jr., and C. N. Dahm. 1990. A perspective on El Niño and La Niña: Global implications for stream ecology. *Journal of the North American Benthological Society* 9:68–76.

Naiman, R. J., C. A. Johnston, and J. C. Kelley. 1988. Alteration of North American streams by beaver. *BioScience* 38:753–762.

Naiman, R. J., J. J. Magnuson, D. M. McKnight, and J. A. Stanford, eds. 1995. *The freshwater imperative: A research agenda.* Washington, D.C.: Island Press.

Naiman, R. J., and K. H. Rogers. 1997. Large animals and system level characteristics in river corridors. *BioScience* 47:521–529.

Petts, G. E. 1984. *Impounded rivers.* New York: Wiley.

Pister, E. P. 2001. Wilderness fish stocking: History and perspective. *Ecosystems* 4:279–286.

Poff, N. L., J. D. Allan, M. B. Bain, J. R. Karr, K. L. Prestegaard, B. D. Richter, R. E. Sparks, and J. C. Stromberg. 1997. The natural flow regime: A paradigm for river conservation and restoration. *BioScience* 47:769–784.

Poff, N. L., and J. V. Ward. 1990. Physical habitat template of lotic systems: Recovery in the context of historical patterns of spatiotemporal heterogeneity. *Environmental Management* 14:629–645.

Postel, S. 1996. Forging a sustainable water strategy. In *State of the world: A Worldwatch Institute report on progress toward a sustainable society,* ed. L. R. Brown, J. Abramovitz, C. Bright, C. Flavin, G. Gardner, H. Kane, A. Platt, S. Postel, D. Roodman, A. Sachs, and L. Starke, 40–59. New York: Norton.

———. 2000. Entering an era of water scarcity: The challenges ahead. *Ecological Applications* 10:941–948.

Rader, R. B., and T. A. Belish. 1999. Influence of mild to severe flow alterations on invertebrates in three mountain streams. *Regulated Rivers: Research and Management* 15:353–363.

Reetz, G. R. 1998. *Water quality in the West: Report to the Western Water Policy Review Advisory Commission.* On-line at <http://www.waterinthewest.org/reading/readingfiles/fedreportfiles/quality.pdf>.

Resh, V. H., A. V. Brown, A. P. Covich, M. E. Gurtz, H. W. Li, G. W. Minshall, S. R. Reice, A. L. Sheldon, J. B. Wallace, and R. C. Wissmar. 1988. Role of disturbance in stream ecology. *Journal of the North American Benthological Society* 7:433–455.

Resh, V. H., and D. M. Rosenberg. 1984. *The ecology of aquatic insects.* New York: Praeger.

Richter, B. D., D. P. Braun, M. A. Mendelson, and L. L. Master. 1997. Threats to imperiled freshwater fauna. *Conservation Biology* 11:1081–1093.

Rood, S. B., J. M. Mahoney, D. E. Reid, and L. Zilm. 1995. Instream flows and the decline of riparian cottonwoods along the St-Mary River, Alberta. *Canadian Journal of Botany* 73:1250–1260.

Solley, W. B., R. R. Pierce, and H. A. Perlman. 1998. *Estimated use of water in the United States in 1995.* U.S. Geological Survey Circular 1200. Denver, Colo.: U.S. Geological Survey.

Southwood, T. R. 1977. Habitat: The template for ecological strategies? *Journal of Animal Ecology* 46:337–365.

SREP (Southern Rockies Ecosystem Project). 2000. *The state of the southern Rockies ecoregion.* Nederland, Colo.: Southern Rockies Ecosystem Project. On-line at <http://csf.colorado.edu/srep>.

Stanford, J. A., and J. V. Ward. 1984. The effects of regulation on the limnology of Gunnison River: A North American case history. In *Regulated rivers,* ed. A. Lillehammer and S. J. Saltveit, 467–480. Oslo: Universitetsforlaget AS.

———. 1986. Fishes of the Colorado system. In *The ecology of river systems,* ed. B. R. Davies and K. F. Walker, 385–402. Boston: Dr. W. Junk.

————. 1989. Serial discontinuities in a Rocky Mountain river. I. Distribution and abundance of plecoptera. *Regulated Rivers: Research and Management* 3:169–175.

Stanford, J. A., J. V. Ward, W. J. Liss, C. A. Frissell, R. N. Williams, J. A. Lichatowich, and C. C. Coutant. 1996. A general protocol for restoration of regulated rivers. *Regulated Rivers: Research and Management* 12:391–413.

Stibrach, J. S., and T. J. Charles. 2000. Resolution of Endangered Species Act issues in permitting the Plateau Creek pipeline. *Journal of American Water Resource Association* 36:1263–1269.

Tornes, L. H. 1997. *National Water-Quality Assessment Program, northern Rockies intermontane basins.* U.S. Geological Survey Fact Sheet FS-158-97. Washington, D.C.: U.S. Geological Survey.

USACE (U.S. Army Corps of Engineers). 2000. *Water control infrastructure: National Inventory of Dams.* CD-ROM. Washington, D.C.: Federal Emergency Management Agency.

U.S. Bureau of Reclamation. 2002. *DataWeb: Managing water in the American West!* On-line at <http://www.rsgis.do.usbr.gov/html/state_dams.html>.

USDA Forest Service. 1999. *Colorado points of diversion database.* CD-ROM. Denver, Colo.: Inland West Water Initiative.

Vannote, R. L., and B. W. Sweeney. 1980. Geographic analysis of thermal equilibria: A conceptual model for evaluating the effect of natural and modified thermal regimes on aquatic insect communities. *American Naturalist* 115:667–695.

Vinson, M. R. 2001. Long-term dynamics of an invertebrate assemblage downstream from a large dam. *Ecological Applications* 11:711–730.

Voelz, N. J., S. H. Shieh, and J. V. Ward. 2000. Long-term monitoring of benthic macroinvertebrate community structure: A perspective from a Colorado river. *Aquatic Ecology* 34:261–278.

Ward, J. V. 1976. Effects of thermal constancy and seasonal temperature displacement on community structure of stream macroinvertebrates. In *Thermal ecology II: ERDA symposium proceedings,* ed. G. W. Esch and R. W. McFarlane, 302–307. Springfield, Va.: National Technical Information Service.

Ward, J. V., H. J. Zimmerman, and L. D. Cline. 1986. Lotic zoobenthos of the Colorado system. In *The ecology of river systems,* ed. B. R. Davies and K. F. Walker, 403–424. Boston: Dr. W. Junk.

Wohl, E. E. 2000. *Mountain rivers.* Water Resources Monograph 14. Washington, D.C.: American Geophysical Union.

————. 2001. *Virtual rivers: Lessons from the mountain rivers of the Colorado Front Range.* New Haven, Conn.: Yale University Press.

Wolman, M. G., and R. Gerson. 1978. Relative scales of time and effectiveness of climate in watershed geomorphology. *Earth Surface Processes* 3:189–203.

Wolman, M. G., and J. P. Miller. 1960. Magnitude and frequency of forces in geomorphic processes. *Journal of Geology* 68:54–74.

WWPRAC (Western Water Policy Review Advisory Commission). 1998. *Water in the West: Challenge for the next century.* Report of the Western Water Policy Review Advisory Commission. On-line at <http://www.waterinthewest.org/reading/readingfiles/fedreport.htm>.

CHAPTER 7

The Cascading Effects of Fire Exclusion in Rocky Mountain Ecosystems

Robert E. Keane, Kevin C. Ryan, Thomas T. Veblen,
Craig D. Allen, Jesse A. Logan, and Brad Hawkes

▲

The extensive wildfire season of 1910 was a defining moment for wildland fire management in the United States. Although heavy grazing had somewhat altered the primeval role of fire in some areas of the Rocky Mountains since the mid-1800s, the General Land Office had established only a primitive fire control structure to suppress fires in the remote Rocky Mountains prior to 1910. One and a half million hectares (ha), or 5,800 square miles (mi.²), burned during that dry, windy summer of 1910, and the USDA Forest Service initiated an aggressive fire suppression policy (Cohen and Miller 1978). Enactment of the Weeks Law in 1911 improved coordination of fire suppression efforts by providing funding to those states willing to adopt comprehensive fire suppression plans (Babbitt 1995). By 1929, the U.S. fire management organization was fully functional, with hundreds of fire towers built and thousands of men employed. The enlargement of this organization has accelerated in intensity and technological capacity until the present day. Similar advances in fire suppression organizations occurred after 1945 in the Canadian Rocky Mountains (Woodley 1995).

This very effective fire suppression program owes much of its success to strong government support and extensive advertising campaigns. Smokey Bear's message, "Only you can prevent wildfires," was simple and direct, but as we now know, it was shortsighted. In a perfect world, we would have known that there would be adverse consequences of this pervasive fire exclusion policy. But

Box 7.1. Some Terminology

Fire suppression is the act of extinguishing or fighting fires, whereas *fire exclusion* is the de facto policy of trying to eliminate fires from the landscape by means of fire suppression techniques. A *fire regime,* the long-term cumulative fire characteristics of a landscape, is often described by frequency, extent, pattern, severity, and seasonality (Agee 1993). In a *native fire regime,* fires are allowed to burn across the landscape; eventually the character of the vegetation will reflect the character of the fires. It is often assumed that fire regimes prior to 1850 were native fire regimes; however, they may or may not have involved significant numbers of fires caused by Native Americans. *Fire severity* describes the effect of a fire on the biota and is quite different from *fire intensity,* which is the heat output of a fire. *Ecological processes* are those factors that influence the flow of energy in an ecosystem and include transpiration, photosynthesis, and disturbances (Waring and Running 1998).

vegetation grows slowly in the Rocky Mountains, and the buildup of hazardous fuels in forests and rangelands went unnoticed for many years. It was difficult for the first, and even the second, generation of forest and range scientists to observe and agree on the adverse effects of excluding fire from Rocky Mountain ecosystems. Now we are faced with critical ecological issues in the aftermath of our war on forest and range fires. The health of many Rocky Mountain ecosystems is declining because of fire exclusion. Moreover, fires are a fundamental part of many Rocky Mountain ecosystems; exclusion merely postpones the inevitable. This is highlighted by the fire season of 2000, during which more than 3.4 million ha (13,000 mi.^{2}) burned despite a billion-dollar suppression effort. This chapter discusses the diverse and cascading effects of fire exclusion in the Rocky Mountains. A brief glossary is presented in box 7.1.

The Role of Fire in the Rocky Mountains

Early observers recognized the critical role of fire in shaping North American forests. John Muir, Gifford Pinchot, and Aldo Leopold noted the importance of fire in regulating the composition and health of American forests (Pinchot 1899, Leopold 1924). Harold Weaver (1943, 7) remarked that removal of fire would "threaten sound management and protection" of western forests. Yet despite these early warnings, fires continued to be extinguished on the majority of public lands because suppression was the more desirable land management policy. It was not until the late 1970s and early 1980s that wildland fires were allowed to return to some U.S. and Canadian national parks and wilderness areas (Hawkes 1990, Kilgore and Heinselman 1990).

Fire is an essential disturbance that (1) recycles nutrients, (2) regulates succession by selecting and regenerating plants, (3) maintains diversity, (4) reduces biomass, (5) controls insect and disease populations, (6) triggers and regulates interactions between vegetation and animals, and, most important, (7) maintains biological and biogeochemical processes (Crutzen and Goldammer 1993). Fire is neither good nor bad; rather, it is an important ecological process that can produce variable effects. Its removal from the fire-dominated ecosystems of the Rocky Mountains has caused a plethora of cascading effects that have permeated nearly every part of this rugged landscape (Arno and Brown 1989). At first glance, the effects of fire exclusion, such as preservation of timber resources and watershed protection, may seem beneficial to society, but on closer scrutiny there is little doubt that fire exclusion has created many unhealthy features on Rocky Mountain landscapes.

Early native inhabitants of the Rocky Mountains had a profound effect on forest structure and composition, primarily as a result of fires they set (Mullan 1866, Denevan 1992). Native populations started fires for land clearing, wildlife habitat improvement, cultivation, defense, signals, and hunting (Gruell 1985, Kay 1995). Was indigenous burning part of the native fire regime? Did these fires differ substantially in frequency and type from lightning fires? These questions are debated (hotly) in the literature (Barrett and Arno 1982; Fisher, Jenkins, and Fisher 1986; Kay 1995), but in this chapter we assume that Native American ignitions were part of the historical fire regimes of the Rocky Mountains and therefore reflect the native, or natural, fire regimes.

Livestock has played a critical role in the decline of wildland fire in the Rocky Mountains (chapter 5). Extensive grazing by sheep, cattle, and horses from the early 1850s to the present has removed an important layer of fine fuel (i.e., grass and forbs) from the landscape (Covington and Moore 1994). Moreover, the elimination of grass competition allowed rapid conifer encroachment that further reduced grass cover by shading (Hansen, Wyckoff, and Banfield 1995). Intensive grazing on Rocky Mountain landscapes has also exacerbated the effects of modern fire suppression efforts (Swetnam and Baisan 1996).

Extent of the Problem

The effects of fire exclusion are quite different from those of other management actions, such as logging, because they occur gradually and are manifest in nearly every part of the landscape rather than localized to small areas. The effects are also extremely variable in time and space (Agee 1993; Heyerdahl, Berry, and Agee 1995). Today's wildfires differ in severity and aerial extent from those that occurred prior to the exclusion era, circa 1900. Major changes in land use throughout the Rockies, including timber harvest, agricultural development, and urbanization, have completely altered ecosystems, and any discussion of fire exclusion effects must take these changes into account. The role of fire becomes more complex as it interacts with land management.

Only a small fraction of the pre-1900 annual average fire acreage is being burned today. Barrett, Arno, and Menakis (1997) estimated that an average of 2.4 million ha (9,000 mi.^{2}) burned annually in the interior northwestern United States before 1900. Until the extensive fires of 2000, the biggest wildfire years of the century burned less than half the historical average. Approximately two-thirds of annual burning historically occurred in sagebrush and grassland vegetation that today is agricultural land or dry pastureland (chapter 11; Morgan et al. 1998). Presettlement fire maps for the United States reveal that more than half the country experienced fires at intervals of one to twelve years (Frost 1998). Maps of historical and current fire regimes for the interior Columbia River basin show that recent fires have been less frequent and more severe than those that occurred prior to 1900, and the greatest change in fire regimes has been in the shrublands, grasslands, dry forests, and woodlands (Morgan et al. 1998).

Some Rocky Mountain ecosystems have not been affected by fire exclusion. Fire is not an important ecological feature in alpine and desert-scrub ecosystems. In upper subalpine ecosystems, fires have a return frequency of more than 200 years, so there has not been enough time to notice differences from suppression, although there are indications of aging forests in Canadian subalpine systems (Rogeau 1996, Romme and Despain 1989, Veblen et al. 1994).

Effects on Landscapes and Stand Structure

Native fire regimes create shifting mosaics of patches, processes, and habitats on Rocky Mountain landscapes (Agee 1993, Romme 1982). These landscapes become more homogeneous as fire is excluded (figure 7.1; Turner et al. 1994). In Glacier National Park, for instance, plant communities less than ten years old are rare, and forests are aging in Banff National Park (Habeck 1970, Rogeau 1996). After ninety-one years of fire exclusion in the northern Rocky Mountains, there have been major declines in whitebark pine and young lodgepole pine stands, and subalpine fir has greatly increased (Tomback, Arno, and Keane 2001). Fire control policies reduce landscape richness and patchiness in areas

(a)

(b)   *(continued)*

FIGURE 7.1 *Historical and Current Photographs Illustrating Changes in Vegetation Structure and Composition Due to Fire Exclusion.* Warm-dry ponderosa pine stand near Lick Creek in Bitterroot National Forest, Montana: (a) recently cut stand, 1909; (b) change in stand structure from single to multiple strata, circa 1979. Moist Douglas-fir stand near Blake Creek in Lewis and Clark National Forest, Montana: (c) effects of recent wildfires, 1909; (d) extensive regeneration of Douglas-fir on all mountain slopes after some seventy years of fire exclusion, 1980. Crown Mountain, eastern front of the northern Rocky Mountains, Montana: (e) extensive grasslands on ridge in foreground, 1900; (f) grasslands replaced with stands of limber pine, 1981. Photographs (a) and (b) from the U.S. Geological Survey Library, Denver, Colorado, in Gruell 1983; photographs (c–f) reprinted with permission from K. Ross Toole Archives, Maureen and Mike Mansfield Library, University of Montana–Missoula.

(c)

(d)

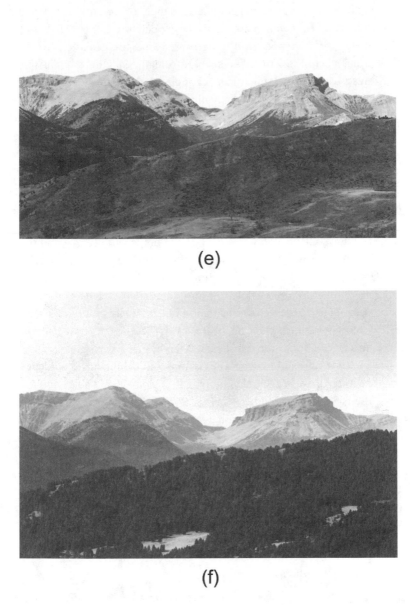

(e)

(f)

such as Yellowstone National Park and throughout the Rockies (Romme 1982, Baker 1992). This creates a "fire exclusion" spiral wherein large forest patches and high homogeneity result in a continuous supply of crown and surface fuels, which foster large fires, which create still larger patches, and so on.

In general, forest composition has changed with fire exclusion from early successional, shade-intolerant tree species to mature, shade-tolerant species. Many forests used to have single-layer canopies; now there are multiple layers. Although individual plant species may differ, the multi-layer structures of these mature stands are now nearly identical all across the Rocky Mountains (figure 7.1; Oliver and Larson 1990; Taylor 1998). This fundamental change in vegetation composition and structure affects myriad other ecosystem characteristics (table 7.1).

Fire exclusion increases stem density, biomass, and number of woody species (Ogle and DuMond 1997). Longer fire return intervals allow fuels to accumulate on the ground. Shade-tolerant species have more biomass in the forest canopy because of their high leaf areas and the branch and twig wood needed for leaf support (Waring and Running 1998, Landsberg and Gower 1997). Since late seral (successional) species are shade-tolerant, there can be many smaller seedlings and saplings present in the understory to take advantage of canopy gaps. Thus, greater crown leaf and branch biomass, coupled with high seedling and sapling densities, can create "ladder" fuels that allow flames from surface fires to climb into the forest canopy and cause crown fires.

Invasion of shrubs and trees into grasslands and shrublands is evident from New Mexico to British Columbia (figure 7.1; Taylor 1998; Veblen and Lorenz 1991; Allen, Betancourt, and Swetnam 1998; Patten 1969). Shade-tolerant conifers have increased in density three- to fivefold in formerly open ponderosa pine forests (Habeck 1994). Southwestern ponderosa pine density has increased tenfold since European settlement (chapter 12; Covington and Moore 1994). In contrast, where natural fires have been allowed to burn in recent decades, such as in Idaho wilderness, major shifts in vegetation composition and structure have not occurred (Brown et al. 1994).

Biodiversity

As ecosystems become more homogeneous without fire, the diversity of plants, animals, and ecological processes declines (chapter 8; Martin and Sapsis 1992, Romme 1982). Rocky Mountain plant diversity decreases with advancing succession because higher numbers of species are adapted to early postfire settings. In the United States as a whole, 135 of the 146 threatened, endangered, and rare

TABLE 7.1. Documented Effects of Fire Exclusion, by Organizational Level and Ecosystem Attribute

Scale	Ecosystem Attribute	Fire Exclusion Effect
Stand	Composition	Increase in number of shade-tolerant species
		Decrease in number of fire-tolerant species, forage quality, plant vigor, biodiversity in plants and animals
	Structure	Increase in vertical stand structure, multi-storied canopies, canopy closure, vertical fuel ladders and continuity, biomass, surface fuel loads, duff and litter depths
	Ecosystem processes	Increase in fire intensity and severity, chance of crown fires, insect and disease epidemics; short-term increase in stand productivity
		Decrease in nutrient cycling, individual plant vigor, decomposition
	Ecosystem dynamics	Increase in leaf area, evapotranspiration, rainfall interception, autotrophic and heterotrophic respiration, snow ablation
	Soil dynamics	Increase in pore space and water-holding capacity, hydrophobic soils, seasonal drought
		Decrease in availability of nutrients (nitrogen, phosphorus, sulfur), soil temperatures
	Wildlife	Increase in hiding and thermal cover, coarse woody debris, insects and disease
		Decrease in forage quality and quantity, biodiversity
	Resources	Increase in timber production, risk to human life and property, fire-fighting efforts, air quality
		Decrease in aesthetics, visitation
Landscape	Composition	Increase in landscape homogeneity, dominance of one patch type
		Decrease in early seral communities, patch diversity
	Structure	Increase in patch evenness, patch size, patch dominance, contagion
	Disturbance	Increase in crown fires, size and severity of fires, insect and disease epidemics and contagion (resulting in more severe epidemics)
	Carbon and water cycles	Increase in water use, drought, emissions of carbon dioxide from respiration, water quality
		Decrease in streamflows, stream sediment
	Resources	Decrease in visitation, visual quality, viewing distance

Note: References for each effect are detailed in the chapter.

plant species benefit from wildland fire or are found in fire-adapted ecosystems (Hessl and Spackman 1995). Although local species extirpation can occur with severe or too frequent fires, locally rare plants have a greater chance of thriving on landscapes with diverse vegetation communities created by diverse disturbance histories (Gill and Bradstock 1995).

The plants that define many fire-adapted ecosystems (e.g., aspen, ponderosa pine, whitebark pine) are often keystone species, critical for the survival of many animals in that ecosystem (deMaynadier and Hunter 1997; Tomback, Arno, and Keane 2001). The open canopy of whitebark and ponderosa pine forests promotes undergrowth forage quality and production. More than 110 animals consume whitebark pine seeds in this important high-elevation ecosystem. DeByle (1985) documented more than 134 bird species and 55 species of mammals that regularly utilize aspen forests. Because of fire exclusion, many of these keystone species are declining.

Stand-replacing fires are important in creating habitat for many Rocky Mountain bird species (Hutto 1995). Approximately fifteen species are associated solely with postburn communities, and more than eighty-seven species are found in burned stands. Landscapes with intact fire regimes have high variability in patch size, shape, and type, which is extremely beneficial for the existence of many avian, insect, and rodent species (Hejl 1992). Fire exclusion, on the other hand, favors generalist bird species that can utilize all stages of succession rather than specialist bird species found primarily on heterogeneous landscapes created by fire (Finch et al. 1997). Populations of small mammals may increase with the number of downed logs as fuels accumulate during succession, but many mice, shrews, and gophers are found mostly in those early seral communities that directly follow fire.

The encroachment of conifers at the expense of grasslands and aspen affects species abundance and distribution of grazing animals (DeByle 1985). The high canopy cover and multi-storied stand structure in late stages of succession improve thermal and security cover for large ungulates. These cluttered stands are difficult to traverse, however, because of the abundance of downed logs and thick understory (figure 7.1). Dense canopies shade out as much as 99% of the shrubs and grasses with high food value. Deer populations increased from 1930 to 1970 because of rapid rangeland succession from grasses to shrubs, although they have declined since (Gruell 1986). In Canada, wood bison require prairie, a vegetation type maintained by frequent fire (Gates et al. 1998). Fire can be beneficial to animal health through parasite reduction. Bighorn sheep have reduced lungworm infections and other ungulates have significantly lower tick abundances with burning (Peek et al. 1985, Drew et al. 1985).

Non-native Species

The introduction of exotic species into Rocky Mountain ecosystems has complicated and, in some cases, intensified fire exclusion effects. Some exotic plant species colonize efficiently following fire, so restoration of fire regimes may actually increase exotic dominance (Covington et al. 1994). Severely burned areas created by the intense wildfires on fire-excluded landscapes might accelerate exotic invasions (chapters 10, 11). Low-severity burns favor native plants adapted to survive fire. The invasion of the non-native annual grass cheatgrass (*Bromus tectorum*) into sagebrush-steppe vegetation types has actually increased fire frequency because of abundant fine fuels. In some places, the increased fire frequency has eliminated sagebrush (Whisenant 1990). Some exotic diseases and pests accelerate the successional cycle, resulting in mid-seral stands having compositions and structures similar to old-growth stands. For example, white pine blister rust (*Cronartium ribicola*) has killed many mature pines in northern Montana and Idaho, rapidly converting stands to subalpine fir (Tomback, Arno, and Keane 2001). Blister rust has also speeded succession in western white pine forests to grand fir, western red cedar, and western hemlock.

Biogeochemical Cycling and Hydrology

In fire-prone ecosystems, fire can directly affect decomposition and nutrient cycling (Neary et al. 1999). Fire increases soil pH as a result of ash accretion, which directly increases the availability of many nutrients. Although there is abundant nitrogen in organic matter, decomposition alone releases only a small amount to plants. Combustion releases nitrogen and phosphorus sequestered in fuels, consumes volatile organic compounds that inhibit decomposition, and may stimulate bacterial growth via soil warming, enhancing nitrogen (N) availability (Neary et al. 1999). The absence of fire lowers rates of nutrient cycling and also decomposition because cooler soil temperatures lower microbial metabolism, enhancing the buildup of even thicker duff layers. Endo- and ectomycorrhizae, soil fungi that live commensally with vascular plants, are particularly sensitive to soil heating by fire because they are concentrated in the organic and upper mineral soil layers. Although historical fires killed some of these microorganisms, severe fires can greatly reduce their populations (DeBano, Neary, and Ffolliott 1998; Neary et al. 1999). Carbon stores in woody biomass and forest floors can dramatically increase without fire, but this increase is temporary, of course, until the next conflagration (Tilman et al. 2000).

Transpiration, snow ablation, and canopy rainfall interception increase with the higher leaf areas that result from fire suppression (table 7.1). This causes periodic depletion of soil water, increased canopy evaporation, and decreased streamflow (Waring and Running 1998). Less solar radiation penetrates to the forest floor, and this, when coupled with lower soil moisture, can delay soil thaw (Kaufmann et al. 1987). When thick organic horizons finally burn, organic matter may form a water-repellent layer that impedes infiltration. This enhances water runoff and erosion. In grasslands, fire suppression has encouraged establishment of deep-rooted shrubs; these persist because they tap into groundwater (Link et al. 1990).

Hydrologic changes are especially pronounced when stand-replacing wildfires inevitably occur. Severe fires outside historical fire frequencies cause excessive erosion, which degrades water quality and aquatic habitat (Covington et al. 1994). Snow melts faster from the large patches created by modern wildfires. Peak flows usually increase severalfold after large, intense wildfires. The increased vegetation cover near streams on fire-excluded landscapes decreases stream water temperatures, increases long-term inputs of coarse woody debris to streams, and delays and reduces peak runoffs. However, when wildfires eventually occur on these protected watercourses, their high intensity can severely reduce shading, increase sediment inputs, and increase water temperatures by 3°C to 10°C (Amaranthus, Jubas, and Arthur 1989).

Human–Fire Interactions

Effects of human–fire interactions range from influence on aesthetic and recreational preferences to endangerment of life and property. Dense tree growth in forests without fire restricts viewing and detracts from the outdoor experience. Open-grown, park-like stands of ponderosa pine created by frequent surface fires have high aesthetic value and are preferred by today's outdoor enthusiasts (Warskow 1978).

Air quality has improved with fire exclusion policies (Covington et al. 1994). Smoke emission production from prehistoric wildland fires in British Columbia is estimated to have been three to six times greater than the average annual contemporary production because of the vast area burned prior to the 1900s (Taylor 1998). Less smoke from fires lowers atmospheric particulate levels, improves visibility, and decreases natural pollution, but this is only a short-term advantage because fires are inevitable (Leenhouts 1998).

Fire exclusion will continue to heighten the fire hazard to forest homes as increasing numbers of people develop and settle lands along the urban-wildland interface (Fischer and Arno 1988). The fires of 2000 burned more than 800 structures in New Mexico, Colorado, and Montana (chapter 12).

Cross-Scale Disturbance Effects

Fires become less frequent and more severe with active suppression on the landscape. Modern wildfires tend to be large, intense, and severe because of high biomass loading, multi-layer stand structure, and high connectivity of the biomass at the stand and landscape levels (Keane et al. 1997, Knight 1987). Covington and colleagues (1994, 59) stated that "the end result of fire exclusion in fire-prone forests is increasingly synchronous landscapes dominated by large, catastrophic disturbance regimes." There is a significant inverse relationship between available fuel and mean fire frequency, so fuels increase with increasing fire return intervals, and with increasing fuels comes increasing fire severity. As illustrated in figure 7.2, the area burned has recently been increasing despite escalating suppression efforts and advanced technology. Fewer fire years will also create less diversity in patch age and size because large areas tend to burn in one year, as demonstrated by the Yellowstone fires of 1988 (Baker 1989, Romme and Despain 1989).

High surface fuel loads and complex vertical stand structures increase the chance that modern surface fires will become crown fires and burn overstory trees (Steele 1994). Early successional tree crowns are heat porous and high

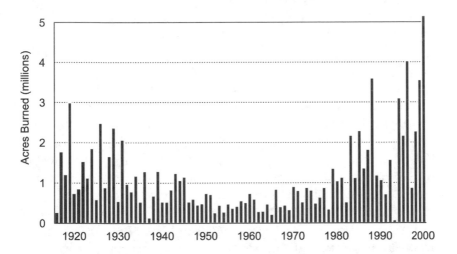

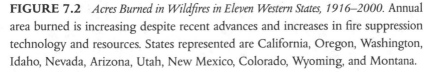

FIGURE 7.2 *Acres Burned in Wildfires in Eleven Western States, 1916–2000.* Annual area burned is increasing despite recent advances and increases in fire suppression technology and resources. States represented are California, Oregon, Washington, Idaho, Nevada, Arizona, Utah, New Mexico, Colorado, Wyoming, and Montana.

off the ground, whereas late seral trees have dense crowns extending nearly the entire length of the stem. High flame lengths due to more surface fuels, coupled with lower and thicker shade-tolerant tree crowns, rapidly turn a surface fire into a crown fire. Once a crown fire has started, the high leaf areas and high crown bulk densities favor expansion of fire throughout other crowns in a stand. Furthermore, these crown fires are more likely to propagate across homogenous landscapes because of high contagion between multilayer stands. Taylor (1998) estimated that the proportion of landscape susceptible to crown fire increased from 7% to 14% from 1952 to 1992 and projected that proportion to increase to 29% by 2032.

Land use changes on Rocky Mountain landscapes have altered ignition and spread patterns of historical fires. Barrett, Arno, and Menakis (1997) noted that the majority of historical fires burned sagebrush grasslands that are now interrupted by agriculture, grazing, and land development (chapter 11). Fires in grasslands often gained access to adjacent forestlands before European settlement and grazing. Currently, the continuity of fine fuels across the non-forest landscape has been reduced or eliminated because of human land use activities, thereby limiting forest ignitions.

Insect and disease processes are affected across a landscape as fires are suppressed (chapter 8). Increases in insect and disease activity are attributed mostly to increased stress and reduced vigor of the early seral, fire-dependent tree species (Harvey 1994, Heinrichs 1988). In Colorado spruce-fir forests, outbreaks of spruce beetle (*Dendroctonus rufipennis*) do not affect post-fire stands younger than eighty years of age, implying that long-term fire exclusion in the subalpine zone will eventually cause increased beetle activity as a larger portion of the landscape enters old-growth stages (Veblen et al. 1994). Outbreaks of mountain pine beetle (*Dendroctonus ponderosae*), bark beetle, and dwarf mistletoe are more common in southwestern United States ponderosa pine forests because tree densities have increased as a result of lack of fire (Covington et al. 1994). The absence of fire is implicated in chronic epidemics of western spruce budworm (*Choristoneura occidentalis*) in many Douglas-fir and true fir stands in the Rockies (Holland 1986, Swetnam and Lynch 1993). Persistent defoliation by budworm outbreak can predispose host trees to infestation by Douglas-fir beetle (*Dendroctonus pseudotsugae*) and root rots. Bark and pine beetle and blister rust epidemics are replaced by root rot and fir decline diseases as the landscape converts from whitebark pine to subalpine fir and spruce cover types (Tomback, Arno, and Keane 2001).

What's Next?

The exclusion of fire on landscapes has had profound implications for natural resource management. Exclusion affects livestock and big game forage, biodiversity, recreational experiences, air quality, and human health and safety. However, restoration of a native fire regime will not be easy. Even though restoration of native fire regimes seems a critical step toward improving the health of many Rocky Mountain ecosystems, the immensity of such an effort is daunting. Future fires will need to burn three to seven times more than at present to make up for past suppression activities. Seventy years of fire suppression has caused unusually high accumulations of live and dead fuel in many stands, which, when ignited, will create abnormally severe fires that will kill most trees, combust much soil organic matter, and possibly kill plant and microbial propagules residing on the forest floor. Land management agencies are limited in their restoration treatments because of competing government regulations and the high cost of implementation, from environmental assessment to execution of treatment. Despite these challenges, a functional restoration program is possible and necessary (Babbitt 1995, Hardy and Arno 1996).

Many believe that silvicultural thinning is the only feasible method to remove some combustible biomass and reduce fire intensities so fire severity will be similar to historical events (Covington and Moore 1994). Baker (1992) believed that landscapes altered by settlement and fire suppression cannot be restored using only the traditional methods of prescribed burning. Moreover, fire restoration cannot be done with just one or two prescribed burns or silvicultural treatments. It may take fifty to seventy-five years and as many as seven fire treatments or rotations to restore native fire regimes where fire has been excluded (Baker 1994, Keane et al. 1997). Additionally, more than one treatment might be required to accomplish the objectives for one prescribed burn. For example, it may take two low-severity prescribed burns to achieve 90% mortality in shade-tolerant species for a stand. Site-specific studies and careful monitoring of the consequences of prescribed burning are essential to achieve goals related to ecosystem restoration.

The role of fire will continue to change in the Rocky Mountains as fire continues to be excluded from landscapes. Landscapes will burn regardless of the intensity of any suppression effort, and when they burn, it is important to reduce the subsequent severity and adverse effects. Modern fires will be large and severe, killing more plants and altering many ecosystem processes. Extreme fire years will burn most plant communities regardless of fuels or ecosystem health, but the severity of these burns at the stand and landscape levels will be dictated by resident fuel loadings. One can only wonder what would happen if the extreme weather conditions of 1910 were to occur today on the fire-excluded landscapes of the Rocky Mountains.

References

Agee, J. K. 1993. *Fire ecology of Pacific Northwest forests.* Washington, D.C.: Island Press.

Allen, C. D., J. L. Betancourt, and T. W. Swetnam. 1998. Landscape changes in the southwestern United States: Techniques, long-term datasets, and trends. In *Perspectives on the land use history of North America: A context for understanding our changing environment,* ed. T. Sisk, 71–84. U.S. Geological Survey Biological Science Report USGS/BRD/BSR-1998-003. Washington, D.C.: U.S. Geological Survey.

Amaranthus, M., H. Jubas, and D. Arthur. 1989. Stream shading, summer streamflow, and maximum water temperature following intense wildfire in headwater streams. In *Proceedings of the symposium on fire and watershed management,* coord. N. H. Berg, 75–91. General Technical Report PSW-109. Berkeley, Calif.: Pacific Southwest Forest and Range Experiment Station.

Arno, S. F., and J. K. Brown. 1989. Managing fire in our forests: Time for a new initiative. *Journal of Forestry* 87:44–46.

Babbitt, B. 1995. Return fire to its place in the West. *Fire Management Notes* 55:6–8.

Baker, W. L. 1989. Effect of scale and spatial heterogeneity on fire-interval distributions. *Canadian Journal of Forest Research* 19:700–706.

———. 1992. Effects of settlement and fire suppression on landscape structure. *Ecology* 73:1879–1887.

———. 1994. Restoration of landscape structure altered by fire suppression. *Conservation Biology* 8:763–769.

Barrett, S. W., and S. F. Arno. 1982. Indian fires as an ecological influence in the northern Rockies. *Journal of Forestry* 80:647–651.

Barrett, S. W., S. F. Arno, and J. P. Menakis. 1997. *Fire episodes in the inland Northwest (1540–1940) based on fire history data.* General Technical Report INT-GTR-370. Ogden, Utah: U.S. Department of Agriculture, Forest Service, Rocky Mountain Research Station.

Brown, J. K., S. F. Arno, S. W. Barrett, and J. P. Menakis. 1994. Comparing the prescribed natural fire program with presettlement fires in the Selway-Bitterroot Wilderness. *International Journal of Wildland Fire* 4:157–168.

Cohen, S., and D. Miller. 1978. *The big burn: The Northwest's forest fire of 1910.* Missoula, Mont.: Pictorial Histories.

Covington, W. W., R. L. Everett, R. Steele, L. L. Irwin, T. A. Daer, and A. N. D. Auclair. 1994. Historical and anticipated changes in forest ecosystems of the inland West of the United States. *Journal of Sustainable Forestry* 2:13–63.

Covington, W. W., and M. M. Moore. 1994. Postsettlement changes in natural fire regimes and forest structure: Ecological restoration of old-growth ponderosa pine forests. *Journal of Sustainable Forestry* 2:153–181.

Crutzen, P. J., and J. G. Goldammer. 1993. *Fire in the environment: The ecological, atmospheric, and climatic importance of vegetation fires.* New York: Wiley.

DeBano, L. F., D. G. Neary, and P. F. Ffolliott. 1998. *Fire's effects on ecosystems.* New York: Wiley.

DeByle, N. V. 1985. Managing wildlife habitat with fire in the aspen ecosystem. In *Fire's effect on wildlife habitat: Symposium proceedings,* ed. J. Lotan and J. Brown, 73–81. General Technical Report INT-186. Ogden, Utah: U.S. Department of Agriculture, Forest Service, Intermountain Research Station.

deMaynadier, P., and M. Hunter. 1997. The role of keystone ecosystems in landscapes. In *Ecosystem management: Applications for sustainable forest and wildlife resources,* ed. M. S. Boyce and A. Haney, 68–76. New Haven, Conn.: Yale University Press.

Denevan, W. M. 1992. The pristine myth: The landscape of the Americas in 1492. *Annals of the Association of American Geographers* 8:369–385.

Drew, M. L., W. M. Samuel, G. M. Lukiwski, and J. N. Willman. 1985. Evaluation of burning for control of winter ticks (*Dermancentor albicuptus*) in central Alberta. *Journal of Wildlife Diseases* 21:313–315.

Finch, D. M., J. L. Ganey, W. Wong, R. T. Kimball, and R. Sallabanks. 1997. Effects and interactions of fire, logging, and grazing. In *Songbird ecology in southwestern ponderosa pine forests,* ed. W. M. Block and D. M. Finch, 103–136. General Technical Report RM-GTR-292. Fort Collins, Colo.: U.S. Department of Agriculture, Forest Service, Rocky Mountain Forest and Range Experiment Station.

Fischer, W. C., and S. F. Arno. 1988. *Protecting people and homes from wildfire in the interior West: Proceedings of the symposium and workshop.* General Technical Report INT-251. Ogden, Utah: U.S. Department of Agriculture, Forest Service, Intermountain Research Station.

Fisher, R. F., J. J. Jenkins, and W. F. Fisher. 1986. Fire and the prairie mosaic of Devils Tower National Monument. *American Midland Naturalist* 117:250–257.

Frost, C. C. 1998. Presettlement fire frequency regimes of the United States: A first approximation. *Tall Timbers Fire Ecology Conference* 20:70–81.

Gates, C. C., T. Chowns, R. Antoniak, and T. Ellsworth. 1998. Succession and prescribed fire in shrublands in northern Canada: Shaping the landscape to enhance bison habitat. In *Fire management under fire (adapting to change): Proceedings of the 1994 Interior West Fire Council Meeting and Program,* ed. K. Close and R. Bartlette, 125–132. International Association of Wildland Fire, P.O. Box 328, Fairfield, WA 99012.

Gill, A. M., and R. Bradstock. 1995. Extinction of biota by fires. In *Conserving biodiversity: Threats and solutions,* ed. R. A. Bradstock, J. D. Auld, D. A. Keith, R. T. Kingsford, D. Lunney, and D. P. Sivertsen, 309–322. Sidney, Australia: Surrey, Beatty and Sons.

Gruell, G. E. 1983. *Fire and vegetative trends in the northern Rockies: Interpretations from 1871–1982 photographs.* General Technical Report INT-158. Ogden, Utah: U.S. Department of Agriculture, Forest Service, Intermountain Research Station.

———. 1985. Indian fires in the interior West: A widespread influence. In *Proceedings of the symposium and workshop on wilderness fire,* coord. J. E. Lotan, B. M. Kilgore, W. C. Fischer, and R. W. Mutch, 68–74. General Technical Report INT-182. Ogden, Utah: U.S. Department of Agriculture, Forest Service, Intermountain Research Station.

———. 1986. *Post-1900 mule deer irruptions in the intermountain West: Principal causes and influences.* General Technical Report INT-206. Ogden, Utah: U.S. Department of Agriculture, Forest Service, Intermountain Research Station.

Habeck, J. R. 1970. *Fire ecology investigations in Glacier National Park: Historical considerations and current observations.* U.S. Department of the Interior, National Park Service, Final Report. On file at Glacier National Park, West Glacier, Montana.

———. 1994. Using General Land Office records to assess forest succession in ponderosa pine–Douglas-fir forests in western Montana. *Northwest Science* 68:69–78.

Hansen, K., W. Wyckoff, and J. Banfield. 1995. Shifting forests: Historical grazing and forest invasion in southwestern Montana. *Forest and Conservation History* 39:66–76.

Hardy, C. C., and S. F. Arno. 1996. *The use of fire in forest restoration.* General Technical Report INT-GTR-341. Ogden, Utah: U.S. Department of Agriculture, Forest Service, Intermountain Research Station.

Harvey, A. E. 1994. Integrated roles for insects, diseases, and decomposers in fire-dominated forests of the inland western United States: Past, present, and future forest health. *Journal of Sustainable Forestry* 2:211–220.

Hawkes, B. C. 1990. Wilderness fire management in Canada: Some new approaches to natural areas. *Western Wildlands* 16:30–34.

Heinrichs, E. A. 1988. *Plant stress–insect interactions.* New York: Wiley.

Hejl, S. J. 1992. The importance of landscape patterns to bird diversity: A perspective from the northern Rocky Mountains. *Northwest Environmental Journal* 8:119–137.

Hessl, A., and S. Spackman. 1995. *Effects of fire on threatened and endangered plants: An annotated bibliography.* Information and Technology Report 2. Washington, D.C.: U.S. Department of the Interior, National Biological Service.

Heyerdahl, E. K., D. Berry, and J. K. Agee. 1995. *Fire history database of the western United States.* EPA/600/R-96/081 NHEERL-COR-851. Washington, D.C.: U.S. Environmental Protection Agency, Office of Research and Development.

Holland, D. G. 1986. The role of forest insects and disease in the Yellowstone ecosystem. *Western Wildlands* 12:19–23.

Hutto, R. L. 1995. Composition of bird communities following stand-replacement fires in northern Rocky Mountains (USA) conifer forests. *Conservation Biology* 9:1041–1058.

Kaufmann, M. R., C. A. Troendle, M. G. Ryan, and H. T. Mowrer. 1987. Trees: The link between silviculture and hydrology. In *Management of subalpine forests: Building on fifty years of research,* coord. C. A. Troendle, M. R. Kaufmann, R. H. Hamre, and R. P. Winokur, 54–67. General Technical Report RM-149. Fort Collins, Colo.: U.S. Department of Agriculture, Forest Service, Rocky Mountain Forest and Range Experiment Station.

Kay, C. E. 1995. Aboriginal overkill and native burning: Implications for modern ecosystem management. *Western Journal of Applied Forestry* 10:121–126.

Keane, R. E., C. C. Hardy, K. C. Ryan, and M. A. Finney. 1997. Simulating effects of fire on gaseous emissions from future landscape of Glacier National Park, Montana, USA. *World Resources Review* 9:177–205.

Kilgore, B. M., and M. L. Heinselman. 1990. Fire in wilderness ecosystems. In *Wilderness management,* 2nd ed., ed. J. C. Hendee, G. H. Stankey, and R. C. Lucas, 297–335. Golden, Colo.: North American Press.

Knight, D. H. 1987. Parasites, lightning, and the vegetation mosaic in wilderness landscapes. In *Landscape heterogeneity and disturbance,* ed. M. G. Turner, 59–83. New York: Springer-Verlag.

Landsberg, J. J., and S. T. Gower. 1997. *Applications of physiological ecology to forest management.* San Diego, Calif.: Academic Press.

Leenhouts, B. 1998. Assessment of biomass burning in the conterminous United States. *Conservation Biology* 2:1–24. On-line at <http://www.consecol.org/vol2/iss1/art1>.

Leopold, A. 1924. Grass, brush, timber, and fire in southern Arizona. *Journal of Forestry* 22:1–10.

Link, S. O., G. W. Gee, M. E. Thiede, and P. A. Beedlow. 1990. Response of a shrub-steppe ecosystem to fire: Soil, water, and vegetational change. *Arid Soil Research and Rehabilitation* 4:163–172.

Martin, R. E., and D. B. Sapsis. 1992. Fires as agents of biodiversity: Pyrodiversity promotes biodiversity. In *Proceedings of the symposium on biodiversity of northwestern California,* ed. R. R. Harris, D. C. Erman, and H. M. Kerner, 150–157. Report 29. Berkeley: University of California, Wildland Resources Center.

Morgan, P., S. C. Bunting, A. E. Black, T. Merrill, and S. Barrett. 1998. Past and present fire regimes in the Columbia River basin. In *Fire management under fire (adapting to change): Proceedings of the 1994 Interior West Fire Council meeting and program,* ed. K. Close and R. Bartlette, 77–82. International Association of Wildland Fire, P.O. Box 328, Fairfield, WA 99012.

Mullan, J. 1866. *Report on military roads.* H.R. Exec. Doc. 44.

Neary, D. G., C. C. Klopatek, L. F. DeBano, and P. F. Ffolliott. 1999. Fire effects on below-ground sustainability: A review and synthesis. *Forest Ecology and Management* 122:51–71.

Ogle, K., and V. DuMond. 1997. *Historical vegetation on national forest lands in the intermountain region.* USDA Forest Service Intermountain Region Report. Ogden, Utah: U.S. Department of Agriculture, Forest Service, Intermountain Research Station.

Oliver, C. D., and B. C. Larson. 1990. *Forest stand dynamics.* New York: McGraw-Hill.

Patten, D. T. 1969. Succession from sagebrush to mixed conifer forest in the northern Rocky Mountains. *American Midland Naturalist* 82:229–240.

Peek, J. M., D. A. Demarchi, R. A. Demarchi, and D. E. Stucker. 1985. Bighorn sheep and fire: Seven case histories. In *Fire's effect on wildlife habitat: Symposium proceedings,* ed. J. Lotan and J. Brown, 36–43. General Technical Report INT-186. Ogden, Utah: U.S. Department of Agriculture, Forest Service, Intermountain Research Station.

Pinchot, G. 1899. The relation of forests and forest fires. *National Geographic* 10:393–403.

Rogeau, M. P. 1996. Understanding age-class distributions in the southern Canadian Rockies. Master's thesis, University of Alberta, Edmonton.

Romme, W. H. 1982. Fire and landscape diversity in subalpine forests of Yellowstone National Park. *Ecological Monographs* 52:199–221.

Romme, W. H., and D. G. Despain. 1989. Historical perspective on the Yellowstone fires of 1988. *BioScience* 39:695–699.

Steele, R. 1994. The role of succession in forest health. *Journal of Sustainable Management* 2:183–189.

Swetnam, T. W., and C. H. Baisan. 1996. Historical fire regime patterns in the southwestern United States since A.D. 1700. In *Proceedings of the second La Mesa Fire Symposium: Fire effects in southwestern forests,* ed. C. D. Allen, 11–33. General Technical Report RM-GTR-286. Fort Collins, Colo.: U.S. Department of Agriculture, Forest Service, Rocky Mountain Forest and Range Experiment Station.

Swetnam, T. W., and A. M. Lynch. 1993. Multicentury regional-scale patterns of western spruce budworm outbreaks. *Ecological Monographs* 64:399–424.

Taylor, S. W. 1998. Prescribed fire in Canada: A time of transition. *Wildfire* 7:34–37.

Tilman, D., P. Reich, H. Phillips, M. Menton, A. Patel, E. Vos, D. Peterson, and J. Knops. 2000. Fire suppression and ecosystem carbon storage. *Ecology* 81:2680–2685.

Tomback, D. F., S. F. Arno, and R. E. Keane, eds. 2001. *Whitebark pine communities: Ecology and restoration.* Washington, D.C.: Island Press.

Turner, M. G., W. W. Hargrove, R. H. Gardner, and W. H. Romme. 1994. Effects of fire on landscape heterogeneity in Yellowstone National Park, Wyoming. *Journal of Vegetation Science* 5:731–742.

Veblen, T. T., K. S. Hadley, E. M. Nel, T. Kitzberger, M. Reid, and R. Villalba. 1994. Disturbance regime and disturbance interactions in a Rocky Mountain subalpine forest. *Journal of Ecology* 82:125–135.

Veblen, T. T., and D. C. Lorenz. 1991. *The Colorado Front Range: A century of ecological change.* Salt Lake City: University of Utah Press.

Waring, R. H., and S. W. Running. 1998. *Forest ecosystems: Analysis at multiple scales.* 2nd ed. San Diego, Calif.: Academic Press.

Warskow, W. L. 1978. Fire impacts on water production in the Southwest. In *Proceedings of the rangeland management and fire symposium, Rocky Mountain Fire Council and Intermountain Fire Council meeting,* 55–58. Missoula: University of Montana, Montana Forest and Conservation Experiment Station.

Weaver, H. 1943. Fire as an ecological and silvicultural factor in the ponderosa pine region of the Pacific slope. *Journal of Forestry* 41:7–14.

Whisenant, S. G. 1990. Changing fire frequencies on Idaho's Snake River plains: Ecological and management implications. In *Proceedings on cheatgrass invasion, shrub die-off, and other aspects of shrub biology,* comp. E. D. McArther, 4–10. General Technical Report INT-276. Ogden, Utah: U.S. Department of Agriculture, Forest Service, Intermountain Research Station.

Woodley, S. 1995. Playing with fire: Vegetation management in the Canadian Parks Service. In *Proceedings: Symposium on fire in wilderness and park management,* ed. J. K. Brown, R. W. Mutch, C. W. Spoon, and R. H. Wakimoto, 30–34. General Technical Report INT-GTR-320. Ogden, Utah: U.S. Department of Agriculture, Forest Service, Intermountain Research Station.

CHAPTER 8

Rocky Road in the Rockies:
Challenges to Biodiversity

Diana F. Tomback and Katherine C. Kendall

▲

To people worldwide, the Rocky Mountains of the United States and Canada represent a last bastion of nature in its purest and rawest form—unspoiled forests teeming with elk and deer stalked by mountain lions and grizzly bears; bald eagles nesting near lakes and rivers; fat, feisty native trout in rushing mountain streams; and dazzling arrays of wildflowers in lush meadows. In fact, the total biodiversity of the Rocky Mountains is considerable, with relatively high diversity in birds, mammals, butterflies, reptiles, and conifers (Ricketts et al. 1999) and with geographic variation in the flora and fauna of alpine, forest, foothill, and adjacent shortgrass prairie and shrub communities over more than 20° of latitude and more than 10° of longitude.

Although the biodiversity of most North American regions has declined because of anthropogenic influences, the perception remains that the biodiversity of the Rocky Mountains is intact. This view exists in part because the Rocky Mountains are remote from urban centers, in part because so much of the land comprises protected areas such as national parks and wilderness areas, and in part because of wishful thinking—that nothing bad could happen to the biodiversity that is so much a part of the history, national self-image, legends, nature films, and movies of the United States and Canada. Despite modern technology and the homogenization and globalization of their cities and towns, at heart North Americans still regard their land as the New World, with pristine nature and untamed landscapes epitomized by the Rockies.

The reality is that the biodiversity of the Rocky Mountains has not been free of anthropogenic influences since the West was settled in the 1800s, and in fact it was altered by Native Americans for centuries prior to settlement. A number of escalating problems and consequences of management choices are currently changing Rocky Mountain ecological communities at a dizzying pace. In order to maintain some degree of natural ecosystem processes and preserve natural biodiversity in light of these challenges, Americans and Canadians are faced with the need for intensive, hands-on management of both ecosystems and selected plant and animal populations.

In this chapter, we first discuss the primary issues regarding the biodiversity of the Rocky Mountains, including the Rocky Mountain portions of Arizona, Colorado, Idaho, Montana, New Mexico, Utah, Wyoming, British Columbia, and Alberta. Next, we survey groups of organisms to examine their status and special problems. Finally, we touch on major challenges to biodiversity that loom in the near future. Given that entire books may be written on these issues, the discussion is brief and general, but with case histories for more detailed examples.

Historical and Current Threats to Rocky Mountain Biodiversity

The changes to Rocky Mountain biodiversity began before western settlement and then continued with farming and ranching economies (chapter 5). Current threats are primarily the results of human intrusion, including the effects of decades of logging, the explosion in recreational use of mountain lands, burgeoning development (the second "western settlement"), and, to some extent, the consequences of earlier management decisions (chapter 1).

Overexploitation of game species and furbearers, such as the Rocky Mountain bighorn sheep (*Ovis canadensis*), bison (*Bos bison*), beaver (*Castor canadensis;* see chapter 6), wolverine (*Gulo gulo*), and river otter (*Lontra canadensis*), historically accounted for the decline and near extirpation of many Rocky Mountain species, from the early days of the French fur trappers to the first part of the twentieth century (box 8.1). Predator and pest control efforts involving hunting, trapping, and poisoning had extirpated the gray wolf (*Canis lupus*) and grizzly bear (*Ursus arctos*) from most regions of the lower Rocky Mountains by the mid-twentieth century, with unintentional casualties, such as the swift fox (*Vulpes velox*). Deliberate eradication efforts, past and present, have also led to a precipitous decline in populations of prairie dogs (*Cynomys* spp.) and their obligate predator, the black-footed ferret (*Mustela nigripes*) (Murray 1987, Finch 1992). The consequences of species loss can be wide-ranging (box 8.2).

Box 8.1. Historical Harvests of Bison

Although the bison was primarily a plains animal, it was historically associated with mountain valleys of the Rocky Mountains (Berger 1991, Singer and Norland 1994). Before the arrival of European settlers, North American bison, popularly known as buffalo, were estimated to total 30 million to 75 million (Sample 1987). Native American hunting methods, such as the use of enclosure traps and buffalo jumps, sometimes resulted in overkill, but their harvests generally did not affect bison numbers. The arrival of white fur traders and hunters with horses and firearms changed the picture as the demand for buffalo meat and robes escalated. Several developments in the 1860s and 1870s accelerated the rate of harvest. An industrial process for tanning leather hides was invented in the 1860s; railroad lines were extended into Colorado, Wyoming, and Montana; and the refrigerated railroad car was invented in the 1870s (Sample 1987). These advances meant that thousands of hides could be shipped back east by the trainload as well as supplying the growing numbers of western settlers. In addition, many people viewed buffalo eradication as the means to weaken Native American plains peoples. By the late 1880s, fewer than three hundred scattered bison remained.

Several farsighted ranchers captured bison calves during the massive slaughter or rounded up some of the scattered individuals afterward, ultimately saving the bison from extinction, and eventually provided the animals for protected herds. By the 1930s, a number of herds existed, including those at the National Bison Range in Montana, Custer State Park in South Dakota, and Yellowstone National Park. The largest herd, in Yellowstone, was started with the few remaining wild bison in the parklands. Bison were protected from poaching in 1886 by the U.S. Cavalry, and buffalo hunting inside park boundaries became illegal soon afterward (Sample 1987).

Today, the Yellowstone herd numbers roughly 3,000 animals, and there are more than 200,000 bison in North America.

The suite of problems affecting Rocky Mountain biodiversity today results from human intrusion. The effects are loosely termed *habitat alteration,* but they include fragmentation of natural communities by roads or clear-cuts (Reed, Johnson-Barnard, and Baker 1996; Hargis, Bissonette, and Turner 1999; Baker and Dillon 2000); recreational and urban development; building on sensitive habitats, such as wetlands; the deliberate or accidental introduction of exotic plants, animals, and pathogens (Louda et al. 1997, Kaiser 1999); disturbance caused by recreational activities, including use of off-road vehicles, hiking and backpacking, and downhill skiing (Youmans 1999; Zabinski, Wojtowicz, and Cole 2000); mining, logging, construction, and hunting (Berger 1991); pollution or habitat degradation resulting from local activities, such as pesticide use, acid mine drainage, and cattle damage to stream banks; and long-distance transport of

---

Box 8.2. Ferrets and Prairie Dogs

Prairie dogs (*Cynomys* spp.) are social herbivores that live in large colonies in prairie and grass-shrub habitats of intermontane basins of the Rocky Mountains. Because prairie dogs serve as prey for several predators and modify habitat structure and landscape dynamics, they are considered a keystone species (Kotliar et al. 1999). Disturbance by intensive grazing and extensive excavating activity within colonies accelerates soil mixing and rates of energy, nutrient, and material flow; alters large-scale processes such as fire and climate variability; and contributes to overall landscape heterogeneity (Kotliar et al. 1999). Prairie dog grazing alters local vegetation structure by changing plant species composition, cover, and height. At a larger scale, prairie dogs increase biodiversity across their range because their colonies support a different complement of plant and animal species from that in uncolonized areas. With a probable historical range exceeding 40 million hectares (Anderson et al. 1986), they once had a marked effect on biodiversity (Kotliar et al. 1999). Populations of all North American species of prairie dog have suffered steep declines. Occupied range of the black-tailed prairie dog (*C. ludovicianus*) declined by 99% during the twentieth century (Cully 1993, USFWS 2000a).

The critically endangered black-footed ferret depends on prairie dogs as its principal prey. This mammal once thrived throughout the Great Plains from southern Saskatchewan to Texas and through the intermountain West. Today, with only about 600 individuals in five reintroduced wild and six captive populations, the black-footed ferret remains one of the rarest mammals in North America. This precarious status is the result of the combined effects of widespread eradication of prairie dog colonies, loss of habitat to agriculture, and disease. Sylvatic plague, accidentally introduced from Asia and spread by fleas, is deadly to both ferrets and their prey. Ultimately, however, the black-footed ferret reintroduction program will not succeed without recovery of prairie dog ecosystems.

pollutants such nitrogen and mercury (Tonnessen 2000). In addition, management policies such as fire suppression in fire-dependent communities or eradication of predators, which allowed some game species to grow beyond carrying capacity, may have altered community composition and fire regimes (Chase 1987; Hess 1993; Tomback, Arno, and Keane 2001).

Wild Ungulates

The Rocky Mountains have the richest diversity of native ungulates of any region in North America. A variety of issues are associated with management of ungulate populations today, including forage availability and range carrying capacity, with specific problems concerning habitat, hunting pressure, predation, and competition among wild species and between wild and domestic species. Wild ungulates also serve as an important prey base for top carnivores. The following discussion highlights some of the more challenging or pressing issues in ungulate management.

Yellowstone and Grand Teton National Parks support more than 3,000 bison (see box 8.1), the only so-called free-ranging herds in the United States. Bison in both herds often leave park boundaries in winter. Those from Grand Teton mix with elk (*Cervus canadensis*) in the National Elk Refuge outside Jackson, Wyoming, and those from Yellowstone leave the park to the west and north where cattle are grazed (Berger 1991). Controversy exists over whether these movements reflect insufficient winter range within the parks or easy access to new foraging grounds via roads snowpacked by snowmobiles (Keiter 1997). However, the winter movements of the Yellowstone bison endanger the future security of the herd. Because a percentage of bison are infected with brucellosis (*Brucella abortus*), a bacterial disease that causes pregnant cattle to abort spontaneously, bison that move into cattle rangeland in Montana and Idaho are shot by park and state officials. The cattle industry in these states fears losing its "brucellosis-free" status if cattle and bison mix freely, although there is no evidence to date that bison can transmit the disease (Wuerthner 1995, Keiter 1997). About 1,000 bison were shot in 1997 in the largest control effort to date (Jensen 1997). Elk also carry brucellosis and intermingle with bison and cattle, but they have not been targeted for control.

Elk populations in most of the Rocky Mountain region are on the rise, although recent declines have occurred in British Columbia as a result of severe winters and in Idaho as a result of successional changes from open- to closed-canopy forests (B. Warkentin, pers. comm.; J. Beecham, pers. comm.). In nearly every valley with elk in the Rocky Mountains, some winter range has been lost to land development.

Elk management in both Yellowstone and Rocky Mountain National Parks has been controversial. Critics suggest that elk populations have exceeded their carrying capacity, particularly in the absence of their top predator, wolves. The perception is that elk are damaging park ecosystems and preventing regeneration of aspen (*Populus tremuloides*) (Chase 1987, Hess 1993, Wagner et al. 1995; but see Romme et al. 1995). The parks have followed a "natural regulation" policy since 1968, which assumes that populations self-regulate by food limitation (Wagner et al. 1995). Recent research shows that carrying capacity is dynamic and that elk mortality is in part a consequence of winter snow depth (Coughenour and Singer 1996).There may, however, be more top-down control of both elk numbers and aspen communities than previously understood (Ripple et al. 2001). In 1995, wolves were reintroduced into Yellowstone National Park, and they are not only reducing elk populations but also altering elk foraging patterns (Ripple et al. 2001). Elk avoid areas routinely used by wolves, and aspen appears to be growing taller in these areas.

For several decades, populations of mule deer (*Odocoileus hemionus*) have decreased in some regions of the Rocky Mountain West. Successional conversion of grasslands to shrublands as a result of lower fire frequencies, competition with elk and domestic cattle, predation, hunting pressure, drought, and habitat destruction all appear to be causative factors (Hunting Information Systems 1998 for Arizona and Colorado; L. Kuck, pers. comm., Idaho; S. Knapp, pers. comm., Montana; K. Olson, pers. comm., Wyoming; D. Weybright, pers. comm., New Mexico; E. Bruns, pers. comm., Alberta; Gill et al. 1999). Recent declines in mule deer populations in British Columbia resulted from the harsh winter of 1997–1998 (B. Warkentin, pers. comm.).

Bighorn sheep require intensive management to maintain populations through time, including herd augmentation, introductions, and reintroductions. Although bighorn sheep populations fluctuate with winter severity, populations have remained small but reasonably stable in the United States and Canada. Populations have been diminished in the past by unrestricted hunting and more recently by resource competition with wild and domestic ungulates and the interaction of stress and disease (Finch 1992, Singer and Norland 1994, Laundré 1994). Bighorns are susceptible to diseases carried by domestic sheep, such as pneumonia and lungworm infestation (Wakelyn 1987; Miller, Hobbs, and Williams 1991). Today, habitat alteration, including successional changes caused by fire suppression, and disease remain the greatest challenges to the survival of bighorn sheep. To avoid disease, reintroduced bighorn sheep must remain twenty-five miles from domestic sheep (M. Welch, pers. comm.). Scientists worry that small reintroduced populations may lose genetic diversity through time and thus be vulnerable to inbreeding depression (Fitzsimmons, Buskirk, and Smith 1997).

Birds

Every Rocky Mountain state or province has a list of high-priority or threatened and endangered bird species. However, the focus on threatened and endangered species often diverts attention from other species that are rapidly declining. We address problems faced by three groups: songbirds, birds of prey, and game birds.

Although a few avian species actually thrive in association with humans and their altered landscapes, many Rocky Mountain species are challenged by habitat alteration. Songbirds, both neotropical migrants and year-round residents, are particularly vulnerable to habitat fragmentation, which disrupts natural continuity and divides continuous habitat into two or more patches (Buskirk et al. 2000). Road building, timber harvest, and subdivision are the principal activities leading to fragmentation (Reed, Johnson-Barnard, and Baker 1996; Hargis, Bissonette, and Turner 1999). Fragmentation not only decreases the effective area of available habitat but also creates more "edge" around patches (Wilcove, McClellan, and Dobson 1986; Primack 1993). This leads to lower nesting success, facilitating access by nest predators and a nest parasite, the brown-headed cowbird (*Molothrus ater*) (Wilcove, McClellan, and Dobson 1986; Paton 1994; Ruefenacht and Knight 2000).

Cottonwood-willow streamside (riparian) communities in montane, foothill, and High Plains communities have been greatly altered since the late 1800s, resulting in high levels of cowbird parasitism for nesting neotropical migrants (chapters 5, 6; Schweitzer, Finch, and Leslie 1996). The southwestern willow flycatcher (*Empidonax trailii extimus*), which nests in riparian communities, was listed in 1995 as a federally endangered species; populations of flycatchers have experienced sharp declines since the late 1960s and subsequent local extirpations (Finch 1992; Schweitzer, Finch, and Leslie 1996). Disturbances caused by recreational activities present further problems for many songbirds and other birds (Marzluff 1997, Hamann et al. 1999).

Birds of prey have special habitat requirements and are particularly sensitive to disturbance by humans; maintaining viable populations will be an increasing challenge in future decades (Finch 1992). Populations of the bald eagle (*Haliaeetus leucocephalus*) and peregrine falcon (*Falco peregrinus*) are recovering under federal protection and management, and these species have been proposed for delisting. Organochlorine residues remain in some areas, as evidenced by eggshell thinning and DDE levels in some individuals—the original reason for their decline (Cade et al. 1997).

Grassland habitat destruction and grazing affect the northern harrier (*Circus cyaneus*) and ferruginous hawk (*Buteo regalis*), and logging of old-growth forests affects northern goshawks (*Accipter gentilis*), Mexican spotted owls (*Strix occidentalis lucida*), flammulated owls (*Otus flammeolus*), and boreal owls (*Aegolius funereus*) (Finch 1992, Plumpton and Andersen 1998).

Game birds have also had their problems. Duck populations in general have increased after severe declines in the 1980s caused by wetland destruction, drought, and lead poisoning. The use of lead shot was banned by the United States in 1991 to aid their recovery. However, breeding harlequin ducks (*Histrionicus histrionicus*) declined greatly in number, and the trend continues (Finch 1992). This unusual duck nests near fast-running freshwater creeks but overwinters in the surf along rocky seashores. It is thus subject to oil spills, habitat loss, and nesting disturbance (Turbak 1996). Habitat destruction and fragmentation, exotic species invasion, and disturbance in sagebrush (*Artemisia* spp.) communities harm both the sage grouse (*Centrocercus urophasianus*) and the newly described Gunnison sage grouse (*C. minimus*), which is now restricted to a small part of its former range (Braun 1995, Webb 2000).

Added to these problems are accumulations of agricultural pesticides and industrial chemical pollutants in the environment, particularly estrogen mimics, organic compounds that act like estrogen if accumulated in body tissues (Fry 1995, McLachlan and Arnold 1996). These chemical contaminants have potentially adverse effects on development, survival, and reproduction in all birds.

Carnivores

Many predator populations declined sharply in the late eighteenth century and early nineteenth century as a result of unregulated hunting, government bounty programs, and unofficial control measures by farmers and ranchers. Accounts of huge predator kills during this period abound. In one account from 1848, five hunters took 700 grizzly pelts in a single year (box 8.3; Grzimek 1965). Heavy market and subsistence hunting of prey species, such as deer and elk, and habitat loss from agricultural conversion and livestock grazing reduced food availability. An influx of people armed with guns came in contact with animals formerly at the top of the food chain. Low reproductive rates and large range requirements, along with a lack of human tolerance, have helped keep most predator numbers low. The challenges of maintaining viable populations of carnivores are illustrated by the following examples.

Martens (*Martes americana*) and fishers (*M. pennanti*) inhabit wet, late successional coniferous forests. They had disappeared from the southern Rocky Mountains by the early 1900s because of forest clearing. Farther north, overtrapping and habitat disturbance caused local extinctions. Protection, habitat improvement, and reintroductions have restored populations in a number of

Box 8.3. Grizzly Bears: Past versus Present

Grizzly bears (*Ursus arctos*) once flourished in western North America. Between 1800 and 1975, grizzly bear populations south of Canada plummeted from perhaps 50,000 to fewer than 1,000 animals (USFWS 1993). Prior to the use of guns and steel traps, grizzly bears were hard to kill. By the latter 1800s, they were heavily harvested for sport and commerce. Historical accounts from Glacier National Park hint at the magnitude of the slaughter: "From the early [eighteen] eighties to the time when Glacier Park was created, in 1910, this was one of the most popular regions for hunting grizzly bears in the whole United States, and many were killed each year by sportsmen, and others were caught by the numerous trappers of the region. In 1895, I found lines of bear traps (in the southwest corner of what was to become the park) up to late in June. Even then some of the trappers who were thoroughly familiar with the methods of killing big game for bear bait considered bear trapping the greatest menace to the game of the region. Traps were baited with mountain sheep, goats, and deer, and I was told that at least 500 elk and moose were killed every year for bait" (Bailey and Bailey 1918, 97).

Government programs to control coyotes and cougars (mountain lions) used strychnine in Glacier National Park from 1914 to 1931, and Compound 1080 was used in bait stations in surrounding national forest and tribal lands during the 1940s and 1950s (figure 8.1). These programs unintentionally killed bears and nontargeted carnivores. Informal strychnine poisoning of bears and other predators was ubiquitous among area ranchers (McCracken 1957). Government agents and bounty hunters eliminated bears to protect huge flocks of domestic sheep grazing along the eastern boundary of the park. Mervin DeRuwe, a sheep rancher in this area from 1946 to 1969, reported "lots of bear problems." One of his herders reportedly killed 350 bears (both black and grizzly) during his thirty-four-year tenure, and another shot 11 bears in a single thirty-day period (M. DeRuwe, Blackfeet Indian Agency, unpublished manuscript).

In 1975, with the grizzly bear range in the lower forty-eight states limited to remnant populations in the Rocky Mountains of Montana, Idaho, and Wyoming, the species was listed as threatened. Despite efforts to protect and improve habitat, control disturbance, and prevent interactions with humans, progress toward recovery has been slowed by mortality resulting from management actions, habitat disturbance, and illegal killing. The difficulties of estimating bear numbers from year to year prevent us from determining the effectiveness of conservation measures in augmenting threatened populations. However, as the human population grows in the Rocky Mountains, conservation of grizzly bears becomes ever more challenging. New and wider roads with higher traffic volumes will accelerate habitat fragmentation and genetic isolation (Gibeau 2000). The best course of action is to protect large tracts of relatively undisturbed habitat to benefit grizzly bears and to secure habitat links between core conservation areas.

areas, although fishers remain extremely rare and are designated as critically imperiled in Wyoming and Colorado.

Cougars (*Puma concolor*), also known as mountain lions, originally ranged from northern British Columbia to the Strait of Magellan in South America (Russell 1978). Relentless persecution of cougars, coupled with dramatic reductions of ungulate populations, their major prey, resulted in precipitous declines (figure 8.1). After being eradicated from most of North America by 1940, cougars rebounded in number throughout the Rocky Mountains in response to protective measures enacted in 1965. Factors contributing to recovery include an increased prey base, including white-tailed deer (*Odocoileus virginianus*), elk, and bighorn sheep, and greater public acceptance of cougars (Riley and Malecki 2001). Long-term conservation of these large predators depends on societal tolerance.

Gray wolves once inhabited most of North America. Euro-American settlers began killing wolves to reduce predation on game and livestock. Although hunters and trappers killed many, government-sponsored predator control programs and the widespread use of poisons during the 1800s and early 1900s eliminated wolves from most of their range (USFWS 2000b). Wolves were extirpated from the U.S. Rocky Mountains by about 1920. By the 1970s, their distribution was mostly limited to Canada and Alaska (Finch 1992). Today, Rocky

FIGURE 8.1 *Predator Control in the Early Years of Glacier National Park.* Park Ranger Dan Doody is shown with skins of cougars (mountain lions) and coyotes killed in 1920. Photograph courtesy of Glacier National Park Archives; photographer unknown.

Mountain wolf populations of more than 250 animals are thriving in Idaho, Montana, and Wyoming. A population of about 60 wolves in northwestern Montana resulted from individuals dispersing from Canada beginning in the early 1980s. The reintroduction of wolves into west-central Idaho and Yellowstone National Park in 1995–1996 has been highly successful. Rocky Mountain wolf populations are proposed for reclassification from endangered to threatened status (USFWS 2000b). Continuing wolf recovery will depend on maintenance of low mortality, habitat protection, agencies that work with ranchers to reduce predation, compensation to ranchers for livestock losses, and continued public support.

Amphibians and Reptiles

Wetland habitat destruction through urban development, agriculture, road building, and water pollution have taken a major toll on populations of amphibians and reptiles in the Rocky Mountain region (Orchard 1994a, b; Hammerson 1999). Writing about Colorado, Hammerson (1999) stated, "Thousands, probably tens of thousands, of amphibians and reptiles are killed by vehicles each year as they attempt to cross roads linking the ever-growing urban and commercial areas." Acid mine drainage, timber harvest, predatory trout, and introduction of the bullfrog (*Rana catesbeiana*) account for losses of eggs, larvae, and adult amphibians; other factors that harm amphibian populations include water development projects, such as water diversion and storage, and hydroelectric power and recreation (Hammerson 1999, 39; Maxell and Hokit 1999). Wetland destruction in British Columbia appears to be harming garter snakes (*Thamnophis* spp.), and the pet trade may be reducing populations of the rubber boa (*Charina bottae*) (Orchard 1994b).

Some amphibian species in the United States have experienced unexplained declines in recent decades, contemporaneously with declines and extinctions in other parts of the world (Wake 1991). Amphibian declines in British Columbia have been attributed to habitat destruction and disturbance (Orchard 1994a). Widespread extinctions of boreal toads (*Bufo boreas*) in the southern Rocky Mountains are attributed to environmentally induced stresses that cause immunosuppression, in turn leading to infection by the fungus *Batrachochytrium dendrobatidis* (Carey 1993, Loeffler 2001). This fungus has been implicated in the declines of other Rocky Mountain amphibians and may be naturally endemic in populations (Loeffler 2001). Studies have eliminated other proposed causes, such as ultraviolet radiation (Corn 1998) and acidification of aquatic breeding sites (Vertucci and Corn 1996). The environmental stresses that lead to a decline in immune system function are currently unknown.

Fishes

In the Rocky Mountains, historically rich native fisheries have fallen prey to over-exploitation, widespread introductions of exotic species, and habitat destruction (box 8.4; chapters 6, 14). A picture of the natural abundance of fish in the Rocky Mountains comes from Cecil Kavanagh, who avidly fished the high lakes in Glacier National Park from 1920 to 1960 and wrote a column in the early 1980s for the *Kalispell (Montana) Weekly News*. Describing one fishing trip to Lincoln Creek, he noted: "We found the creek to be as full of Cutthroat as a hatchery, almost, but they were small. We got strikes on every cast and when we added an extra fly, or even two, got strikes on each. We kept about 20 fish" (Kavanagh 1983, 4). Not all lakes were great sport: "Fishing wasn't good in Cobalt. I never tried it, but 15-inch cutts were planted there prior to an expected visit by President Hoover, an avid fisherman, who never showed up. Grayling had been planted in Upper Two Medicine, but didn't thrive" (Kavanagh 1982, 4).

In general, the fish communities of the entire Rocky Mountain region are in poor shape (table 8.1). The numbers of threatened, endangered, or at-risk fishes have increased sharply since the 1980s. The most important threats to fish populations are introductions, which are implicated in the declines of 25% of fish species (Richter et al. 1997, Kohler and Courtenay 2002). Other factors include habitat destruction and altered hydrology, particularly from water impoundments and hydroelectric dams (Richter et al. 1997; chapter 6).

Box 8.4. Lake Trout in Yellowstone Lake

Yellowstone Lake and its tributaries once provided the Yellowstone cutthroat trout (*Oncorhynchus clarkii bouvieri*) with protection and security in Yellowstone National Park. In 1994, however, lake trout (*Salvelinus namaycush*) were discovered in Yellowstone Lake, the result of an illegal introduction. Multiple age classes of the lake trout confirmed that they had been reproducing. Native to the Great Lakes, lake trout are large predatory fish known to displace smaller western trout. The Yellowstone cutthroat trout provides an important prey base in the park, sustaining endangered species such as the grizzly bear and bald eagle and providing food for other animals, including ospreys (*Pandion haliaetus*) and white pelicans (*Pelecanus erythrorhynchos*). Because lake trout tend to occupy deep waters, they are unavailable to most of these fish-eating birds and mammals. Lake trout cannot be eradicated, so management plans are to gillnet lake trout annually in deep water to keep their populations as low as possible (Olliff 1995).

TABLE 8.1. Numbers of Native, Introduced, and Federally Listed or At-Risk Fishes in the Rocky Mountain Region

Number of Fish Species in State or Province

	Alberta	British Columbia	Arizona	Colorado	Idaho	Montana	New Mexico	Utah	Wyoming
Total species[1]	43	34	18	33	39	42	58	27	31
Extinct species[2]	0	1	2	0	0	0	1	0	3
Non-native species[2]	27	13	76	99	62	52	73	76	54
Federally listed/at-risk species[3]	4	3	24	17	4	4	1	11	7
Candidates for listing[4]	—	—	1	1	1	2	2	2	1

Note: Numbers are based on estimates of species that occur in mountains, high plains, and upland river systems.
[1]Obtained from U.S. state lists for 1998. For fishes of Alberta, see Jackson 2001; for British Columbia, see Desrochers 1998.
[2]Data for U.S. states from U.S. Geological Survey 1998; includes fish species native to the state but introduced outside their native range, failed introductions, and eradicated populations of species. The lists for Alberta and British Columbia include introduced species.
[3]Data from USFWS 2002b, WWF Canada 1998, CDC 2002.
[4]Data for U.S. states from USFWS 2002a. Candidate species are not available for Alberta and British Columbia.

Invertebrates

The invertebrate fauna of the entire Rocky Mountain region is very poorly known. Cannings (1994) speculates that British Columbia alone has 35,000 insect species, but only about 15,000 have been described. Arthropods, particularly the insects, represent the biggest gap in biodiversity knowledge in the Rockies. Ironically, these taxa not only account for the preponderance of terrestrial and aquatic animal life but also are more important than vertebrates to ecosystem function (Wilson 1987, Samways 1993). Their dominant role in ecosystem processes and the valuable ecological services they provide, such as pollination, decomposition, and biocontrol, make both community inventories and conservation efforts imperative (Kim 1993).

Because invertebrates in general are sedentary organisms, rarity and restricted distribution, as well as exotic invasions, put some populations at risk. Listing fifty terrestrial insects of concern in British Columbia, Cannings (1994) highlighted several species that are associated with threatened wetlands or that require other specialized habitats. Guppy (1994) discussed butterflies and moths at risk and the harmful effects of habitat destruction and degradation on sensitive species. It is difficult to speculate on invertebrate futures when so little information is available about the status of these taxa, but continued habitat destruction will certainly result in the loss of species, many never described.

In one of the most intensive insect studies in the Rocky Mountains, Ivie, Ivie, and Gustafson (1998) inventoried beetles (Coleoptera) for five years in part of Glacier National Park. They collected about 1,200 species, dramatically increasing the known number in the park. However, the inventory was only about 50% complete. Most vegetation types and the eastern slope of the park remained unsampled. Their collection included one new genus and three new species of beetle. Most of the species were first records for Montana, and one species was new for the United States. They also found that 5% of the beetle species sampled were exotic.

Aquatic invertebrates are wonderfully diverse in floodplains that have not been drastically transformed (see chapter 14). Aquatic invertebrates, however, are particularly at risk today because of fish stocking, nutrient pollution from agricultural sources, introductions of exotic organisms, and water impoundments and diversion projects (Knapp, Corn, and Schindler 2001; Richter et al. 1997; Schindler 2000). Fish introductions, particularly in fishless lakes, can greatly alter invertebrate communities (chapter 9).

The region-wide disturbance and destruction of wetland habitats has resulted in a particularly precarious existence for snails in the Rocky Mountains (Schindler 2000), especially in Utah and Idaho. Many land and freshwater snails

(Gastropoda: Mollusca) occur in uplands, foothills, and higher-elevation communities as well as in river valleys. Lower-elevation species are particularly affected by hydroelectric development and accompanying fluctuations in water levels, by water pollution, and by competition from exotic mollusks. Portions of the Snake River and tributary streams in Idaho still represent a unique intact ecosystem supporting a number of sensitive, threatened, and endangered snails (Beacham 1994).

Plants

Plants in general pose more challenges than do animals for determining their conservation status: they can be patchily distributed, and their demographics, reproductive patterns, and genetic structure must be determined (Schemske et al. 1994). Plants that are naturally rare are considered most at risk. Rarity occurs either because a plant's geographic range is small or because it occurs at low densities over a broad geographic range in a very restricted habitat type (Rabinowitz, Cairns, and Dillon 1986; Roemer 1994). Depending on the kind of rarity, plants are vulnerable to habitat destruction, mining, logging, and urbanization.

The few nationally recognized threatened and endangered species barely scratch the surface of at-risk taxa. For all Rocky Mountain states and provinces, there are lists of plants frequently numbering in the hundreds that range in status from rare to imperiled, although only twenty-three are actually listed across Canada and the United States (Wyoming Natural Diversity Database 2001, Colorado Natural Heritage Program 1995, USFWS 2002, Canadian Botanical Conservation Network 2001). One-third of the listed plants are wetland species, endangered through habitat loss.

Habitat specificity certainly leads to vulnerability. Ute ladies'-tresses (*Spiranthes diluvialis*), an orchid, is found in five Rocky Mountain states in moist soils of riparian zones, lakeshores, springs, and wet meadows. Urbanization, recreation, water diversion, and habitat invasion by exotics are reducing its populations (USFWS 1995). Penland alpine fen mustard (*Eutrema penlandii*) is found exclusively in the Mosquito Range of Colorado. An extreme habitat specialist, it occurs in wet meadows downslope of permanent snowfields. Mining activities that alter high-elevation hydrology, trampling by hikers and backpackers, and destruction of alpine wetlands all threaten this species (Colorado Native Plant Society 1997). In British Columbia, most rare species are associated with specific habitat types (Roemer 1994). However, everywhere in the Rockies, plants are damaged by off-road vehicles, snowmobiles, horses, hikers, campsites, motorcycles, and mountain bikes (Douglass, Hamann, and Joslin 1999).

The status of lichens and bryophytes is poorly known. Air pollution is a particular threat to lichens near urbanized areas (Goward 1994, Rogers et al. 2001). In British Columbia, where as many as 70% of the province's rare lichens occur in forests, logging is another major threat.

Exotic Species

One of the greatest threats to the biodiversity of the Rocky Mountains has been the introduction of exotic, or nonindigenous, animals and plants, an escalating problem worldwide (Vitousek et al. 1996). Some exotics pose a threat to native flora and fauna; others result in major economic losses to agriculture, ranching, waterways, and forestry, as well as incurring large control costs (Kaiser 1999, Malakoff 1999). With global transport and global economies, even extreme vigilance may be insufficient to head off future problems.

Inadvertent early vertebrate introductions include Old World rats and mice that hitchhiked on boats and ships. The house sparrow (*Passer domesticus*) and the European starling (*Sturnus vulgaris*) were deliberately introduced in the 1880s; these two species have since spread throughout much of North America (American Ornithologists' Union 1998). Most subsequent bird and mammal introductions into the Rocky Mountains have been for hunting. For example, mountain goats (*Oreamnos americanus*), natives of the Canadian and northern U.S. Rockies and competitive with bighorn sheep, were brought to Colorado and Wyoming (Laundré 1994). Chukars (*Alectoris chukar*) and ring-necked pheasants (*Phasianus colchicus*), natives of Europe and Asia, respectively, now occur in most Rocky Mountain states and provinces. As previously discussed, fish introductions into the Rocky Mountains were numerous and undertaken primarily for sport, but some were inadvertent, and many have had unintended ecological consequences. The flathead catfish (*Pylodictis olivaris*), for example, was widely introduced from the eastern United States as an "outstanding sportfish" but became an aggressive predator, devouring native fish (Stein and Flack 1996, 12). The widely introduced bullfrog preys on smaller, native amphibians. Lists of invertebrate introductions are incomplete. Aquatic exotics of the Rocky Mountains include snails, shrimps (*Mysis* spp.), crayfish (*Orconectes* spp.), and the Asian clam (*Corbicula fluminea*), which is a notorious biofouler, clogging water intake pipes of power plants and various industries.

Introductions of insects have been both inadvertent, such as introduction of the European gypsy moth (*Lymantria dispar*), which defoliates deciduous trees, and deliberate, for biological control (biocontrol) of other introduced insects or invasive plants (Malakoff 1999). For example, the Eurasian weevil (*Rhinocyllus conicus*) has been used to control introduced thistles (*Cirsium* spp.) in national parks and nature preserves but was recently found to attack five native thistles

(Strong 1997, Louda et al. 1997). More problems are emerging with insects introduced for biocontrol. In surveys of U.S. Rocky Mountain national parks for *Coccinella,* a common genus of ladybird beetle, the proportion of non-native species ranged from 30% to 80% (K. Keating, pers. comm.). Some previously common native species were rare or not found at all. Most of the alien ladybird beetles had been introduced by the U.S. Department of Agriculture as biocontrol agents. The seven-spotted ladybird beetle (*C. septempunctata*), brought from Eurasia to western states in 1984, threatens native species in natural areas. It is now geographically widespread, and sharp declines in several native *Coccinella* populations coincide with its appearance (K. Keating, pers. comm.).

Invasive plant species are particularly problematic in the Rocky Mountain region. Invasive plants have been implicated in the decline of 43% of the plants federally listed in the United States as threatened and endangered (Stein and Flack 1996). Many agricultural weeds were inadvertently included in imported seeds more than a century ago; others are escaped ornamentals. Successful invaders reproduce rapidly and displace native species, often forming monocultures and thus decreasing community diversity. Some now occur in national parks, having entered from roadside corridors and dispersed outward (Tyser and Worley 1992). Tamarisks (*Tamarix* spp.), for example, are introduced riparian species that send their roots deep into water tables, altering local hydrology (Stein and Flack 1996). Grazing cattle prefer native willows and cottonwoods to tamarisk; this, along with prolific seed production, gives tamarisk an advantage over its competitors. Cheatgrass (*Bromus tectorum*), which is widespread throughout the High Plains, shortens fire return intervals, so native shrubs are replaced (chapter 11; West 1988). The widespread wetland invader purple loosestrife (*Lythrum salicaria*) displaces native cattails (*Typha latifolia*) (Stein and Flack 1996).

Diseases, Parasites, and Pests

Under natural conditions, endemic diseases, parasites, and pests usually do not pose a significant danger to most native plant and animal populations. However, when populations are stressed from drought (e.g., plants), habitat destruction, or disturbance, endemic pathogens and pests can cause drastic declines and, in extreme cases, extirpation. The introduction of exotic diseases and pests has resulted in serious population losses in North American forests and wildlife.

Plant Pathogens and Pests

Native pests and diseases play an important role in forest renewal in the Rocky Mountains. The western spruce budworm (*Choristoneura occidentalis*), a widely distributed, destructive forest defoliator, and the mountain pine beetle (*Dendroctonus ponderosae*) together kill millions of trees each year in the Rockies (Leatherman and Cranshaw 1983, Logan and Powell 2001). Dwarf mistletoe (*Arceuthobium* spp.), which occurs in 35% to 60% of forest stands, is a parasite of western conifers that retards tree growth, reduces wood quality, increases susceptibility to fungal and insect infestation, and may cause death (Hawksworth and Wiens 1996).

Although many insects and diseases are a natural part of the ecosystem, human interference can increase the damage by these agents. Fire suppression spreads and intensifies dwarf mistletoe infestations. Since the mid-nineteenth century, fire exclusion, logging, and replanting all have increased the vulnerability of Rocky Mountain forests to bark beetle attack by homogenizing stand age and composition and by increasing stand density (Samman and Logan 2000, Logan and Powell 2001). Endemic mountain pine beetle infestations historically resulted in patchy tree mortality throughout a stand. But given the right tree size, age, and density, beetle outbreaks can kill more than 80% of the trees within a stand over five to seven years. Such outbreaks end up as stand-replacing events because fire, fueled by the abundance of dead trees, usually follows within fifteen years.

Many destructive plant diseases result from exotic pathogens. White pine blister rust (*Cronartium ribicola*), native to Asia, arrived in western North America on infected nursery stock in 1910. Blister rust quickly spread through populations of almost all susceptible trees—the five-needled white pines. Native white pines of the Rocky Mountains have little natural resistance to blister rust, and the fungus has defied massive, multi-pronged control efforts (McDonald and Hoff 2001). To date, there have been major losses in forests of western white pine (*Pinus monticola*), sugar pine (*P. lambertiana*), whitebark pine (*P. albicaulis*), and limber pine (*P. flexilis*) from blister rust infection; foxtail pine (*P. balfouriana*) and southwestern white pine (*P. strobiformis*) are infected as well (McDonald and Hoff 2001). Whitebark pine, a species with little commercial value but great ecosystem value, has been especially hard hit (Tomback, Arno, and Keane 2001). In the northwestern United States and southwestern Canada, nearly half the trees are dead and more than 80% of the remaining live trees are infected with rust (Kendall and Keane 2001). Because the disease cannot be controlled, conservation measures now focus on (1) employing forest management practices that use wildfire to maintain sites suitable for whitebark pine regeneration, (2) enhancing natural selection for rust resistance by creating areas where competing species are cleared away from regenerating white pines, and (3) developing rust-resistant pines (Hoff et al. 2001). The USDA Forest Service is developing rust-resistant whitebark pine, but seeds from the first generation

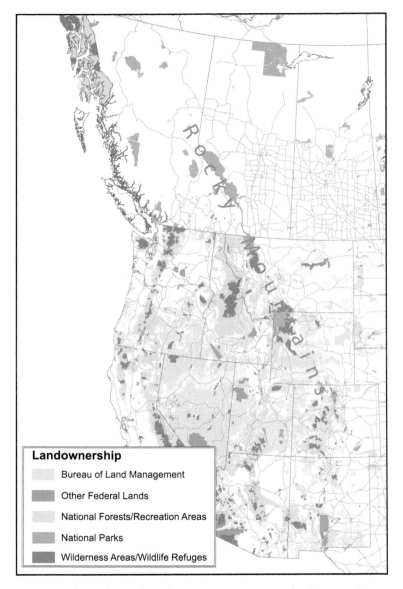

Landownership

- Bureau of Land Management
- Other Federal Lands
- National Forests/Recreation Areas
- National Parks
- Wilderness Areas/Wildlife Refuges

PLATE 1 *Landownership in the Rocky Mountain Region.* Data for the United States are from the U.S. Geological Survey's *National Atlas of the United States,* federal and Indian lands coverage. Data for Canada are from ESRI 2000.

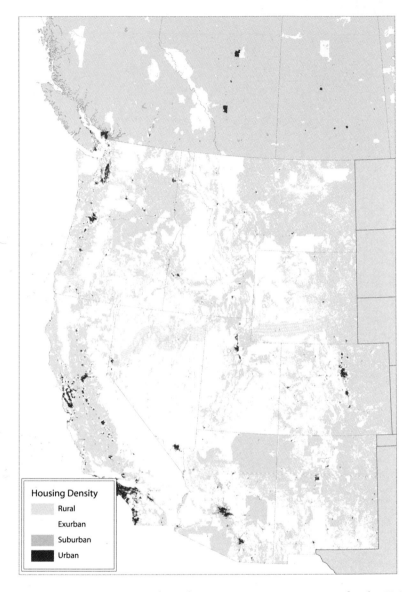

PLATE 2 *Housing Density in the Rocky Mountain Region, 2000.* Data for the United States are from the U.S. Bureau of the Census for block groups in 2000; data for Canada are from Statistics Canada for municipalities in 1996. White areas indicate public lands. Urban housing density is greater than 1 unit per 0.4 hectares (ha), suburban density is 1 unit per 0.4–0.8 ha, and exurban density is 1 unit per 0.9–16.1 ha.

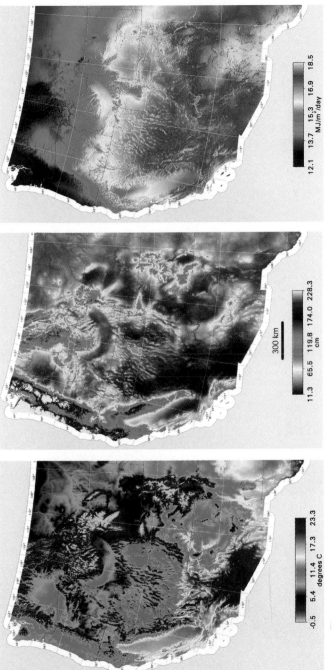

PLATE 3 *High-Resolution Mean Climatology of the Western United States, 1980–1997.* Left panel: annual mean temperature (°C). Center panel: annual total precipitation (cm). Right panel: annual mean daily radiation (MJ m⁻² day⁻¹). Spatial resolution is 1 km. From U.S. Daymet data set (Thornton, Running, and White 1997).

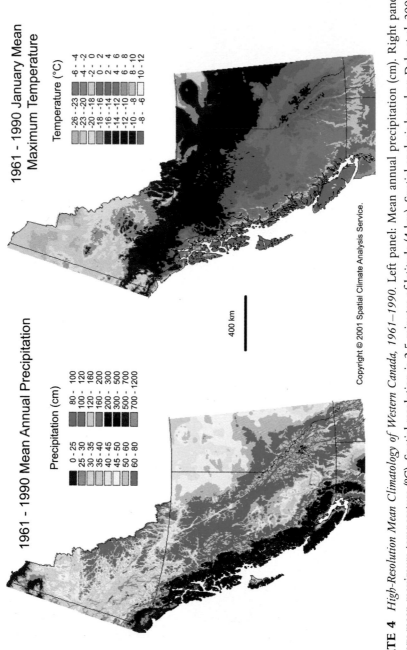

PLATE 4 *High-Resolution Mean Climatology of Western Canada, 1961–1990.* Left panel: Mean annual precipitation (cm). Right panel: January mean maximum temperature (°C). Spatial resolution is 2.5 minutes of latitude (4 km). Spatial analysis based on Daly et al. 2001, 2002; maps provided by Spatial Climate Analysis Service and used by permission.

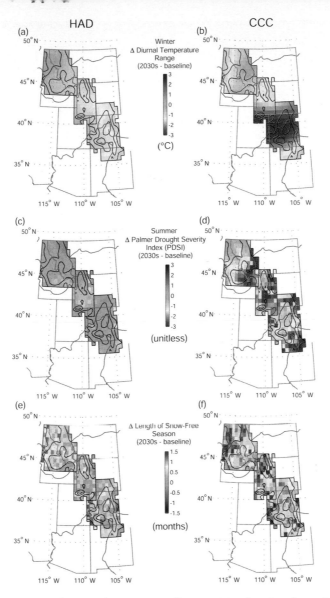

PLATE 5 *Sensitivity of U.S. Rocky Mountain Climates to Transient Greenhouse Gases and Sulfate Aerosol Forcing.* Values are as simulated by two coupled global climate models (HAD and CCC; see text) for the ten-year period 2025–2034 relative to a 1961–1990 baseline. (a, b) Changes in winter mean diurnal temperature range (monthly mean maximum temperature–monthly mean minimum temperature, °C). (c, d) Changes in summer Palmer Drought Severity Index (PDSI). (e, f) Changes in snow-free period (months). Elevation is contoured as plotted in figure 4.1 (500 m interval). Winter is December–February; summer is June–August. Snow-free season was calculated with the terrestrial ecosystem model Biome-BGC (Running and Coughlan 1988) using daily precipitation, temperature, radiation, and humidity (from Kittel et al. 2000) to estimate snow accumulation and melt. The average number of snow-free months was calculated for each 0.5° grid cell for the baseline period (1961–1990) and for HAD and CCC future climate scenarios.

PLATE 6 *Landsat Image of Rio Arriba, the Upper Rio Grande Region of Northern New Mexico and Southern Colorado.* North is toward the top of the image, which represents an area approximately 300 km long by 200 km wide. The dark green forests of the Sangre de Cristo Mountains extend along the. The Rio Grande runs south through the valleys in the center of the image, originating in the San Juan Mountains in the northwestern corner. The volcanic Jemez Mountains in the southwest include bright green grasslands within the circular Valles Caldera. Green and blue irrigated fields dominate the broad San Luis Valley in southern Colorado, and riparian vegetation and irrigated agriculture narrowly line the main rivers in New Mexico. Reservoirs (black-blue) visible include Heron, El Vado, and Abiquiu on the Rio Chama, the major tributary of the Rio Grande, which comes from the northern side of the Jemez Mountains. Cochiti Reservoir plugs the mainstem of the Rio Grande, and the small Jemez Reservoir is near the mouth of the Jemez River at Santa Ana Pueblo. Landscape scars from recent fires are tan or reddish interruptions of dark green montane forests in this composite of scenes taken in fall 2001. Evidence of the 2000 Viveash Fire is prominent in the center of the southern end of the Sangre de Cristo Mountains. Large fires have burned the eastern flank of the Jemez Mountains, including the La Mesa (1977), Dome (1996), Oso (1998), and Cerro Grande (2000) Fires, which burned the area adjoining the bright green Los Alamos townsite. Image courtesy of Karl Key, U.S. Geological Survey.

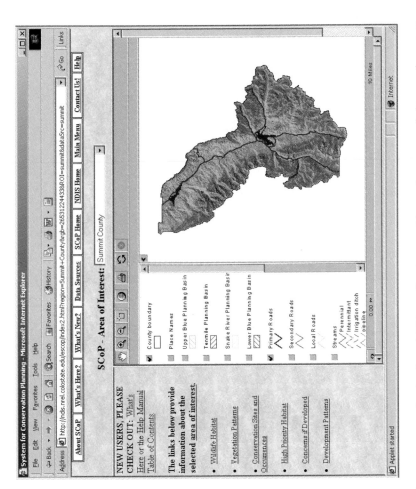

PLATE 7 *The System for Conservation Planning (SCoP).* This application provides ready access to habitat and vegetation maps, lists of species, photographs, and life history information. It is accessible via Internet browser and is powered by customized programs written with Java, JavaScript, HTML, the Avenue scripting language, and ArcView Internet Map Server mapping software.

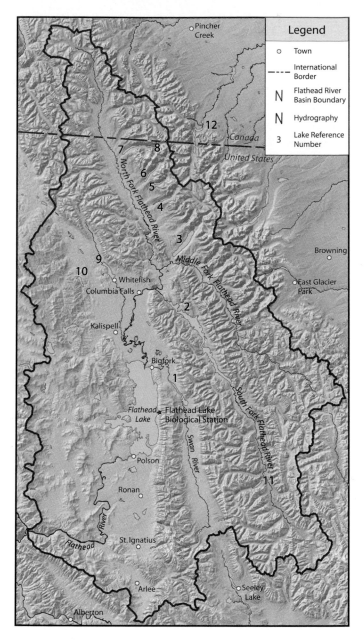

PLATE 8 *Lakes and Reservoirs of the Flathead River Basin.* Shown here are (1) Swan Lake, (2) Hungry Horse Reservoir, (3) McDonald Lake, (4) Logging Lake, (5) Quartz Lake, (6) Bowman Lake, (7) Kintla Lake, (8) Upper Kintla Lake, (9) Whitefish Lake, (10) Tally Lake, (11) Big Salmon Lake, and (12) Waterton Lake (Saskatchewan River basin).

will not be available until about 2015, and it is possible that the pathogen may overcome host resistance (Hagle, McDonald, and Norby 1989; M. Mahalovich, pers. comm.).

Animal Pathogens and Parasites

Nematode parasites that infect the lungs of ungulates in the Rocky Mountains include those in the Dictyocaulinae, which infect elk and white-tailed deer, and those in the Protostrongylinae, which affect bighorn sheep (Thorne et al. 1982, Kocan 1990). Infection rates in sheep populations in Wyoming and Colorado may reach 100%. Stressed bighorn sheep may be further infected by pathogenic bacteria, forming a lethal lungworm-pneumonia complex (Thorne et al. 1982).

Bluetongue and epizootic hemorrhagic disease, typically fatal, are caused by viruses transmitted by a biting gnat, *Culicoides variipennis*. Their clinical symptoms are indistinguishable. Both diseases occur in white-tailed deer, but bluetongue also affects bighorn sheep, mule deer, pronghorn (*Antilocapra americana*), and elk. Cattle may serve as a reservoir for the viruses, often exhibiting no symptoms (Lance 1981, Thorne et al. 1982). Bluetongue in particular may kill in epidemic proportions. A 1976 outbreak in Wyoming killed at least 3,100 pronghorn and 1,000 deer (Thorne et al. 1982).

Chronic wasting disease (CWD), a transmissible spongiform encephalopathy (TSE) of mule deer, white-tailed deer, and elk, is an emerging issue. To date, CWD has been found in game farm elk and free-ranging deer and elk in southeastern Wyoming and northern Colorado (Miller et al. 2000, USDA Animal and Plant Health Inspection Service 2001, Thorne 2001). CWD is characterized by behavioral changes resulting from deterioration of the brain, and chronic weight loss leading to death (Miller, Wild, and Williams 1998). It is unknown whether CWD may also be transmitted to humans.

Canine distemper occurs worldwide and is common in the Rocky Mountain region (Thorne et al. 1982). It threatens the critically endangered black-footed ferret. Canine parvovirus was first documented in North America in 1978. Possibly of European origin, it is now ubiquitous in populations of domestic and wild canids and threatens wolf populations south of Canada (Thorne et al. 1982).

Whirling disease, caused by the introduced parasite *Myxobolus cerebralis,* has become epidemic in native Rocky Mountain trout populations. The disease may affect only trout and salmon, with rainbow trout (*Salmo gairdneri*) particularly at risk (Bennett et al. 1996). Accidentally introduced into the United States from Europe in 1958, the parasite has spread throughout Rocky Mountain watersheds. In Montana, whirling disease was responsible for a 90% reduction in the rainbow trout population in the Madison River in just four years (Montana Fish, Wildlife, and Parks n.d.). There is no cure for whirling disease, and once the parasite is in a river, there is no way to arrest its spread.

Avian cholera (*Pasteurella multocida*), a highly contagious bacterial disease, most commonly infects ducks, geese, coots, gulls, and crows. Acute infections can cause death within hours, whereas chronic infection involves a longer incubation time and less dramatic losses. Explosive die-offs involving 1,000 or more birds per day occur in physiologically stressed populations, such as those exposed to insecticides and other chemical pollutants. The spread of avian cholera has been aided by denser concentrations of migratory birds resulting from loss of habitat (Friend 1987).

The Long and Rocky Road

As human population grows, so will the problems of habitat destruction, fragmentation, urbanization, pollution, and the introduction of exotic species, along with their challenges to Rocky Mountain biodiversity. On the horizon, however, are equally serious problems: (1) Dwindling freshwater supplies already generate conflicts between the needs of ecological communities, particularly populations of threatened and endangered aquatic species, and the needs of humans (Naiman and Turner 2000). This pernicious dilemma will reach crisis proportions in the future, particularly in years of low snowpack. (2) Human-driven global climate change will provide additional challenges to maintaining biodiversity in rapidly changing terrestrial and aquatic ecosystems (see, e.g., Hauer et al. 1997, Inouye et al. 2000). (3) There will be an escalation in local conflicts between human demand for access to public lands for recreational, hunting, or economic purposes and the need to protect biodiversity from further degradation. For example, professional mushroom and huckleberry collectors invaded national forests in great numbers during the 1990s, with unknown consequences to ecosystems. Backcountry outfitters, river-rafting companies, mountain bikers, off-road vehicle users, and snowmobilers are increasingly powerful voices with respect to management decisions. Those who value and endeavor to preserve natural biodiversity in the Rocky Mountains face a truly rocky road in the decades to come.

Acknowledgments

We are particularly grateful to the students in Diana F. Tomback's Conservation Biology course, spring 1998, University of Colorado at Denver, for their help in researching topics, compiling references and state and federal lists of species, and interviewing experts: Rachel Aragon, Pamela Black, Suzanne Bonola, Meegan Carlson, Lance Carpenter, Greg Davis, John DuWaldt, Carrie Frederick,

Mary Goldade, Tom Grant, Victoria Hernandez, Steve Hine, Kim Johnson, Ken Keefover-Ring, Kim Larson, Paul Lozano, Kristy McGovern, Cory Maes, Kyung Moon, Kendra Morrison, Steve Murphy, Karen Nunley, Darcy O'Connor, Gordon Rattray, Ken Schwartz, Jeffrey Sipple, Sumaya Vanderhorst, Rick Willard, and Steve Yarbrough. We also thank Jackie Boss, Colorado Division of Wildlife, for providing some of the literature cited in this chapter; Margo Coleman and the library staff at the U.S. Geological Survey's Midcontinent Ecological Science Center, for assistance in locating and obtaining reference materials; and Jeff Stetz, for help with literature searches.

References

American Ornithologists' Union. 1998. *Check-list of North American birds.* 7th ed. Washington, D.C.: American Ornithologists' Union.

Anderson, E., S. C. Forrest, T. W. Clark, and L. Richardson. 1986. Paleobiology, biogeography, and systematics of the black-footed ferret, *Mustela nigripes* (Audubon and Bachman), 1851. *Great Basin Naturalist Memoirs* 8:11–62.

Bailey, V., and F. M. Bailey. 1918. *Wild animals of Glacier National Park.* Washington, D.C.: U.S. Government Printing Office.

Baker, W. L., and G. K. Dillon. 2000. Plant and vegetation responses to edges in the southern Rocky Mountains. In *Forest fragmentation in the southern Rocky Mountains,* ed. R. L. Knight, F. W. Smith, S. W. Buskirk, W. H. Romme, and W. L. Baker, 221–245. Boulder: University Press of Colorado.

Beacham, W., ed. 1994. *The official World Wildlife Fund guide to endangered species of North America.* Vol. 4. Washington, D.C.: Beacham.

Bennett, R. E., D. K. Krieger, T. P. Nesler, L. E. Harris, and R. B. Nehring. 1996. The influence of dwarf mistletoe on bird communities in Colorado ponderosa pine forests. *Ecological Applications* 6:899–909.

Berger, J. 1991. Greater Yellowstone's native ungulates: Myths and realities. *Conservation Biology* 5:353–363.

———. 2001. A mammalian predator-prey imbalance: Grizzly bear and wolf extinction affect avian neotropical migrants. *Ecological Applications* 11:947–960.

Braun, C. E. 1995. Distribution and status of sage grouse in Colorado. *Prairie Naturalist* 27:1–9.

Buskirk, S. W., W. H. Romme, F. W. Smith, and R. L. Knight. 2000. An overview of forest fragmentation in the southern Rocky Mountains. In *Forest fragmentation in the southern Rocky Mountains,* ed. R. L. Knight, F. W. Smith, S. W. Buskirk, W. H. Romme, and W. L. Baker, 3–14. Boulder: University Press of Colorado.

Cade, T. J., J. H. Enderson, L. F. Kiff, and C. M. White. 1997. Are there enough good data to justify de-listing the American peregrine falcon? *Wildlife Society Bulletin* 25:730–738.

Canadian Botanical Conservation Network. 2001. On-line at <http://www.rbg.ca/cbcn/en/> (click on "Endangered plants" and then select province of interest).

Cannings, S. 1994. Endangered terrestrial and freshwater invertebrates in British Colum-
bia. In *Biodiversity in British Columbia: Our changing environment,* ed. L. E. Harding and E.
McCullum, 47–51. Quebec: Environment Canada, Canadian Wildlife Service, Pacific and
Yukon Region.

Carey, C. 1993. Disappearance of boreal toads. *Conservation Biology* 7:355–362.

CDC (British Columbia Conservation Data Centre). 2002. *B.C. Species Explorer.* On-line at
<http://srmwww.gov.bc.ca/atrisk/index.html>.

Chase, A. 1987. *Playing God in Yellowstone: The destruction of America's first national park.*
Orlando, Fla.: Harcourt Brace Jovanovich.

Colorado Native Plant Society. 1997. *Rare plants of Colorado.* 2nd ed. Billings, Mont.: Falcon
Press.

Colorado Natural Heritage Program. 1995. *Colorado natural heritage: Rare and imperiled animals,
plants, and natural communities.* Fort Collins: Colorado Natural Heritage Program.

Corn, P. S. 1998. Effects of ultraviolet radiation on boreal toads in Colorado. *Ecological Applications* 8:18–26.

Coughenour, M. B., and F. J. Singer. 1996. Elk population processes in Yellowstone National
Park under the policy of natural regulation. *Ecological Applications* 6:573–593.

Cully, J. F. 1993. Plague, prairie dogs, and black-footed ferrets. In *Management of prairie dog
complexes for the reintroduction of the black-footed ferret,* ed. J. Oldemeyer, D. E. Biggins, B. J.
Miller, and R. Crete, 38–40. Biological Report 13. Denver, Colo.: U.S. Fish and Wildlife
Service.

Desrochers, B. 1998. *Fisheries Information Summary System (FISS). Data compilation and mapping procedures.* Appendix 9A, B.C. Fish species codes: Taxonomic groupings. Prepared
for British Columbia Ministry of Environment, Lands and Parks Resources Inventory
Branch, Victoria, B.C., and Fisheries and Oceans Canada, Vancouver, B.C. On-line at
<http://srmwww.gov.bc.ca/risc/pubs/aquatic/fiss/fiss94-15.htm#p3766_109691>.

Douglass, K. S., J. Hamann, and G. Joslin. 1999. Vegetation, soils, and water. In *Effects of recreation on Rocky Mountain wildlife: A review for Montana,* coord. G. Joslin and H. Youmans,
9.1–9.12. Montana Chapter of The Wildlife Society, Committee on Effects of Recreation
on Wildlife. On-line at <http://www.montanatws.org/pages/page4.html>.

Finch, D. M. 1992. *Threatened, endangered, and vulnerable species of terrestrial vertebrates in the Rocky
Mountain region.* General Technical Report RM-215. Fort Collins, Colo.: U.S. Department
of Agriculture, Forest Service, Rocky Mountain Forest and Range Experiment Station.

Fitzsimmons, N. N., S. W. Buskirk, and M. H. Smith. 1997. Genetic changes in reintroduced
Rocky Mountain bighorn sheep populations. *Journal of Wildlife Management* 61:863–872.

Friend, M. 1987. Avian cholera. In *Field guide to wildlife diseases,* vol. 1, ed. M. Friend and C.
J. Laitman, 69–82. Resource Publication 167. Washington, D.C.: U.S. Department of
the Interior, U.S. Fish and Wildlife Service.

Fry, D. M. 1995. Reproductive effects in birds exposed to pesticides and industrial chemicals. *Environmental Health Perspectives* 103 (suppl. 7): 165–171.

Gibeau, M. L. 2000. A conservation biology approach to management of grizzly bears in
Banff National Park. Ph.D. diss., University of Calgary.

Gill, R. B., T. D. I. Beck, C. J. Bishop, D. J. Freddy, N. T. Hobbs, R. H. Kahn, M. W. Miller, T. M.

Pojar, and G. C. White. 1999. *Declining mule deer populations in Colorado: Reasons and responses. A report to the Colorado legislature.* Denver: Colorado Division of Wildlife. On file with the Colorado Division of Wildlife.

Goward, T. 1994. Rare and endangered lichens in British Columbia. In *Biodiversity in British Columbia: Our changing environment,* ed. L. E. Harding and E. McCullum, 77–80. Quebec: Environment Canada, Canadian Wildlife Service, Pacific and Yukon Region.

Grzimek, B. 1965. *Wild animal, white man.* New York: Hill and Wang.

Guppy, C. 1994. British Columbia's butterflies and moths. In *Biodiversity in British Columbia: Our changing environment,* ed. L. E. Harding and E. McCullum, 53–56. Quebec: Environment Canada, Canadian Wildlife Service, Pacific and Yukon Region.

Hagle, S. K., G. I. McDonald, and E. A. Norby. 1989. *White pine blister rust in northern Idaho and western Montana: Alternatives for integrated management.* General Technical Report INT-261. Ogden, Utah: U.S. Department of Agriculture, Forest Service, Intermountain Research Station.

Hamann, B., H. Johnston, P. McClelland, S. Johnson, L. Kelly, and J. Gobielle. 1999. Birds. In *Effects of recreation on Rocky Mountain wildlife: A review for Montana,* coord. G. Joslin and H. Youmans, 3.1–3.34. Montana Chapter of The Wildlife Society, Committee on Effects of Recreation on Wildlife. On-line at <http://www.montanatws.org/pages/page4.html>.

Hammerson, G. A. 1999. *Amphibians and reptiles in Colorado.* 2nd ed. Boulder: University Press of Colorado and Colorado Division of Wildlife.

Hargis, C., J. Bissonette, and D. Turner. 1999. The influence of forest fragmentation and landscape pattern on American martens. *Journal of Applied Ecology* 36:157–172.

Hauer, F. R., J. S. Baron, D. H. Campbell, K. D. Fausch, S. W. Hostetler, G. H. Leavesley, P. R. Leavitt, D. M. McKnight, and J. A. Stanford. 1997. Assessment of climate change and freshwater ecosystems of the Rocky Mountains, USA and Canada. *Hydrological Processes* 11:903–924.

Hawksworth, F. G., and D. Wiens. 1996. *Dwarf mistletoes: Biology, pathology, and systematics.* Agricultural Handbook 709. Washington, D.C.: U.S. Department of Agriculture, Forest Service.

Hess, K. Jr. 1993. *Rocky times in Rocky Mountain National Park: An unnatural history.* Niwot: University Press of Colorado.

Hoff, R. J., D. E. Ferguson, G. I. McDonald, and R. E. Keane. 2001. Strategies for managing whitebark pine in the presence of white pine blister rust. In *Whitebark pine communities: Ecology and restoration,* ed. D. F. Tomback, S. F. Arno, and R. E. Keane, 346–366. Washington, D.C.: Island Press.

Hunting Information Systems. 1998. *Hunting the West: What hunters can expect to encounter this fall on their treks to great hunting in the western United States.* State-by-state status reports on game population trends. On-line at <http://www.huntinfo.com/west/>.

Inouye, D. W., B. Barr, K. B. Armitage, and B. D. Inouye. 2000. Climate change is affecting altitudinal migrants and hibernating species. *Proceedings of the National Academy of Sciences* 97:1630–1633.

Ivie, M. A., L. L. Ivie, and D. L. Gustafson. 1998. *The effects of the Red Bench fire of 1988 on beetle communities in Glacier National Park, Montana, USA, 1989–1993.* National Park Service

Cooperative Agreement No. CA 1268-1-9017. Bozeman: Montana State University.

Jackson, K. L. 2001. *Ichthyology Web Resources.* Fish taxa of Alberta, Canada. On-line at <http://www.biology.ualberta.ca/jackson.hp/IWR/Regions/North_America/Alberta/Taxa.php>.

Jensen, M. 1997. Buffaloed. *National Parks* 71:43–45.

Kaiser, J. 1999. News focus: Stemming the tide of invading species. *Science* 285:1836–1841.

Kavanagh, C. 1982. Fishing tales way back when. *Kalispell (Montana) Weekly News,* 13 October 1982.

———. 1983. Fishing tales way back when. *Kalispell (Montana) Weekly News,* 30 March 1983.

Keiter, R. B. 1997. Greater Yellowstone bison: Unraveling of an early American wildlife conservation achievement. *Journal of Wildlife Management* 61:1–11.

Kendall, K. C., and R. E. Keane. 2001. Whitebark pine decline: Infection, mortality, and population trends. In *Whitebark pine communities: Ecology and restoration,* ed. D. F. Tomback, S. F. Arno, and R. E. Keane, 221–242. Washington, D.C.: Island Press.

Kim, K. C. 1993. Biodiversity, conservation, and inventory: Why insects matter. *Biodiversity and Conservation* 2:191–214.

Knapp, R. A., P. S. Corn, and D. E. Schindler. 2001. The introduction of nonnative fish into wilderness lakes: Good intentions, conflicting mandates, and unintended consequences. *Ecosystems* 4:275–278.

Kocan, A. 1990. Lungworm. In *Review of wildlife disease status in game animals in North America,* 33–34. Saskatoon: Saskatchewan Agriculture Development Fund.

Kohler, C. C., and W. R. Courtenay Jr. 2002. *American Fisheries Society position on introductions of aquatic species.* On-line at <http://www.afsifs.vt.edu/afspos.html>.

Kotliar, N. B., B. W. Baker, A. D. Whicker, and G. Plumb. 1999. A critical review of assumptions about the prairie dog as a keystone species. *Environmental Management* 24:177–192.

Lance, W. R. 1981. Bluetongue–epizootic hemorrhagic disease complex. In *Manual of common wildlife diseases in Colorado,* ed. W. J. Adrian, 31–34. Denver: Colorado Division of Wildlife.

Laundré, J. W. 1994. Resource overlap between mountain goats and bighorn sheep. *Great Basin Naturalist* 54:114–121.

Leatherman, D. A., and W. S. Cranshaw. 1983. *Western spruce budworm.* Service in Action No. 5.543. Fort Collins: Colorado State University Cooperative Extension.

Loeffler, C., coord./ed. 2001. *Conservation plan and agreement for the management and recovery of the southern Rocky Mountain population of the boreal toad (Bufo boreas boreas).* Boreal Toad Recovery Team and Technical Advisory Group. On file with the Colorado Division of Wildlife.

Logan, J. A., and J. A. Powell. 2001. Ghost forests, global warming, and the mountain pine beetle (Coleoptera: Scolytidae). *American Entomologist* 47:160–173.

Louda, S. M., D. Kendall, J. Connor, and D. Simberloff. 1997. Ecological effects of an insect introduced for the biological control of weeds. *Science* 277:1088–1090.

McCracken, H. 1957. *The beast that walks like man.* London: Oldbourne Press.

McDonald, G. I., and R. J. Hoff. 2001. Blister rust: An introduced plague. In *Whitebark pine communities: Ecology and restoration,* ed. D. F. Tomback, S. F. Arno, and R. E. Keane, 193–220.

Washington, D.C.: Island Press.

McLachlan, J. A., and S. F. Arnold. 1996. Environmental estrogens. *American Scientist* 84:452–461.

Malakoff, D. 1999. News focus: Fighting fire with fire. *Science* 285:1841–1843.

Marzluff, J. L. 1997. Effects of urbanization and recreation on songbirds. In *Songbird ecology of southwestern ponderosa pine forests: A little review,* ed. W. M. Block and D. M. Finch, 80–102. General Technical Report RM-GTR-292. Fort Collins, Colo.: U.S. Department of Agriculture, Forest Service, Rocky Mountain Forest and Range Experiment Station.

Maxell, B., and G. Hokit. 1999. Amphibians and reptiles. In *Effects of recreation on Rocky Mountain wildlife: A review for Montana,* coord. G. Joslin and J. Youmans, 2.1–2.29. Montana Chapter of The Wildlife Society, Committee on Effects of Recreation on Wildlife. On-line at <http://www.montanatws.org/pages/page4.html>.

Miller, M. W., N. T. Hobbs, and E. S. Williams. 1991. Spontaneous pasteurellosis in captive Rocky Mountain bighorn sheep (*Ovis Canadensis*): Clinical, laboratory, and epizootiological observations. *Journal of Wildlife Diseases* 27:534–542.

Miller, M. W., M. A. Wild, and E. S. Williams. 1998. Epidemiology of chronic wasting disease in captive Rocky Mountain elk. *Journal of Wildlife Diseases* 34:532–538.

Miller, M. W., E. S. Williams, C. W. McCarty, R. R. Spraker, T. J. Kreeger, C. T. Larsen, and E. T. Thorne. 2000. Epizootiology of chronic wasting disease in free-ranging cervids in Colorado and Wyoming. *Journal of Wildlife Diseases* 36:676–690.

Montana Fish, Wildlife, and Parks. N.d. *Whirling disease and Montana's trout.* Helena: Montana Fish, Wildlife, and Parks.

Murray, J. A. 1987. *Wildlife in peril: The endangered mammals of Colorado.* Boulder, Colo.: Roberts Rinehart.

Naiman, R. J., and M. G. Turner. 2000. A future perspective on North American freshwater ecosystems. *Ecological Applications* 10:958–970.

Olliff, T. 1995. A draft plan of action for controlling expansion of the lake trout population in Yellowstone Lake. In *The Yellowstone Lake crisis: Confronting a lake trout invasion,* ed. J. D. Varley and P. Schullery, 34–35. Report to the director of the National Park Service. Yellowstone National Park, Wyo.: Yellowstone Center for Resources. On-line at <http://www.nps.gov/yell/planvisit/todo/fishing/laketroutweb/olliff.html>.

Orchard, S. A. 1994a. Amphibians in British Columbia: Forestalling endangerment. In *Biodiversity in British Columbia: Our changing environment,* ed. L. E. Harding and E. McCullum, 127–131. Quebec: Environment Canada, Canadian Wildlife Service, Pacific and Yukon Region.

———. 1994b. Reptiles in British Columbia. In *Biodiversity in British Columbia: Our changing environment,* ed. L. E. Harding and E. McCullum, 119–125. Quebec: Environment Canada, Canadian Wildlife Service, Pacific and Yukon Region.

Paton, P. W. C. 1994. The effect of edge on avian nest success: How strong is the evidence? *Conservation Biology* 8:17–26.

Plumpton, D. L., and D. E. Andersen. 1998. Anthropogenic effects on winter behavior of ferruginous hawks (*Buteo regalis*). *Journal of Wildlife Management* 62:340–346.

Primack, R. B. 1993. *Essentials of conservation biology.* Sunderland, Mass.: Sinauer.

Rabinowitz, D., S. Cairns, and T. Dillon. 1986. Seven forms of rarity and their frequency in the flora of the British Isles. In *Conservation biology: The science of scarcity and diversity,* ed. M. E. Soulé, 182–204. Sunderland, Mass.: Sinauer.

Reed, R. A., J. Johnson-Barnard, and W. L. Baker. 1996. Contribution of roads to forest fragmentation in the Rocky Mountains. *Conservation Biology* 10:1098–1106.

Richter, B. D., D. P. Braun, M. A. Mendelson, and L. L. Master. 1997. Threats to imperiled freshwater fauna. *Conservation Biology* 11:1081–1093.

Ricketts, T. H., E. Dinerstein, D. M. Olson, C. J. Loucks, W. Eichbaum, D. DellaSala, K. Kavanagh, P. Hedao, P. T. Hurley, K. M. Carney, R. Abell, and S. Walters. 1999. *Terrestrial ecoregions of North America: A conservation assessment.* Washington, D.C.: Island Press.

Riley, S. J., and R. A. Malecki. 2001. A landscape analysis of cougar distribution and abundance in Montana, USA. *Environmental Management* 28:317–323.

Ripple, W. J., E. J. Larsen, R. A. Renkin, and D. W. Smith. 2001. Trophic cascades among wolves, elk, and aspen on Yellowstone National Park's northern range. *Biological Conservation* 102:227–234.

Roemer, H. 1994. Rare and endangered vascular plants in British Columbia. In *Biodiversity in British Columbia: Our changing environment,* ed. L. E. Harding and E. McCullum, 91–95. Quebec: Environment Canada, Canadian Wildlife Service, Pacific and Yukon Region.

Rogers, P., D. Atkins, M. Frank, and D. Parker. 2001. *Forest health monitoring in the interior West: A baseline summary of forest issues, 1996–1999.* General Technical Report RMRS-GTR-75. Fort Collins, Colo.: U.S. Department of Agriculture, Forest Service, Rocky Mountain Research Station.

Romme, W. H., M. G. Turner, L. L. Wallace, and J. S. Walker. 1995. Aspen, elk, and fire in northern Yellowstone National Park. *Ecology* 76:2097–2106.

Ruefenacht, B., and R. L. Knight. 2000. Songbird communities along natural forest edges and forest clearcut edges. In *Forest fragmentation in the southern Rocky Mountains,* ed. R. L. Knight, F. W. Smith, S. W. Buskirk, W. H. Romme, and W. L. Baker, 249–269. Boulder: University Press of Colorado.

Russell, K. R. 1978. Mountain lion. In *Big game of North America: Ecology and management,* ed. J. L. Schmidt and D. L. Gilbert, 207–226. Harrisburg, Pa.: Stackpole Books.

Samman, S., and J. Logan. 2000. *Assessment and response to bark beetle outbreaks in the Rocky Mountain area. Report to Congress from Forest Health Protection, Washington Office, Forest Service, USDA.* General Technical Report RMRS-GTR-62. Ogden, Utah: U.S. Department of Agriculture, Forest Service, Rocky Mountain Research Station.

Sample, M. S. 1987. *Bison: Symbol of the American West.* Billings, Mont.: Falcon Press.

Samways, M. J. 1993. Insects in biodiversity conservation: Some perspectives and directives. *Biodiversity Conservation* 2:258–282.

Schemske, D. W., B. C. Husband, M. H. Ruckelshaus, C. Goowille, I. M. Parker, and J. H. Bishop. 1994. Evaluating approaches to the conservation of rare and endangered plants. *Ecology* 75:584–606.

Schindler, D. W. 2000. Aquatic problems caused by human activities in Banff National Park, Alberta, Canada. *Ambio* 29:401–407.

Schweitzer, S. H., D. M. Finch, and D. M. Leslie Jr. 1996. Reducing impacts of brood parasitism by brown-headed cowbirds on riparian-nesting migratory songbirds. In *Desired future conditions for southwestern riparian ecosystems: Bringing interests and concerns together,* coord.

D. W. Shaw and D. M. Finch, 267–276. General Technical Report RMRS-GTR-272. Fort Collins, Colo.: U.S. Department of Agriculture, Forest Service, Rocky Mountain Research Station.

Singer, F. J., and J. E. Norland. 1994. Niche relationships within a guild of ungulate species in Yellowstone National Park, following release from artificial controls. *Canadian Journal of Zoology* 72:1383–1394.

Stein, B. A., and S. R. Flack. 1996. *America's least wanted: Alien species invasions of U.S. ecosystems.* Arlington, Va.: Nature Conservancy.

Strong, D. R. 1997. Fear no weevil? *Science* 277:1058–1059.

Thorne, E. T., N. Kingston, W. R. Jolley, and R. C. Bergstrom, eds. 1982. *Diseases of wildlife in Wyoming.* 2nd ed. Cheyenne: Wyoming Game and Fish Department.

Thorne, T. 2001. *Chronic wasting disease briefing statement.* Overview of disease, cause, and current research efforts. Wyoming Game and Fish Department. On-line at <http://gf.state.wy.us/html/admin/chronic.htm>.

Tomback, D. F., S. F. Arno, and R. E. Keane. 2001. The compelling case for management intervention. In *Whitebark pine communities: Ecology and restoration,* ed. D. F. Tomback, S. F. Arno, and R. E. Keane, 3–25. Washington, D.C.: Island Press.

Tonnessen, K. A. 2000. Protecting wilderness air quality in the United States. In *Wilderness ecosystems, threats, and management,* comp. D. N. Cole, S. F. McCool, W. T. Borrie, and J. O'Laughlin, 74–96. Vol. 5 of *Proceedings: Wilderness Science in a Time of Change conference.* Proceedings RMRS-P-15-VOL-5. Ogden, Utah: U.S. Department of Agriculture, Forest Service, Rocky Mountain Research Station.

Turbak, G. 1996. The bizarre life of the harlequin duck. *National Wildlife* 35:34–40.

Tyser, R. W., and C. A. Worley. 1992. Alien flora in grasslands adjacent to road and trail corridors in Glacier National Park, Montana (U.S.A.). *Conservation Biology* 6:253–262.

USDA Animal and Plant Health Inspection Service. 2001. Information about chronic wasting disease, current programs, and press releases. On-line at <http://www.aphis.usda.gov> (click on "Chronic wasting disease").

USFWS (U.S. Fish and Wildlife Service). 1993. *Grizzly bear recovery plan.* Missoula, Mont.: U.S. Fish and Wildlife Service.

———. 1995. *Ute ladies'-tresses (Spiranthes diluvialis) recovery plan.* Denver, Colo.: U.S. Fish and Wildlife Service.

———. 2000a. *News release: Citing higher priority species, U.S. Fish and Wildlife Service will not list black-tailed prairie dog at this time.* On-line at <http://www.r6.fws.gov/pressrel/00-04.htm>.

———. 2000b. *News release: Gray wolves rebound; U.S. Fish and Wildlife Service proposes to reclassify, delist wolves in much of United States.* On-line at <http://www.r6.fws.gov/pressrel/00-18.htm>.

———. 2002a. *Candidate Conservation Program.* On-line at <http://endangered.fws.gov/candidates/index.html> (click on "List of candidate species" and select category of interest).

———. 2002b. *Species information: Threatened and endangered animals and plants.* On-line at <http://endangered.fws.gov/wildlife.html#Species>.

U.S. Geological Survey. 1998. *Nonindigenous Aquatic Species (NAS) information resource.* Maintained by the Florida Caribbean Science Center. On-line at <http://nas.er.usgs.gov>.

Vertucci, F. A., and P. S. Corn. 1996. Evaluation of episodic acidification and amphibian declines in the Rocky Mountains. *Ecological Applications* 6:447–453.

Vitousek, P. M., C. M. D'Antonio, L. L. Loope, and R. Westbrooks. 1996. Biological invasions as global environments change. *American Scientist* 84:468–478.

Wagner, F. H., R. Foresta, R. B. Gill, D. R. McCullough, M. R. Pelton, W. F. Porter, and H. Salwasser. 1995. *Wildlife policies in the U.S. national parks.* Washington, D.C.: Island Press.

Wake, D. B. 1991. Declining amphibian populations. *Science* 253:860.

Wakelyn, L. A. 1987. Changing habitat conditions on bighorn sheep ranges in Colorado. *Journal of Wildlife Management* 51:904–912.

Webb, R. 2000. Status review and petition to list the Gunnison sage grouse (*Centrocercus minimus*). Net Work Associates Ecological Consulting. On file with the Colorado Division of Wildlife.

West, N. E. 1988. Intermountain deserts, shrub steppes, and woodlands. In *North American terrestrial vegetation,* ed. M. G. Barbour and W. D. Billings, chap. 7, 209–230. Cambridge: Cambridge University Press.

Wilcove, D. S., D. H. McClellan, and A. P. Dobson. 1986. Habitat fragmentation in the temperate zone. In *Conservation biology: The science of scarcity and diversity,* ed. M. E. Soulé, 237–256. Sunderland, Mass.: Sinauer.

Wilson, E. O. 1987. The little things that run the world (the importance and conservation of invertebrates). *Conservation Biology* 1:344–346.

Wuerthner, G. 1995. The battle over bison. *National Parks* 69:36–40.

WWF Canada. 1998. *Canadian species at risk.* On-line at <http://www.wwfcanada.org/en/cons_pgms/ESRF/SpeciesAtRisk.asp>.

Wyoming Natural Diversity Database. 2001. *Species of special concern list.* On-line at <http://wwfcanada.net/en/cons_pgms/ESRF/SpeciesAtRisk.asp>.

Youmans, H. 1999. Project overview. In *Effects of recreation on Rocky Mountain wildlife: A review for Montana,* coord. G. Joslin and H. Youmans, 1.1–1.18. Montana Chapter of The Wildlife Society, Committee on Effects of Recreation on Wildlife. On-line at <http://www.montanatws.org/pages/page4.html>.

Zabinski, C., T. Wojtowicz, and D. Cole. 2000. The effects of recreation disturbance on subalpine seed banks in the Rocky Mountains of Montana. *Canadian Journal of Botany* 78:577–582.

SYNTHESIS OF HUMAN INFLUENCES ON DIFFERENT ECOLOGICAL ZONES

▲

The chapters in part III describe Rocky Mountain ecosystems, from the alpine zone at the top to the valley bottoms and plains below. They are more than descriptions of the systems themselves, however. Each of the three chapters explores the cumulative effects of past, present, and projected future human activities on tundra, subalpine and montane areas, and valleys and grasslands. Slicing ecosystems zonally is convenient for us, but that distinction is artificial for native animals, which were once more abundant than today. As noted in chapter 11, many migratory species such as elk, bears, and wolves made use of all elevations: alpine areas, forests, wetlands, and grasslands were their habitat in different seasons. The *mountains* were their home, not an altitudinal slice of them. A recurrent theme throughout these chapters is that barriers now restrict the movements of species, to the impoverishment of all ecosystems.

The emphases on different human-caused disturbances differ, depending on which area of the mountain is being discussed. Alpine reaches, for example, have not been logged, but they bear the marks of hardrock mining. Some areas, especially mountaintops and lakeshores, are currently being loved to death by outdoor enthusiasts in all seasons. Alpine lakes, a popular destination, are all the more popular because of a continent-wide campaign to stock non-native trout for anglers. Chapter 9 suggests that because alpine reaches are relatively free from continuous direct human disturbances, more subtle, indirect human alterations become all the more apparent. Climate change, increasing solar ultraviolet B radiation (UVB), and inputs of atmospherically deposited nutrients and toxic chemicals are readily observed in the absence of other, confounding human influences. Alpine ecosystems may be more sensitive to UVB than lower-elevation environments because high elevations receive greater solar input in the thinner atmosphere. Harsh climates and slow-growing oligotrophic alpine ecosystems may also be more vulnerable to fertilization from increased deposition of atmospheric nitrogen. The ecological responses in tundra and lake communities in regions where deposition of nitrogen is increasing are unique in the 12,000 years since glaciation (Wolfe, Baron, and Cornett 2001; Bowman, Theodose, and Fisk 1995).

Forested systems suffered the brunt of logging and mining activities during the nineteenth and twentieth centuries, as noted in chapter 10. Grasslands were transformed early by irrigation and agriculture, as discussed in chapter 11. Both forests and grasslands now are heavily altered by fire suppression, invasive species incursions, road building, and, especially, development.

These chapters provide a clear picture that Rocky Mountain ecosystems bear only a superficial resemblance to their condition before Euro-American settlement. Although we can peel back layer after layer of human activity to describe what once was, we could not reconstruct a presettlement ecosystem in today's world even if we wanted to. Modern society continues to alter ecosystem components and processes. Mitigation of further stress is possible, as discussed here and elsewhere in the book, but only if it is approached broadly and multiple stressors, from local to global scales, are addressed simultaneously.

References

Bowman, W. D., T. A. Theodose, and M. C. Fisk. 1995. Physiological and production responses of plant growth forms to increases in limiting resources in alpine tundra: Implications for differential community response to environmental change. *Oecologia* 101:217–227.

Wolfe, A. P., J. S. Baron, and R. J. Cornett. 2001. Anthropogenic nitrogen deposition induces rapid ecological changes in alpine lakes of the Colorado Front Range (USA). *Journal of Paleolimnology* 25:1–7.

CHAPTER 9

Islands in the Sky: Alpine and Treeline Ecosystems of the Rockies

William D. Bowman, David M. Cairns, Jill S. Baron, and Timothy R. Seastedt

▲

The scenic alpine and treeline zones found at the highest elevations of the Rocky Mountains are home to attractive carpets of flowers and grasses, jagged peaks, and jewel-like lakes. The beauty of the alpine zone belies the harsh environment in which it is found. The cold, windy climate, short growing season, and poor soils seem uninviting from a human perspective, yet the animal, plant, and microbial inhabitants of the alpine zone are well adapted to this environment. The inhospitable environment has resulted in few permanent human settlements. However, rich mineral deposits have been found and extracted, and despite relatively low rates of plant growth the alpine zone continues to be used for livestock grazing.

The most serious direct threats to alpine environments today come from recreation. The alpine zone is an alluring destination; the open terrain provides excellent skiing, climbing, hiking, and sightseeing opportunities. Soils and vegetation become trampled, and native animals are disturbed. Alpine lakes have become increasingly popular with anglers because of a hundred years of non-native trout stocking, which has profoundly altered original aquatic food webs.

Indirect changes, from the regional to global scales, affect all Rocky Mountain ecosystems, but they are more readily detected in the alpine zone, partly because of the lack of prior disturbance and partly because there is little environmental buffer to mask or delay the responses. Indirect effects are caused by changes in atmospheric deposition of pollutants, primarily a regional problem, and increasing UVB radiation and climate change, which are global environmental concerns. Shifts in plant and algal species composition, changes in stream and lake chemistry, variation in snow distribution and depth, and movement of treelines are all sensitive indicators of broad-scale environmental changes in the Rocky Mountain region. This chapter provides a brief overview of treeline and alpine ecosystems and evaluates the direct and indirect influences humans impose on these ecosystems.

Rocky Mountain Treelines

The alpine treeline ecotone is one of the most visually dramatic transitions of vegetation in the Rockies. Subalpine trees change from tall, upright columns in forests to patches of trees surrounded by herbs and shrubs and finally to stunted, wind-sculpted krummholz in a sea of alpine plants (figure 9.1). The width of this transition belt can vary greatly, from less than 200 meters (m) to 500 m, or less than 650 to 1,640 feet (ft.), because of the presence of debris flows, rock and snow avalanches, and disturbances such as fire (Becwar and Burke 1982; Butler, Malanson, and Walsh 1992; Butler and Walsh 1994). Tree

FIGURE 9.1 *Various Shapes and Forms of Tree Islands and Krummholz.* The triangular shape of this tree is produced by dieback on the windward side and growth on the leeward side. The tree is capable of movement because new roots are produced by branches buried in detritus beneath the tree. Photograph by Timothy R. Seastedt.

"islands" at the upper part of the treeline-alpine transition may creep across the alpine zone at a pace of 3–4 centimeters (cm) per year (yr.), or 1–2 inches (in.) per year, as the windward sides are blasted by wind and ice during the winter while the leeward sides produce new roots and shoots (Marr 1977).

The elevation of treeline in the Rockies declines with increasing latitude. Treeline ranges from around 3,660 m (12,000 ft.) in New Mexico to 1,100 m (3,600 ft.) in Yukon Territory (Arno and Hammerly 1984). The dominant tree species vary with site history and latitude and include Engelmann spruce (*Picea engelmannii*), subalpine fir (*Abies lasiocarpa*), and limber pine (*Pinus flexilis*) in the south. More northern treeline species are whitebark pine (*P. albicaulis*) and subalpine fir to the north (Wardle 1974, Kearney 1982).

Summer temperatures and length of growing season are the most important determinants of treeline elevation (chapter 3; Daubenmire 1954, Cairns and Malanson 1997). Duration and depth of the snowpack also affect tree persistence. Snow insulates the soil during winter, determines the start of the growing season, and provides moisture during the growing season (Walsh et al. 1994). When the snowpack covers needles and branches, snow mold infection (*Herpotrichia* spp.) can damage tissues (Marr 1977). High winter winds blow ice crystals across needles, abrading the protective cuticles of conifers and causing water stress at the onset of the growing season (Hadley and Smith 1986; van Gardingen, Grace, and Jeffree 1991). Differences in soil characteristics, disturbances such as fire and timber cutting, and random establishment all influence the patterns of treeline in the Rocky Mountains (Peet 1981, Baker and Weisberg 1995, Malanson 1997).

Alpine Zone

From a distance, the alpine zone appears as a relatively homogeneous landscape consisting of low vegetation. On closer examination, the flora and fauna of the alpine are quite diverse. The species density of alpine vegetation in the southern Rocky Mountains is higher than that of representative arctic, grassland, and desert ecosystems (Gough et al. 2000). Differential snow distribution is the most important determinant of landscape biotic variation (Billings 1973, 1988; figure 9.2). Strong winds and steep topography result in substantial snow accumulation in some areas, whereas others remain relatively free of snow throughout winter. This creates a mosaic of growing season lengths and soil moistures that strongly affects species composition and the functional attributes of communities (Walker et al. 1993; Oberbauer and Billings 1981; Fisk, Schmidt, and Seastedt 1998).

Floristic and faunal similarities in the alpine zone are strong among the different mountain ranges in the Rockies and have close affinities with those in the

FIGURE 9.2 *Alpine Landscape Gradient on Niwot Ridge, Colorado.* Snow distribution varies, with east-facing slopes accumulating deep snow and west-facing slopes little or no snow. Vegetation distribution is strongly linked to the differential distribution of snow and topography, with fell-field communities found in the most windswept locations, dry meadows in areas of low snow cover, moist meadow communities at the base of snowfields, wet meadows in flat areas with substantial snowmelt drainage, and snow beds under the deepest snow cover. Photograph by William D. Bowman.

Arctic (Bowman and Damm 2002). Some endemism does occur, primarily where breaks in the continuity of the alpine zone occur between mountain ranges (Billings 1988). Fell-fields are characterized by low snow cover, coarse soils, and sparse vegetative cover dominated by cushion plants. Sedge- and grass-dominated dry meadows and herb- and grass-dominated moist meadows are found in sites with intermediate snow cover. Lush meadows dominated by alpine avens (*Acomastylis rossii*) and tufted hair grass (*Deschampsia caespitosa*) occur near the base of snowfields, receiving water and nutrient subsidies during the growing season. Alpine wetlands and moist meadows in poorly drained areas are dominated by sedges. Snow-bed communities are found under and adjacent to the deepest snowpacks. Substantial areas of the alpine zone can be bare rock, with variable amounts of lichen and moss cover, depending on snow cover and geomorphic activity.

Most alpine vertebrates are warm-blooded, although some amphibians make it to the alpine zone, including boreal toads, tiger salamanders, and striped chorus frogs (Hammerson 1982). Currently, the most abundant ungulate herbivores include mule deer and elk. Bighorn populations are much reduced from pre-Euro-American settlement days, and small remnant bands require constant maintenance in order to persist (chapter 8; Armstrong, Halfpenny, and Southwick 2001; Singer and Gudorf 1999). Mountain goats vary from having been extirpated in much of their natural range to having been introduced in places such as central Colorado, where there is no history of their prior residence. Vertebrate predators include coyotes and red foxes. Grizzly bears and wolves are found in the Rockies north of Colorado but no longer occur farther south. All these "charismatic megafaunae" are transients in the alpine zone, using it primarily in summer and early autumn. Year-round residents associated with the alpine zone include marmots, pikas, and ptarmigan (white-tailed and willow). Other vertebrates important to the alpine zone include the northern pocket gopher and voles (red-backed, heather, montane, and long-tailed) (Armstrong, Halfpenny, and Southwick 2001).

Alpine Lakes

G. Evelyn Hutchinson, one of the great limnologists of the twentieth century, defined a lake district as a geographically distinct cluster of lakes of similar origins and general characteristics (Hutchinson 1957). By this definition, approximately 15,000 high-elevation lakes along the 4,800 kilometer (km), or 3,000 mile (mi.), spine of the Rocky Mountains from northern New Mexico to northern Canada are part of the Rocky Mountain lake district. Alpine and subalpine lakes are similar in their genesis through montane glacial activity. All are ice-covered for some, if not most, of the year and are dominated hydrologically by spring snowmelt. Despite these similarities, the lakes differ in their climate, bedrock chemistry, and biotic history and in the degree to which their basins have been disturbed by human activity (Hauer et al. 1997).

High-elevation lakes formed following the retreat of Pleistocene glaciers. Many are cirque lakes (lakes in steep-walled hollows) that developed from gouging and rotation of glacial ice masses and are adjacent to steep rocky walls or talus (angular rock debris) fields. Others were formed by dams and debris flows. The recent glacial retreat (only 11,000–13,000 years ago) and harsh climates at high elevations result in minimal soil and vegetation development surrounding alpine and subalpine lakes. Lakes may have alternated between alpine and subalpine status since their formation; sediment pollen and macrofossil records from the San Juan Mountains and Front Range of Colorado suggest that treeline has migrated up and down between 60 and 120 m (about 200–400 ft.) in response to warming and cooling periods over time (Reasoner and Jodry 2000).

Most high-elevation lakes are small, clear, and relatively shallow, being less than 10 hectares (ha), or 25 acres, in expanse and 10 m (33 ft.) deep, on average. Alpine lakes can be ice-covered seven to ten months of the year and strongly influenced by snowmelt for another month, so water residence time during the growing season is low. The lakes are consequently nutrient-poor, or oligotrophic.

The glacial origin of high-elevation lakes has greatly shaped aquatic communities. Approximately 95% of all high mountain lakes are found upstream of hanging valleys and other Pleistocene-age barriers and have been fishless since their origin (Bahls 1992; Adams, Frissell, and Rieman 2001). Without fish, alpine lakes developed complex food webs that in some cases included amphibians (Pilliod and Peterson 2001). Top predators are crustaceans such as *Daphnia* (water fleas), *Hesperodiaptomus* (a copepod), *Gammarus* (an amphipod), *Branchinecta* (fairy shrimp), and other predatory zooplankton, such as rotifers. Clams, snails, and leeches are often found in the sediments of high mountain lake bottoms. Insect larvae, including those of caddis flies, stone flies, midges, and various beetles, also colonize high mountain lakes.

The algal population of Rocky Mountain lakes is not remarkably diverse when compared with lower-elevation lakes and ponds. High-elevation lakes lack the habitat and seasonal diversity that characterize lakes with greater temperature, nutrient, and microtopographic ranges. There are species found only in high-elevation lakes of the western United States, however, and the degree of endemism, or uniqueness, has been poorly explored (Sarah Spaulding, pers. comm.).

Direct Human Influences on Treeline and Alpine Ecosystems

Direct human influences on the alpine zone include both past and current mining activities, overgrazing by domestic livestock and wild ungulates, recreation, and introduction of non-native species into aquatic ecosystems.

Mining

The severity of the alpine climate has not deterred miners from exploring and developing mines above treeline. Precious metals and molybdenum have been mined since the mid-nineteenth century (chapter 5; Lavender 1975, Fox 1997). The largest gold nuggets ever found in Colorado were from the alpine zone of the Mosquito Range in Colorado (U.S. Department of the Interior, Bureau of Mines 1991). Many mines and associated tailings can be found above treeline in the Rockies, primarily in the southern Rockies in Colorado. Most large alpine mines (e.g., Climax Molybdenum in the Tenmile Range in Colorado) operate intermittently today, depending on the cyclical price of minerals.

Mining and construction of access roads disrupts soils and exposes mineralized rocks to weathering. Mine water seepage damages aquatic ecosystems. Prior to the Surface Mining Control and Reclamation Act of 1977, no effort was invested in mine reclamation. Hence, mines have permanently disfigured the landscape. Current environmental laws in the United States and Canada require mitigation of mining damage, and efforts have increased to improve reclamation efforts (Fox 1997).

The relatively strict environmental laws in the United States and Canada, along with encouragement from developing countries for development of their own mineral resources, have resulted in displacement of environmental damage to the Southern Hemisphere (Fox 1997). However, breakdowns in regulation and environmental law enforcement still occur, as painfully exemplified by the Summitville mine in the San Juan Mountains of Colorado (chapter 5).

Grazing

Grazing of alpine vegetation in the Rocky Mountains has occurred naturally for millennia, although the cast of herbivores has changed (Elias 1996). Current native herbivores include permanent residents such as pikas and pocket gophers and seasonal herbivores such as elk and grizzly bears. Since the late nineteenth century, Euro-American influences have resulted in both extirpation of some native grazers and introduction of domestic livestock. Both activities may have significantly altered the structure and functioning of the alpine zone.

In contrast to the situation in the temperate grasslands, the intensity and frequency of herbivory in the alpine zone prior to European settlement was probably low. Comparisons with more chronically grazed alpine areas in Eurasia support this hypothesis (Bock, Jolls, and Lewis 1995). These comparisons show that North American alpine plants (1) are generally unable to overcompensate (produce more tissue than consumed) or even compensate (replace lost tissue) when consumed and (2) appear to have, on average, less secondary plant metabolites that are used to discourage or reduce herbivory (Bock, Jolls, and Lewis 1995). Of the native herbivores, the pocket gopher appears to have the strongest influence on alpine vegetation and soils (Marr 1964, Sherrod and Seastedt 2001). This is due less to grazing than to the gopher's burrowing and mounding activities, which may cover a substantial percentage of the alpine landscape (Thorne 1982). This physical disturbance of the alpine soil surface generates a successional process of vegetation recovery that requires decades, if not centuries, to complete in many alpine habitats.

Changes in the abundance of native herbivores due to human activities are not well documented, but two important examples highlight potential changes during the twentieth century. The loss of grizzly bears from the southern Rocky

Mountains may have led to substantially lower vegetative and surface disturbance. First, in the northern Rockies, excavation of belowground storage organs of plants is common in alpine and subalpine meadows, leading to maintenance of a seral, or early successional, plant community (Tardiff and Stanford 1998). Second, increases in the abundance of elk may be associated with lower predation pressures. Where high densities of elk occur, such as in Rocky Mountain National Park, higher grazing intensity on alpine vegetation, particularly on willow species, is notable, potentially disrupting populations of other herbivores, such as ptarmigan (Hess 1993). Overgrazing by native herbivores in U.S. and Canadian national parks is problematic because there is strong public pressure to maintain dense herds, and they are sometimes protected by law from culling (Hess 1993).

Domestic cattle and sheep have grazed alpine areas in many areas of the Rockies since Euro-American settlement. Cattle have been a minor component in many alpine areas because of a high-altitude-induced disease that affects survivorship of the livestock (Marr 1964). Sheep are not as susceptible to the disease. The major effects of sheep grazing are trampling, trail cutting, and erosion because sheep tend to congregate (Paulsen 1960). When the animals stay dispersed, there appear to be few short-term effects. We anticipate that in the future, use of the alpine zone for grazing of domestic livestock will be substantially, if not entirely, limited as grazing leases expire within wilderness areas.

Recreation

Recreational use of the alpine zone has increased with increased access via road development, ski lifts and resort expansion, and trails (Price, Moss, and Williams 1997; Inyan and Williams 2001). Road and trail construction in the alpine zone has been relatively widespread. One can drive to the summits of Pikes Peak (4,300 m, or 14,110 ft.) and Mount Evans (4,347 m, or 14,264 ft.). Colorado is the only state that boasts of its many mountain passes, but they are important conduits to alpine areas in all Rocky Mountain states and provinces. Alpine trails are present in virtually all mountain ranges in the Rockies. On a typical weekend during summer, as many as fifty people may be concurrently on the summit of any of Colorado's 4,300 m (14,000 ft.) peaks, making trampling a serious concern.

Trails and roads result in compacted soil, encourage erosion, and displace vegetation, and they also reduce the quality of animal habitat by increasing human presence (Willard and Marr 1970). Roads and trails facilitate the spread of nonnative plant species through revegetation efforts and human vectoring (the carrying of seeds on clothing or with pack animals); fortunately, few invasions have occurred, possibly because most non-native species lack the adaptations required to survive the harsh alpine climate (Greller 1974, Zwinger and Willard 1972).

Introduction of Non-native Trout into Alpine Lakes

Stocking of non-native trout has been pervasive across the Rockies (chapter 6). According to Bahls (1992), 60% of all U.S. mountain lakes and 95% of the larger, deeper lakes now contain non-native brook, rainbow, and cutthroat trout. Twenty percent of the lakes in Canada's national parks have been stocked (Leavitt et al. 1994). Stocking began in the late 1800s and rapidly evolved into a large industry including fish hatcheries, fleets of airplanes, and armies of state and provincial fish managers to supply the growing multi-million-dollar industry of sportfishing (Pister 2001).

Fish introductions dramatically alter native communities and extirpate native fishes, amphibians, zooplankton, and benthic invertebrates (Knapp, Corn, and Schindler 2001; Knapp, Matthews, and Sarnelle 2001). In some lakes, fish introductions increased lake primary production by reducing the number of algal grazers and increasing availability of the vital nutrient phosphorus (Leavitt et al. 1994). This is consistent with trophic cascade theory (Kitchell 1992). Primary production has not responded in other lakes, possibly because of very low original productivity and temperatures (Parker et al. 2001; Wolfe, Baron, and Cornett 2001).

U.S. and Canadian national park managers realized some time ago that introductions of non-native fish were inconsistent with management of natural ecosystems. Stocking practices were eliminated between the 1960s and the 1980s, and non-native trout persist now only where there are reproducing populations or elderly survivors of earlier introductions. Stocking still continues in thousands of nonpark wilderness lakes of the Rockies, but even where lakes are no longer stocked and nonreproducing populations have died out, some native species have not returned (Knapp, Matthews, and Sarnelle 2001).

Indirect Human Influence on Treeline and Alpine Ecosystems

The indirect effects of human activities, especially those involving climate change, are present through all the ecosystems discussed in this book. In the alpine zone, however, they can be observed more readily because in most alpine areas there are fewer direct human influences to interfere with detection. Changes in ultraviolet radiation and atmospheric deposition disproportionately influence the alpine zone because it is more exposed to the atmosphere and less able to buffer atmospheric inputs.

Climate Change

Climate change in Rocky Mountain ecosystems is likely to be nonuniform, with altitudinally and latitudinally dependent differences in temperature and precipitation (chapter 4). The warming observed during the twentieth century should affect the treeline boundary. Climate-induced ecological change in the alpine zone is likely to be mediated primarily through changes in snow distribution and abundance, which, as noted earlier, are important controls on biotic distribution and function (Walker et al. 1993).

Palynological data (pollen records from lake and bog sediments) indicate that the current treeline elevation in Wyoming was established approximately 3,000 years ago (Fall, Davis, and Zielinski 1995). Despite significant warming trends in the northern Rockies, repeat photography indicates that treeline elevation has been stable since at least the beginning of the twentieth century (Butler, Malanson, and Cairns 1994). Treelines in Colorado are thought to be relics of a previous warm period (Ives and Hansen-Bristow 1983). Thus, although the treeline-alpine ecotone appears potentially useful for monitoring environmental change, inertial constraints may limit its sensitivity as a climate change indicator (Kupfer and Cairns 1996, Baker and Weisberg 1995).

Some predictions suggest that the spatial extent of the alpine zone will decline as a result of forest expansion due to climate change (see, e.g., Smith, Richels, and Miller 2000). Although there is no evidence that treeline is creeping upslope, there have been changes in treeline vegetation structure. There is more seedling establishment around tree islands and in the upper subalpine zone (Hessl and Baker 1997; Moir, Rochelle, and Schoettle 1999). Leader growth is greater in krummholz patches, suggesting that krummholz growth forms may be undergoing a phenotypic transformation to a true tree growth habit (Weisberg and Baker 1995).

Snow is an important water source for plants during the growing season. It also controls the movement of nutrients and helps determine the length of the growing season (Oberbauer and Billings 1981, Bowman 1992, Walker et al. 1993). Sites with intermediate snow cover (0.5–1.5 m, or 1.6–5.0 ft.) are optimal for plant productivity (Walker et al. 1994). Changes in the distribution and abundance of snow will change resource abundance, triggering a number of consequences. Species establishment rates and competitive interactions will be altered. Species dependent on sexual reproduction for population maintenance may be outcompeted by asexual reproducers that are rapid consumers of water and moisture (Theodose and Bowman 1997, Galen and Stanton 1995, Bell and Bliss 1979).

The development of snowfields in early autumn facilitates wintertime activity by soil microorganisms. Soil microbes are more active in the insulated soils under snow than in surrounding areas with lower snow cover (Brooks, Williams, and Schmidt 1996; Sommerfeld, Mosier, and Musselman 1993). Decomposition of plant litter and soil organic matter and chemical transformation of soil compounds are therefore enhanced by early snow accumulation. Although rates are lower, the magnitude of these processes is as great or greater in winter than during the short growing season. Changes in the timing and amount of snow cover will therefore have important implications for the carbon and nutrient balances of alpine soils and ultimately will influence plants and the animals dependent on them for food and cover (Walker et al. 1993).

Changes in snow cover and depth will influence the abundance and activity of resident animal species by altering soil microclimate. Species active under the snow during winter, including pocket gophers and voles, will benefit from a greater snowpack, potentially leading to greater irruptions of these herbivore populations. Species that do not forage under the snow and that cache their winter food supply, such as pikas, will be detrimentally affected by a longer snow-covered season. Longer winters limit foraging time, during which these animals collect winter food resources, and lengthen the time they are dependent on cached food.

The potential for increases in growing season temperatures in the alpine zone has been experimentally addressed in conjunction with experiments in arctic tundra (Welker et al. 1997, Henry and Molau 1997). Increased soil and air temperatures stimulate soil respiration rates and transform dry alpine sites, dominated by *Dryas octopetala,* from carbon sinks to carbon sources (Welker et al. 1997). Growth of some plant species is enhanced by warming, and there is a delay in the senescence of plants at the end of the growing season (P. L. Turner and M. D. Walker, unpublished data). In general, the optimum temperatures for growth of most alpine plant species are near current temperatures. An increase in growing season temperature therefore is likely to lead to changes in resource availability, possibly leading to changes in species composition (Körner and Larcher 1988).

Changes in Atmospheric Ultraviolet Transmission

The transmittance of ultraviolet B (UVB) radiation through Earth's atmosphere has increased in recent years as a result of industrial emissions of compounds such as chlorinated fluorocarbons (CFCs) that reduce the stratospheric ozone layer. Increases in UVB radiation to midlatitude alpine areas have been noted (Madronich et al. 1998, Blumthaler and Ambach 1990). There is significant potential for detrimental effects on animals, plants, and microorganisms resulting from direct physiological damage, damage to DNA, and potential increased susceptibility to pathogens, predators, and competitors (Caldwell et al. 1998, Licht and Grant 1997).

High-altitude ecosystems naturally experience greater UVB irradiance because of lower atmospheric absorption, so treeline and alpine biota are already subject to greater radiation stress than lowland biota. Alpine plants exhibit lower sensitivity to increased UVB relative to lowland species (Caldwell et al. 1982, Rau and Hofmann 1996). However, rapid changes in UVB transmittance from further stratospheric ozone depletion could exceed the tolerances of some species. Amphibians and treeline conifers during foliar development are thought to be especially vulnerable (Nagl and Hofer 1997; Licht and Grant 1997; DeLucia, Day, and Vogelman 1992). Differential susceptibilities of grazers and plankton to UVB radiation may alter trophic interactions in some, but not all, aquatic ecosystems. In oligotrophic shallow alpine lakes, plankton and invertebrate grazers appear equally susceptible (Bothwell, Sherbot, and Pollock 1994; Vinebrooke and Leavitt 1999). Aquatic ecosystems are most vulnerable to the effects of UVB radiation during mid- to late summer, when water levels are at their lowest and UVB transmittance is at its highest (Kiffney, Clements, and Cady 1997).

There is legitimate concern about the potential effects of increased UVB radiation in high-altitude ecosystems of the Rocky Mountains, but several factors may minimize future damage. There are more clouds at high elevations, and cloud cover is increasing with global warming (chapter 4). Cloudiness may lower UVB transmittance (Caldwell, Robberecht, and Billings 1980). Urban pollution increases tropospheric ozone, creating a regional haze that also lowers UVB transmittance (Böhm 1992). And finally, although stratospheric ozone loss is expected to continue until 2010, a recovery is projected during the mid-twenty-first century, assuming continued adherence to the Montreal Protocol on Substances That Deplete the Ozone Layer.

Atmospheric Deposition

Increasing nitrogen (N) deposition to ecosystems is an important global environmental concern (Vitousek et al. 1997). Although Earth's atmosphere is 78% inert nitrogen gas, reactive nitrogen, formed from nitrogen-fixing microbes, production of synthetic fertilizer, and combustion of fossil fuels, directly affects human health, ecosystem productivity, and species biodiversity. Elevated levels of N deposition are most apparent in the Rocky Mountains near urban, agricultural, and industrial centers. Elevated N deposition occurs in the Colorado Front Range, in the Wasatch Range and Uinta Mountains of Utah, in the Park Range of western Colorado, and in the southern San Juan Mountains downwind of large coal-fired power plants. Low rates are found elsewhere in the Rocky Mountain alpine zone (National Atmospheric Deposition Program 2001). Although the rates of N deposition are low relative to sites in the northeastern United States and central Europe, the potential for ecological change in the Rocky Mountain alpine zone is great. Low vegetative cover, short growing seasons, and high rates of snowmelt flushing lead to a depressed ability of ecosystems to take up and utilize N (Baron et al. 2000, Williams and Tonnessen 2000).

Nitrate concentrations in high mountain lakes on the eastern side of the Colorado Front Range, adjacent to the populous Denver metropolitan urban corridor and rich agricultural lands of the South Platte River valley, are significantly higher than in other lakes in the West, and episodic acidification has been reported in one basin (Baron et al. 2000, Caine 1995). Sediment records show that the aquatic flora was typical of oligotrophic alpine lakes until the middle of the twentieth century, at which time it began to reflect species common to more nutrient-rich conditions. The timing is commensurate with an increase in human and livestock populations and use of synthetic fertilizers (Baron et al. 2000; Wolfe, Baron, and Cornett 2001). Lakes in the Uinta Mountains east of Salt Lake City also show high concentrations of nitrate (Eilers et al. 1987). The end result of nitrogen enrichment in high mountain lakes will be acidification, but it is not known how much of an increase in emissions will cause this to occur or how long it will take to alter watershed and lake buffering capacity.

Alpine plant communities will respond to increased atmospheric N deposition through changes in structure (biotic composition and abundance) and function (production and nutrient cycling). Although primary production may increase with N fertilization, some species, notably grasses, take up N more readily than others (Bowman et al. 1993; Bowman, Theodose, and Fisk 1995). Observations from the alpine zone are similar to those worldwide, where added N leads to increased dominance by a few nitrogen-responsive species and loss of many other plant species (Vitousek et al. 1997). Nitrogen additions also affect soil microbial assemblages, directly influencing nutrient cycling and the fluxes of trace gases (Fisk and Schmidt 1996, Neff et al. 1994).

Approximately half of the annual N deposition occurs during winter. Blowing snow redistributes N across the landscape such that some communities are subject to higher inputs of N than others (Bowman 1992). Plant communities that receive high inputs of snowmelt, particularly the moist meadows and treeline, are also subject to high inputs of N derived from snowpack. This sets up a cascade of responses as a result of changes in plant species composition (Bowman and Steltzer 1998, Steltzer and Bowman 1998). Nitrogen inputs enhance growth of plant species associated with higher rates of N cycling and nitrate production. Coincidentally, these plant species and their associated microbial flora enhance nitrate leaching. Higher nitrate leaching increases the potential for acidification of soils and surface waters (Aber et al. 1989) as well as alteration of algal species composition (McKnight et al. 1990; Wolfe, Baron, and

Cornett 2001). Thus, the potential for a nonlinear response of the alpine zone to increased N deposition exists, exacerbating the environmental problems associated with anthropogenic N deposition.

Nitrogen is not the only pollutant to fall from the sky onto alpine ecosystems. Polychlorinated biphenyls (PCBs), fluoranthene, dieldrin, and other organochlorines have been found in the sediments and snowpack of Rocky Mountain lakes and in tissue of fish in the lakes (Blais et al. 1998; Heit, Klusek, and Baron 1984). These compounds are transported for long distances through the atmosphere. Organochlorines volatilize in warm environments and condense in cooler environments. In this way, they "leapfrog" their way to high elevations, where they persist. In Alberta and British Columbia, snowpack concentrations of organochlorines were a hundredfold greater at elevations of 3,100 m (10,200 ft.) than at lower elevations (Blais et al. 1998). Trace metals such as lead and mercury have increased in the sediments of high mountain lakes with time, indicative of industrialization since the mid-nineteenth century (Baron et al. 1986, Krabbenhoft et al. 2002). Lead, for instance, began to increase above background levels with the rise of mining in the West, and it continued to increase through the twentieth century in part because of the combustion of automotive leaded gasoline (Baron et al. 1986).

In the Future . . .

Much of the high-elevation terrain of the Rockies is under some legal protection, and many alpine areas are protected in national parks and wilderness areas. In the southern Rocky Mountains, 56% of all alpine areas is found in national parks and wilderness areas, and another 38% is managed for multiple use (SREP 2000). Only 5% is privately owned. Many human activities directly affecting alpine and treeline ecosystems have been curtailed since the mid-twentieth century as a result of environmental regulation, economics, and shifting societal values. A notable exception is recreation, which continues to increase. Management of recreation in alpine areas is already challenging because of inadequate funding of management agencies, which consequently cannot support adequate patrols. Recently, a consortium of environmental and civic groups established the Colorado Fourteeners Initiative to educate outdoorsmen on low-impact use and to establish trails to the summits to minimize erosion. Restoration of badly eroded sites using revegetation techniques shows some promise (Conlin and Ebersole 2001; Chambers, Brown, and Johnston 1984). A notable effort to increase communication about revegetation strategies in the alpine zone is the annual "High-Altitude Revegetation Workshop" sponsored by a consortium of mining companies, environmental consultants, and the Colorado Water Resources Research Institute.

Alpine areas will continue to be important sites for monitoring the indirect influence of human activities on the environment. Changes in climate, UVB transmittance, and atmospheric chemistry and deposition can perhaps be more readily interpreted in alpine locations, where direct human influence is minimal. It is clear that mountain ranges near urban, industrial, and agricultural centers will continue to see increases in emissions and subsequent deposition of N. Our evidence suggests that alpine ecosystems will continue to respond to N deposition with changes in biodiversity, lake eutrophication, and ultimately lake acidification (Baron et al. 2000, Bowman and Steltzer 1998). It is our hope that clean air legislation will precede these changes.

References

Aber, J. D., K. J. Nadelhoffer, P. A. Steudler, and J. M. Melillo. 1989. Nitrogen saturation in northern forest ecosystems. *BioScience* 39:378–386.

Adams, S. B., C. A. Frissell, and B. E. Rieman. 2001. Geography of invasion of mountain streams: Consequences of headwater lake fish introductions. *Ecosystems* 4:296–307.

Armstrong, D. M., J. C. Halfpenny, and C. H. Southwick. 2001. Vertebrates. In *Structure and function of an alpine ecosystem: Niwot Ridge, Colorado,* ed. W. D. Bowman and T. R. Seastedt, 128–156. New York: Oxford University Press.

Arno, S. F., and R. P. Hammerly. 1984. *Timberline: Mountain and arctic forest frontiers.* Seattle: Mountaineers Books.

Bahls, P. F. 1992. The status of fish populations and management of high mountain lakes in the western United States. *Northwest Science* 66:183–193.

Baker, W. L., and Weisberg, P. J. 1995. Landscape analysis of the forest-tundra ecotone in Rocky Mountain National Park, Colorado. *Professional Geographer* 47:361–375.

Baron, J., S. A. Norton, D. R. Beeson, and R. Herrmann. 1986. Sediment diatom and metal stratigraphy from Rocky Mountain lakes, with special reference to atmospheric deposition. *Canadian Journal of Fisheries and Aquatic Science* 43:1350–1362.

Baron, J. S., H. M. Rueth, A. M. Wolfe, K. R. Nydick, E. J. Allstott, J. T. Minear, and B. Moraska. 2000. Ecosystem responses to nitrogen deposition in the Colorado Front Range. *Ecosystems* 3:352–368.

Becwar, M. R., and M. J. Burke. 1982. Winter hardiness limitations and physiography of woody timberline flora. In *Plant cold hardiness and freezing stress: Mechanisms and crop implications,* vol. 2, ed P. H. Li and A. Sakai, 307–323. New York: Academic Press.

Bell, K. L., and L. C. Bliss. 1979. Autecology of *Kobresia belardii:* Why winter snow accumulation limits local distribution. *Ecological Monographs* 49:377–402.

Billings, W. D. 1973. Arctic and alpine vegetations: Similarities, differences, and susceptibility to disturbance. *BioScience* 23:697–704.

———. 1988. Alpine vegetation. In *North American terrestrial vegetation,* ed. M. G. Barbour and W. D. Billings, 391–420. Cambridge: Cambridge University Press.

Blais, J. M., D. W. Schindler, D. C. G. Muir, L. E. Kimpe, D. B. Donald, and B. Rosenberg. 1998. Accumulation of persistent organochlorine compounds in mountains of western Canada. *Nature* 395:585–588.

Blumthaler, M., and W. Ambach. 1990. Indication of increasing solar ultraviolet-B radiation flux in alpine regions. *Science* 248:206–208.

Bock, J. H., C. L. Jolls, and A. C. Lewis. 1995. The effects of grazing on alpine vegetation: A comparison of the Central Caucasus, Republic of Georgia, with the Colorado Rocky Mountains, USA. *Arctic and Alpine Research* 27:130–136.

Böhm, M. 1992. Air quality and deposition. In *The response of western forests to air pollution,* ed. R. K. Olson, D. Binkley, and M. Böhm, 63–152. Ecological Studies 97. New York: Springer-Verlag.

Bothwell, M. L., D. M. J. Sherbot, and C. M. Pollock. 1994. Ecosystem response to solar ultraviolet-B radiation: Influence of trophic-level interactions. *Science* 265:97–100.

Bowman, W. D. 1992. Inputs and storage of nitrogen in winter snowpack in an alpine ecosystem. *Arctic and Alpine Research* 24:211–215.

Bowman, W. D., and M. Damm. 2002. Causes and consequences of alpine vascular plant diversity in the Rocky Mountains. In *Mountain biodiversity: A global assessment,* ed. Ch. Körner and E. Spehn, 35–47. Elmsford, N.Y.: Pergamon Press.

Bowman, W. D., and S. Steltzer. 1998. Positive feedbacks to anthropogenic nitrogen deposition in Rocky Mountain alpine tundra. *Ambio* 27:514–517.

Bowman, W. D., T. A. Theodose, and M. C. Fisk. 1995. Physiological and production responses of plant growth forms to increases in limiting resources in alpine tundra: Implications for differential community response to environmental change. *Oecologia* 101:217–227.

Bowman, W. D., T. A. Theodose, J. C. Schardt, and R. T. Conant. 1993. Constraints of nutrient availability on primary production in two alpine communities. *Ecology* 74:2085–2098.

Brooks, P. D., M. W. Williams, and S. K. Schmidt. 1996. Microbial activity under alpine snow packs, Niwot Ridge, Colorado. *Biogeochemistry* 32:93–113.

Butler, D. R., G. P. Malanson, and D. M. Cairns. 1994. Stability of alpine treeline in Glacier National Park, Montana, U.S.A. *Phytocoenologia* 22:485–500.

Butler, D. R., G. P. Malanson, and S. J. Walsh. 1992. Snow-avalanche paths: Conduits from the periglacial alpine to the subalpine-depositional zone. In *Periglacial geomorphology,* ed. J. C. Dixon and A. D. Abrahams, 185–202. New York: Wiley.

Butler, D. R., and S. J. Walsh. 1994. Site characteristics of debris flows and their relationship to alpine treeline. *Physical Geography* 15:181–199.

Caine, N. 1995. Temporal trends in the quality of streamwater in an alpine environment: Green Lakes Valley, Colorado Front Range, U.S.A. *Geografiska Annaler* 77A:207–220.

Cairns, D. M., and G. P. Malanson. 1997. Evaluation of the carbon balance hypothesis of treeline location in Glacier National Park, Montana. *Physical Geography* 18:125–145.

Caldwell, M. M., L. O. Bjorn, J. F. Bornman, S. D. Flint, G. Kulandaivelu, A. H. Teramura, and M. Tevini. 1998. Effects of increased solar ultraviolet radiation on terrestrial ecosystems. *Journal of Photochemistry and Photobiology B: Biology* 46:40–52.

Caldwell, M. M., R. Robberecht, and W. D. Billings. 1980. A steep latitudinal gradient of solar ultraviolet-B radiation in the arctic-alpine life zone. *Ecology* 61:600–611.

Caldwell, M. M., R. Robberecht, R. S. Nowak, and W. D. Billings. 1982. Differential photosynthetic inhibition by ultraviolet radiation in species from the arctic-alpine life zone. *Arctic and Alpine Research* 14:195–202.

Chambers, J. C., R. W. Brown, and R. S. Johnston. 1984. Examination of plant successional stages in disturbed alpine ecosystems: A method of selecting revegetation sites.

In *Proceedings: High-Altitude Revegetation Workshop no. 6,* ed. T. A. Colbert and R. L. Cuany, 215–224. Information Series No. 53. Fort Collins: Colorado State University, Colorado Water Resources Research Institute.

Conlin, D. B., and J. J. Ebersole. 2001. Restoration of an alpine disturbance: Differential success of species in turf transplants, Colorado, USA. *Arctic, Antarctic, and Alpine Research* 33:340–347.

Daubenmire, R. F. 1954. Alpine timberlines in the Americas and their interpretation. *Butler University Botanical Studies* 1:119–136.

DeLucia, E. H., T. A. Day, and T. C. Vogelman. 1992. Ultraviolet-B and visible light penetration into needles of two species of sub-alpine conifers during foliar development. *Plant Cell and Environment* 15:921–929.

Eilers, J. M., P. Kanciruk, R. A. McCord, W. S. Overton, L. Hook, D. J. Blick, D. F. Brakke, P. E. Keller, M. S. DeHaan, M. E. Silverstein et al. 1987. *Data compendium for selected physical and chemical variables.* Vol. 2 of *Characteristics of lakes in the western United States.* EPA/600/3-86/054b. Washington, D.C.: U.S. Environmental Protection Agency.

Elias, S. A. 1996. *Ice age environments of national parks in the Rocky Mountains.* Washington, D.C.: Smithsonian Institution Press.

Fall, P. L., P. T. Davis, and G. A. Zielinski. 1995. Late Quaternary vegetation and climate of the Wind River Range, Wyoming. *Quaternary Research* 43:393–404.

Fisk, M. C., and S. K. Schmidt. 1996. Microbial responses to excess nitrogen in alpine tundra soils. *Soil Biology and Biochemistry* 28:751–755.

Fisk, M. C., S. K. Schmidt, and T. R. Seastedt. 1998. Topographic patterns of above- and below-ground production and N cycling in alpine tundra. *Ecology* 79:2253–2266.

Fox, D. J. 1997. Mining in the mountains. In *Mountains of the world. A global priority,* ed. J. D. Ives and B. Messerli, 171–198. London: Parthenon.

Galen, C., and M. L. Stanton. 1995. Responses of snowbed plant species to changes in growing-season length. *Ecology* 76:1546–1557.

Gough, L., C. W. Osenberg, K. L. Gross, and S. L. Collins. 2000. Fertilization effects on species density and primary productivity in herbaceous plant communities. *Oikos* 89:428–439.

Greller, A. M. 1974. Vegetation of roadcut slopes in the tundra of Rocky Mountain National Park, Colorado. *Biological Conservation* 6:84–93.

Hadley, J. L., and W. K. Smith. 1986. Wind effects on needles of timberline conifers: Seasonal influence on mortality. *Ecology* 67:12–19.

Hammerson, G. A. 1982. *Amphibians and reptiles in Colorado.* Denver: Colorado Division of Wildlife.

Hauer, F. R., J. S. Baron, D. H. Campbell, K. D. Fausch, S. W. Hostettler, G. H. Leavesley, P. R. Leavitt, D. M. McKnight, and J. A. Stanford. 1997. Assessment of climate change and freshwater ecosystems of the Rocky Mountains, USA and Canada. *Hydrologic Processes* 11:903–924.

Heit, M., C. Klusek, and J. Baron. 1984. Evidence of deposition of anthropogenic pollutants in remote Rocky Mountain lakes. *Water, Air, Soil Pollution* 22:403–406.

Henry, G. H. R., and U. Molau. 1997. Tundra plants and climate change: The International Tundra Experiment (ITEX). *Global Change Biology* 3 (suppl. 1): 1–9.

Hess, K. Jr. 1993. *Rocky times in Rocky Mountain National Park: An unnatural history.* Niwot: University Press of Colorado.

Hessl, A. E., and W. L. Baker. 1997. Spruce and fir regeneration and climate in the forest-tundra ecotone of Rocky Mountain National Park, Colorado, U.S.A. *Arctic and Alpine Research* 29:173–183.

Hutchinson, G. E. 1957. *Geography and physics of lakes.* Vol. 1 of *A treatise on limnology.* Chichester: Wiley.

Inyan, B. J., and M. W. Williams. 2001. Protection of headwater catchments from future degradation: San Miguel River basin, Colorado. *Mountain Research and Development* 21:54–60.

Ives, J. D., and K. J. Hansen-Bristow. 1983. Stability and instability of natural and modified upper timberline landscapes in the Colorado Rocky Mountains, USA. *Mountain Research and Development* 3:149–155.

Kearney, M. S. 1982. Recent seedling establishment at timberline in Jasper National Park, Alta. *Canadian Journal of Botany* 60:2283–2287.

Kiffney, P. M., W. H. Clements, and T. A. Cady. 1997. Influence of ultraviolet radiation on the colonization dynamics of a Rocky Mountain stream benthic community. *Journal of the North American Benthological Society* 16:520–530.

Kitchell, J. F., ed. 1992. *Food web management: A case study of Lake Mandota.* New York: Springer-Verlag.

Knapp, R. A., P. S. Corn, and D. E. Schindler. 2001. The introduction of nonnative fish into wilderness lakes: Good intentions, conflicting mandates, and unintended consequences. *Ecosystems* 2:275–278.

Knapp, R. A., K. R. Matthews, and O. Sarnelle. 2001. Resistance and resilience of alpine lake faunal assemblages to fish introductions. *Ecological Monographs* 71:401–421.

Körner, Ch., and W. Larcher. 1988. Plant life in cold climates. In *Plants and temperature,* ed. S. P. Long and F. I. Woodward, 25–57. Cambridge: Company of Biologists.

Krabbenhoft, D. P., M. L. Olson, J. F. Dewild, D. W. Clow, R. G. Striegl, M. M. Dornblaser, and P. VanMetre. 2002. Mercury loading and methylmercury production and cycling in high-altitude lakes from the western United States. *Water, Air, and Soil Pollution,* 2002.

Kupfer, J. A., and D. M. Cairns. 1996. The suitability of montane ecotones as indicators of global climatic change. *Progress in Physical Geography* 20:253–272.

Lavender, D. 1975. *The Rockies.* New York: Harper and Row.

Leavitt, P. R., D. E. Schindler, A. J. Paul, A. K. Hardie, and D. W. Schindler. 1994. Fossil pigment records of phytoplankton in trout-stocked alpine lakes. *Canadian Journal of Fisheries and Aquatic Science* 51:2411–2423.

Licht, L. E., and K. P. Grant. 1997. The effects of ultraviolet radiation on the biology of amphibians. *American Zoologist* 37:137–145.

McKnight, D. M., R. L. Smith, J. P. Bradbury, J. S. Baron, and S. A. Spaulding. 1990. Phytoplankton dynamics in three Rocky Mountain alpine lakes, Colorado, USA. *Arctic and Alpine Research* 22:264–274.

Madronich, S., R. L. McKenzie, L. O. Bjorn, and M. M. Caldwell. 1998. Changes in biologically active ultraviolet radiation reaching the earth's surface. *Journal of Photochemistry and Photobiology B: Biology* 46:5–19.

Malanson, G. P. 1997. Effects of feedbacks and seed rain on ecotone patterns. *Landscape Ecology* 12:27–38.

Marr, J. W. 1964. Utilization of the Front Range tundra, Colorado. In *Grazing in terrestrial and marine environments,* ed. D. J. Crisp, 109–118. Oxford: Blackwell Scientific.

————. 1977. The development and movement of tree islands near the upper limit of tree growth in the southern Rocky Mountains. *Ecology* 58:1159–1164.

Moir, W. H., S. G. Rochelle, and A. W. Schoettle. 1999. Microscale patterns of tree establishment near upper treeline, Snowy Range, Wyoming, U.S.A. *Arctic, Antarctic, and Alpine Research* 31:379–388.

Nagl, A. M., and R. Hofer. 1997. Effects of ultraviolet radiation on early larval stages of the alpine newt, *Triturus alpestris,* under natural and laboratory conditions. *Oecologia* 110:514–519.

National Atmospheric Deposition Program. 2001. *National Atmospheric Deposition Program 2000 annual summary.* NADP Data Report 2001-01. Champaign: Illinois State Water Survey, National Atmospheric Deposition Program Office.

Neff, J. C., W. D. Bowman, E. A. Holland, and S. K. Schmidt. 1994. Fluxes of nitrous oxide and methane from nitrogen amended soils in the Colorado alpine. *Biogeochemistry* 27:23–33.

Oberbauer, S., and W. D. Billings. 1981. Drought tolerance and water use by plants along an alpine topographic gradient. *Oecologia* 50:325–331.

Parker, B. R., D. W. Schindler, D. B. Donald, and R. S. Anderson. 2001. The effects of stocking and removal of a nonnative salmonid on the plankton of an alpine lake. *Ecosystems* 4:334–345.

Paulsen, H. A. Jr. 1960. Plant cover and forage use of alpine sheep ranges in the central Rocky Mountains. *Iowa State Journal of Science* 34:731–748.

Peet, R. K. 1981. Forest vegetation of the Colorado Front Range. *Vegetatio* 45:3–75.

Pilliod, D. S., and C. R. Peterson. 2001. Local and landscape effects of introduced trout on amphibians in historically fishless watersheds. *Ecosystems* 4:322–333.

Pister, E. P. 2001. Wilderness fish stocking: History and perspective. *Ecosystems* 4:279–286.

Price, M. F., L. A. G. Moss, and P. W. Williams. 1997. Tourism and amenity migration. In *Mountains of the world: A global priority,* ed. J. D. Ives and B. Messerli, 249–280. London: Parthenon.

Rau, W., and H. Hofmann. 1996. Sensitivity to UV-B of plants growing in different altitudes in the Alps. *Journal of Plant Physiology* 148:21–25.

Reasoner, M. A., and M. A. Jodry. 2000. Rapid response of alpine timberline vegetation to the Younger Dryas climate oscillation in the Colorado Rocky Mountains, USA. *Geology* 28:51–54.

Sherrod, S. K., and T. R. Seastedt. 2001. Effects of the northern pocket gopher (*Thomomys talpoides*) on alpine soil characteristics, Niwot Ridge, Colorado. *Biogeochemistry* 55:195–218.

Singer, F. J., and M. A. Gudorf. 1999. *Restoration of bighorn sheep metapopulations in and near fifteen national parks: Conservation of a severely fragmented species.* U.S. Geological Survey Open-File Report 99-102. Fort Collins, Colo.: U.S. Geological Survey, Midcontinent Ecological Science Center.

Smith, J. B., R. Richels, and B. Miller. 2000. Potential consequences of climate variability and change for the western United States. In *Climate change impacts on the United States,* comp. National Assessment Synthesis Team, U.S. Global Change Research Program, 1–44. Washington, D.C.: U.S. Global Change Research Program.

Sommerfeld, R. A., A. R. Mosier, and R. C. Musselman. 1993. CO_2, CH_4, and N_2O flux through a Wyoming snowpack. *Nature* 361:140–143.

SREP (Southern Rockies Ecosystem Project). 2000. *The state of the southern Rockies ecoregion.* Nederland, Colo.: Southern Rockies Ecosystem Project. On-line at <http://csf.colorado.edu/srep>.

Steltzer, H., and W. D. Bowman. 1998. Differential influence of plant species on soil N trans-formations within moist meadow alpine tundra. *Ecosystems* 1:464–474.

Tardiff, S. E., and J. A. Stanford. 1998. Grizzly bear digging: Effects on subalpine meadow plants in relation to mineral nitrogen availability. *Ecology* 79:2219–2228.

Theodose, T. A., and W. D. Bowman. 1997. Nutrient availability, plant abundance, and species diversity in two alpine tundra communities. *Ecology* 78:1861–1872.

Thorne, C. E. 1982. Gopher disturbance: Its variability by Braun-Blanquet vegetation units in the Niwot Ridge alpine tundra zone, Colorado Front Range, U.S.A. *Arctic and Alpine Research* 14:45–51.

U.S. Department of the Interior, Bureau of Mines. 1991. *Annual research report.* Washington, D.C.: U.S. Department of the Interior, Bureau of Mines.

van Gardingen, P. R., J. Grace, and C. E. Jeffree. 1991. Abrasive damage by wind to the nee-dle surfaces of *Picea sitchensis* (Bong.) Carr. and *Pinus sylvestris* L. *Plant, Cell, and Environment* 14:185–193.

Vinebrooke, R. D., and P. R. Leavitt. 1999. Differential responses of littoral communities to ultraviolet radiation in an alpine lake. *Ecology* 80:223–237.

Vitousek, P. M., J. D. Aber, R. W. Howarth, G. E. Likens, P. A. Matson, D. W. Schindler, W. H. Schlesinger, and D. G. Tilman 1997. Human alteration of the global nitrogen cycle: Sources and consequences. *Ecological Applications* 7:737–750.

Walker, D. A., J. C. Halfpenny, M. D. Walker, and C. A. Wessman. 1993. Long-term studies of snow–vegetation interactions. *BioScience* 43:287–301.

Walker, M. D., P. J. Webber, E. A. Arnold, and D. Ebert-May. 1994. Effects of interannual cli-mate variation on aboveground phytomass in alpine vegetation. *Ecology* 75:393–408.

Walsh, S. J., D. R. Butler, T. R. Allen, and G. P. Malanson. 1994. Influence of snow patterns and snow avalanches on the alpine treeline ecotone. *Journal of Vegetation Science* 5:657–672.

Wardle, P. 1974. Alpine timberlines. In *Arctic and alpine environments,* ed. J. D. Ives and R. G. Barry, 371–402. London: Methuen.

Weisberg, P. J., and W. L. Baker. 1995. Spatial variation in tree seedling and krummholz growth in the forest-tundra ecotone of Rocky Mountain National Park, Colorado, U.S.A. *Arctic and Alpine Research* 27:116–129.

Welker, J. M., U. Molau, A. N. Parsons, C. H. Robinson, and P. A. Wookey. 1997. Responses of *Dryas octopetala* to ITEX environmental manipulations: A synthesis with circumpolar comparisons. *Global Change Biology* 3:61–73.

Willard, B. E., and J. W. Marr. 1970. Effects of human activities on alpine tundra ecosys-tems in Rocky Mountain National Park, Colorado. *Biological Conservation* 2:257–265.

Williams, M. W., and K. A. Tonnessen. 2000. Critical loads for inorganic nitrogen deposi-tion in the Colorado Front Range, USA. *Ecological Applications* 10:1648–1665.

Wolfe, A. P., J. S. Baron, and R. J. Cornett. 2001. Anthropogenic nitrogen deposition induces rapid ecological changes in alpine lakes of the Colorado Front Range (USA). *Journal of Paleolimnology* 25:1–7.

Zwinger, A. H., and B. E. Willard. 1972. *Land above the trees.* New York: Harper and Row.

CHAPTER 10

The Heart of the Rockies: Montane and Subalpine Ecosystems

Thomas J. Stohlgren, Thomas T. Veblen, Katherine C. Kendall, William L. Baker, Craig D. Allen, Jesse A. Logan, and Kevin C. Ryan

▲

Nestled between the tundra and the plains, the montane and subalpine ecosystems could be considered the pounding heart of the Rocky Mountains. These ecosystems filter runoff and snowmelt to supply one-quarter of the nation's freshwater for agricultural and domestic use. Millions of visitors to state and national parks, forests, and wildlife refuges support service industries that circulate billions of dollars into local, regional, and national economies. The forests pump millions of tons of fresh oxygen into the atmosphere and supply timber for human use. Their wetlands and aspen stands contribute disproportionately to the diversity of the Rocky Mountain landscape. The montane and subalpine ecosystems of the Rockies also provide critical habitat for thousands of plant and animal species.

Natural resources in these ecosystems have been exploited since the beginning of the nineteenth century (Lavender 1975). Beavers (*Castor canadensis*) had been trapped to near extinction by the 1830s. Significant deposits of gold, silver, copper, lead, molybdenum, tungsten, and zinc have been exploited in prospecting and mining. Most species of predator, such as gray wolves (*Canis lupus*), grizzly bears (*Ursus arctos*), and coyotes (*Canis latrans*), have been hunted and poisoned. The forests have been logged for railroad ties, mine supports, timber, and firewood. Livestock have long been moved between low-elevation winter pastures and high-elevation summer pastures. Indeed, human history has dealt significant and often detrimental change to Rocky Mountain natural resources (part III).

Since the 1960s and 1970s, the transformation has continued but in different ways. Human population growth now exceeds 3% per year in many places, and demands for water have left few rivers wild. Air pollution adds nitrogen, organochlorines, and mercury to Rocky Mountain ecosystems. Exotic plants, fishes, mammals, and diseases have been introduced throughout the montane and subalpine zones. Fire suppression dominates in landscapes that once had much more frequent natural fires. And though the rate of commercial logging has decreased in most Rocky Mountain states and provinces, it continues at a rapid pace in Idaho, Montana, British Columbia, and Alberta (chapter 5).

In light of these threats, we evaluate the status of the region's montane and subalpine ecosystems. After a brief description of these ecosystems, we discuss the individual and cumulative effects of climate change and land use change, resource extraction, fire and water management, and species extirpations and invasions on montane and subalpine ecosystems in the Rocky Mountains.

Description of the Montane and Subalpine Forests

The different vegetation types of the Rocky Mountains have been described by several authors (Alexander 1985; Peet 1988; Allen, Peet, and Baker 1991; Cooper, Neiman, and Roberts 1991; Knight 1994) and in chapter 2 of this book. Here, we generally follow the description of forest types provided by Peet (1988).

Montane Coniferous Forests

Ponderosa pine (*Pinus ponderosa*) forests dominate the lower montane zone of the central and southern Rocky Mountains. They vary in appearance from scattered individuals in low-elevation or rocky areas to dense forests at higher elevations or in deeper soils (Peet 1981, 1988; Knight 1994). Other tree species, such as Douglas-fir (*Pseudotsuga menziesii*) and Rocky Mountain juniper (*Juniperus scopulorum*), can codominate. At lower treeline, montane forests are savanna-like, interspersed with grasses and shrubs such as bitterbrush, sagebrush, and cinquefoil (Emerick 1995).

Douglas-fir occurs from Mexico to northern Canada, generally from near lower treeline upward to spruce-fir forests. In Colorado, Douglas-fir ranges from about 1,650 meters (m), or 5,400 feet (ft.), to 2,700 m (8,900 ft.), often in mixed stands with ponderosa pine, blue spruce (*Picea pungens*), or lodgepole pine (*Pinus contorta*). Douglas-fir is thick-barked and somewhat tolerant of the frequent, low-intensity surface fires that characterize the lower-elevation ponderosa pine forests. Ponderosa pine is considered a true pyrophyte, or fire-adapted species. Evolved traits such as thick layers of exfoliating bark insulate the pine from recurrent fire. Before European settlement, mean intervals between consecutive fires in open stands of ponderosa pine and Douglas-fir were generally less than 50 years and in some habitats less than 10 years (chapter 7; Keane, Arno, and Brown 1990; Goldblum and Veblen 1992; Veblen, Kitzberger, and Donnegan 1996). Toward higher elevations within the montane zone, in denser forests dominated by Douglas-fir or lodgepole pine, fires occurred at intervals of 50 to more than 100 years (Loope and Gruell 1973, Gruell 1985).

The Cascadian forest includes several tree species commonly associated with the Cascade Range and occurs on the rain-swept western slopes of the northern Rockies from Wyoming to central Alberta and British Columbia. Common tree species include western hemlock (*Tsuga heterophylla*), western red cedar (*Thuja plicata*), grand fir (*Abies grandis*), mountain hemlock (*Tsuga mertensiana*), and larches (*Larix* spp.), all of which are subject to infrequent (e.g., 80- to 110-year intervals), stand-replacing fires (Johnson, Fryer, and Heathcott 1990).

Lodgepole pine forests interspersed with stands of quaking aspen (*Populus tremuloides*) are fire-resilient forests that dominate the central and north-central Rocky Mountains (Peet 1988). Usually found between 2,500 m (8,200 ft.) and 3,200 m (10,500 ft.) in Colorado, lodgepole pine and aspen grow rapidly after fire in relatively even-aged stands. The intervals between fires typically range from 100 to 300 years (Romme and Knight 1981).

Montane Aspen Forests

Aspen is the most widely distributed tree species in North America, and even in the Rocky Mountain montane zone, aspen exists within a diversity of ecological settings. Aspen stands are a prominent feature, serving as critical habitat for hundreds of birds and mammals. Aspen seedlings, saplings, and small trees are especially important forage for deer (*Odocoileus* spp.) and elk (*Cervus elaphus*) (Mueggler 1993). Aspen trees more than eighty years old are valuable avian habitat; sapsuckers, woodpeckers, boreal owls, and buffleheads build nest cavities in trees that have been invaded by heartrot fungi (Hart and Hart 2001). Approximately thirty-four avian species nest in aspen trees, and at least one, the red-naped sapsucker, may be an obligate aspen nester. Once cavities are constructed and abandoned, they become homes for many other nesters, including other birds and mammals (DeByle and Winokur 1985).

Aspen stands and wetlands (discussed in the next section) are noted for their high diversity of vascular plants (Peet 1978). Aspen ecosystems are also rich in number and species of animals, especially in comparison with nearby coniferous forest types. They provide important habitat and food supply for ungulates, beavers, and butterflies. A characteristic of aspen stands that makes them especially valuable habitat is multi-layered undergrowth. The open, sunny habit of aspen stands allows development of a mixed layer of shrubs and herbs that provides important host plants and microhabitats for insects. The large insect populations found in aspen stands are important food resources for many wildlife species, especially birds and bats (Simonson et al. 2001, DeByle and Winokur 1985).

Aspen may occur in pure stands without any other tree species. Large expanses of aspen on upland slopes, such as occur in the San Juan Mountains of southwestern Colorado and parts of Utah and northern New Mexico, persist for hundreds of years as a landscape mosaic of different-aged aspen stands. Romme, Floyd-Hanna, and Hanna (2001) suggest that short fire intervals may have eliminated coniferous seedlings prior to fire suppression and aspen currently persists because of patch clear-cutting practices.

Farther north, aspen is much less abundant. It occurs as small, mostly discrete patches within a landscape dominated by sagebrush, steppe, and coniferous forests. Many of these stands are successional and are eventually replaced by coniferous forests. In both stable and successional stands, most reproduction is through vegetative sprouting, and it responds positively to fire, moderate logging, and grazing (Romme, Floyd-Hanna, and Hanna 2001). Seedling establishment was observed after intense fires in Yellowstone National Park in 1988 and in Arizona as a result of a combination of heavy seed production by mature aspen, exposed soil where competition was greatly reduced, and cool, moist early summer conditions following the fires (Romme, Floyd-Hanna, and Hanna 2001; Quinn and Wu 2001).

Wetlands

Wetlands deserve their own extended chapter in any study of the ecological state of the Rocky Mountains, but it is surprising how little is actually known. Wetlands are found at all elevations throughout the Rockies, but they broadly occur in mountain valleys or intermountain basins where the water table is high or where there is periodic flooding. Scientifically, wetlands are transitional areas between terrestrial and open-water systems. Legally, however, their definition requires spatial delineation, and disputes over what is and is not classified as wetland have contributed greatly to the lack of overall understanding of wetland status in the Rocky Mountains (NRC 1992). For example, there is a 700% difference in the area of wetlands mapped for the 445,170 hectare (ha), or 1.1 million acre, Bighorn National Forest in Wyoming by two credible federal agencies (D. J. Cooper, pers. comm.). Wetlands in the Rockies consist of forested wetlands, willow wetlands, fens (flooded peat marshes with nonacidic soil), marshes, bogs, alpine snow glades, wet meadows, salt meadows, bottomland shrublands, shallow ponds, and even playa lakes (temporary desert lakes). They are the most diverse and biologically productive landscapes of the region and offer important habitat for plants and animals far in excess of their total area. The Southern Rockies Ecosystem Project (SREP) reports that more than 450 vertebrate species (excluding fish) make use of wetland and riparian areas of northern New Mexico, Colorado, and southern Wyoming. The next richest ecosystems for vertebrates, lowland grasslands, piñon juniper woodlands, and mountain shrublands, all have fewer than 200 vertebrate species (SREP 2000). For instance, South Park, Colorado, is the highest large intermountain basin in North America. Its peatlands have more unique, rare, and disjunct plant communities than any other ecosystem type in Colorado and possibly in the Rocky Mountains. South Park wetlands support a striking combination of communities whose nearest relatives are in Mongolia, circumpolar regions, and the mountains of Chihuahua (Cooper 2002).

There are twenty national wildlife refuges in the U.S. Rocky Mountains, all of them surrounding either wetlands or riparian areas (Windell et al. 1986). They are stopover sites for thousands of migratory waterfowl and shorebirds, including sandhill cranes, avocets, snowy egrets, ducks, and geese (SREP 2000). Wetlands are important habitat for moose, grizzly bears, and beavers and support other aquatic mammals, such as river otters.

Subalpine Forests

The subalpine forests of the Rocky Mountains are characterized by spruce and fir and are floristically and structurally similar to northern boreal conifer forests. Dominant tree species in the southern Rockies include Engelmann spruce (*Picea engelmannii*) and subalpine fir (*Abies lasiocarpa*). In the Black Hills of South Dakota and in northern British Columbia and Yukon Territory, white spruce (*Picea glauca*) replaces Engelmann spruce. Lodgepole pine often dominates in the lower half of the subalpine zone but can extend to near treeline. In contrast to the typically low-intensity surface fires of the lower montane zone, most extensive fires in the subalpine zone are stand-replacing fires that may burn thousands of square kilometers in single events (Romme 1982, Peet 1988). Fires that replace stands occur typically at 100- to 400-year intervals (Romme and Knight 1981, Veblen et al. 1994). In some habitats, major outbreaks of bark beetle occur more frequently (Baker and Veblen 1990, Veblen et al. 1991).

On exposed, dry slopes at high elevations, spruce-fir forests are replaced by subalpine white pine forests. Common species of the white pine forests include bristlecone pine (*Pinus aristata*) in the southern Rockies, limber pine (*P. flexilis*) in the central and north-central Rockies, and whitebark pine (*P. albicaulis*) in the northern Rockies. Typical intervals between fires range from 50 to 300 years (Tomback, Arno, and Keane 2001). The white pines are tolerant of extreme environmental conditions and can be important postfire successional species.

Treeline rises steadily at the rate of 100 m (330 ft.) per degree of latitude from the northern to the southern Rockies (chapter 9). Dominant treeline species, including spruce, fir, and white pine, often take on a shrub-like physiognomy called krummholz to withstand the harsher, windswept conditions. Under favorable climatic conditions, krummholz trees can begin to take a tree-like form or can increase seedling establishment (Hessl and Baker 1997a, b).

Current Stressors to Montane and Subalpine Ecosystems

Today's mix of human influences includes increased human settlement with associated land use change and habitat loss, climate change, and introductions of non-native species. Combinations of all these occur and, of course, are superimposed on past disturbances, including fire suppression.

Human Population Growth: The New Pioneers and Tourists

Human population has grown rapidly in the montane zones in Rocky Mountain states since the 1950s (chapter 1; Stohlgren 1999). Several mountain towns, such as the village of Estes Park, Colorado, doubled their population during this time. As an outstanding case, Jackson Hole, Wyoming, increased by 260% (from 1,244 to 4,472 residents) in forty years (figure 10.1). Additionally, tourism exceeds 3 million visitors per year in Yellowstone and Rocky Mountain National Parks, with the majority of visitor hours in montane and subalpine ecosystems. Population growth of this proportion has escalated the demand for water, power, and natural resources in these ecosystems. Where residential development is exurban, it fragments the landscape, allowing increased predation on native birds and mammals by pets, cowbirds, and birds of prey (Knight et al. 1999). Development in montane forests encourages fire suppression activities, making restoration of native fire regimes impractical.

Climate and Land Use Change

The popular press often suggests that the greenhouse effect will increase the frequency of wildfire, and extensive fires in 1988 and 2000 do not dispute this trend. Although there is good evidence linking the occurrence of fire to climatic variation, the association of trends in areas burned per year with long-term climatic trends is complex. For Yellowstone National Park in the period 1895–1989, a trend toward increasing extent of fires is possibly associated with trends of increasing summer temperatures and decreasing January–June precipitation (Balling, Meyer, and Wells 1992). However, there are substantial differences in temperature and precipitation trends according to seasonality, latitude, and elevation in response to many influences, including latitude, topography, and

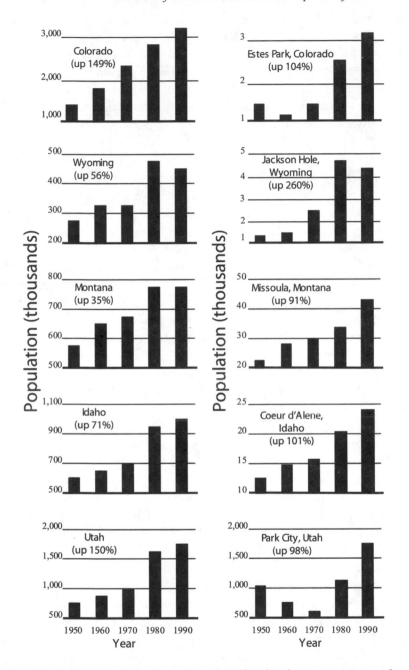

FIGURE 10.1 *Human Population Growth in Selected Rocky Mountain States and Cities, 1950–1990.* From Stohlgren 1999.

atmospheric circulation (chapter 4). Although there is a natural synergism between insect-caused tree mortality and fire in lodgepole pines of the montane zone, fire suppression may enhance unnatural outbreaks in other pine species, which in turn may increase fire hazards (Logan and Powell 2001, Hadley and Veblen 1993, Swetnam and Lynch 1993). It is plausible that the recent increases in wildfire may reflect a synergism of human influence on fuel accumulation (mainly through fire suppression) and fire-promoting climatic variation.

Habitat Loss

Extensive logging and human-set fires decimated old-growth forest resources between 1850 and 1920 (figure 5.3; Gruell 1983; Veblen and Lorenz 1991). During the period of early Euro-American settlement, fires were set to aid prospecting, to kill trees in order to justify salvage logging, to clear brush, and as a weapon between warring sheep and cattle ranchers (Sudworth 1899, Jack 1899). For much of the central Rocky Mountains, this was a time of increased fire occurrence in comparison with the period before Euro-American settlement (figure 7.2; Veblen and Lorenz 1991; Goldblum and Veblen 1992; Kipfmueller 1997) and a time when the extent of old-growth forests probably decreased widely. Regan (1998) estimated that more than 30% of some portions of Lincoln National Forest in New Mexico was old-growth forest in the late nineteenth century, compared with just 5%–6% today.

Although much of the logging of old-growth resources in the United States occurred prior to 1950, logging of old growth continues at a low level today (Stohlgren 1999, Powell et al. 1993). In the intermountain region (Arizona, New Mexico, Colorado, Wyoming, Utah, Idaho, and Montana), the total volume of softwood sawtimber from large trees decreased by 31.1% between 1952 and 1992, representing a change in sawtimber volume from 151.9 x 10^6 cubic meters (m^3), or 43,648 million board feet (mbf), to 104.6 x 10^6 m^3 (30,067 mbf) (figure 10.2).

In Canada, the rate of logging accelerated throughout the twentieth century, with 4% of Alberta's forests and 9% of British Columbia's forests harvested between 1975 and 1996. Much of the forested land in these provinces is not in the Rocky Mountains, but this serves to illustrate that Canada relies heavily on wood products for its economy (Smith and Lee 2000). Harvesting of forests in Yukon Territory, a region of remote, slow-growing forests, increased sharply in 1993. Of the subalpine forests in Canada that are not protected as national parks, 68% are licensed to timber companies for harvest (Smith and Lee 2000). The effects of harvesting are discussed in greater detail in chapter 5.

Habitat loss often causes species decline, as exemplified in old-growth forests of the Rockies. Many threatened, endangered, and vulnerable wildlife species are largely dependent on intact old-growth ecosystems (Finch 1992, Knight

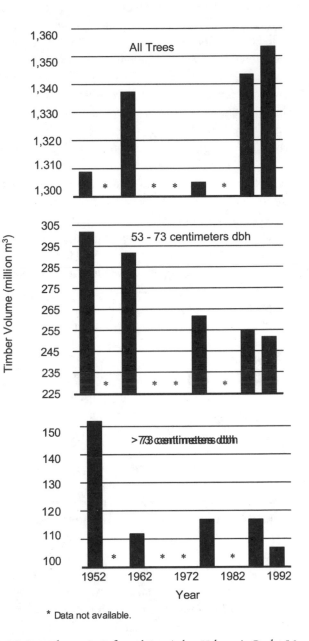

FIGURE 10.2 *Change in Softwood Sawtimber Volume in Rocky Mountain States, 1952–1992.* States represented are Arizona, New Mexico, Colorado, Wyoming, Utah, Idaho, and Montana (dbh is diameter [in cm] at breast height). From Stohlgren 1999.

et al. 1999). The effects of logging, road building, and recreation are therefore especially harmful to these organisms. Caribou (*Rangifer tarandus caribou*) in northern Idaho and British Columbia feed on lichens found only in old-growth hemlock and cedar forests. Wolverines, martens (*Martes americana*), Abert's squirrels (*Sciurus aberti ferreus*), and fishers (*Martes pennanti*) are associated almost exclusively with old-growth forests (Finch 1992). The red-backed vole (*Clethrionomys gapperi*) is more abundant and has better body condition in old-growth spruce-fir forests (Nordyke and Buskirk 1991). Several bird species, such as the northern goshawk (*Accipiter gentilis*), flammulated owl (*Otus flammeolus*), Mexican spotted owl (*Strix occidentalis lucida*), boreal owl (*Aegolius funereus*), and olive-sided flycatcher (*Contopus borealis*), depend on old-growth conifer resources for either nesting or foraging (Finch 1992, Hayward and Verner 1994).

Neotropical forest-dwelling songbirds that breed in the Rocky Mountains and winter in Central and South America are declining in number. Population declines may be due, in part, to increased predation and brood parasitism. Brood parasitism by cowbirds (*Molothrus* spp.) increases as a result of nearby logging (Evans and Finch 1994). In conifer forests in west-central Idaho, common songbirds benefited from timber harvest, whereas the abundance of rare species that inhabit old-growth forests, such as hermit thrush (*Catharus guttatus*), Swainson's thrush (*Catharus ustulatus*), and pileated woodpecker (*Dryocopus pileatus*), declined (Evans and Finch 1994).

Bighorn sheep populations are roughly 2% to 8% what they were at the time of Euro-American settlement as a result of unregulated harvesting, overgrazing of livestock on rangelands (causing loss of habitat), and diseases transmitted by domestic sheep (Singer 1995). In recent years, 115 translocations were made to reintroduce bighorn sheep into the Rocky Mountains and many national parks; only 39% of these in six states have been somewhat successful. A combination of lack of open suitable habitat, partly from fire suppression and partly from habitat fragmentation, and proximity to domestic sheep disease vectors prevents bighorn populations from ever reaching a stable persistent state (Singer 1995).

Species Introductions

Deliberate introductions of the Rocky Mountain goat and the moose into Colorado have allowed breeding populations to establish. The house mouse (*Mus musculus*) and the Norway rat (*Rattus norvegicus*) were accidentally introduced into Colorado and Wyoming (Armstrong 1993). European cheatgrass (*Bromus tectorum*) has invaded significant portions of the western piñon-juniper woodlands and ponderosa pine and Douglas-fir areas in the Rocky Mountains (Peters and Bunting 1994). Many native shrubs and perennial grasses cannot survive the increased competition from cheatgrass (chapter 11; Barbour, Burk, and Pitts 1987), and its dense cover has increased the fire frequency in many of these areas. More than 1.4 million ha (3.4 million acres) of Oregon, Washington, Idaho, and Montana are covered with spotted knapweed (*Centaurea maculosa*) (Langner and Flather 1994). We cannot estimate accurately just how much of this is in the Rocky Mountains. Purple loosestrife (*Lythrum salicaria*), another European weed, is beginning to invade Rocky Mountain wetlands and stream-sides. Purple loosestrife spreads quickly and crowds out native plants that animals use for food and shelter. This invader has no natural enemy in the United States and therefore spreads unchecked (Thompson, Stuckey, and Thompson 1987). The effects of introduced species on native forest ecosystems are poorly understood (Stohlgren 1999).

Multiple Stressors

Changes to Rocky Mountain forest ecosystems caused by human disturbance come from many directions. Disturbances rarely occur one at a time, and management solutions will need to address many stresses at once. Some examples follow.

Aspen stands are declining in some, but not all, parts of the Rocky Mountains as a result of a combination of causes. Chronic heavy browsing of aspen by elk and cattle coupled with fire suppression is most often cited, although climate change may add additional pressure (Romme, Floyd-Hanna, and Hanna 2001). A management prescription designed to restore degraded stands, which are found in and adjacent to large national parks, including Rocky Mountain, Yellowstone, Banff, Jasper, Yoho, and Kootenay National Parks, must address at least grazing and fire (or logging) simultaneously. Prescribed fires to restore habitat may lead to overgrazing of young shoots if browsing controls are not placed on large ungulates and cattle (Binkley 2001). Fencing to keep grazers out is often impractical, but reintroduction of predators may work; aspen regeneration increased in the 1970s after wolves were reintroduced into Jasper National Park (White, Olmsted, and Kay 1998).

Wetlands have never been extensive in the Rocky Mountains, but they have been severely altered by conversion to croplands, by river flow regulation, and recently by mountain residential development. Because they are the lowlands to which waters drain, they have also become the repository of pollution runoff from development activities. The eastern bullfrog and purple loosestrife are examples of non-native species that invade and alter wetland communities. According to estimates by the U.S. Fish and Wildlife Service, Idaho and Colorado have both lost 50% or more of the wetland area that was present before Euro-American settlement. Utah, New Mexico, and Wyoming have lost between 30% and 40% of their original wetlands, and Montana has lost 27% (table 10.1; NRC 1992). In

TABLE 10.1. Wetland Area Lost in U.S. Rocky Mountain States, 1800s and 1980s

State	Area in 1800s, in acres (ha)	Area in 1980s, in acres (ha)	% Loss of Wetland Area
Idaho	877,000 (355,000)	385,700 (156,100)	56
Colorado	2,000,000 (809,400)	1,000,000 (404,700)	50
Wyoming	2,000,000 (809,400)	1,250,000 (505,900)	38
New Mexico	720,000 (291,400)	481,900 (195,000)	33
Utah	802,000 (324,600)	558,000 (225,800)	30
Montana	1,147,000 (464,200)	840,300 (340,100)	27

Source: Estimates are from NRC 1992.

the southern Rocky Mountains, only 16% of wetland and riparian areas is protected from further loss or degradation (SREP 2000). Although restoration of wetlands has gained national favor and fervor, restoration technologies often ignore the complexities of multi-dimensional and variable flow, water quality needs, and delicate species balances that are required for success (Malakoff 1998).

Future Rates of Change

On the basis of previous rates of ecological change and extinctions documented in the paleoecology literature, we project that rates of change in species and habitat loss will continue to greatly exceed background levels (Cole 1995). Human population growth in montane and subalpine ecosystems will bring increasing demands for safety from wildfire and predators. Natural areas are becoming increasingly insular, and habitat fragmentation will increase in nature reserves and urban areas. Continued species decline, habitat loss, water development, and introductions of species and diseases will continue to affect the components and processes of montane and subalpine ecosystems.

References

Alexander, R. R. 1985. *Major habitat types, community types, and plant communities in the Rocky Mountains.* General Technical Report RM-123. Fort Collins, Colo.: U.S. Department of Agriculture, Forest Service, Rocky Mountain Forest and Range Experiment Station.

Allen, R. B., R. K. Peet, and W. L. Baker. 1991. Gradient analysis of latitudinal variation in southern Rocky Mountain forests. *Journal of Biogeography* 18:123–139.

Armstrong, D. M. 1993. *Lions, ferrets, and bears: A guide to the mammals of Colorado.* Denver: Colorado Division of Wildlife and University of Colorado Museum.

Baker, W. L., and T. T. Veblen. 1990. Spruce beetles and fires in the nineteenth century subalpine forests of western Colorado, U.S.A. *Arctic and Alpine Research* 22:65–80.

Balling, R. C. Jr., G. A. Meyer, and S. G. Wells. 1992. Climate change in Yellowstone National Park: Is the drought-related risk of wildfires increasing? *Climatic Change* 22:35–45.

Barbour, M. G., J. H. Burk, and W. D. Pitts. 1987. *Terrestrial plant ecology.* 2nd ed. Menlo Park, Calif.: Benjamin-Cummings.

Binkley, D. 2001. We already know all about aspen. In *Sustaining Aspen in Western Landscapes: Symposium proceedings,* ed. W. Shepperd, D. Binkley, D. L. Bartos, T. J. Stohlgren, and L. G. Eskew, 1–2. Proceedings RMRS-P-18. Fort Collins, Colo.: U.S. Department of Agriculture, Forest Service, Rocky Mountain Research Station.

Cole, K. L. 1995. Vegetation change in national parks. In *Our living resources, 1995: A report to the nation on the distribution, abundance, and health of U.S. plants, animals, and ecosystems,* ed. E. T. LaRoe, G. S. Farris, C. E. Puckett, P. D. Doran, and M. J. Mac, 224–227. Washington, D.C.: U.S. Department of the Interior, National Biological Service.

Cooper, D. J. 2002. The modern environment, flora, and vegetation of South Park, Colorado. In *Porcupine Cave, South Park: Biodiversity through time,* ed. T. Barnosky, chap. 2. Berkeley: University of California Press.

Cooper, S. V., K. E. Neiman, and D. W. Roberts. 1991. Forest habitat types of northern Idaho: A second approximation. General Technical Report INT-236. Ogden, Utah: U.S. Department of Agriculture, Forest Service, Intermountain Research Station.

DeByle, N. V., and R. Winokur, eds. 1985. *Aspen: Ecology and management in the western United States.* General Technical Report RM-119. Fort Collins, Colo.: U.S. Department of Agriculture, Forest Service, Rocky Mountain Forest and Range Experiment Station.

Emerick, J. C. 1995. *Rocky Mountain National Park natural history handbook.* Niwot, Colo.: Roberts Rinehart.

Evans, D. M., and D. M. Finch. 1994. Relationships between forest songbird populations and managed forests in Idaho. In *Sustainable ecological systems: Implementing an ecological approach to land management,* coord. W. W. Covington and L. F. DeBano, 308–314. General Technical Report RM-247. Fort Collins, Colo.: U.S. Department of Agriculture, Forest Service, Rocky Mountain Forest and Range Experiment Station.

Finch, D. M. 1992. *Threatened, endangered, and vulnerable species of terrestrial vertebrates in the Rocky Mountain region.* General Technical Report RM-215. Fort Collins, Colo.: U.S. Department of Agriculture, Forest Service, Rocky Mountain Forest and Range Experiment Station.

Goldblum, D., and T. T. Veblen. 1992. Fire history of a ponderosa pine/Douglas-fir forest in the Colorado Front Range. *Physical Geography* 13:133–148.

Gruell, G. E. 1983. *Fire and vegetative trends in the northern Rockies: Interpretations from 1871–1982 photographs.* General Technical Report INT-158. Ogden, Utah: U.S. Department of Agriculture, Forest Service, Intermountain Forest and Range Experiment Station.

———. 1985. Indian fires in the interior West: A widespread influence. In *Proceedings: Symposium and workshop on wilderness fire,* ed. J. E. Lotan, 68–74. General Technical Report INT-GTR-182. Ogden, Utah: U.S. Department of Agriculture, Forest Service, Intermountain Research Station.

Hadley, K. S., and T. T. Veblen. 1993. Stand response to western spruce budworm and Douglas fir bark beetle outbreaks, Colorado Front Range. *Canadian Journal of Forest Research* 23:479–491.

Hart, J. H., and D. L. Hart. 2001. Heartrot fungi's role in creating picid nesting sites in living aspen. In *Sustaining Aspen in Western Landscapes: Symposium proceedings,* ed. W. Shepperd, D. Binkley, D. L. Bartos, T. J. Stohlgren, and L. G. Eskew, 207–213. Proceedings RMRS-P-18. Fort Collins, Colo.: U.S. Department of Agriculture, Forest Service, Rocky Mountain Research Station.

Hayward, D. G., and J. Verner, eds. 1994. *Flammulated, boreal, and great gray owls in the United States: A technical conservation assessment.* General Technical Report RM-253. Fort Collins, Colo.: U.S. Department of Agriculture, Forest Service, Rocky Mountain Forest and Range Experiment Station.

Hessl, A. E., and W. L. Baker. 1997a. Spruce and fir regeneration and climate in the forest-tundra ecotone of Rocky Mountain National Park, Colorado, U.S.A. *Arctic and Alpine Research* 29:173–183.

———. 1997b. Spruce-fir growth form changes in the forest-tundra ecotone of Rocky Mountain National Park, Colorado, USA. *Ecography* 20:356–367.

Jack, J. G. 1899. *Pikes Peak, Plum Creek, and South Platte Reserves: Twentieth annual report of the United States Geological Survey to the secretary of the interior, 1898–1899.* Washington, D.C.: U.S. Government Printing Office.

Johnson, E. A., G. I. Fryer, and M. J. Heathcott. 1990. The influence of man and climate on frequency of fire in the interior wet belt forest, British Columbia. *Journal of Ecology* 78:403–412.

Keane, R. E., S. F. Arno, and J. K. Brown. 1990. Simulating cumulative fire effects in ponderosa pine/Douglas-fir forests. *Ecology* 7:189–203.

Kipfmueller, K. F. 1997. A fire history of a subalpine forest in southeastern Wyoming. Master's thesis, University of Wyoming, Laramie.

Knight, D. H. 1994. *Mountains and plains: The ecology of Wyoming landscapes.* New Haven, Conn.: Yale University Press.

Knight, D. H., F. W. Smith, S. W. Buskirk, W. H. Romme, and W. L. Baker, eds. 1999. *Forest fragmentation in the southern Rocky Mountains.* Boulder: University Press of Colorado.

Langner, L. L., and C. H. Flather. 1994. *Biological diversity: Status and trends in the United States.* General Technical Report RM-244. Fort Collins, Colo.: U.S. Department of Agriculture, Forest Service, Rocky Mountain Forest and Range Experiment Station.

Lavender, D. 1975. *The Rockies.* New York: Harper and Row.

Logan, J. A., and J. A. Powell. 2001. Ghost forests, global warming, and the mountain pine beetle (Coleoptera: Scolytidae). *American Entomologist* 47:160–173.

Loope, L. L., and G. E. Gruell. 1973. The ecological role of fire in Jackson Hole, northwestern Wyoming. *Quaternary Research* 3:425–443.

Malakoff, D. 1998. Restored wetlands flunk real-world test. *Science* 280:371–372.

Mueggler, W. F. 1993. Forage. In *Aspen: Ecology and management in the western United States,* ed. N. V. DeByle and R. P. Winokur, 129–134. General Technical Report RM-119. Fort Collins, Colo.: U.S. Department of Agriculture, Forest Service, Rocky Mountain Forest and Range Experiment Station.

Nordyke, K. A., and S. W. Buskirk. 1991. Southern red-backed vole, *Clethrionomys gapperi,* populations in relation to stand succession and old-growth character in the central Rocky Mountains. *Canadian Field-Naturalist* 105:330–334.

NRC (National Research Council). 1992. *Restoration of aquatic ecosystems.* Washington, D.C.: National Academy Press.

Peet, R. K. 1978. Forest vegetation of the Colorado Front Range: Patterns of species diversity. *Vegetatio* 37:65–78.

———. 1981. Forest vegetation of the Colorado Front Range. *Vegetatio* 45:3–75.

———. 1988. Forests of the Rocky Mountains. In *North American terrestrial vegetation,* ed. M. G. Barbour and W. D. Billings, 63–101. New York: Cambridge University Press.

Peters, E. F., and S. C. Bunting. 1994. Fire conditions pre- and post-occurrence of annual grasses on the Snake River plain. In *Proceedings: Ecology and Management of Annual Rangelands,* ed. S. B. Monsen and S. G. Kitchen, 31–36. General Technical Report INT-GTR-313. Ogden, Utah: U.S. Department of Agriculture, Forest Service, Intermountain Research Station.

Powell, D. S., J. L. Faulkner, D. R. Darr, Z. Zhu, and D. W. MacCleery. 1993. *Forest resources of the United States, 1992.* General Technical Report RM-234. Fort Collins, Colo.: U.S. Department of Agriculture, Forest Service, Rocky Mountain Forest and Range Experiment Station.

Quinn, R. D., and L. Wu. 2001. Quaking aspen reproduce from seed after wildfire in the mountains of southeastern Arizona. In *Sustaining Aspen in Western Landscapes: Symposium proceedings,* ed. W. Shepperd, D. Binkley, D. L. Bartos, T. J. Stohlgren, and L. G. Eskew, 369–376. Proceedings RMRS-P-18. Fort Collins, Colo.: U.S. Department of Agriculture, Forest Service, Rocky Mountain Research Station.

Regan, C. M. 1998. Characteristics of old-growth mixed conifer forests in a southwestern landscape. Ph.D. diss., Colorado State University.

Romme, W. H. 1982. Fire and landscape diversity in Yellowstone National Park. *Ecological Monographs* 52:199–221.

Romme, W. H., L. Floyd-Hanna, and D. D. Hanna. 2001. Aspen's ecological role in the West. In *Sustaining Aspen in Western Landscapes: Symposium proceedings,* ed. W. Shepperd, D. Binkley, D. L. Bartos, T. J. Stohlgren, and L. G. Eskew, 243–260. Proceedings RMRS-P-18. Fort Collins, Colo.: U.S. Department of Agriculture, Forest Service, Rocky Mountain Research Station.

Romme, W., and D. H. Knight. 1981. Fire frequency and subalpine forest succession along a topographic gradient in Wyoming. *Ecology* 62:319–326.

Simonson, S., P. A. Opler, T. J. Stohlgren, and G. W. Chong. 2001. Rapid assessment of butterfly diversity in a montane landscape. *Biodiversity and Conservation* 10:1369–1386.

Singer, F. 1995. *Bighorn sheep: Our living resources.* Washington, D.C.: U.S. Department of the Interior, National Biological Service.

Smith, W., and P. Lee, eds. 2000. *Canada's forests at a crossroads: An assessment in the year 2000.* Global Forest Watch Canada Report. Washington, D.C.: World Resources Institute. On-line at <http://www.globalforestwatch.org>.

SREP (Southern Rockies Ecosystem Project). 2000. *The state of the southern Rockies ecoregion.* Nederland, Colo.: Southern Rockies Ecosystem Project. On-line at <http://csf.colorado.edu/srep>.

Stohlgren, T. J. 1999. The Rocky Mountains. In *Status and trends of the nation's biological resources,* ed. M. J. Mac, P. A. Opler, C. E. Puckett, K. C. Haecker, and P. D. Doran, vol. 2, 473–504. Reston, Va.: U.S. Geological Survey, Biological Resources Division.

Sudworth, G. B. 1899. White River Plateau Timber Land Reserve. In *Forest Reserves,* 117–179, pt. V of *Twentieth annual report of the United States Geological Survey.* Washington, D.C.: U.S. Government Printing Office.

Swetnam, T. W., and A. M. Lynch. 1993. Multi-century, regional-scale patterns of western spruce budworm outbreaks. *Ecological Monographs* 63:399–424.

Thompson, D. Q., R. L. Stuckey, and E. B. Thompson. 1987. *Spread, impact, and control of purple loosestrife (Lythrum salicaria) in North America wetlands.* USDI Fish and Wildlife Service Research 2. Washington, D.C.: U.S. Department of the Interior, U.S. Fish and Wildlife Service.

Tomback, D. F., S. F. Arno, and R. E. Keane, eds. 2001. *Whitebark pine communities: Ecology and restoration.* Washington, D.C.: Island Press.

Veblen, T. T., K. S. Hadley, E. M. Nel, T. Kitzberger, M. Reid, and R. Villalba. 1994. Disturbance regime and disturbance interactions in a Rocky Mountain subalpine forest. *Journal of Ecology* 82:125–135.

Veblen, T. T., K. S. Hadley, M. S. Reid, and A. J. Rebertus. 1991. Stand response to spruce beetle outbreak in Colorado subalpine forests. *Ecology* 72:213–231.

Veblen, T. T., T. Kitzberger, and J. Donnegan. 1996. *Fire ecology in the wildland/urban interface of Boulder County.* Report to the City of Boulder Open Space Department, Boulder, Colorado.

Veblen, T. T., and D. C. Lorenz. 1991. *The Colorado Front Range: A century of ecological change.* Salt Lake City: University of Utah Press.

White, C. A., C. E. Olmsted, and C. E. Kay. 1998. Aspen, elk, and fire in Rocky Mountain national parks of North America. *Wildlife Society Bulletin* 26:449–462.

Windell, J. T., B. E. Willard, D. J. Cooper, S. Q. Foster, C. F. Knud-Hansen, L. P. Rink, and G. N. Kiladis. 1986. *An ecological characterization of Rocky Mountain montane and subalpine wetlands.* Biological Report 86 (11). Washington, D.C.: U.S. Department of the Interior, U.S. Fish and Wildlife Service, Division of Wildlife and Contaminant Research, National Ecology Center.

CHAPTER 11

Base Camps of the Rockies:
The Intermountain Grasslands

Timothy R. Seastedt

▲

The intermountain grasslands of the Rocky Mountain region are a composite of prairie grasslands, shrublands, and savannas. The literature clearly indicates that there were many types of intermountain grassland, but little remains today because of extensive settlement and grazing use. The shortgrass steppe and mixed grass prairies reached the Rockies from the east. The desert grasslands intercept the Rockies from the south, and the intermountain grasslands, also called the shrub-steppe, are found both within the larger valleys and plateaus of the Rocky Mountains and to the west of this region (figure 11.1; Risser et al. 1981; Brown 1985; Sims and Risser 2000; West and Young 2000). Small pockets of mountain grassland, usually associated with ponderosa pine forest, collectively occupied an additional 24 million hectares (ha), or 60 million acres, of land (Risser et al. 1981). All of these distinct grasslands contributed to the flora of the intermountain grasslands, making the extended intermountain grassland region floristically very rich by North American standards.

The intermountain grasslands have experienced the greatest extent of environmental transformation of any ecosystem type in the Rocky Mountain region. Settlers deliberately replaced the dominant native plants and animals with their own favorites, and in the process they brought along some serious Euro-trash, a plethora of undesirable weeds (Mack 1986, 1989). Not only were resident species harmed by these intrusions; those species that made only seasonal use of the bottomland corridors also suffered. The wholesale modification of this integral part of the Rocky Mountain system has altered the entire region in very important ways.

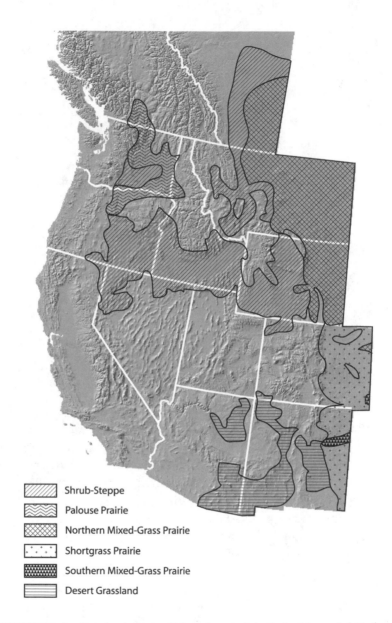

Shrub-Steppe
Palouse Prairie
Northern Mixed-Grass Prairie
Shortgrass Prairie
Southern Mixed-Grass Prairie
Desert Grassland

FIGURE 11.1 *Grassland Areas within and around the Rocky Mountains.* Redrawn from maps in Risser et al. 1981 and Sims and Risser 2000.

Managing the vegetation . . . so that it reflects presettlement conditions is a goal that may be impossible once certain introduced species become established. (Knight 1994, 105)

The introduced species referred to in the quote are nonindigenous plants. However, the Euro-American settlers themselves perhaps best epitomize the statement. These individuals were introduced into the bottomlands and intermountain plains during the mid- to late nineteenth century. Euro-American settlement has comprised a progression of trappers, miners, ranchers, and recreationists and the "support groups" required to maintain all the above. By the time the current populations of tourists, owners of second homes, and retirees arrived in the Rockies, the intermountain flora of the region had long since been substantially altered (Mack 1986).

In this chapter I briefly describe the intermountain grasslands and document how human-generated modifications have altered the region. I then attempt to show that the current suite of environmental issues interact to produce the current ecological status of these areas. I argue that the remaining bottomlands are a synthetic product of human interventions that have collectively transformed the preexisting landscape. Conservation efforts within these areas therefore require a proactive suite of rehabilitation techniques. True restoration of intermountain grasslands is probably ecologically and economically infeasible. However, retention and enhancement of desirable biotic assemblages with a matrix of synthetic landscapes can be fostered.

The Presettlement Valleys and Intermountain Plains

Prairies, even when located adjacent to mountains, seem to get little respect.

Those residing in the more populous parts of the country often have regarded the region as an unused wasteland roamed only by a few cowboys, miners, and shepherds, and where "nuisance" activities such as military research and training, electricity-generating stations, and nuclear wastes might be placed. (West 1988, 227)

Rogers and Rickard (1988) suggest this bias began with the earliest Euro-American visitors. Meriwether Lewis and William Clark and subsequent explorers first moved through the intermountain areas in midsummer. The growing season was over, and what they saw was a brown and—compared with spring on the Great Plains—barren landscape. Although these lands were not the Great American Desert, they apparently held similarities. Nonetheless, by the 1880s extensive homesteading had followed the railroads into the area (Rogers and Rickard 1988). The lowland intermountain areas may not have been pretty in late summer, but the fact that they could support cattle quickly became known.

The Great Plains had the honor of being "the inland sea of grass," but the intermountain grassland region was the largest expanse of grassland in North America (figure 11.1; Risser et al. 1981). Grassland purists, however, may protest, given that the region included landscapes dominated not only by grasses but also by sagebrush and other shrubs. Bluebunch steppe was dominated by a mixture of bluebunch wheatgrass and sagebrush (Joern and Keeler 1995). The vegetation of the valley bottoms and plains interdigitating among the various mountain ranges included grasslands, savannas, shrublands, and even deserts. No clear boundaries between these ecosystems are offered here, and probably none ever existed.

Within this heterogeneous mix of grasslands and shrublands, a single true prairie, the Palouse prairie, was found in southwestern Canada, eastern Washington and Oregon, southwestern Idaho, and western Montana (Sims and Risser 2000). A major feature that distinguished the Palouse prairie from other North American grasslands was the seasonal pattern of precipitation (Stoddart 1941). The Palouse region receives only 30%–50% of annual rainfall during the growing season; grasslands in the Great Plains receive a higher fraction of rainfall during this interval. Low summer rainfall favors cool-season grasses—bluebunch wheatgrass (*Agropyron spicatum*) in the western and southern areas and Idaho fescue (*Festuca idahoensis*) along the eastern and northern boundaries (Humphrey 1945). Along with June grass, needlegrass, and Sandberg bluegrass, these grasses constituted at least 85% of the plant cover. Sagebrush, rabbit brush, annual bromes, and fescues made up no more than 5% of the original cover.

The Palouse prairie was clearly a grassland at the time of Euro-American discovery. Brown (1985) noted that the word *prairie* is French for lawn, which suggests a true grassland, something very different from the sagebrush-rich landscape reported for other intermountain areas. The dominance by cool-season grasses would explain the brown, senescent grasses found by the early explorers in mid- to late summer. The Palouse prairie was generated in part by the presence of particularly fine-textured and fertile soils generated by volcanic activity or from lake sediments deposited by Pleistocene epoch Lake Missoula. The fertile soils were desirable for conversion to croplands, and the area has been largely transformed by cultivation, grazing, and introductions of nonindigenous species (Mack 1981, Sims and Risser 2000, West 1988).

On the eastern slopes of the Rockies, sagebrush dominates much of the Wyoming landscape, with grasslands interwoven, depending on soil texture and moisture availability (Knight 1994). Elsewhere on the eastern boundaries of the mountains, shortgrass and mixed grass prairies extend up the foothills of the mountains. Remarkably, a thin 322 kilometer (km), or 200 mile (mi.), swath of tallgrass prairie with the same dominant plant species found in Iowa, big bluestem, extended from about the Wyoming border down the Colorado Front Range of the southern Rockies. Rainfall along these foothills is about 50 centimeters (cm), or 20 inches (in.), less than an amount believed necessary to support these species, and it appears the tallgrass prairie is a relic from the end of the last ice age. When rainfall in the area decreased, the species were able to persist because of the particularly rocky soils that formed from glacial debris (Livingston 1952; Branson, Miller, and McQueen 1965). These soils can hold water deeper in the soil, a factor that favored the tallgrass species. Spring runoff may have flood-irrigated bottomlands to provide additional water to this community. Like the Palouse prairie, the fertile bottomland soils that supported tallgrass prairie were, for the most part, quickly converted to agricultural lands. Subsequently, the eastern slopes became the largest urban and suburban development adjacent to the Rockies.

Farther south and west, the black grama desert grasslands intermix with the Great Basin shrublands. Vegetation is strongly influenced by soil surface assemblages of bacteria, lichens, and mosses. These crusts are known by many names, including cryptogamic, microbiotic, and microphytic crust. Soil texture, pH, and moisture determine the presence or absence of a crust, and the importance of these ancient organisms cannot be overstated. The crusts function much like grass roots, holding the soil together and preventing surface erosion from summer thunderstorms and winter winds. The presence of crusts attests to the general absence of large grazers in these regions. Foot traffic by both cattle and humans significantly reduces the extent and functioning of the crusts, and trampling damages both the biota and soils of these sites (West 1990; Belnap 1993).

Presettlement intermountain grasslands were characterized by moderate to frequent fire intervals. Variables of topography, climate, and vegetational lifeform influence fire return intervals (chapter 7). Smaller, more isolated valleys probably had a lower fire frequency than large expanses of prairie. The relatively moist eastern side of the Rockies in Colorado had surface (grass) fire return intervals as high as once every 7–12 years (Veblen 1996). This interval lengthened to once every 80 years in the sagebrush-dominated steppe in Utah (Whisenant 1990). Wright and Bailey (1982) and others suggest that fire return intervals for the relatively low-fuel and rough-topography areas of the Wyoming plains were around 25–30 years. The cooler and cloudier climates of the northwestern intermountain grasslands particularly favored the development and persistence of grass-dominated ecosystems with high fire frequency. The Hanford Ecological Research site, a reserve in eastern Washington, experienced four wildfires in a 20-year period from the 1950s to the 1970s (Rogers and Rickard 1988). Thus, the intermountain grasslands, like grasslands elsewhere in North America, were both created and maintained by recurring fires.

Much of the vegetation of the western intermountain region and Great Basin apparently had no large ungulate grazers for the past 12,000 years (Rogers and Rickard 1988). The dominant plant species of shortgrass and mixed grass prairies to the east of the Rockies were much more tolerant of grazing by large ungulates (Mack and Thompson 1982). Pronghorn constituted the only common large grazer in the Great Basin; elk and mule deer functioned as browsers, feeding mostly on herbaceous and woody plants.

The top carnivores, wolves, and the top omnivores, grizzly bears, inhabited the valley bottoms and plains adjacent to the Rockies to a great extent, just as they now occupy these areas in Yellowstone National Park. All of the large terrestrial mammals in the Rocky Mountains used elevational gradients to extend the season of high-quality food supplies (Klein 1970). By following snowmelt from the valley floor to the alpine reaches, deer, elk, and, along the eastern side of the Rockies, bison, benefited from the extended spring flush of vegetative growth. Predators and omnivores followed the grazers. Certain species, such as gophers (*Thomomys talpoides*), inhabit a very wide distribution of ecosystem types. Species such as gophers can be periodically eradicated from individual communities as a result of a variety of mortality factors, but populations are reestablished by emigration from adjacent communities. Thus, from the perspective of many of the dominant species, the plains to the alpine regions often formed a single "home," not a series of distinct ecosystems.

The Transformation of the Intermountain Lowlands

Natural, recurring disturbances to the intermountain grasslands include fire, drought, cold snaps, flood scour in lower areas, insect outbreaks, and, at smaller scales, burrowing by prairie dogs, ground squirrels, and gophers. These natural disturbances influenced the evolution of the biological systems within this region; species were adapted to the natural range and frequency of these disturbance events. Recall, however, that these species have colonized or recolonized the intermountain area only since the end of the last glaciation. Thus, although many of the plants and animals may have coevolved in a similar environment elsewhere, their establishment and present distribution within the Rockies region is a fairly recent phenomenon. Human alterations and species introductions over the past few centuries have substantially altered the natural range and frequencies of disturbances, and this has affected native biological systems.

Native Americans had horses for perhaps 100–200 years before Euro-American settlement, and horse herds may have modified intermountain grasslands to a limited extent before the arrival of cattle. With settlement, new disturbances occurred to the grasslands. Plowing, irrigation, hay mowing, domestic grazing, road building, and the soil disturbances associated with human habitations were added to the list of natural grassland disturbances. Settlers attempted to remove two natural disturbances, fire and flooding. Ironically, catastrophic events late in the twentieth century attest to the success of those efforts. Fire suppression resulted in accumulation of fuel loads, which contributed to widespread fires in 1988 and 2000. Channeling and levy construction successfully contain all but the largest of floods. However, life-threatening flash floods along the Colorado Front Range as well as major flooding in the Great Plains and the Pacific Northwest have demonstrated the flaws in current water containment strategies. The intermountain region may soon experience temperature and moisture regimes outside nominal ranges, and concentrations of carbon dioxide (CO_2), nitrate (NO_3^-), and ammonium (NH_4^+) in atmospheric inputs already exceed—in some cases greatly exceed—levels experienced prior to Euro-American settlement. Although the effects of all these changes can be discussed individually, species and ecological communities respond to the composite interaction of these changes. The intermountain grasslands are the recipient of multiple stressors. We should expect large changes in the species composition and functional activity of these regions.

Invasive Nonindigenous Species

The introduction of many plant species to this region was deliberate and mostly beneficial to the human inhabitants. Horses, cattle, and sheep appeared to thrive in what was previously a much less intensively grazed grassland. Selective grazing of the palatable species soon took a toll. Among the ecological consequences of heavy selective grazing were increased dominance of less preferred plant species, such as sagebrush. This might have been the worst-case scenario except that a group of Eurasian plant species exploited the vacuum created by overgrazing. The intermountain grasslands now provide textbook examples of environmental problems associated with invasions by nonindigenous plant species (figure 11.2).

Even in the parts of the West where bison had toughened native vegetation to the depredations of livestock, the aridity of the region and mismanagement of cattle and sheep still led to degraded land. In the bison-free intermountain West, land suffered worse yet. In 40 or 50 years, cattle reduced much of the region's robust grasslands to gaunt shadows of what they were formerly. Sometimes cattle left little but dirt in their wake. Or to put it another way, cattle turned much of the intermountain West into cheatgrass heaven. (Devine 1998, 57)

The Eurasian *Bromus tectorum,* downy brome or cheatgrass, arrived in the United States in the late nineteenth century (Mack 1981). Two preeminent ecologists of the twentieth century, Aldo Leopold, a wildlife biologist, and W. Dwight Billings, a plant physiologist, were struck by the ability of cheatgrass to exclude other plants and, by its presence, impoverish the biotic diversity of areas where it has become abundant (Leopold 1949, Billings 1990).

Cheatgrass is an annual grass; it completes its life cycle from seed to flowering plant to seed in a single year. The grass often germinates in fall, and its roots may continue to grow in unfrozen soils throughout much of the winter. The plant quickly flowers and sets seed in the spring. This growth strategy effectively preempts certain other plants from obtaining needed water. It is unusual to find a single species that can function as both a good invader and a good competitor and is capable of maintaining itself through many generations within a single area. Ecological studies have generally shown that change or

FIGURE 11.2 *Invasive Bindweed, Cheatgrass, and Diffuse Knapweed Competing for a Patch of Prairie in the Colorado Front Range.* A native species, western wheatgrass, surrounds this patch of weeds. A previous disturbance to the soil by machinery is responsible for the weed patch, but all three species are now common in so-called undisturbed prairie as well. Photograph by Timothy R. Seastedt.

succession in plant communities involves a progression of plant species with one or more known end points that usually involve species not present during the earlier stages. During this process, soils are modified, usually increasing in organic matter content and total nutrient reserves. Cheatgrass monocultures, however, do not undergo succession, nor do the underlying soils. Cheatgrass is therefore an apparent exception to the rule of ecological succession. Cheatgrass may share this characteristic with other invasive weeds, such as the knapweeds (LeJeune and Seastedt 2001).

> Once cheatgrass becomes established on rangelands, it persists for decades and interferes with the reinvasion by the native perennial plants even when native taxa seed sources are adjacent. . . . The success of cheatgrass in eastern Washington . . . is attributable to its inherent genetic capacity to be stress tolerant, competitive and ruderal, depending upon the particular site. (Rickard and Vaughan 1988, 152)

Cheatgrass establishes itself in existing grasslands, using a strategy for rapid growth and resource exploitation, and then changes the rules that determine the outcome for subsequent competitors. Cheatgrass areas are fire-prone, and the grass very significantly alters the area's fire frequency. The fire return interval in southern Idaho and Utah drops from about 80 years to 4 years when cheatgrass becomes established (Whisenant 1990). Often, the extent of fires increases (Knapp 1997). Fires occur after the grass has set seed, and these seeds are not harmed and will germinate with autumn rains. In contrast, competing perennial grasses and shrubs lose substantial amounts of live biomass during the fires. The cheatgrass grows in fall and early spring, when the now-stressed competitive vegetation is largely dormant. Frequent fires maintain this successful life history strategy. Cheatgrass uses fire to keep the canopy open and maintain a nitrogen-poor soil during at least portions of the growing season, thus starving competitors, which become more vulnerable to the frequent fires (West 1988). Since cheatgrass itself can be harmed by nitrogen limitation, fire behavior is a two-edged sword that may be modified to the detriment of the invader.

A number of Eurasian knapweeds, including yellow star thistle, have also contributed to the transformation of much of the northern and western grasslands. Knapweeds are capable of both invading a site and persisting on it. To persist, these species may maintain the soil in a disturbed state (low carbon, high available nitrogen). Knapweeds have a high demand for phosphorus, another vital nutrient for plant growth, and can outcompete native species for phosphorus (LeJeune and Seastedt 2001). Unlike the native grasses these weeds replace, knapweeds produce taproots rather than fibrous roots and do a poor job of protecting the soil from erosion. The soil-building processes associated with grasslands are either halted or reversed, and soil fertility can be reduced. If the soil does not undergo succession, neither does the vegetation. Knapweeds and leafy spurge, another non-native invader, produce compounds that may inhibit the growth of other plants (Callaway and Aschehoug 2000). Unpalatable secondary plant metabolites inhibit grazers such as cattle from feeding on the mature plants, but their effects on soil chemistry may also be significant.

> There is a tendency to denounce all alien invaders as undesirable and to see these invasions as punishment for our greed. Downy brome (cheatgrass), at least from a cattle rancher's point of view, is not absolutely bad. (Brown 1985, 80)

The ecological services (benefits to other species, including humans) provided by an invasive species are sometimes well below those provided by the native plants they replace, but invasive weeds still provide more positive ecosystem services than do most suburban lawns. Evans and Evans (1991) found something good to say about Russian thistle (the "tumbling tumbleweed" of the old cowboy song). Although "these are pestiferous weeds of the worst kind," the authors point out, "when the first shoots appear above the ground, in the spring or after a summer shower, they are tender and succulent. Many a pioneer, supplies exhausted, has survived on them until other food became available" (p. 131). If noxious weeds were more palatable, we would probably call them crops.

Most noxious weeds obtain their name because they reduce the profit margin of agricultural activities. However, an additional undesired and often unrecognized consequence is loss of biodiversity (Vitousek et al. 1996). Not only are native plants replaced, but there may also be associated loss of wildlife and beneficial microbes. The focus on only a subset of invasive species, the noxious weeds, may be inappropriate. Grasslands along the foothills of the eastern Rockies by Boulder, Colorado, are now reported to have about 40% non-native plant species cover (Barrett 1997). Much effort is spent in attempting to control the noxious weed component of these invasives, but many non-native species, such as Kentucky bluegrass and smooth brome, are not controlled. These non-native species are achieving dominance over native species in many areas. Ultimately, these species—and not the noxious weeds—may replace the native dominants.

Hobbs and Humphries (1995) put this problem into perspective. Most non-indigenous species are unlikely to threaten native biodiversity. Threats by invasive species are probably site specific. A species is unlikely to be a threat to biodiversity over its entire range or in diverse habitats within various communities (or, conversely, certain species are better competitors and limit the effects of the invader). Hobbs and Humphries conclude that a focus on the ecosystem and its management is equally as important as an understanding of the population biology of the invader. Collectively, research is desperately needed to identify the true threats to native biodiversity, not just those species causing economic harm to agroindustry. It is possible that invaders in combination have properties not observed singly. And collectively, invaders plus fire suppression, habitat fragmentation, flood control, and air pollution may be able to transform native communities in much the same manner as noxious weeds (Simberloff and Von Holle 1999).

Modification of Fire Return Intervals

The current intermountain grasslands contain areas where fire frequency has increased as a result of invasion by grasses such as cheatgrass. The conversion of sagebrush-dominated areas to cheatgrass is one of the few examples of "grasslandification" found in North America. Additional examples due to nonindigenous invasive species can be found in Hawaii, Arizona, and northern Mexico. More commonly, however, fire frequency has been reduced as a result of human activities. Removal of vegetation associated with crop production produces effective barriers to the spread of fire. Fuel reduction by intensive grazing is also very effective in reducing fire frequencies or the spatial extent of fires. This is particularly true in areas where late-summer thunderstorms are common. Road building and other fragmentation activities put barriers on the widespread movement of fires.

Besides directly affecting survivorship, fire greatly alters the relative abundance of resources to plants (see, e.g., Knapp et al. 1998). The relative availability and absolute amounts of light, nutrients, and water are changed. Fire suppression therefore changes competitive relationships. Those plants not adapted to fire increase in abundance, and if fire is suppressed for a long enough period, the community is altered to the point at which fire may not function effectively as a renewal agent.

Grasses usually are not killed by fires, even those that occur during the growing season. However, with sufficient periods of fire suppression, grasses are replaced by woody species. With time, grass propagules in the soil are lost. A fire may kill the woody species, but if the seed bank does not contain the preexisting grass species, grasses obviously cannot regenerate.

Fire return cycles provide an example of a natural disturbance frequency. Once fire suppression exceeds this frequency, ecosystems can surpass their historical range of variation (chapter 7; Swanson et al. 1993; Wallin, Swanson, and Marks 1994; Wallin et al. 1996). For example, with 100 years of fire suppression in the Colorado Front Range that had an average 10-year return frequency, the system exceeded its historical range of variation tenfold. In contrast, many subalpine mountain forests had fire return intervals of 200–400 years, so some areas are still not outside their historical range of variability. From a fire suppression standpoint, therefore, the grassland areas are potentially the most altered ecosystems found in the Rockies.

The grassland-shrubland biotic communities that form under extended periods of fire suppression are very different from presettlement communities. Add the nonindigenous species to this combination and the changes are potentially even greater. Suppression of fires has therefore triggered a variety of atypical successional responses that are essentially new and synthetic communities that did not exist prior to Euro-American settlement.

Climate and Atmospheric Change

Moderate temperature and moisture fluctuations around a long-term mean are unlikely to have major effects on grasslands (Seastedt et al. 1994). This is because the dominant species are well adapted to climatic extremes (Knapp and Seastedt 1998). Native plants that are dominants in drier regions become dominant in areas that historically were wetter if the climate becomes drier, and vice versa under wetter conditions (Knapp and Seastedt 1998). Trends in temperature regimes may, however, alter the competitive relationships among plant species (Alward, Detling, and Milchunas 1999), and this becomes a more urgent problem in the presence of invasive plant species. Interactions of climate change with other changes in grassland disturbance may, in fact, be very significant. Effects of one stressor may be amplified by the presence of another.

Atmospheric chemistry changes are potentially much more significant to plant species composition than are changes in temperature and moisture. The intermountain grasslands are composed of a mix of species that are differentially responsive to CO_2 concentrations. Thus, increases in amounts of CO_2 will change the competitive relationships among species. The amount of atmospheric nitrogen that plants can readily use for growth greatly increased in the last few decades of the twentieth century. Current intermountain grasslands often have low-acidity (high-pH) soils and lots of cows. The result can be a plume of ammonia (NH_3) that is emitted from soil, mixes with rainfall, and returns to Earth as fertilizer. Cows in feedlots produce so much manure that soils, regardless of their initial chemistry, will not hold this nitrogen. Automobiles, trucks, trains, heavy construction and farm machinery, and many power plants release substantial amounts of nitrogen oxides (NO_x) that also add fertilizer. Together, these sources contribute to increased deposition of atmospheric nitrogen. Small amounts function to stimulate plant growth, but larger amounts cause undesirable changes in soil and water characteristics. Again, the abundance of nitrogen can change the rules that determine the dominant plants within a community.

For example, the addition of nitrogen to grassland plant communities has been shown to increase the presence and densities of exotic plants (Lauenroth, Dodd, and Simms 1978; Hobbs et al. 1988; Wedin and Tilman 1996).

Habitat Destruction and Fragmentation

The intermountain grasslands represent by far the most fragmented component of the Rocky Mountains. When big pieces are made into little pieces, the rules governing plant species composition are changed. By definition, fragmentation creates more borders per unit area of ecosystem. Fragmentation changes local microclimate and hydrology (Saunders, Hobbs, and Margules 1991). With every new road and trail, a new, usually warmer and drier, microhabitat is generated. Water availability increases adjacent to paths; thus, the disturbance is measurable beyond the zone of direct vegetation disturbance. Preexisting vegetation may not be adapted to the changes in climate and soil moisture, and the consequences are fairly consistent. Edges become zones where early successional species, including invasive species, are found. Once established, even natural disturbances, such as flood scours, fires, and gopher mounds, become potential entryways for nonindigenous species to invade otherwise healthy fragments. Fragmentation also provides barriers that reduce the spread of fire.

Fragmentation affects species immigration, colonization, and extinction rates within grassland remnants (see, e.g., Collins and Glenn 1995). Densities of many native animal species are inversely related to the size of the remnants (Bock, Bock, and Bennett 1999). Almost all authors agree that as the size of native areas of grassland diminish and the distances between these fragments increase, losses of native species are almost certain.

A Future for Intermountain Grasslands?

The lands adjacent to and within the Rocky Mountain region were composed of a variety of grassland and shrubland community types that exhibited a unique biotic structure and high biotic diversity relative to adjacent forested areas. Ecosystem processes (energy flow and materials cycling) differed substantially from those of adjacent forests, with more biotic activity occurring in the soils rather than in the vegetation canopy. These ecosystems also had a unique historical range of variability with regard to specific disturbance events such as fire, flood, defoliation, and the like. The grasslands were the most likely of all Rocky Mountain ecosystems to experience fire and, in lowland meadows, flooding. The dominant species in this system were adapted to such disturbances.

The early settlers and their agronomic practices substantially altered the composition of the intermountain grasslands. Human transformation continues today in the most desirable and scenic areas as newcomers build on the remaining flat areas. Permanent human occupancy of intermountain valleys, foothills, and savannas provides the base camps for incursions to the more scenic montane and alpine regions of the Rockies. Urban and suburban development requires power, and the hydroelectric dams constructed in the 1930s have been supplemented with a regional grid of coal-burning power plants serving both local and distant sources. Coal and natural gas combustion, combined with the burning of fossil fuels by local industries and motor vehicles, releases substantial amounts of pollutants into the atmosphere.

The intermountain grasslands now represent the most human-influenced ecosystem of the Rocky Mountain region. Within the southern Rockies, only 5% of the more than 5 million ha (12 million acres) of grasslands and shrublands have protected status (SREP 2000). Once frequently burned, many areas have not experienced fire for more than a century. Once largely ungrazed or infrequently grazed, these same grasslands and shrublands have been exposed to chronic grazing for an equal or longer time. Species new to the continent have imposed their own characteristics on fire frequencies and soil chemistries, and in doing so they have altered the rules that govern the organization of grassland communities. Urban, suburban, and agricultural development have greatly fragmented the landscape. Fragmented areas are more likely to lose native species, more likely to be invaded by non-native species, and more likely to exhibit changes in biogeochemical characteristics that both influence and are influenced by the biota. Removal of many introduced species appears neither ecologically or economically feasible.

Subsequent changes to the intermountain grasslands will result from interactions among the components of global change, not necessarily from the direct effect of a single factor. Thus, the research questions confronting those who want the intermountain grasslands to function as a healthy, sustaining system are many and complex. What percentage of the species can persist with the combined changes induced by the interactions among fragmentation, disturbance, invasive species, and atmospheric and climate change? How can essential or desirable ecosystem services be maximized, given the current status and prognosis for human activities in this system?

The ecological variables such as recurring fire and limited grazing that were responsible for the original vegetation composition of the presettlement intermountain grasslands are unlikely to be restored to conditions that prevailed before Euro-American settlement. Thus, preservation, in a strict sense, is impossible, even if there existed pristine grasslands to preserve. However, some restoration and certainly rehabilitation of ecosystems is possible. A key management assumption is that if future landscapes resemble historical landscapes, there exists a higher likelihood of retaining native habitats, species, and ecological functions. To that end, appropriate use of fire and grazing (or, in many areas, the absence of grazing) in the intermountain regions is clearly important. From an ecosystem management perspective, we should attempt to maintain the dominant and keystone species, where they can be identified. Those species created the environment for the presettlement communities; they also create the microclimate in which the rare species can most likely exist. If we can maintain the historically dominant species and mimic historical disturbance activities, we quite likely can sustain the highest percentage of native species within these areas.

Acknowledgments

This chapter benefited from reviews by Jill S. Baron, Kate LeJeune, and Katie Suding. Support for the research summarized here was provided by National Science Foundation–Long-Term Ecological Research (NSF-LTER) grants and by additional funding to the author from the National Science Foundation and the U.S. Department of Agriculture.

References

Alward, R. D., J. K. Detling, and D. G. Milchunas. 1999. Grassland vegetation changes and nocturnal global warming. *Science* 283:229–231.

Barrett, B. C. 1997. Vegetation of the grasslands on the city of Boulder open space. Ph.D. diss., University of Colorado at Boulder.

Belnap, J. 1993. Recovery rates of cryptobiotic crusts: Inoculant use and assessment methods. *Great Basin Naturalist* 53:89–95.

Billings, W. D. 1990. *Bromus tectorum,* a biotic cause of ecosystem impoverishment in the Great Plains. In *The earth in transition: Patterns and processes of biotic impoverishment,* ed. G. M. Woodwell, 301–322. New York: Cambridge University Press.

Bock, C. E., J. H. Bock, and B. C. Bennett. 1999. Songbird abundance in grasslands at a suburban interface on the Colorado High Plains. In *Ecology and conservation of grassland birds of the Western Hemisphere,* ed. P. D. Vickery and J. R. Herkert, 131–136. Vol. 19 of *Studies in Avian Biology.* Camarillo, Calif.: Cooper Ornithological Society.

Branson, F. A., R. F. Miller, and I. S. McQueen. 1965. Plant communities and soil moisture relationships near Denver, Colorado. *Ecology* 46:311–319.

Brown, L. 1985. *Grasslands.* New York: Knopf.

Callaway, R. M., and E. T. Aschehoug. 2000. Invasive plants versus their new and old neighbors: A mechanism for exotic invasion. *Science* 290:521–523.

Collins, S. L., and S. M. Glenn. 1995. Grassland ecosystem and landscape dynamics. In *The changing prairie: North American grasslands,* ed. A. Joern and K. H. Keeler, 128–156. New York: Oxford University Press.

Devine, R. 1998. *Alien invasion: America's battle with non-native animals and plants.* Washington, D.C.: National Geographic Society.

Evans, H. E., and M. A. Evans. 1991. *Cache la Poudre: The natural history of a Rocky Mountain river.* Bolder: University Press of Colorado.

Hobbs, R. J., S. L. Gulmon, V. J. Hobbs, and H. A. Mooney. 1988. Effects of fertilizer addition and subsequent gopher disturbance on a serpentine annual grassland community. *Oecologia* 75:291–295.

Hobbs, R. J., and S. E. Humphries. 1995. An integrated approach to the ecology and management of plant invasions. *Conservation Biology* 9:761–770.

Humphrey, R. R. 1945. *Range condition: A classification of the Palouse grass type.* Portland, Oreg.: U.S. Department of Agriculture, Soil Conservation Service, Region 7.

Joern, A., and K. H. Keeler. 1995. Getting the lay of the land: Introducing North American native grasslands. In *The changing prairie: North American grasslands,* ed. A. Joern and K. H. Keeler, 11–24. New York: Oxford University Press.

Klein, D. R. 1970. Food selection by North American deer and their response to over-utilization of preferred plant species. In *Animal populations in relation to their food resources,* ed. A. Watson, 25–44. Oxford: Blackwell Scientific.

Knapp, A. K., J. M. Briggs, D. C. Hartnett, and S. C. Collins, eds. 1998. *Grassland dynamics: Long-term ecological research in tallgrass prairie.* New York: Oxford University Press.

Knapp, A. K., and T. R. Seastedt. 1998. Grasslands, Konza prairie, and long-term ecological research. In *Grassland dynamics: Long-term ecological research in tallgrass prairie,* ed. A. K. Knapp, J. M. Briggs, D. C. Hartnett, and S. C. Collins, 3–15. New York: Oxford University Press.

Knapp, P. A. 1997. Spatial characteristics of regional wildfire frequencies in intermountain West grass-dominated communities. *Professional Geographer* 49:39–51.

Knight, D. H. 1994. *Mountains and plains.* New Haven, Conn.: Yale University Press.

Lauenroth, W. K., J. L. Dodd, and P. L. Simms. 1978. The effects of water- and nitrogen-induced stresses on plant community structure in a semiarid grassland. *Oecologia* 36:211–222.

LeJeune, K. D., and T. R. Seastedt. 2001. *Centaurea* species: The forb that won the West. *Conservation Biology* 15:1568–1574.

Leopold, A. 1949. Cheat takes over. In *A Sand County almanac, and sketches here and there.* New York: Oxford University Press.

Livingston, R. B. 1952. Relict true prairie communities in central Colorado. *Ecology* 33:72–86.

Mack, R. N. 1981. Invasion of *Bromus tectorum* L. into western North America: An ecological chronicle. *AgroEcosystems* 7:145–165.

———. 1986. Alien plant invasion into the intermountain West: A case history. In *Ecology of biological invasions of North America and Hawaii,* ed. H. A. Mooney and J. A. Drade, 191–213. New York: Springer-Verlag.

———. 1989. Temperate grasslands vulnerable to biological invasions: Characteristics and consequences. In *Biological invasions: A global perspective,* ed. J. A. Drake, H. A. Mooney, F. di Castri, R. H. Groves, F. J. Krueger, M. Remjmanek, and M. Williams, 115–180. New York: Wiley.

Mack, R. N., and J. N. Thompson. 1982. Evolution in steppe with few large, hooved animals. *American Naturalist* 119:757–773.

Rickard, W. H., and B. E. Vaughan. 1988. Plant community characteristics and responses. In *Shrub-steppe: Balance and change in a semi-arid terrestrial ecosystem,* ed. W. H. Rickard, L. E. Rogers, B. E. Vaughan, and S. F. Liebetrau, 106–180. Amsterdam: Elsevier Science.

Risser, P. G., E. C. Birney, H. D. Blocker, S. W. May, W. J. Parton, and J. A. Wiens. 1981. *The true prairie ecosystem.* Stroudsburg, Penn.: Hutchinson Ross.

Rogers, L. E., and W. H. Rickard. 1988. Introduction: Shrub-steppe lands. In *Shrub-steppe: Balance and change in a semi-arid terrestrial ecosystem,* ed. W. H. Rickard, L. E. Rogers, B. E. Vaughan, and S. F. Liebetrau, 1–12. Amsterdam: Elsevier Science.

Saunders, D. A., R. J. Hobbs, and C. R. Margules. 1991. Biological consequences of ecosystem fragmentation: A review. *Conservation Biology* 5:18–32.

Seastedt, T. R., C. C. Coxwell, D. S. Ojima, and W. J. Parton. 1994. Controls of plant and soil carbon in a semihumid temperate grassland. *Ecological Applications* 4:344–353.

Simberloff, D., and B. Von Holle. 1999. Positive interactions of nonindigenous species: Invasional meltdown? *Biological Invasions* 1:21–32.

Sims, P. L., and P. G. Risser. 2000. Grasslands. In *North American terrestrial vegetation,* 2nd ed., ed. M. B. Barbour and W. D. Billings, 323–356. Cambridge: Cambridge University Press.

SREP (Southern Rockies Ecosystem Project). 2000. *The state of the southern Rockies ecoregion.* Nederland, Colo.: Southern Rockies Ecosystem Project. On-line at <http://csf.colorado.edu/srep>.

Stoddart, L. A. 1941. The Palouse grassland association of northern Utah. *Ecology* 22:158–163.

Swanson, F. J., J. A. Jones, D. O. Wallin, and J. H. Cissel. 1993. Natural variability: Implications for ecosystem management. In *Eastside forest ecosystem health assessment,* ed. M. E. Jensen and P. S. Bourgeron, 89–106. Vol. 2 of *Ecosystem management: Principles and applications.* PNW-GTR-318. Portland, Oreg.: U.S. Department of Agriculture, Forest Service, Pacific Northwest Research Station.

Veblen, T. 1996. *Fire ecology in the wildland/urban interface of Boulder County.* Report to the City of Boulder Open Space Department, Boulder, Colorado.

Vitousek, P. M., C. M. D'Antonio, L. L. Loope, and R. Westbrooks. 1996. Biological invasions as global environmental change. *American Scientist* 84:468–478.

Wallin, D. O., F. J. Swanson, and B. Marks. 1994. Landscape pattern response to changes in pattern generalization rules: Land-use legacies in forestry. *Ecological Applications* 4:569–580.

Wallin, D. O., F. J. Swanson, B. Marks, J. H. Cissel, and J. Kertis. 1996. Comparison of managed and pre-settlement landscapes dynamics in forests of the Pacific Northwest, USA. *Forest Ecology and Management* 85:291–309.

Wedin, D., and D. Tilman. 1996. Influence of nitrogen loading and species composition on the carbon balance of grasslands. *Science* 274:1720–1723.

West, N. E. 1988. Intermountain deserts, shrub steppes, and woodlands. In *North American terrestrial vegetation,* ed. M. B. Barbour and W. D. Billings, 209–230. Cambridge: Cambridge University Press.

———. 1990. Structure and function of soil microphytic crusts in wildland ecosystems of arid and semiarid regions. *Advances in Ecological Research* 20:179–223.

West, N. E., and J. A. Young. 2000. Intermountain valleys and lower mountain slopes. In *North American terrestrial vegetation,* 2nd ed., ed. M. B. Barbour and W. D. Billings, 255–284. Cambridge: Cambridge University Press.

Whisenant, S. G. 1990. *Changing fire frequencies on Idaho's Snake River plains: Ecological and management implications.* General Technical Report INT-276. Ogden, Utah: U.S. Department of Agriculture, Forest Service, Intermountain Research Station.

Wright, H. A., and A. W. Bailey. 1982. *Fire ecology.* New York: Wiley.

PART IV

CASE STUDIES

▲

From Alberta to New Mexico, the Rocky Mountain region displays a consistent theme of rapid human population growth and land use change in valleys, amid an extensive matrix of wild, rugged uplands. However, there are substantial regional permutations and variations on this theme, from Banff in the north to Santa Fe in the south. The Rockies have gone through a period in which economies were sustained by natural resource development, the topic of chapter 5. Some parts of the Rockies are still in this mode; others have moved into a postextraction economy wherein natural processes are being restored and growth planning is incorporating ecological knowledge and tools. The examples that follow describe four parts of the Rocky Mountains and how each region is (or is not) addressing ecological integrity. In northern New Mexico, a kaleidoscope of peoples and agencies are coming together to restore fire and natural hydrologic flow regimes (chapter 12). In the resort community of Summit County, Colorado, a geographic information systems (GIS) tool that locates and describes important wildlife habitat is being applied to county planning (chapter 13). The Flathead Lake country of Montana and British Columbia is remarkably ecologically intact, although introduced non-native species are making an inroad into this complex system. Chapter 14, about the Flathead River valley, clearly shows the connectedness of the entire basin, emphasizing that the aquatic ecosystem provides essential resources for terrestrial ecosystems. The province of Alberta is experiencing rapid increases in tourism and population growth while still relying heavily on mining and timber cutting for revenue, as described in chapter 15.

In none of these examples did planning precede development. Even Summit County is late in adopting the concept of environmental planning to protect natural ecosystems. "Act first, think later" seems to be the experience in the Rocky Mountains. Some of the undesirable consequences of this type of behavior are irreversible, such as the universal stocking of non-native fish. Some, however, may be remediated if there is community and government willpower to make it happen.

CHAPTER 12

Rumblings in Rio Arriba:
Landscape Changes in the Southern
Rocky Mountains of Northern New Mexico

Craig D. Allen

▲

This chapter focuses on human effects on the landscape ecology of the south-ernmost realm of the Rocky Mountains, the Rio Arriba region of northern New Mexico. Here the Rocky Mountains end with the Sangre de Cristo and Jemez Mountains, which flank the eastern and western sides, respectively, of the Rio Grande valley (plate 6). I define the Rio Arriba (Upper River) area to be the mountainous region astride the Rio Grande from the Colorado border south to the mouth of the Jemez River at Santa Ana Pueblo. Large upland portions of Rio Arriba are contained in Santa Fe National Forest and Carson National Forest, which together constitute about 1.6 million hectares (ha), or 4 million acres.

Human Societies and Land Use History of Rio Arriba

The landscapes of Rio Arriba bear the imprint of a long history of human activ-ity. Paleo-Indian presence extends back approximately 11,000 years, and these hunters very likely contributed to the extinctions of many large mammal species during that time (Stuart and Gauthier 1988, Alroy 2001). Resident hunting and gathering peoples had only modest effects on the regional landscape because of their small numbers and high mobility, their level of technology, and the ubiquity of natural fire ignitions in this region (Allen 2002). Over the past 3,000 years, the ancestors of modern Puebloan peoples, the Anasazi, adopted an agricultural lifestyle. By 1200 B.P., Rio Arriba was a major zone of settlement for ancestral Puebloans, as documented by the extremely high densities of archaeological sites found today (see, e.g., Powers and Orcutt 1999). These agricultural peoples developed large populations and affected their environment through clearing of woodlands, agriculture, and hunting (Betancourt and Van Devender 1981, Periman 1996, Allen 1996). By the time of Spanish contact in the sixteenth century, the Puebloans of Rio Arriba had moved from upland mesas to adjoining river valleys, except in the vicinity of modern Jemez Springs. Today, fourteen long-settled Puebloan communities are still found along the major valley steams in Rio Arriba; all these sites have been occupied for 400 to 800 years. These long-enduring people see Western civilization as unsustainable and are planning to outlast it (Stuart 2000).

Spaniards colonized Rio Arriba in 1598 B.P., establishing missions among the Puebloans. The Spanish introduced additional food crops, new technologies and cultural practices, and domestic livestock. Hispanic settlements and land uses were focused on the lowlands and valleys of Rio Arriba, where there was suitable agricultural land, water, and communal protection from the attacks of nomadic Navajos, Utes, Apaches, and Comanches. These dangerous tribes used the uplands until the 1860s, constraining use of the mountains by the more settled Indo-Hispanic peoples of the valleys (deBuys 1985). Northern New Mexico remained a remote peripheral territory of first New Spain and later Mexico, after Mexican independence in 1821.

Anglo-American penetration of the region in the 1820s eventually led to the Mexican War and annexation by the United States. With the Treaty of Guadalupe Hidalgo in 1848, which ended the war, Rio Arriba became part of the United States. Large portions of communal land grants awarded during Spanish and Mexican governance were lost to Hispanic villages and eventually ended up in Santa Fe and Carson National Forests, where controversy persists between rural Hispanic communities and others over control and management of these lands (deBuys 1985, Atencio 2001).

The arrival of railroads in Rio Arriba in 1880 reduced the economic isolation of the region, leading to intensification of commercial livestock grazing and logging activities (deBuys 1985, Rothman 1992). Communities such as Española sprang up at railheads. New Mexico became the forty-seventh state in 1912. A modest tourism industry developed. Until World War II, the Land of Enchantment remained a sparsely populated, relatively unknown state with an impoverished agricultural economy.

The successful creation of the first atomic bomb in 1945 by the secret Manhattan Project at Los Alamos transformed the economy of this region, leading to broad landscape changes (Rothman 1992). Los Alamos became the nation's preeminent nuclear weapons laboratory. By importing highly educated scientific personnel from throughout the country, "the Lab" created an affluent island of external cultural values amid the traditional agrarian cultures of Rio Arriba.

The development of Santa Fe as a major arts center and tourist destination has further fueled economic and population growth in Rio Arriba. New Mexico in general, and Rio Arriba in particular, have experienced rapid population and economic growth in recent decades (figure 1.1). New Mexico's population increased by 78.9% from 1970 to 2000, growing from 1.0 million to 1.8 million people. With a 20.1% growth rate during the 1990s, it ranked twelfth nationwide, ahead of Montana and Wyoming but lagging behind the extraordinary growth of the other Rocky Mountain states. The five New Mexico counties that constitute the bulk of Rio Arriba all experienced rapid population growth after 1990, with the exception of tiny, landlocked Los Alamos County, where a shortage of privately owned land constrains population expansion.

Increasing affluence and changing lifestyles regionally and nationally have driven substantial land use changes in Rio Arriba, reflected in the growing prominence of year-round recreation and tourism attractions. Northern New Mexico has become a magnet for a variety of visitors. The Jemez Mountains attract outdoor enthusiasts to Santa Fe National Forest, Bandelier National Monument, a state park, three designated wilderness areas, a wild and scenic river, Jemez National Recreation Area, and the newly established Valles Caldera National Preserve. Seven ski areas attract winter use. Native Americans are cashing in on tourism too, with four pueblos developing golf courses and resort centers. Casinos have sprouted across Rio Arriba on seven pueblos and on Jicarilla Apache land. This leads to such ironies as the Cities of Gold Casino at Pojoaque Pueblo, where Native Americans have found an easy way to collect money from the descendants of European conquistadores and colonists.

Rio Arriba is no longer an isolated economic and cultural backwater of the United States; it is a desirable and trendy place to live, like many other portions of the Rocky Mountains. With population growth and increased incomes has come substantial conversion of agricultural lands to residential use, with a proliferation of both house trailers and trophy homes. Substantial upgrades of highway networks contribute to the accelerating sprawl by reducing driving time from outlying areas. With increased use of flexible work schedules, the emergence of telecommuting, affluent retirees, and the demand for vacation homes, no place is too remote to develop anymore.

This has brought substantial changes in the landscape around Los Alamos, as an example (Allen 1989). Human-dominated cover accounted for only 0.9% of the 86,000 ha, or 212,000 acre, landscape in 1935, primarily as dry-farmed fields. By 1981, humanized patches covered 6.3% of the landscape as farms were replaced by Los Alamos National Laboratory and the townsites of Los Alamos, White Rock, and Cochiti Lake. Other new cultural features by 1981 included two golf courses, a ski area, Cochiti Dam and Reservoir, and multiple pumice mines and stock ponds. Such developments increasingly fragment the montane wildlands of the southern Rockies.

With the arrival of well-to-do immigrants, property values in Rio Arriba have skyrocketed, putting increased economic (and cultural) pressure on natives. Santa Fe, the City Different, is turning into a wealthy pseudo-adobe caricature of itself, where many natives can no longer afford to live. Pockets of poverty and affluence often occur in close proximity, highlighting trends of increasing disparity. Yet the winter pall of wood smoke increasingly hangs over all Rio Arriba communities alike, whether from subsistence heating and cooking stoves in rural Las Trampas or from decorative fireplaces in the upscale Las Campañas development near Santa Fe. Regional quality of life increasingly depends on communal appreciation and thoughtful management of the shared environment.

In the sections that follow, I amplify two particular land use topics: (1) human alteration of upland forests and grasslands and (2) development and degradation of water resources in Rio Arriba.

Anthropogenic Alteration of Upland Forests and Grasslands

Forests in the southern Rockies have been extensively exploited for timber production for more than a century (deBuys 1985, Rothman 1992). Historical forest harvest practices include targeted removal of most old-growth trees and the construction of extensive road networks to support timber extraction (see, e.g., Allen, Betancourt, and Swetnam 1998). However, the most pervasive human effects on Rio Arriba forests have been indirectly caused by the combination of historical livestock grazing and fire suppression.

There were 5.4 million sheep and 1.4 million cattle present in New Mexico by the mid- to late 1880s (chapter 5; Wooton 1908). Consumption of herbaceous plants and trampling contributed significantly to accelerated erosion rates and arroyo development (Cooperider and Hendricks 1937, Davenport et al. 1998). Cattle numbers remained fairly constant and sheep numbers dropped tenfold in the twentieth century (Bogan et al. 1998), yet the consequences of grazing remain an ecological and social problem in parts of Rio Arriba, particularly in riparian areas, where cattle tend to congregate. Elk, reintroduced into Rio Arriba in the 1900s, also cause substantial ecological effects through herbivory of herbaceous and woody plants (Allen 1996).

A major consequence of intensive landscape-wide grazing was inadvertent suppression of surface fires from many forests and grasslands as livestock ate the herbaceous fuels that had previously allowed low-intensity fires to spread (Swetnam, Allen, and Betancourt 1999). Active fire suppression then became institutionalized as policy by the federal government after severe fires in 1910 (chapter 7). Regional vegetation changes caused by both grazing and fire suppression include invasion of grasslands by trees and shrubs, increased density of woody species and accelerated erosion rates in piñon-juniper woodlands, and conversion of many open ponderosa pine and mixed conifer forests into thickets dominated by young trees (chapters 10, 11).

Consider the decline of montane grasslands in the Jemez Mountains. Montane grasslands are found on the upper south-facing slopes of nearly all the larger summits and ridge crests. Deep prairie-type soils indicate that grasslands have persisted on these sites for thousands of years, yet a tidal wave of young ponderosa pine, Douglas-fir, and aspen have been invading since the 1920s (Allen 1989; Swetnam, Allen, and Betancourt 1999). Between 1935 and 1981, tree invasion reduced the area of open montane grasslands by 55% across the southeastern Jemez Mountains (Allen 1989; Allen, Betancourt, and Swetnam 1998). Similar tree and shrub invasions are also observed in many other open vegetation types throughout northern New Mexico, including blue spruce encroachment on moist meadows in Valles Caldera National Preserve, Engelmann spruce invasion of subalpine parks in the Pecos Wilderness and San Pedro Parks Wilderness, and the spread of juniper, sagebrush, and snakeweed into valley grasslands (Bogan et al. 1998).

The regional land use history of overgrazing and fire suppression has altered many piñon-juniper woodlands, which were formerly more open and had well-developed herbaceous ground covers. Since the late 1800s, fire-sensitive piñon and juniper trees became established in higher densities, competing with the remaining grasses for water and nutrients. Thus, a positive feedback cycle was initiated that favors tree invasion and decreased herbaceous ground cover in these semi-arid woodlands, where intense thunderstorms on exposed soil generate substantial runoff and accelerated erosion.

Woodland soils in Bandelier National Monument are eroding at rates of about 1 centimeter (cm), or 0.4 inch (in.), per decade (Davenport et al. 1998; Sydoriak, Allen, and Jacobs 2000). Given soil depths averaging only 30–60 cm (12–24 in.) in many areas, these erosion rates are clearly unsustainable and will result in the loss of entire soil bodies across extensive areas. Accelerated runoff and erosion has damaged more than 90% of inventoried archaeological sites at Bandelier (Sydoriak, Allen, and Jacobs 2000). In this park, my colleagues and I have found as many as 1,040 cultural artifacts (mostly potsherds) moved by a single thunderstorm into a sediment trap draining only 0.1 ha, or about 11,000 square feet ($ft.^2$), of gentle hillslope. The park's biological productivity and cultural resources are literally washing away. Similar histories and high erosion rates characterize many piñon-juniper woodlands, resulting in considerable transport of sediment through watersheds, with associated effects on water quality (Bogan et al. 1998). Without management intervention, this human-induced episode of accelerated soil erosion appears to be irreversible (Sydoriak, Allen, and Jacobs 2000).

Tree densities have burgeoned approximately tenfold in many ponderosa pine and mixed conifer forests over pre-1900 norms as the result of a century of fire suppression (Bogan et al. 1998; Swetnam, Allen, and Betancourt 1999). Relatively open forests dominated by older trees and with herbaceous ground cover have been converted into thickets of young trees with heavy fuel loadings of needles and logs on the forest floor. Fire-sensitive and shade-tolerant species such as white fir and Engelmann spruce now dominate, increasing the potential for widespread outbreaks of western spruce budworm (Swetnam and Lynch 1993). Montane forests in Rio Arriba are increasingly experiencing stand-replacing crown fires, such as the 1977 La Mesa Fire, the 1996 Dome and Hondo Fires, the 1998 Oso Fire, and the 2000 Cerro Grande and Viveash Fires (plate 6, figure 12.1). Extensive crown fires are not natural in lower-elevation forests in this region (Allen 2002) and cause many undesirable ecological and social effects. The Cerro Grande Fire killed nearly every tree in a 39 square kilometer (km^2), or 15 mi.^{2}, patch adjoining Los Alamos that included key habitat for the endemic Jemez Mountains salamander and threatened Mexican spotted owl (figure 12.1). The fire triggered downstream flooding that has affected the infrastructure of the townsite and national laboratory because such fires increase peak flows approximately a hundredfold (Veenhuis 2002). The Cerro Grande Fire was the first fire in American history in which postfire watershed rehabilitation cost more than the fire suppression efforts, reflecting the regional trends of increased fire severity and human values at risk.

Trees in overcrowded forests and woodlands are subject to more water stress in dry years. When multi-year drought returns to this region, as occurs every few decades, extensive forest dieback and enormous wildfires are likely (Allen and Breshears 1998, Swetnam and Betancourt 1998). Global climate change will quite likely increase the frequency and magnitude of extreme climatic events such as drought, along with associated dieback and fires (Breshears and Allen 2002).

Agua es Vida: Development and Degradation of Water Resources

Agua es vida is a familiar slogan in Rio Arriba, meaning "Water is life." Water availability has long limited human societies in this region because conditions are dry in the lowlands, where people cultivate food crops. People here have

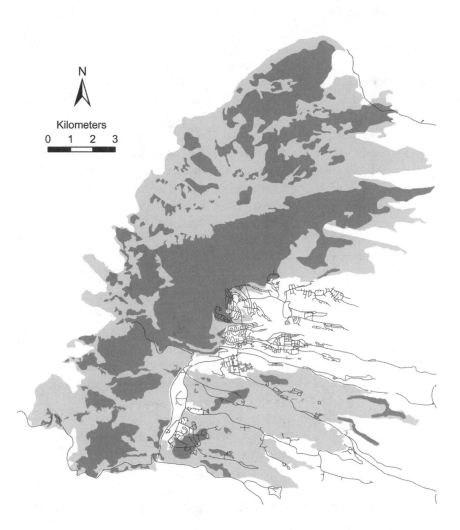

FIGURE 12.1 *Map of the Cerro Grande Fire near Los Alamos.* Lines are paved roads, highlighting urban and industrial land uses embedded in a wildland matrix of montane forests. Dark patches represent areas of crown fire with nearly total tree mortality. Lighter patches represent lower fire intensity. In May 2000, this fire burned into the western side of the townsite of Los Alamos, destroying almost 400 homes. The fire also burned across much of Los Alamos National Laboratory, causing extensive damage.

manipulated water flows for agricultural use and domestic consumption for at least the past 1,000 years. Ancestral Puebloans developed sophisticated means of increasing water availability for their crops, including terraces, check dams, grid gardens, cobble mulch gardens, irrigation diversions, and reservoirs (Powers and Orcutt 1999). Given the substantial human population of this region by the 1500s B.P., agricultural practices must have affected substantial portions of both upland and riparian landscape settings (Periman 1996, Powers and Orcutt 1999).

Local ditch systems known as acequias were developed with Spanish colonization (Rivera 1998). Stream valleys large and small show patchworks of long, narrow fields oriented at right angles to the streams and bordered by acequias. Acequia associations continue to serve as the beating heart of living rural communities in Rio Arriba, maintaining historical patterns of cultural persistence, community cooperation, and agricultural lands as increasingly valuable open space today.

Larger-scale commercial agriculture developed after 1870, particularly in the San Luis Valley of Colorado. The ecology and hydrology of the San Luis Valley was transformed from native grasslands, shrublands, and wetlands into farm fields, facilitated by the construction of extensive drainage and irrigation works across the valley (plate 6). By the late 1800s, flows were substantially reduced in the mainstem of the Rio Grande, sometimes even causing the river to run dry before reaching the Colorado–New Mexico border.

Rio Arriba rivers have been markedly altered by the construction of dams to control floods, reduce downstream sediment loads, and store water. The completion of Cochiti Dam in 1975 (figure 12.2) altered the ecology and hydrology of the Rio Grande both upstream and downstream (Allen, Hanson, and Mullins 1993; Crawford et al. 1993). This huge dam protects the middle Rio Grande valley downstream (including Albuquerque) from floods, reducing peak flows—historically more than 24,000 cubic feet per second (cfs), or 680 cubic meters per second (m^3/sec.)—to no more than 10,000 cfs (283 m^3/sec.). With the elimination of large flood flows, the ecology of the riparian zone has been greatly altered, resulting in invasion of Russian olive, tamarisk, and Siberian elm at the expense of native cottonwoods and willows (Crawford et al. 1993, Hanscom 2001). Most riparian sloughs and wetlands have also been lost (Crawford et al. 1993). Similar changes have occurred on the Rio Chama, caused by Heron, El Vado, and Abiquiu Dams.

Rio Arriba contains many additional dams on other Rio Grande tributary streams, including the Santa Cruz, Nambe, Jemez, Galisteo, and Santa Fe Rivers (figure 12.3). These dams have had similar downstream effects, individually and cumulatively, of pervasively altering the hydrology of this region by reduc-

FIGURE 12.2 *Cochiti Dam, on the Rio Grande at the Foot of the Jemez Mountains.* A public highway can be seen on the dam crest. This huge earth-fill dam provides flood and sediment control for human purposes downstream. Photograph by Craig D. Allen.

ing peak flows while storing water and sediment. The water and sediment impounded by these dams also have major upstream effects on rivers, ranging from drowning of terrestrial vegetation and blocking of fish migrations to development of new lake ecosystems. Ecosystem development in reservoirs is highly dependent on the magnitude and timing of water fluctuations behind each dam, which vary not only with the vagaries of natural precipitation but also with the authorized purposes of each reservoir and the perspectives of water managers.

Streamflows have obviously been markedly reduced by the extensive diversion of surface water and groundwater for consumptive human purposes, with perennial flows increasingly reduced to unnaturally low levels. Water yields have also declined from mountain watersheds in Rio Arriba because of the great increases in forest density over the past century (figure 12.3). Water yields have dropped because the increasingly closed forest canopies capture more snowfall, which can then sublimate (vaporize) directly back to the sky, and more trees pump more water out of the soil through evapotranspiration. The upper Santa Fe watershed is thought to be yielding 20% less water annually than it did in the early twentieth century (USDA Forest Service 2001).

FIGURE 12.3 *McClure Reservoir, one of Two Storage Reservoirs on the Santa Fe River.* Together, the reservoirs provide approximately 40% of the municipal water supply of Santa Fe. McClure Reservoir had been drawn down to low levels after two dry winters when this photograph was taken, in fall 2000. Dense forests in the background are at risk of extensive crown fire, threatening the security of the city's downstream infrastructure and water supply. Photograph by P. S. Tharnstrom.

Water quality in the major streams has been degraded by a variety of human land uses. Extensive road networks and livestock grazing in uplands trigger accelerated soil erosion, resulting in excess sediment and more turbid water in streams. Cattle prefer to graze in riparian zones, trampling stream banks and defecating in streams. As human populations have grown, so have water contamination problems from sewage, solid waste, industrial and household products, and fertilizer and biocide residues from agricultural activities. Biocides that were applied to Rio Arriba forests in efforts to control natural insect "pests" still persist. For example, 423,000 kilograms (kg), or 1,133,622 pounds (lb.), of DDT was sprayed on 478,055 ha (1,846 mi.^{2}) of Santa Fe National Forest and Carson National Forest from 1955 to 1963 in operations against western spruce budworm, and DDT was repeatedly used against tent caterpillars and bark beetles at Bandelier National Monument in 1948–1962 (Allen 1989). A legacy of DDT-contaminated fish and soil remains along lower Frijoles Creek in Bandelier, which remains closed to fishing. A unique variety of heavy metal and radioactive contaminants are also part of the Rio Grande system, a legacy of almost sixty years of nuclear weapons research at Los Alamos National Laboratory (Graf 1994).

Altered fish communities provide another measure of human effects on Rio Arriba waters. The native fish communities of Rio Arriba have been decimated by modification of stream habitats and water quality, range fragmentation resulting from dams and engineered channels, and competition from introduced species (Platania 1991). The Rio Grande and Rio Chama, from Abiquiu Dam to Cochiti Dam, were historically inhabited by thirteen native fish species. Of these, six were extirpated in the twentieth century, and seven introduced non-native species are now present (Platania 1991). One of these extirpated species, the Rio Grande silvery minnow (*Hybognathus amarus*), is a federally listed endangered species that is at the center of controversies over how to manage this river basin (Hanscom 1999). The precarious existence of the silvery minnow reflects the magnitude of ecological change imposed on the Rio Grande since the late 1800s.

Current Trends and Causes for Hope

As is the case elsewhere in the Rocky Mountains, the juggernaut of pervasive human-caused change is sweeping across the landscapes of northern New Mexico. Yet hope for a more sustainable future is brewing in Rio Arriba. There is much cultural and natural continuity and persistence, a certain timelessness, associated with this region. The native Indo-Hispano peoples of Rio Arriba have a long-term affection, a *querencia,* for this land that resists the short-term economic imperatives and carpetbagger ethics of our footloose modern world (Atencio 2001). Newcomers are attracted to this legacy of connectedness and quickly form commitments to the landscape. Even the land management bureaucracies have begun to recognize the value of place-focused approaches to stewardship. Throughout Rio Arriba, efforts are under way to support healthier and more sustainable ecosystems and human communities in the southern Rockies.

Ranchers, environmentalists, and federal land managers are beginning to work together in new ways to solve problems to the benefit of all interests. The Quivira Coalition, based in Santa Fe, has been working to constructively improve rangeland conditions, sustain small-scale Hispanic ranchers in Rio Arriba, keep progressive ranchers on the land, and protect their remaining open spaces from "ranchettization" (Atencio 2001). Toward these goals, The Quivira Coalition and the Santa Fe Group of the Sierra Club recently sponsored a report on environmental justice and public land ranching in northern New Mexico. The Valle Grande Grass Bank fosters restoration of USDA Forest Service grazing allotments through collaboration among Santa Fe National Forest, The Conservation Fund, and small-scale Hispanic ranchers in groups such as the Santa Barbara Grazing Association, The Quivira Coalition, and the New Mexico Environment Department. The new Valles Caldera National Preserve protects the heart of the Jemez Mountains from subdivision and aims to establish a new model for science-based land management that will support healthy ecosystems and include livestock grazing by local ranchers.

Initial forest restoration efforts are encouraging. Degraded woodlands are treated by thinning young piñon and juniper trees, with the cut branches used to mulch the barren interspaces between older remnant trees (Sydoriak, Allen, and Jacobs 2000). Broad-based coalitions are initiating understory thinning and prescribed burning in overdense forests (USDA Forest Service 2001, Allen et al. 2002). Tree invasion of grasslands and meadows is being checked by similar management efforts (Swetnam, Allen, and Betancourt 1999). These restoration efforts shift ecological dominance back toward the natural pattern of more abundant herbaceous vegetation in most local ecosystems. This should also help resolve public range management conflicts by providing additional grazing capacity in upland settings, away from the environmental conflicts associated with grazing in riparian zones.

Water managers are adopting ecologically friendly approaches to reservoir operations. Episodes of highly fluctuating and long-term water storage in Cochiti Reservoir from 1978 to 1988 killed all vegetation that existed before construction of the reservoir, leaving bare sediment along the river and a dead zone like a bathtub ring extending as far as 37 m, or 120 feet (ft.), above river level and more than 24 stream km, or 15 stream mi., above the dam (see the photograph of McClure Reservoir in figure 12.3). Yet the legal authorization for this dam supports its use only for short-term floodwater storage that can be managed to mimic natural patterns of flooding (Allen, Hanson, and Mullins 1993). A permanent pool of 486 surface ha (1,200 surface acres) has been established at Cochiti Reservoir for conservation of fish and wildlife resources and recreation. Interactions among biologists and water managers from many entities, including pueblos and multiple agencies, resulted in more sensitive management of Cochiti Reservoir since the early 1990s, providing a measure of stability to the upstream environment that is allowing productive new ecosystems to develop. An ever-growing wedge of delta sediments at the slack headwaters of the reservoir is creating a complex environment of sediment bars, wetlands, and sloughs that resembles the preregulated condition of the Rio Grande (Allen, Hanson, and Mullins 1993; Crawford et al. 1993).

There has been a striking resurgence of ecological health in the reservoir area as vegetation has grown back in the delta, including extensive wetlands and exuberant young thickets of native willow and cottonwood, which are rare elsewhere today along the flood-starved Rio Grande. This is a modest ecosystem management success story. If well managed, Cochiti Reservoir will continue to develop as a diverse and productive ecosystem occupying a strategic position on the Rio Grande flyway, a major migratory bird corridor. Already the reservoir is used by thousands of migratory waterfowl and songbirds as well as overwintering bald eagles. Alternatively, if Cochiti Reservoir is managed like a bathtub, solely for external human purposes and with indifference to its ecological condition and potential, it could end up a degraded and unproductive mudhole, as it was in the late 1980s. Given the unrelenting pressure for increased utilitarian efficiency and control of water resources in New Mexico, the ultimate fate of the Rio Grande and Cochiti Reservoir will be determined by choices yet to be made by our society.

Success at sustaining ecological health in the southern Rockies is uncertain. Yet Rio Arriba is abuzz with myriad creative efforts to build a harmonious landscape community. Involvement occurs at all levels: acequia associations and environmentalists, land trusts and federal agencies, river runners and ranchers, scientists and schoolchildren. Unique approaches to land stewardship will arise as local Native American and Hispanic people reassert their sovereignty and their cultural traditions of land as a community to which humans belong, and as newcomers become more deeply rooted and make commitments to this place. I am hopeful that these diverse efforts will collectively weave a strong fabric of long-term care for the wonderful landscapes of Rio Arriba.

Acknowledgments

I thank Kay Beeley and Scott Wiggers of Bandelier National Monument, and Carl H. Key, David Sawyer, Diane Schneider, and Tammy Fancher of the U.S. Geological Survey, for support in preparation of the figures. And I especially appreciate Jill S. Baron's vision in pursuing this book and am grateful for her persistence and patience in support of this chapter.

References

Allen, C. D. 1989. Changes in the landscape of the Jemez Mountains, New Mexico. Ph.D. diss., University of California, Berkeley.

———. 1996. Elk response to the La Mesa Fire and current status in the Jemez Mountains. In *Fire effects in southwestern forests: Proceedings of the second La Mesa Fire Symposium,* ed. C. D. Allen, 179–195. General Technical Report RM-GTR-286. Fort Collins, Colo.: U.S. Department of Agriculture, Forest Service, Rocky Mountain Forest and Range Experiment Station.

————. 2002. Lots of lightning and plenty of people: An ecological history of fire in the upland Southwest. In *Fire, native peoples, and the natural landscape,* ed. T. R. Vale, chap. 5. Washington, D.C.: Island Press.

Allen, C. D., J. L. Betancourt, and T. W. Swetnam. 1998. Landscape changes in the southwestern United States: Techniques, long-term datasets, and trends. In *Perspectives on the land use history of North America: A context for understanding our changing environment,* ed. T. D. Sisk, 71–84. Biological Science Report USGS/BRD/BSR-1998-0003. U.S. Department of the Interior, U.S. Geological Survey. On-line at <http://biology.usgs.gov/luhna/chap9.html>.

Allen, C. D., and D. D. Breshears. 1998. Drought-induced shift of a forest/woodland ecotone: Rapid landscape response to climate variation. *Proceedings of the National Academy of Sciences of the United States of America* 95:14839–14842.

Allen, C. D., B. Hanson, and C. Mullins, eds. 1993. Cochiti Reservoir reregulation interagency biological report. Unpublished report on file with the U.S. Army Corps of Engineers, Albuquerque, N.M.

Allen, C. D., M. Savage, D. A. Falk, K. F. Suckling, T. W. Swetnam, T. Schulke, P. B. Stacey, P. Morgan, M. Hoffman, and J. Klingel. 2002. Ecological restoration of southwestern ponderosa pine ecosystems: A broad perspective. *Ecological Applications,* 2002.

Alroy, J. 2001. A multispecies overkill simulation of the end-Pleistocene megafaunal mass extinction. *Science* 292:1893–1896.

Atencio, E. 2001. *Of land and justice: Environmental justice and public lands ranching in northern New Mexico.* Report for The Quivira Coalition and the Santa Fe Group of the Sierra Club, Santa Fe, N.M.

Betancourt, J. L., and T. R. Van Devender. 1981. Holocene vegetation in Chaco Canyon, New Mexico. *Science* 214:656–658.

Bogan, M. A., C. D. Allen, E. H. Muldavin, S. P. Platania, J. N. Stuart, G. H. Farley, P. Melhop, and J. Belnap. 1998. Southwest. In *Status and trends of the nation's biological resources,* ed. M. J. Mac, P. A. Opler, C. E. Puckett Haecker, and P. D. Doran, 543–592. 2 vols. Reston, Va.: U.S. Department of the Interior, U.S. Geological Survey.

Breshears, D. D., and C. D. Allen. 2002. The importance of rapid, disturbance-induced losses in carbon management and sequestration. *Global Ecology and Biogeography* 11:1–15.

Cooperider, C. K., and B. A. Hendricks. 1937. Soil erosion and stream flow on range and forest lands of the upper Rio Grande watershed in relation to land resources and human welfare. USDA Technical Bulletin No. 567. Washington, D.C.: U.S. Department of Agriculture.

Crawford, C. S., A. C. Cully, R. Leutheuser, M. S. Sifuentes, L. H. White, and J. P. Wilber. 1993. *Middle Rio Grande ecosystem: Bosque biological management plan.* Albuquerque, N.M.: U.S. Department of the Interior, U.S. Fish and Wildlife Service.

Davenport, D. W., D. D. Breshears, B. P. Wilcox, and C. D. Allen. 1998. Viewpoint: Sustainability of piñon-juniper ecosystems: A unifying perspective of soil erosion thresholds. *Journal of Range Management* 51 (2): 229–238.

deBuys, W. 1985. *Enchantment and exploitation: The life and hard times of a New Mexico mountain range.* Albuquerque: University of New Mexico Press.

Graf, W. L. 1994. *Plutonium and the Rio Grande.* New York: Oxford University Press.

Hanscom, G. 1999. A tiny fish cracks New Mexico's water establishment. *High Country News,* 11 October. On-line at <http://www.hcn.org/servlets/hcn.Article?article_id=5305>.

————. 2001. Bringing back the bosque. *High Country News,* 19 November. On-line at <http://www.hcn.org/servlets/hcn.Article?article_id=10856>.

Periman, R. D. 1996. The influence of prehistoric Anasazi cobble-mulch agricultural features on northern Rio Grande landscapes. In *Desired future conditions for southwestern riparian ecosystems,* coord. D. Shaw and D. Finch, 181–188. General Technical Report RM-GTR-272. Fort Collins, Colo.: U.S. Department of Agriculture, Forest Service, Rocky Mountain Forest and Range Experiment Station.

Platania, S. P. 1991. Fishes of the Rio Chama and upper Rio Grande, New Mexico, with preliminary comments on their longitudinal distribution. *Southwest Naturalist* 36:186–193.

Powers, R. P., and J. D. Orcutt, eds. 1999. *The Bandelier archeological survey.* Vols. 1, 2. Intermountain Cultural Resources Management Professional Paper No. 57. Denver, Colo.: U.S. Department of the Interior, National Park Service, Intermountain Region.

Rivera, J. A. 1998. *Acequia culture: Water, land, and community in the Southwest.* Albuquerque: University of New Mexico Press.

Rothman, H. K. 1992. *On rims and ridges: The Los Alamos area since 1880.* Lincoln: University of Nebraska Press.

Stuart, D. E. 2000. *Anasazi America.* Albuquerque: University of New Mexico Press.

Stuart, D. E., and R. P. Gauthier. 1988. *Prehistoric New Mexico.* Albuquerque: University of New Mexico Press.

Swetnam, T. W., C. D. Allen, and J. L. Betancourt. 1999. Applied historical ecology: Using the past to manage for the future. *Ecological Applications* 9:1189–1206.

Swetnam, T. W., and J. L. Betancourt. 1998. Mesoscale disturbance and ecological response to decadal climatic variability in the American Southwest. *Journal of Climate* 11:3128–3147.

Swetnam, T. W., and A. M. Lynch. 1993. Multi-century, regional-scale patterns of western spruce budworm history. *Ecological Monographs* 63:399–424.

Sydoriak, C. A., C. D. Allen, and B. F. Jacobs. 2000. Would ecological landscape restoration make the Bandelier Wilderness more or less of a wilderness? In *Wilderness ecosystems, threats, and management,* comp. D. N. Cole, S. F. McCool, W. T. Borrie, and J. O'Laughlin, 209–215. Vol. 5 of *Proceedings: Wilderness Science in a Time of Change conference.* Proceedings RMRS-P-15-VOL-5. Ogden, Utah: U.S. Department of Agriculture, Forest Service, Rocky Mountain Research Station.

USDA Forest Service. 2001. *Santa Fe Municipal Watershed Project, Environmental Impact Statement.* Santa Fe, N.M.: Santa Fe National Forest.

Veenhuis, J. E. 2002. *Effects of wildfire on the hydrology of Capulin and Rito de los Frijoles Canyons, Bandelier National Monument, New Mexico.* Water Resources Investigations Report 02-4152. Albuquerque, N.M.: U.S. Department of the Interior, U.S. Geological Survey.

Wooton, E. O. 1908. The range problem in New Mexico. Agriculture Experiment Station Bulletin No. 66, New Mexico College of Agriculture and Mechanic Arts. *Albuquerque Morning Journal,* Albuquerque, New Mexico.

CHAPTER 13

Collaborative Development of a Conservation Planning System: A Case Study of Summit County, Colorado

David M. Theobald and N. Thompson Hobbs

▲

The foremost threat to maintaining vigorous and diverse populations of wildlife in the Rocky Mountain region is the loss of intact, high-quality habitat as a result of agricultural to residential conversion. Demographic and economic trends suggest that residential development on private land will continue to degrade wildlife habitat during the first decade of the twenty-first century (Rudzitis and Streatfield 1992; Power 1996; Beyers 1996; Baron, Theobald, and Fagre 2000; Theobald 2000). The U.S. Rocky Mountain region swelled by more than 4.5 million new residents during the 1990s, so population growth averaged nearly 3% annually, compared with 1% for the remainder of the United States (Bureau of the Census 2001). Growth is contributing to urban sprawl throughout the United States, where the density of cities decreases while the overall population increases (Diamond and Noonan 1996). More than half of the West's counties are also experiencing rural sprawl, wherein locations outside city and town limits grow faster than urban areas (plate 2; Bureau of the Census 2001).

Population growth will force fundamental changes in private land use and land cover throughout the region. For example, in the early 1990s, about 36,000 ha, or 90,000 acres, of agricultural land in Colorado were converted annually to other uses, primarily residential development and associated infrastructure, and this pace quickened to about 57,000 ha (141,000 acres) per year from 1987 to 1997 (Colorado Department of Agriculture 2000). Before development, more than 60% of the agricultural land was native rangeland that provided important wildlife habitat.

Concern over loss of habitat is especially great for private land because listed species found on private land are declining in abundance faster than are those on public land, and because private land supports areas of high biodiversity (Noss, O'Connell, and Murphy 1997; Bean and Wilcove 1997). Fewer than 10% of endangered species occur exclusively on public land (GAO 1994). It follows that land use planning affecting private land is fundamentally important to conserving biodiversity nationwide (Dale et al. 2000). Careless development of private lands will cause long-term declines in the abundance and distribution of many species.

Regional changes in land use are the result of many local decisions made one at a time: a ranch is converted to a subdivision; a mountainside is developed for skiing; a valley is dotted with vacation homes. This is problematic because planners have assumed that habitat lost in one place can be compensated by habitat remaining undisturbed elsewhere. However, it is becoming clear that this assumption cannot hold forever—many small, seemingly benign effects accumulate to cause large, harmful effects on environmental values such as wildlife habitat. Thus, society is challenged to accommodate growth while preserving natural features that contribute to a region's high quality of life.

Local communities have a timely opportunity to meet this challenge. In many counties in the West, geographic information systems (GIS) are being developed to guide land use planning. At the same time, state and federal agencies are assembling spatial data on vegetation, hydrology, and distributions of wildlife species. As a result of these efforts, a large amount of data is accumulating in county and agency offices that can help citizens and decision makers understand and predict the effects of land use change on the environment. Although there is great potential for such information to guide effective land use planning, analytical tools are needed to bring those data to bear on decisions.

We initiated a project called the System for Conservation Planning (SCoP) in order to provide such tools. The goal of the SCoP project was to provide local communities with readily accessible information about the consequences of development for wildlife (Theobald et al. 2000). We developed an interactive GIS that allows planners, decision makers, and citizens to foresee how changes in land use might accumulate over time and space and how these cumulative changes might affect the extent and distribution of habitat for wildlife.

Study Area

The SCoP system was initially developed for Summit County, Colorado. Summit County is located in central Colorado, about 112 kilometers (km), or 70 miles (mi.), west of Denver. It is flanked by the Continental Divide on the east and is bisected by U.S. Interstate 70, which connects the Front Range to the mountain resorts of Breckenridge, Vail, and Keystone. Easy access to once-remote mountain counties was provided by completion in 1973 of the Eisenhower Memorial Tunnel underneath the Continental Divide. Since then, Summit County has grown particularly rapidly, and it has tripled its population since 1975.

Collaborative Design Process

We were committed to designing a system that reflects the needs of users. In particular, we wanted to avoid developing analytical tools influenced by scientists' viewpoints alone. We believed that the utility of the system would depend on the extent to which we could integrate scientific information with the diverse views of information users, particularly those who have a stake in the decisions the information system would support. To ensure that the information system would meet the needs of a diverse set of clients, we initiated a process we call collaborative design.

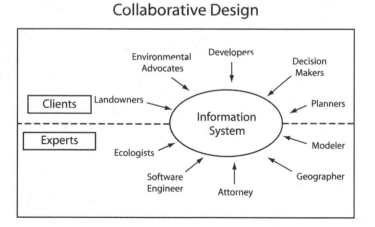

FIGURE 13.1 *Diagram Illustrating the Collaborative Design of the Biological Information System SCoP (System for Conservation Planning).* The eventual users of the system helped design it from the outset.

Collaborative design is based on the idea that the best products result from interactions between people who know how to make products and people who will ultimately use them (figure 13.1). Our collaborative design process proceeded in four stages: (1) formation of the design team, (2) creation of a series of content primers, (3) identification of goals and development of preliminary sketches, and (4) design specification. Our design team included a county commissioner, a planner, a developer, a landowner, a wildlife manager, and three environmental advocates. Ecologists, geographers, a land use attorney, and computer programmers contributed technical expertise. We held a series of one-day primers on subject matter relevant to land use change and habitat conservation. Topics of these sessions included principles of conservation biology and landscape ecology, land use law and planning, human geography, and GIS. The purpose of the primers was to provide a common understanding of some technical issues relevant to the information system.

We spent most of our time in the third stage, identifying goals for the information system and developing preliminary sketches of how the system would work. This required an additional half-dozen meetings with the design team. Each session followed an iterative cycle of listening to users' needs, getting feedback, and designing as a group, resulting in incremental development of the system. Our main technique was simply to prime discussions by asking several questions, such as the following:

• Imagine a situation (real or hypothetical) that is typical of your role in working with wildlife and development in Summit County. What insights about effects of development on wildlife would help you play your role more effectively?

• Describe a situation in which you wanted to include wildlife concerns in land use planning or in your work in development but were unable to do so effectively. Be as specific as possible and try to choose an example that differs from the first one you discussed.

• The goal of the SCoP project is "to support land use planning by local communities by providing state-of-the-art information on the effects of development on wildlife and by identifying actions that can be taken to minimize those effects." What do you consider to be important, tangible measures of success in meeting that goal?

• Imagine yourself ten years from now in Summit County. What specific things will you look for to indicate that Summit County is succeeding in meeting its goals for wildlife protection?

We found that iterative design is important because users frequently are not able to express what they want until they have a chance to use it (Norman 1998).

At each meeting, we reviewed what had been discussed in the previous meeting and brought out a rough sketch or mock-up of the system as it emerged through our discussions. This was especially helpful in the fourth stage, when we specified a formal design. The comments that emerged in response to these questions were drawn together into statements of goals for the information system.

Local Land Use Decision Making

Biological information must be carefully linked to the decisions routinely made during the planning process to ensure its use in local land use planning (Duerkson et al. 1997). In the western United States, local land use decisions are made predominantly by county governments, and the basis for county oversight of wildlife resource protection originates from state land use control acts. For example, Colorado's Local Government Land Use Control Enabling Act of 1974 states the need for "protecting lands from activities which would cause immediate or foreseeable material danger to significant wildlife habitat and would endanger a wildlife species."

Two types of planning typically occur at the county level: master planning and site review. Master, or comprehensive, planning provides a county-wide "vision" and establishes the goals and policies for long-term land use decisions. These master plans are advisory, not regulatory, and implementation of the policies depends largely on the political will of local elected officials and the support of their constituency. Master plans are also important because they typically guide policy beyond the duration of individual officials' tenures.

The site review process is triggered as individual developments and zoning changes are proposed. Criteria for decision making during site review include compliance with zoning regulations; adequate water supply and sewage disposal; compatibility with soils, topography, and hazards; adequate access to transportation systems; and maintenance of affordable housing. Site reviews also typically consider effects on environmental values such as wildlife habitat and wetlands. A major challenge facing ecologists is to offer scientific information and analyses in the planning process when varied and frequently competing objectives are brought together (Rockwood 1995).

Implementation Strategy

The design team identified four goals for the information system: education, screening of local environmental effects, assessment of habitat values, and projection of cumulative effects (table 13.1).

The collaborative design team believed strongly that SCoP should educate

TABLE 13.1. Information System Goals and Modules, with Descriptions

Goal	System Module	Description
Education	Wildlife habitat	Identify wildlife found in the area of interest. For each species, get vegetation affinities, elevation range and water constraints, legal status, distribution maps, photographs, and documentation.
	Vegetation patterns	Identify vegetation found in the area of interest, using maps of all types or individual vegetation types, statistics, photographs, and documentation.
Screening	Conservation sites and occurrences	Identify Colorado Natural Heritage Program (CNHP) conservation areas or element occurrences found in the area of interest. Show maps and profiles for each site or occurrence.
	Concerns if developed	Identify suitable habitat for federally listed and state-listed threatened and endangered species and species designated by the CNHP as imperiled. Identify known distributions and activity areas for economically important species.
Habitat value assessment	High-priority habitat	Identify areas of high value for different groups of species, including rare (legally listed) and economically important species.
Projection of cumulative effects	Development patterns	Create housing density maps and growth projections covering the years 1900–2020.

the citizens of Summit County about their wildlife. The information system should allow citizens to learn about the distribution of wildlife species and their habitats; it should inform them about the species' status, life histories, habitat requirements, and sensitivities to environmental effects. Users should be able to locate an area on a map and find out what species use the area. He or she should also be able to identify a species and learn about the distribution of its habitat.

The developer and an environmental advocate on the design team asked that the system offer a coarse screening of environmental effects of future development at a given site. The developer wanted to be able to identify an area on a map and learn about development concerns that might be raised about effects on wildlife habitat at that site. This was important because the developer was willing to do his best to avoid sensitive areas but needed to know about such sensitivities up front, that is, before he invested a great deal of time and money in preparing a formal development proposal for review by the county.

The citizen advocate asked for virtually the same function. He wanted to allocate his advocacy time to the development with the greatest potential to affect wildlife. Therefore, he wanted a tool to distinguish areas in urgent need of comment from those less urgent. He also wanted a sound scientific source of information to use in formulating his comments.

All members of the design team believed that SCoP should map areas of the landscape according to relative habitat value. A map of habitat value is useful in identifying alternative development paths during master planning by offering a rationale for steering development away from valuable areas and toward areas of lesser value.

It is clear that effects of development accumulate over time and space and that the aggregate consequences of these many results must be overcome if planning is to effectively conserve wildlife habitat. The effects of a single development on the abundance and distribution of wildlife may be minor, but the effects of 100 developments are not. The design team asked that we develop a way to foresee how future development might spread in relation to existing wildlife habitats. They asked that the system help them evaluate different management approaches. These include traditional regulatory approaches, such as zoning and growth caps, but also incentive-based approaches such as cluster development and transfer of development rights. Building on the work of SCoP, we further developed a series of build-out scenarios and evaluated their effects on habitat (Theobald and Hobbs 2002).

System Implementation

The system makes use of currently available data, including maps of species distribution and maps of potentially suitable habitat derived from satellite images. The system currently tracks fifty-two vertebrate species that are listed by state or federal agencies as threatened, endangered, of special concern, imperiled, sensitive, rare, or economically important. Because it is difficult to map actual distribution ranges for this number of species and because it is important to identify likely habitat, we modeled potentially suitable habitat maps using the best information available on factors influencing known species distributions. Our approach was based on identification of species affinities for vegetation types using elevational and water constraints similar to those used by White and colleagues (1997).

Locations in the county became potentially suitable habitat for each species if they met three criteria:

1. The location must contain vegetative cover appropriate for the species.
2. The location must be at an elevation within the upper and lower elevation limits for the species.
3. The location must be sufficiently close to water for species that require lakes or streams as part of their habitat.

Vegetation was mapped by classifying a Landsat Thematic Mapper satellite image in terms of fourteen types of vegetative cover (table 13.2). Species affinities for each type were derived from standard literature sources (e.g., Andrews and Righter 1992; Fitzgerald, Meaney, and Armstrong 1981; Hammerson 1986) and by consultation with local biologists.

Analysis Procedures: Habitat Value

We were challenged to identify measures of habitat quality that did not overly simplify the biological complexity of habitat quality and species distribution yet did not overwhelm citizens with too much information. We settled on three measures (table 13.3) that by and large incorporate conservation planning principles: local diversity, neighborhood diversity, and patch value (Murphy and Noon 1992; Noss, O'Connell, and Murphy 1997; Peck 1998). Conservation planning principles include the following: (1) species that are well distributed across their historical range are less prone to extinction; (2) large patches of habitat that support large populations support them for longer periods of time; (3) patches that are continuous (less fragmented) support long-term viability; (4) patches that are sufficiently close together allow dispersal and thus support long-term viability; (5) patches that are connected by corridors provide better dispersal; (6) patches that have minimal or no human influence (e.g., have no roads) are better; and (7) populations that naturally fluctuate widely are more vulnerable than stable populations.

To identify areas that support particularly diverse assemblages of species—biological hot spots—on the basis of resources present at a given location, we developed the Local Diversity index. This index shows the number of species that have potentially suitable habitat at each grid cell, weighted by biological rank. A species' biological rarity was ranked with a score of 0–100 (Gross and Melcher 1998). To identify areas that support a large number of species because of the configuration and arrangement of different vegetation types, we developed the Neighborhood Diversity index. This index was calculated by centering a circular window (0.5 km, or approximately 0.3 mi., radius) on each grid

TABLE 13.2. Definitions of Land Cover Classes Used to Map Summit County, Colorado

Class	Definition
Water	Includes all types of open water: lakes, ponds, and reservoirs.
Conifer (denser)	Medium- to high-density stands of single and mixed species, including lodgepole pine (*Pinus contorta*), Engelmann spruce (*Picea engelmannii*), blue spruce (*Picea pungens*), subalpine fir (*Abies lasiocarpa*), and Douglas-fir (*Pseudotsuga menziesii*).
Conifer (sparser)	Sparse to medium-density stands of lodgepole pine (*Pinus contorta*), Engelmann spruce (*Picea engelmannii*), blue spruce (*Picea pungens*), subalpine fir (*Abies lasiocarpa*), and Douglas-fir (*Pseudotsuga menziesii*). Subdominant cover types range from bare soil and rock to willow, grass-forbs, and to a lesser degree aspen (*Populus tremuloides*). This class also includes a small amount of water edge.
Conifer-aspen	Stands of aspen (*Populus tremuloides*) mixed with various conifer species.
Aspen	Primarily aspen (*Populus tremuloides*) but also cottonwood (*Populus* spp.).
Irrigated	Primarily irrigated native meadows and hayfields.
Willow	Primarily willows.
Aspen-irrigated-willow	All three cover types are represented.
Grass-forbs	Dominated by grasses and/or forbs; may also include sparse shrubs. Includes alpine meadows as well as lower-elevation grasslands.
Sage	Dominated by big sage (*Artemisia tridentata*). Subdominant cover types include grasses, bare soil, and other shrub species (e.g., gray sage, bush cinquefoil, rabbit brush, and saltbrush).
Mixed shrub	A mixed general class consisting primarily of willows, sage, and limited amounts of serviceberry and chokecherry.
Soil-dominated	Dominated by bare soil, often with sparse vegetation. Also includes areas of human development and a significant portion of U.S. Interstate 70.
Rock	Includes talus slopes, mine tailings, dam faces, and bare soil (including dry tailings ponds).
Snow	Includes permanent and temporary snowfields.

TABLE 13.3. Indices Used to Assess Habitat Value

Index	Objective
Local diversity	Identifies areas of the county that offer high levels of species diversity resulting from overlap of habitats of individual species
Neighborhood diversity	Identifies areas of the county that offer high levels of species diversity resulting from juxtaposition of vegetation types
Patch value	Identifies large intact patches of vegetation and weights them by relative rarity of species habitat

cell, determining the number of species (weighted by biological rank) that had potentially suitable habitat within the circle, and assigning that number to the grid cell. Finally, to identify areas that offer high-quality habitat because they are relatively intact, we developed the Patch Value index. The index was calculated for all patches of vegetation containing more than fifty contiguous cells. For each patch, we counted the number of species with potentially suitable habitat within the patch. We then calculated the ratio of patch area to total area of potential suitable habitat for each species found within an individual patch. Thus, the patch value map identified large intact patches of vegetation and weighted them by relative rarity of species habitat. Small patches were given greater weight if they constituted a large proportion of a species' habitat. Large patches of vegetation offering habitat for specialist species received high scores for patch value.

Simulating Land Use Change

We developed a stochastic model forecasting the distribution of housing units across the county (Theobald and Hobbs 1998). The model was based on historical data from the county assessor on housing density in each quarter-section of the county. The probability that an undeveloped cell (i.e., one in which housing density is zero) will develop during any given year is a function of the densities of the neighboring quarter-sections; areas with higher neighborhood housing density are more likely to develop. We fit a linear regression model to the historical density data describing the growth rate of developing cells. The predictions of the model can be adjusted by changing assumptions about population growth rates, the likelihood of development in certain areas (e.g., by phased development), the spatial restrictions (e.g., zoning) that limit the number of building units, and the spatial pattern of development (e.g., clustering). We assumed that each building was the center of a circular disturbance zone extending outward 50–500 meters (m), or 164–1,640 feet (ft.), and that the value of habitat was substantially reduced within the disturbance zone, in order to examine potential effects of development on habitat (Theobald, Miller, and Hobbs 1997). The method was sensitive to both density and pattern. Cumulative effects were estimated by summing the total area contained within disturbance zones with different development patterns.

Discussion

The goal of the SCoP project was to help citizens and their governments make choices about land use that achieve a reasonable balance between the need of wildlife for intact landscapes and the need of people for economic vitality. Many of the notable successes of bringing science to bear on environmental policy involve a top-down model wherein scientific information flows upward in a government hierarchy and regulations and policy flow downward through that hierarchy. This model does not serve well in the case of private land use change because the political authority for decisions about land use reside at the local level (Dale et al. 2000). As a result, scientists are challenged to bring their knowledge to many local decisions, decisions that are inherently diffuse in time and space.

Originally, the SCoP application resided at the Natural Resource Ecology Laboratory at Colorado State University. Citizens, planners, and decision makers could gain access to the information system through a public terminal housed in the Summit County government offices or through direct Internet connections. We quickly found that use of the system was limited because of specialized computer and software needs, so we redesigned the system to take advantage of emerging Internet browser technology. This substantially broadened our user base and, more important, forced us to rethink, simplify, and standardize the application's design and functionality (plate 7). Currently, SCoP uses ArcView Internet Map Server mapping software, JavaScript, and HTML and can be accessed via the Internet (NDIS 2002). Bearly and colleagues (1998) describe the technical details of this site.

Remaining Challenges

SCoP has been in place in Summit County since the fall of 1998. Wildlife habitat data from the system have been incorporated into basin and sub-basin plans. Information from the system has been used to identify ptarmigan winter habitat areas in development of the Copper Mountain Subbasin Plan. Maps of development patterns were also used to inform a citizen growth conference.

The main difficulty to overcome is ensuring that data continue to be used to inform decisions. Although we have simplified and streamlined the system's interface and ease of use, it can still be daunting for potential users. We conduct training sessions to help users, particularly planners, understand how to use the system and how to gather the information required for a particular planning process.

Perhaps the most significant challenge of this project has been the gap between the information scientists provide and the information desired by decision makers in public processes. Traditionally, scientists have been expected to provide precise answers to scientific questions. In the search for precision, many scientists narrow their focus, losing relevancy in solving real-world problems. In a plea for ecologists to engage in more relevant research, Holling (1997) suggested that scientists should seek approximate answers to the right questions, not precise answers to the wrong questions. At the same time, public decision makers must be willing to base their decisions on limited, but credible, scientific information. Frequent turnover of elected officials complicates the incorporation of biological information into private land use planning because it disrupts the accumulation of knowledge.

In conclusion, the wisdom of decisions made in a democracy depends on access to information by citizens and decision makers. We believe that improving the quality of information about wildlife and natural communities and enhancing access to it will improve conservation decisions in Colorado and elsewhere.

Acknowledgments

The project described in this chapter was supported by the Great Outdoors Colorado Trust Fund, the Rocky Mountain Elk Foundation, and the Colorado Division of Wildlife. We thank all design team participants in both Summit and Larimer Counties for their willingness to participate and their insightful contributions.

References

Andrews, R., and R. Righter. 1992. *Colorado birds: A reference to their distribution and habitat.* Denver, Colo.: Denver Museum of Natural History.

Baron, J. S., D. M. Theobald, and D. B. Fagre. 2000. Management of land use conflicts in the United States Rocky Mountains. *Mountain Research and Development* 20:24–27.

Bean, M. J., and D. S. Wilcove. 1997. The private-land problem. *Conservation Biology* 11:1–2.

Bearly, T., D. M. Theobald, N. T. Hobbs, and J. Zack. 1998. Disseminating natural diversity information using ArcView IMS: Design issues and technical considerations. *Proceedings of the ESRI User Conference '98.* On-line at <http://gis.esri.com/library/userconf/proc98/PROCEED/TO200/PAP184/P184.HTM>.

Bearly, T., J. Zack, C. Johnson, D. M. Theobald, and N. T. Hobbs. 1998. The natural diversity information source. On-line at <http://ndis.nrel.colostate.edu>.

Beyers, W. B. 1996. *Explaining the new service economies of the rural West.* Presentation at Pacific Northwest Regional Economics Conference, Portland, Oregon, 4 May. On-line at <http://www.upa.pdx.edu/PNREC/>.

Bureau of the Census. 2001. *Census 2000.* Washington, D.C.: U.S. Department of Commerce, Bureau of the Census.

Colorado Department of Agriculture. 2000. *Tracking agricultural land conversion in Colorado.* Denver: Colorado Department of Agriculture, Division of Resource Analysis.

Dale, V. H., S. Brown, R. A. Haeuber, N. T. Hobbs, N. Huntly, R. J. Naiman, W. E. Riebsame, M. G. Turner, and T. J. Valone. 2000. Ecological principles and guidelines for managing the use of land: A report from the Ecological Society of America. *Ecological Applications* 10:639–670.

Diamond, H. L., and P. F. Noonan. 1996. *Land use in America.* Washington, D.C.: Island Press.

Duerkson, C. J., N. T. Hobbs, D. L. Elliott, E. Johnson, and J. R. Miller. 1997. *Managing development for people and wildlife: A handbook for habitat protection by local governments.* PAS No. 470/471. Chicago: American Planning Association.

Fitzgerald, J. P., C. A. Meaney, and D. M. Armstrong. 1981. *Mammals of Colorado.* Denver, Colo.: Denver Museum of Natural History.

GAO (U.S. General Accounting Office). 1994. Endangered Species Act: information on species protection on nonfederal lands. GAO/RCED-95-16. Washington, D.C.: U.S. General Accounting Office.

Gross, J. E., and C. P. Melcher. 1998. COVERS: Identifying species at risk and setting priorities for conservation of vertebrates in Colorado. Unpublished report submitted to the Colorado Division of Wildlife, Fort Collins, Colorado.

Hammerson, G. A. 1986. *Amphibians and reptiles in Colorado.* Denver: Colorado Division of Wildlife.

Holling, C. S. 1997. The inaugural issue of *Conservation Ecology. Conservation Ecology* 1:1. On-line at <http://www.consecol.org/vol1/iss1/art1>.

Murphy, D. D., and B. R. Noon. 1992. Integrating scientific methods with habitat conservation planning: Reserve design for northern spotted owls. *Ecological Applications* 2:3–17.

NDIS (Colorado Natural Diversity Information Source). 2002. GIS-based application providing information about Colorado's natural diversity. On-line at <http://ndis.nrel.colostate.edu/>.

Norman, D. A. 1998. *The invisible computer.* Cambridge, Mass.: MIT Press.

Noss, R. F., M. A. O'Connell, and D. D. Murphy. 1997. *The science of conservation planning: Habitat conservation under the Endangered Species Act.* Washington, D.C.: Island Press.

Peck, S. 1998. *Planning for biodiversity: Issues and examples.* Washington, D.C.: Island Press.

Power, T. M. 1996. *Lost landscapes and failed economies: The search for a value of place.* Washington, D.C.: Island Press.

Rockwood, P. 1995. Landscape planning for biodiversity. *Landscape and Urban Planning* 31:379–385.

Rudzitis, G., and R. A. Streatfield. 1992. The importance of amenities and attitudes: A Washington example. *Journal of Environmental Systems* 22:269.

Theobald, D. M. 2000. Fragmentation by inholdings and exurban development. In *Forest fragmentation in the central Rocky Mountains,* ed. R. L. Knight, F. W. Smith, S. W. Buskirk, W. H. Romme, and W. L. Baker, 155–174. Boulder: University Press of Colorado.

Theobald, D. M., and N. T. Hobbs. 1998. Forecasting rural land use change: A comparison of regression- and spatial transition–based models. *Geographical and Environmental Modelling* 2:57–74.

———. 2002. A framework for evaluating land use planning alternatives: Protecting biodiversity on private land. *Conservation Ecology* 6:5. On-line at <http://www.consecol.org/vol6/iss1/art5>.

Theobald, D. M., N. T. Hobbs, T. Bearly, J. Zack, T. Shenk, and W. E. Riebsame. 2000. Incorporating biological information into local land-use decision making: Designing a system for conservation planning. *Landscape Ecology* 15:35–45.

Theobald, D. M., J. M. Miller, and N. T. Hobbs. 1997. Estimating the cumulative effects of development on wildlife habitat. *Landscape and Urban Planning.* 39:25–36.

White, D., P. G. Minotti, M. J. Barczak, J. C. Sifneos, K. E. Freemark, M. V. Santelmann, C. F. Steinitz, A. R. Kiester, and E. M. Preston. 1997. Assessing risks to biodiversity from future landscape change. *Conservation Biology* 11:1–13.

CHAPTER 14

Natural and Cultural Influences on Ecosystem Processes in the Flathead River Basin (Montana and British Columbia)

Jack A. Stanford and Bonnie K. Ellis

▲

Although the mountains of the Flathead River basin reach elevations of 3,500 meters (m), or 11,500 feet (ft.), most of the basin's landscape is below 1,700 m (6,000 ft.) and is dominated by the Flathead River, its tributaries, and its floodplains. Our ongoing hypothesis is that the large floodplains are centers of organization that control regional biodiversity. Ungulates and their predators, such as mountain lions and wolves, congregate on the floodplains in winter (Foresman 2001). The forested and wetland, or riparian, corridors of the rivers and their lateral tributaries are the linkage zones for animal migrations between upland and lowland forest types. The floodplain itself is a marvelously complex and dynamic landform that is continually changing, creating a shifting habitat mosaic that on the surface comprises permanent and ephemeral channels, spring brooks, and wetlands embedded in the successional template of cottonwood-spruce riparian forest (Stanford et al. in press). In this chapter, we describe the Flathead River–Flathead Lake ecosystem, review the natural and cultural drivers of the ecosystem's structure and function, and conclude with some thoughts about the future of this relatively pristine Rocky Mountain ecosystem.

The Flathead River is a large Rocky Mountain tributary of the Columbia River that more than doubles the size of the Clark Fork River. The Clark Fork flows north through Pend Oreille Lake in Idaho to join the main-stem Columbia River near the intersection of the borders of Washington, Idaho, and British Columbia. The Flathead drains extensive montane landscapes sculpted by Quaternary period glaciation. Flathead Lake, one of the 300 largest lakes in the world, occupies a glacial and tectonic basin at the terminus of the Rocky Mountain Trench that contained a long lobe of the Pleistocene epoch continental glacier that extended south from Canada. In addition to Flathead Lake, there are other large glacial lakes in the basin, notably those in Glacier National Park on the eastern side of the North Fork valley, along with Whitefish and Swan Lakes (plate 8). McDonald Lake on the Middle Fork and Tally Lake on the Stillwater River are the deepest lakes, at 520 m (1,706 ft.) and 480 m (1,575 ft.), respectively. All are oligotrophic (nutrient-poor) or ultra-oligotrophic, owing to great depth and generally low nutrient dissolution from the catchment.

The Flathead River basin is 22,241 square kilometers (km²), or 8,590 square miles (mi.²), in extent and is drained by six fifth-order tributaries of the mainstem river (plate 8). Expansive mountain valleys with wide floodplains fed by steep-gradient streams characterize these tributaries. The basin includes 2,300 km² (888 mi.²) of British Columbia, making it subject to jurisdiction of the International Joint Commission, which oversees transboundary issues between the United States and Canada.

Almost half (42%) of the basin is included in Glacier National Park and the Bob Marshall–Great Bear–Scapegoat Wilderness complex of the USDA Forest Service and therefore is completely protected from development, except for the east–west highway (U.S. Highway 2) and railroad corridor along the Middle Fork. Several segments of the North, Middle, and South Forks are included in the National Wild and Scenic Rivers System. The rest of the mountain areas of the basin are managed forestlands in private, state, provincial, federal, and tribal (Confederated Salish and Kootenai Tribes of the Flathead Indian Reservation) ownership.

The valley bottom above Flathead Lake, the Kalispell Valley, historically was a ponderosa pine savanna. The Mission Valley below Flathead Lake historically was a Palouse prairie unit of intermountain grasslands (chapter 11; Küchler 1964). About 80,000 people now live in the Kalispell and Mission Valleys, which have been farmed since settlement and are being rapidly converted to urban and fragmented exurban landscapes. The rest of the basin is essentially uninhabited, except for recreational traffic that has become increasingly congested along the rivers (white-water sports), along the Going-to-the-Sun Highway in Glacier National Park, and at popular camping sites in the park and the wilderness areas.

Limnology of the Flathead River System

Headwater streams in the Flathead River basin begin almost exclusively as springs below talus slopes (glacially formed rocky slopes) or in deep groundwater that has followed complex flow paths in cracked bedrock or through karstic (limestone) pathways. Fens and bogs fed by groundwater occur at all elevations. The headwater streams flow across highly variable glacial landscapes but in exposed meadows where summer water temperatures can exceed 20°C for short periods in summer. From their headwaters, streams enter subalpine and slope forests, where they achieve very high gradients and stay very cold all the way to the valley floors, owing to heavy forest cover, high elevations, and side flows from cold springs.

The lower-gradient rivers in the mountain valleys exchange water with their floodplains above- and belowground. Indeed, groundwater flow and recharge of surface waters in expansive floodplain settings is a predominant feature of the Flathead system and has received considerable study (detailed in Stanford et al. in press). The floodplains reflect the legacy of river flood and sediment dynamics interacting with forest succession. Floodplain rivers continuously jump their beds to cut new channels, leaving behind exposed gravel bars, sandbars, and old riverbeds. Active floodplain rivers are thus constantly altering vegetation successional trajectories. River water seeps into the aquifers and flows downslope through them, emerging wherever river scour has downcut sufficiently to intersect the water table. The volume of the aquifer system varies with river stage, and the aquifer system naturally stores water during floods and discharges during base flow. Indeed, most of the base flow of Flathead streams and rivers is derived from groundwater, some that has been underground for months or years and other from short flow paths connecting directly to the river. This creates the shifting habitat mosaic.

The shifting habitat mosaic is habitat for many species of resident and migratory biota. Floodplain ponds contain robust populations of boreal toads as more obvious components of complex aquatic food webs. Juvenile fishes are abundant in the shallow water habitats on the fringe of channels, where temperatures are moderated by the upwelling groundwater and predation from larger fish is reduced. Algal production is greatly enhanced in channels, ponds, and wetlands fed by groundwater owing to the decomposition of organic matter within the groundwater flow path by interstitial biofilms of bacteria and fungi. Bioavailable nitrogen and phosphorus are typically an order of magnitude higher in upwelling groundwater than in the main channel (Ellis, Stanford, and Ward 1998). The stream channel itself is actually a rather small compartment of the floodplain: the shifting habitat mosaic is the hot spot of biodiversity. Uniquely adapted biota reside in the alluvial aquifers, including six species of stone fly (Plecoptera) that mature in the aquifer and move great distances through the zones of preferential flow to emerge as flying adults from the river channels.

Elk populate the uplands during summer but must reside on the valley floodplains in winter. There they find moderate snow depths and temperatures and plentiful food supplies in the form of browse-adapted plants such as willows and dogwood. The various successional stages of the cottonwood forest provide food in the early stages and thermal cover in the old growth. The floodplains are a primary site for elk calving because they are the first places in the altitudinal gradient to produce new, high-protein plant shoots in the spring, providing immediate nutrition for mother and calf.

The complex, nonlinear nature of these floodplains remains to be fully illuminated. But they clearly are nodes in the corridors that connect the terrestrial and aquatic components of the ecosystem.

Faunal Pattern and Process

All the Rocky Mountain megafauna occur in the Flathead River basin, including reasonably robust populations of grizzly bears, bald eagles, gray wolves, wolverines, and lynx, which have been extirpated to the south and are not abundant anywhere in the Rockies. Mountain goats, Rocky Mountain sheep, and hoary marmots characterize the alpine zone; mule deer and elk, the middle elevations and ponderosa savannas; and white-tailed deer are common at lower elevations. Moose range throughout the forested zone. Cyclic populations of meadow vole and montane vole (*Microtus pennsylvanicus, M. montanus*) are prey for coyotes, red foxes, badgers, and other mammals, even an occasional grizzly bear, as well as a notably rich raptor fauna. Raptors include northern species such as snowy owls in winter on the intermountain grasslands and old-field farmlands of the Mission Valley.

Other faunal assemblages, especially insects, are species-rich and underscore the melting pot zoogeography of the Flathead basin. In a long-term study, Michael Ivie and colleagues at Montana State University, Bozeman, collected more than 1,184 species of beetle (Coleoptera) in the lowland forests of Glacier National Park (M. Ivie, pers. comm.; Ivie, Ivie, and Gustafson 1998). Seventy percent (105 species) of the stone flies known in the entire Rocky Mountain area, from Alaska to Mexico, occur in the Flathead River system (Stanford 1975; Baumann, Gaufin, and Surdick 1977). More than 400 species of macroinvertebrates inhabit lotic (running water) environments on the floodplain reaches of the rivers, and predictable faunal replacements occur in relation to temperature patterns longitudinally along the tributary streams from mountain divides to valley bottoms (Stanford, Hauer, and Ward 1988; Stanford et al. in press; Hauer et al. 2000).

The native fish fauna of the Flathead River, on the other hand, is depauperate in comparison with those of the Columbia River mainstem and the Missouri River system (table 14.1; Holton and Johnson 1996). None of the anadromous salmonids that so characterize the Columbia River were able to colonize the Flathead, owing to impassable falls downstream on the Clark Fork. Moreover, some species, notably longnose dace, are abundant in the Clark Fork and in the Flathead River downstream of the substantial cataract where Kerr Dam was constructed to raise the level of Flathead Lake. Longnose dace are very widely distributed throughout the western United States and characteristically inhabit fast-flowing streams and rivers. Nonetheless, they were not able to pass the rapids below the outlet of Flathead Lake, and today upstream fish passage is blocked by the dam. Hungry Horse Dam, on the South Fork, also blocks fish passage (plate 8). This has prevented colonization of non-native species, and the South Fork drainage, the largest of the three main tributaries, retains the native Flathead fish fauna.

Isolation and protection of native species are important because many non-native fishes were introduced into the basin, mainly in Flathead Lake, and some established strong populations. Management agencies purposefully introduced sport fish decades ago to increase angling opportunities (chapter 8). More recent introductions were surreptitious, by anglers desiring more diverse fishing, or accidental, via bait buckets. Non-native species introductions are now illegal in Montana. Unfortunately, competition for limited food supplies in the oligotrophic waters of the Flathead, and interbreeding with non-natives, reduced the vitality of the natives, especially native salmonids. Adfluvial, or lake-dwelling but river-spawning, cutthroat trout historically were the dominant predator in Flathead Lake, but they were substantially reduced by competition with introduced kokanee salmon by the 1950s (Elrod 1929; Brunson, Pennington, and Bjorklund 1952). Flathead Lake adfluvial cutthroats have not been extirpated but are rare today, as are their natural predators, bull trout. Fluvial cutthroat and bull trout are more abundant upstream, and the populations in the South Fork, including adfluvials from the reservoir, are comparatively robust. Cutthroat, especially fluvial populations, may genetically mix with rainbow trout and are excluded from juvenile habitat in the floodplain reaches by the more aggressive non-native brook trout (Cavallo 1997). Brook trout can interbreed with bull trout, and hybrids have been observed in the Swan River basin, where brook trout are widely distributed (Leary, Allendorf, and Forbes 1993; Baxter 1997).

TABLE 14.1. Origin, Habitat, and Status of Fishes of the Flathead River Basin

Name	Species	Origin, Habitat[1]	Status[2]
Bull trout	*Salvelinus confluentus*	N, a, f	A, D
Westslope cutthroat trout	*Oncorhynchus clarkii lewisi*	N, a, f	A, D
Rocky Mountain whitefish	*Prosopium williamsoni*	N, a, f	A, S
Pygmy whitefish	*Prosopium coulteri*	N, a	R, S
Largescale sucker	*Catostomus macrocheilus*	N, l	C, S
Longnose sucker	*Catostomus catostomus*	N, a, f	A, S
Northern pikeminnow	*Ptychocheilus oregonensis*	N, l, f	A, S
Peamouth minnow	*Mylocheilus caurinus*	N, l	C, S
Redside shiner	*Richardsonius balteatus*	N, l	A, S
Longnose dace	*Rhinichthys cataractae*	N, f$_{LR}$	C, S
Slimy sculpin	*Cottus cognatus*	N, l, f	A, S
Shorthead sculpin	*Cottus confusus*	N, l, f	A, S
Lake whitefish	*Coregonus clupeaformis*	I (1890), a	C, E
Arctic grayling	*Thymallus arcticus*	I (1960s), a	R[3], S
Kokanee salmon	*Oncorhynchus nerka*	I (1916), a	R, D
Yellowstone cutthroat trout	*Oncorhynchus clarkii bouvieri*	I (1910s), a	R[3], S
Lake trout	*Salvelinus namaycush*	I (1905), l	A, E
Brook trout	*Salvelinus fontinalis*	I (1913), l, f	A, E
Rainbow trout	*Oncorhynchus mykiss*	I (1914), f	C, S
Golden trout	*Oncorhynchus mykiss aguabonita*	I (1960s), a	R[3], S
Brown trout	*Salmo trutta*	I (1910s), f$_{LR}$	C, E
Yellow perch	*Perca flavescens*	I (1910), l	A, S
Northern pike	*Esox lucius*	I (1960s), l, f	R[4], E
Pumpkinseed sunfish	*Lepomis gibbosus*	I (1910), l	C, S
Bluegill sunfish	*Lepomis macrochirus*	I (?), l	R[3], ?
Black bullhead	*Ameiurus melas*	I (1910), l	C, S
Yellow bullhead	*Ameiurus natalis*	I (?), l	R, ?
Largemouth bass	*Micropterus salmoides*	I (1898), l	R, S
Smallmouth bass	*Micropterus dolomieu*	I (1960s), f$_{LR}$	C, E
Central mudminnow	*Umbra limi*	I (1990s), l	R, ?

Source: Holton and Johnson 1996 and unpublished records.

[1]Native (N) or non-native (I) populations in basin lakes (l) or rivers and streams (f), sometimes with adfluvial (a) life cycle (adults in lakes, spawning in tributary streams); f$_{LR}$ are restricted to the lower Flathead River downstream of the cataract where Kerr Dam was built, in 1935.

[2]Distributed throughout the basin (A), common (C), or restricted (R); population size stable (S), declining (D), or expanding (E). Bull trout are listed (L) under the Endangered Species Act of 1973. Status based on state and tribal census programs (unpublished data).

[3]Introduced adfluvial population in a few small lakes in the basin.

[4]Restricted to the littoral zone of Flathead Lake, where it is rarely caught; a few small, shallow lakes in the Kalispell Valley; and the lower Flathead River and the sloughs and oxbows immediately upstream of Flathead Lake.

The most pervasive change in the fish fauna was caused by the unfortunate but purposeful introduction in the late 1970s of *Mysis relicta,* the freshwater opossum shrimp, whose native range includes the glacial lakes of the Canadian Shield and the Laurentian Great Lakes. The shrimp were obtained from native habitat in Waterton Lake, on the eastern side of Glacier National Park; they were stocked in lowland lakes upstream of Flathead Lake (plate 8). They were discovered in Flathead Lake in the early 1980s and then expanded exponentially, feeding on the cladoceran (water flea) zooplankton. Because they migrate from the bottom of the lake to feed at night, the mysids are unavailable to the pelagic (open-water) fishes, particularly the very abundant and very popular kokanee salmon. Indeed, the mysids were introduced to increase the production of salmon, on the basis of misleading information from trial stockings in Kootenay Lake, British Columbia. They were intended to promote production of native kokanee in that lake. Early results were promising but changed for the worse over the longer term. Unfortunately, mysid introduction had become an accepted management practice for kokanee fisheries all over the western United States before the actual effects were documented. In the Flathead, as elsewhere, the results were a disaster for kokanee fisheries and for native fishes in general.

Mysids become abundant in lakes by substantially reducing the large zooplankton. They avoid visual feeders such as kokanee and cutthroat in the lighted layers of the lakes by residing in very cold water on the dark lake bottom in the daytime. They are, however, excellent forage for juvenile lake trout and lake whitefish, which also were introduced from the Canadian Shield lakes, where mysids are their natural food. This relationship allowed lake trout and whitefish to substantially increase, creating a voracious predator trap. The kokanee received a double whammy from the mysids: their food resources were substantially reduced and their predators substantially increased (Spencer, McClelland, and Stanford 1991). Mysid numbers declined from their exponential high of 180 per square meter (m^2), or 16 per square foot ($ft.^2$), in 1986 and have oscillated around $40/m^2$ ($4/ft.^2$) in recent years. Of course, the native zooplankton were substantially altered, with large cladocerans declining and small forms, including rotifers, substantially increasing. The cascading effects of the mysid introduction included eagles and grizzlies that fed on the spawning salmon. Eagle numbers, especially, declined.

Because planktivorous fish occur in very low numbers, the subadult and adult lake trout have little to feed on other than mysids. They have begun to disperse upstream and downstream out of the lake. Lake trout are often now caught in the rivers, and they have invaded the front country lakes where mysids were not introduced. This presents an interesting natural experimental design for long-term research of food web dynamics and the strong interactive effects of the mysids with and without lake trout (table 14.2).

TABLE 14.2. Natural Experimental Design Created by Mysid and Lake Trout Establishment in Deep Oligotrophic Lakes of the Flathead River Basin

Treatments	Lake Trout Recently Colonizing	Lake Trout Well Established	Native Fish Only (Natural Control Lakes)
MYSIDS ESTABLISHED	SWAN LAKE, TALLY LAKE Small-sized zooplankton; native planktivorous fish declining; bull trout status erratic or declining	WHITEFISH LAKE, FLATHEAD LAKE Small-sized zooplankton, epilimnial refugium for Cladocera; planktivorous fish extirpated; bull trout in steep decline; conversion to benthic-oriented food web	WATERTON LAKE[1] Small-sized zooplankton, copepods dominate; no planktivorous fish; no bull trout; benthic-oriented food web well established
MYSIDS ABSENT	LOGGING LAKE, BOWMAN LAKE Large cladoceran zooplankton common; planktivorous fish declining; bull trout stable	McDONALD LAKE, KINTLA LAKE Large cladoceran zooplankton common; planktivorous fish declining; bull trout declining	QUARTZ LAKE[2], BIG SALMON LAKE[3], UPPER KINTLA LAKE[4] Large cladoceran zooplankton common, insects and gammarids in water column; planktivorous fish stable (if present)[4], cutthroat dominant; bull trout stable; pelagic-oriented food web well established

[1] Waterton Lake is outside the Flathead River basin (in the Saskatechwan River basin; see plate 8) but is germane because it is the source of *Mysis relicta* introduced into the Flathead and it contains the *native* mysid–lake trout food web of the Canadian Shield.

[2] Non-native access is blocked by a falls below the outlet; contains the complete Flathead native fish fauna.

[3] Non-native fish access is blocked by Hungry Horse Dam; contains the complete Flathead native fish fauna.

[4] Non-native access is blocked by a falls below the outlet; contains only bull trout.

The cumulative effects on cutthroat trout and bull trout are not clear, but populations clearly are declining. Gill net sets in Flathead Lake catch mostly lake trout and lake whitefish today, whereas prior to the establishment of *Mysis,* kokanee, mountain whitefish, and bull trout were the dominant catches. Native salmonids are rarely taken in nets or by anglers today, whereas they were abundant in the early 1900s (Elrod 1929). Bull trout redd (nest) counts declined in relation to the mysid and lake trout expansion (Rieman and McIntyre 1996).

These observations do not bode well for Flathead bull trout in the long term. Bull trout are present only in lakes where they have passed falls or cascades that prevent immigration of lake trout (cf. Donald and Alger 1993). In the Swan River system, bull trout populations are more robust in streams whose basins remain unroaded (Baxter, Frissell, and Hauer 1999).

Limnology of Flathead Lake

Flathead Lake is one of the least culturally eutrophied (nutrient-enriched) large lakes in the Northern Hemisphere (figure 14.1). With an area of 480 km^2 (185 mi.^{2}) and volume of 23.3 cubic kilometers (km^3), or 5.6 cubic miles (mi.^{3}), seasonal heating and cooling is slow, and the lake moderates regional temperature and precipitation patterns. Surface temperatures range from freezing during midwinter in very cold years to a maximum of 22°C during late summer in hot years. Summer stratification is intense, however, and a thin layer of warm water, the epilimnion, lies above most of the volume of the lake. Below the epilimnion, water temperatures never exceed 6°C–8°C. The lake circulates to the bottom all winter in most years, with the entire water column reaching 2°C during very cold winters and briefly freezing over during calms. Stratification initiates in June, and fall turnover typically occurs in late October. The less dense water near shore circulates counterclockwise around the colder water in the main part of the lake, owing to gravitational force associated with Earth's rotation. This Coriolis current entrains the inflow from the Flathead and Swan Rivers and pulls the river water down the western shore. This is very observable during spring freshet (snowmelt), when the river is turbid and warmer than the main lake. The turbidity plume of river water overflows the denser, colder lake water and moves down the western shore, the dirty brown water appearing in strong contrast to the blue waters in the deeper parts of the lake. The Coriolis current persists all year but is less observable in fall.

Most of the year, Flathead Lake is crystal clear. Fine sediments from the Flathead River freshet reduce clarity during spring, depending on the intensity of the runoff. Nonetheless, the average depth of visibility, or Secchi disk, since 1975 has been 9 m (30 ft.), with values exceeding 20 m (66 ft.) often recorded

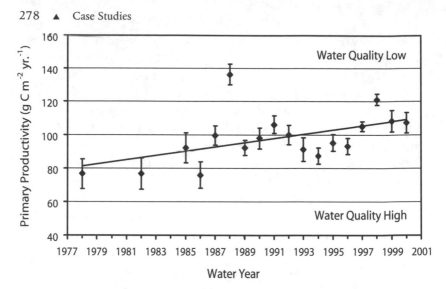

FIGURE 14.1 *Water Quality in Flathead Lake Measured as Annual Rate of Primary Production, 1977–2001.* Primary production was measured with ^{14}C uptake in 4 hr. midday incubations using methods of Pregnall 1991. Data are means (±1 standard deviation) of 12–15 measures throughout each year. The trend line is significant ($P < 0.01$): water quality is deteriorating as primary production increases.

in fall. Biomass in the lake is uniformly low (1.0 microgram [μg] of chlorophyll per liter [L] of water) year-round. Pelagic primary production is limited by paucity of nitrogen (N) and phosphorus (P) (figure 14.1; Spencer and Ellis 1990). As noted earlier, the river system does not export much of a nutrient load. Surprisingly, as much as 30% of the annual N and P load during the 1980s and 1990s was fallout from the atmosphere. This was mainly fugitive dust from local rural roads and smoke particulates from forest fires and agricultural burning inside and often far outside (usually west of) the Flathead basin. Nutrient loading from human sources upstream of Flathead Lake has steadily increased since the 1970s, and annual loading weakly correlates with increasing primary production.

Organisms smaller than 10 μm (microplankton), mostly bacteria and very small green and blue-green algae, are responsible for 90% of the total primary production (Ellis and Stanford 1982). But diatoms (more than 400 species and varieties), dinoflagellates, and other macroalgae are always very visible in plankton samples. A vernal bloom of large diatoms occurs in spring along with the microplankton in response to elevated nutrient levels, increasing day length, and warming water. By late summer, when the lake is thermally stratified, primary production and sinking of plankton to the bottom depletes nutrients in the surface waters, and productivity begins to decline.

In 1984 and 1994, lakewide blooms of macroalgae, *Anabaena flos-aquae* and *Botryococcus,* were documented prior to fall turnover. These algae had never been observed in Flathead Lake during 100 years of lake studies. The algae collected in windrows on the shoreline and clearly represented sudden and alarming declines in water quality. *Anabaena* and *Botryococcus* were common in late-summer samples in other years but did not reach bloom proportions. These outbreaks of macroalgae very likely are linked to increasing nutrient inputs from human activities. Similar patterns of lake eutrophication, of course, have been documented many times worldwide, and the federal Clean Water Act requires states to reduce nutrient loading in impaired lakes.

Efforts to reduce nutrient pollution from human sources have been initiated in the Flathead basin in response to the apparent decline in water quality associated with steadily increasing primary productivity and the observed *Anabaena* blooms (figure 14.1; Stanford et al. 1997). However, the mechanisms and interactions that cause these rare events in Flathead Lake and other large lakes are not clear. Certainly primary productivity is at or approaching a threshold in which complex interactions favor production of macroplankton over microplankton.

The highest annual rate of primary production occurred in 1988, corresponding with onset of the trophic shift caused by establishment of *Mysis relicta* in the lake (figure 14.1). Mysid numbers peaked in 1986–1987. The food web shift from pelagic (open-water) to benthic (bottom-dwelling) orientation was firmly in place for the first time in 1988. This suggests a top-down stimulus on phytoplankton production: the mysids had virtually eliminated the cladoceran grazers by 1988. This may have altered microbial nutrient cycling to favor microconsumers that cycle biomass and nutrients rapidly, thereby increasing primary production rates. On the other hand, atmospheric fallout of nutrients was very high in the summer of 1988 as a result of extensive forest fires and smoke plumes. Similar levels of smoke occurred during the fire years of 1998 and 2000, and primary production levels were again above the trend line. *Anabaena* did not bloom in 1988, 1998, or 2000.

Conclusions about the mechanisms that control productivity in Flathead Lake remain elusive in spite of the long-term record. However, the record does change the obvious conclusion that *Mysis relicta* is the strong interactor in the lake food web, influencing trophic structure at multiple levels and far beyond expectations based on its biomass alone.

Linking the Rivers and the Lake:
A Conceptual Ecosystem Model

The studies described here show strong biophysical linkages between the river system and Flathead Lake (figure 14.2). The catchment delivers water and nutrients into the lake, and a wide variety of fishes pump nutrients upstream into the catchment. Temperature, precipitation, and light regime are the prime drivers that introduce natural variation in processes controlling structure. Cultural drivers, particularly invasions of non-native biota, eutrophication, and control of river flow and lake levels by Kerr and Hungry Horse Dams, moderate processes. This conceptual construct applies to the other deep lakes in the basin (plate 8) because they all are similarly oligotrophic, have large catchment basins relative to lake surface area, and are inhabited by adfluvial fishes.

The mysid-mediated immigration of lake trout from Flathead Lake is more than

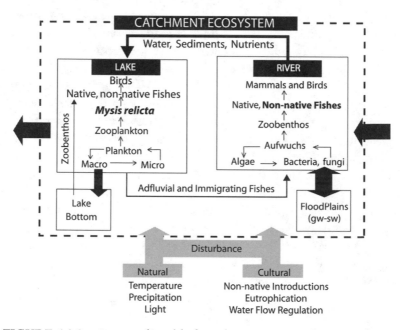

FIGURE 14.2 *Conceptual Model of Trophic Interactions and Drivers That Control Cycling of Materials and Energy in the Flathead River–Flathead Lake Ecosystem.* In this model, heavy arrows indicate materials and energy pathways. *Mysis* and non-native fish interact strongly to elicit cascading changes in trophic structure. *Aufwuchs* refers to attached (to rocks, plants) aquatic organisms; *gw-sw* is groundwater–surface water.

a nutrient pump, however, because they have invaded other large lakes in the basin, thereby changing food webs in potentially predictable ways. Indeed, lake trout establishment, coupled with the pattern of mysid introductions into the deep, oligotrophic lakes of the basin, provides an interesting array of potential trajectories and outcomes of food web change that could shed considerable new light on lake trophic ecology and cascading effects of non-native invasions (table 14.2).

The lake bottom functions as a subsystem because about 40% of the annual nutrient input into the lake is retained, tied up by a steep chemical gradient in the bottom sediments (figure 14.2). The bed sediments of Flathead Lake are dense clays deposited at a rate of about 1 millimeter (mm), or 0.04 inch (in.), per year, depending on location in the lake. Productivity in the lake and delivery of allochthonous organic matter (from the rivers and airshed) are too low to generate a significant organic load in the hypolimnion (bottom waters), where the water column remains oxygen-saturated. Hence, the mud-water interface is aerobic, and nutrients, especially phosphorus, collect on the bottom and remain insoluble (Wetzel 2001). The lake bottom is therefore a materials and energy sink. Very little organic matter actually gets to the lake bottom because of decomposition and extreme nutrient limitation within the water column: organic matter is consumed by microplankton before it settles to the bottom. Moreover, mysids consume zooplankton and organic detritus within the water column and metabolize it on the bottom. Nonetheless, the fishes that now dominate the lake are adapted to life in the deep waters, where they feed on mysids and zoobenthos, such as fingernail clams, midges, and caddis flies. These observations suggest that organic matter conversion is very rapid at the lower trophic levels and the lake remains nutrient-limited.

The river floodplains function as riverine subsystems (figure 14.2). We do not know whether they are net sinks or sources of material and energy for the rivers, but clearly, strong interactions occur. The riparian forests and wetlands provide organic inputs to the river and entrain and cycle nutrients in surface and subsurface flow paths. The river supplies sediments, nutrients, and biota to the floodplains.

Future Conditions

We view the Flathead River system as a headwater node in the larger Columbia River ecosystem. Cultural drivers become more influential downstream, and therefore the Flathead is both a reference area for downstream restoration and a refugium for native biota.

However, the integrity of the Flathead clearly is at stake. Non-native biota are pressing in from every direction and external nutrient loading is increasing, which underscores the open nature of the ecosystem (figure 14.2). Indeed, lake trout and other long-lived fish in Flathead Lake have high burdens of mercury and polychlorinated biphenyls (PCBs), and the only significant sources of these airborne pollutants are far outside the basin.

The press of cultural disturbance is perhaps less in the Flathead basin than elsewhere, owing to the high proportion of protected lands. On the other hand, this only makes real estate valued beyond the income of traditional users, a situation that is rapidly changing local culture and economies (chapter 1). Timber and agricultural activities are phasing out, and high-technology and recreation-based industries are phasing in. It remains to be seen which footprint, extractive or recreational industry, will be larger in the ecological realm.

The dams can be operated to better mimic natural conditions. Hungry Horse Dam recently was retrofitted with a selective release system that allows a more natural temperature regime in downstream waters, whereas prior releases were winter-warm and summer-cool, with strongly negative effects on growth and production of aquatic biota (chapter 6). Release patterns for Hungry Horse and Kerr Dams based on ecological principles, rather than just the usual hydropower and flood control elements, have been devised and justified (Stanford and Hauer 1992, Marotz et al. 1996). But implementation drags and is highly influenced by other interests and economics outside the Flathead basin, such as salmon recovery efforts in the lower Columbia River basin and electricity demand and pricing.

The threats of global warming are superimposed on local and regional disturbances (chapter 4). Although glacial melt has been steady over the past 200 years, most glaciers in Glacier National Park disappeared altogether during the 1980s and 1990s, and the current climatic trend appears to be toward drier and warmer conditions (Fagre et al. 1997, 1999). This has huge implications for population dynamics and distributions of native and non-native biota. New research and modeling of fire fuels and scenarios have promoted management tactics designed to allow fires to burn more naturally in the wilderness areas and national park, but control is difficult in the populated areas of the basin (chapter 7). Moreover, smoke from wildfire and burning slash (limbs and stumps left over from logging) adds significantly to pollution of Flathead Lake and other lakes.

The logical solution is to enhance ecological literacy through effective communication of reasoned scientific research and monitoring. In this context, the numbers of grizzly bears and bull trout matter greatly. They are no longer strong interactors or keystone species, if they ever were, but they are strong indicators of ecosystem integrity.

References

Baumann, R. W., A. R. Gaufin, and R. F. Surdick. 1977. The stoneflies (Plecoptera) of the Rocky Mountains. *Memoirs of the American Entomological Society* 31:1–208.

Baxter, C. V. 1997. Geomorphology, land-use, and groundwater–surface water interaction: A multi-scale, hierarchical analysis of the distribution and abundance of bull trout (*Salvelinus confluentus*) spawning. Master's thesis, University of Montana–Missoula.

Baxter, C. V., C. A. Frissell, and F. R. Hauer. 1999. Geomorphology, logging roads, and the distribution of bull trout (*Salvelinus confluentus*) spawning in a forested river basin: Implications for management and conservation. *Transactions of the American Fisheries Society* 128:854–867.

Brunson, R. B., R. E. Pennington, and R. G. Bjorklund. 1952. On a fall collection of native trout (*Salmo clarkii*) from Flathead Lake, Montana. *Proceedings from the Montana Academy of Science* 12:63–67.

Cavallo, B. J. 1997. Floodplain habitat heterogeneity and the distribution, abundance, and behavior of fishes and amphibians in the Middle Fork Flathead River basin, Montana. Master's thesis, University of Montana–Missoula.

Donald, D. B., and D. J. Alger. 1993. Geographic distribution, species displacement, and niche overlap for lake trout and bull trout in mountain lakes. *Canadian Journal of Zoology* 71:238–247.

Ellis, B. K., and J. A. Stanford. 1982. Comparative photoheterotrophy, chemoheterotrophy, and photolithotrophy in a eutrophic reservoir and an oligotrophic lake. *Limnology and Oceanography* 27:440–454.

Ellis, B. K., J. A. Stanford, and J. V. Ward. 1998. Microbial assemblages and production in alluvial aquifers of the Flathead River, Montana, USA. *Journal of the North American Benthological Society* 17:382–402.

Elrod, M. J. 1929. The fishes of Flathead Lake. In *Montana wild life*. Helena: Montana Fish and Game Commission.

Fagre, D. B., P. L. Comanor, J. D. White, F. R. Hauer, and S. W. Running. 1997. Watershed responses to climate change at Glacier National Park. *Journal of the American Water Resources Association* 33:755–765.

Fagre, D. B., C. H. Key, J. D. White, S. W. Running, F. R. Hauer, R. E. Keane, and K. C. Ryan. 1999. Ecosystem dynamics of the northern Rocky Mountains, USA. In *Global change in the mountains*, ed. M. F. Price, T. H. Mather, and E. C. Robertson, 20–22. London: Parthenon.

Foresman, K. R. 2001. *The wild mammals of Montana*. Special Publication No. 12. Lawrence, Kans.: American Society of Mammalogists.

Hauer, F. R., J. A. Stanford, J. J. Giersch, and W. H. Lowe. 2000. Distribution and abundance patterns of macroinvertebrates in a mountain stream: An analysis along multiple environmental gradients. *Verhandlungen Internationale Vereinigung fuer Limnologie* 27:1–4.

Holton, G. D., and H. E. Johnson. 1996. *A field guide to the fishes of Montana*. Helena: Montana Fish, Wildlife, and Parks.

Ivie, M. A., L. L. Ivie, and D. L. Gustafson. 1998. *The effects of the Red Bench fire of 1988 on beetle communities in Glacier National Park, Montana, USA, 1989–1993*. National Park Service Cooperative Agreement No. CA 1268-1-9017. Bozeman: Montana State University.

Küchler, A. W. 1964. Potential natural vegetation of the conterminous United States. American Geographical Society Special Publication No. 36. New York: American Geographical Society.

Leary, R. F., F. W. Allendorf, and S. H. Forbes. 1993. Conservation genetics of bull trout in the Columbia and Klamath River drainages. *Conservation Biology* 7:856–865.

Marotz, B. L., C. Althen, B. Lonon, and D. Gustafson. 1996. *Model development to establish integrated operational rule curves for Hungry Horse and Libby Reservoirs—Montana.* Final Report DOE/BP-92452-1. Portland, Oreg.: Bonneville Power Administration.

Pregnall, M. 1991. Photosynthesis/translocation: Aquatic. In *Carbon isotope techniques,* ed. D. C. Coleman and B. Fry, 53–74. San Diego, Calif.: Academic Press.

Rieman, B. E., and J. D. McIntyre. 1996. Spatial and temporal variability in bull trout redd counts. *North American Journal of Fisheries Management* 16:132–141.

Spencer, C. N., and B. K. Ellis. 1990. Co-limitation by phosphorus and nitrogen, and effects of zooplankton mortality, on phytoplankton in Flathead Lake, Montana, U.S.A. *Verhandlungen Internationale Vereinigung fuer Limnologie* 24:206–209.

Spencer, C. N., B. R. McClelland, and J. A. Stanford. 1991. Shrimp stocking, salmon collapse, and eagle displacement: Cascading interactions in the food web of a large aquatic ecosystem. *BioScience* 41:14–21.

Stanford, J. A. 1975. Ecological studies of Plecoptera in the upper Flathead and Tobacco Rivers, Montana. Ph.D. diss., University of Utah, Salt Lake City.

Stanford, J. A., B. K. Ellis, J. A. Craft, and G. C. Poole. 1997. Water quality data and analyses to aid in the development of revised water quality targets for Flathead Lake, Montana. Open File Report 142-97. Kalispell, Mont.: Flathead Basin Commission.

Stanford, J. A., and F. R. Hauer. 1992. Mitigating the impacts of stream and lake regulation in the Flathead River catchment, Montana, USA: An ecosystem perspective. *Aquatic Conservation: Marine and Freshwater Ecosystems* 2:35–63.

Stanford, J. A., F. R. Hauer, and J. V. Ward. 1988. Serial discontinuity in a large river system. *Verhandlungen Internationale Vereinigung fur Limnologie* 23:1114–1118.

Stanford, J. A., and twelve others. In press. Biodiversity and ecosystem process controls of a large Rocky Mountain flood plain. *BioScience.*

Wetzel, R. G. 2001. *Limnology.* San Diego, Calif.: Academic Press.

CHAPTER 15

The Eastern Slopes of the Canadian Rockies: Must We Follow the American Blueprint?

David W. Schindler

▲

Since the 1960s, I have watched with dismay as development in the Rocky Mountains and foothills of Alberta, Canada, has followed the path of Colorado and Montana. Today, the Rockies and their foothills in Alberta are at the point of crisis. Unless a plan is quickly put in place to incorporate preservation of key ecosystems into development decisions, the Rockies will lose many species of wildlife. National parks will be loved to death, overrun with tourists and overdeveloped by those anxious to get their share of tourist dollars. Subdivisions of ranchettes and condominiums will fill the valleys that are the critical habitats for grizzlies and cougars. Roads and trails everywhere will leave no ecosystem inaccessible, even to the laziest of hunters and fishermen. Albertans have seen the grizzly, the wolf, the wolverine, the goat, the caribou, and the lynx wiped out in most of the Rockies south of us. Non-native species have replaced natives, and whirling disease has decimated salmonid fishes. Must we let it happen here? In this chapter, I concentrate on the eastern slopes of the Rockies, which lie largely within the province of Alberta. The western slopes, in British Columbia, are in no better shape, but they are affected by a slightly different set of problems.

The National Parks of the Canadian Rockies

The settlement of Alberta's Rockies began only in the late nineteenth century, oddly enough in what are now national parks. In 1883, the Canadian Pacific Railway reached the present site of Banff, then called "Siding 29," twenty-two years before Alberta became a province (Gadd 1995). Two years later, a federal reserve was established around the Cave and Basin Hot Springs, later expanded to become Banff National Park. The townsite was laid out in 1886, and the Banff Springs Hotel was built in 1888. The area was widely advertised in Europe and in the eastern United States and Canada as a destination for adventurers where fishing, big game hunting, mountain climbing, and beautiful scenery were within reach of civilized accommodations in luxury hotels. Banff was successful enough that similar developments were soon growing in Yoho National Park (1886), at Lake Louise in western Banff National Park (1890), and in Jasper National Park (1907), which both the Grand Trunk and Canadian National Railways reached in 1913. Kootenay National Park followed in 1920. The first roads reached Banff in 1909 and Jasper in 1951. In 1940 the Icefields Parkway, originally a single-lane dirt track constructed as a Great Depression–era employment project, was constructed between Jasper and Banff. Several provincial parks and wilderness areas were added to the cluster of national parks over the next few decades (Gadd 1995).

Human settlement in the national parks probably seemed harmless enough in the first half-century. The rest of the mountains and foothills of Alberta were roadless wilderness, so Banff, Lake Louise, and Jasper were tiny islands of civilization. But even though the number of inhabitants and visitors was relatively small, some of the early damage is still evident more than a century later.

Banff and Jasper were developed in the large montane valleys of the Bow and Athabasca Rivers, respectively. Banff could not be located in a worse place for impeding wildlife movement in the Bow River valley. At the time the communities were established, people did not realize how important these valleys were as habitat and travel corridors for large mammals because no one had seen enough of the parks to know that they otherwise consisted largely of rock and ice, which are poor wildlife habitat. The loss of habitat was probably not critical in the nineteenth century because similar habitats were plentiful in the foothills outside the parks.

Damage to fisheries was early and permanent. It was relatively easy to catch huge bull trout (*Salvelinus confluentus*). Fishermen would have their photographs taken with a stringer of fish and then discard them. Shortly after the turn of the century, complaints began about declining sport fisheries, and fish stocking began. The bull trout was considered to be an inferior species, and to replace it, popular sport fishes from eastern North America and Europe were imported by rail. Fish were dumped into the Bow River and its tributaries as well as into many lakes and streams of the mountain parks. A fish hatchery was built in Banff in 1913.

Fortunately, many of the stocked species did not survive. Unfortunately, the few that did wreaked havoc with native fishes and other aquatic species. Eastern brook trout (*Salvelinus fontinalis*) and lake trout (*S. namaycush*) eliminated native bull trout in lakes. The brook trout grows and matures faster and feeds more voraciously, displacing the bull trout from spawning habitat. "Splake" was a hybrid of brook and lake trout developed at the hatchery in Banff (Stenton 1950). Even though touted as a superfish, splake did not thrive in the wild, and today there are few remaining stocks. Only six of the original twenty-six bull trout lakes in Banff remain occupied by bull trout today, and only one contains a stock that has not been compromised by introductions from other lakes.

In the Bow River and its tributaries, brook trout occupy 100% of the reaches that were once used by bull trout. Although the latter are still present in small numbers, brook trout predominate (Schindler and Pacas 1996, Schindler 2000). Other native fish, such as westslope cutthroat trout and grayling, either have had their gene pools compromised or have been extirpated from their original range.

Even nonsport species were not safe. The Banff hot springs were popular with early tourists. But tourists found the mosquitoes bothersome, so tropical *Gambusia* (mosquito fish) were introduced to eat mosquito larvae. Later, anonymous residents disposed of unwanted tropical fish from aquariums. These introductions, together with modifications to reroute the hot springs into pools for human use, caused extinction of the Banff longnose dace (*Rhinichthys cataractae smithi*), the only native fish. The endemic hot spring snail *Physella johnsoni* was also affected by development, and today it is considered endangered (Schindler 2000).

Rainbow trout (*Oncorhynchus mykiss*) were native to the Athabasca River drainage in Jasper, in the form of a special subspecies known as Athabasca rainbow. They are believed to have invaded from the Fraser River 10,000 years ago (Nelson and Paetz 1992). They are the only native rainbows in Alberta, although many lakes now contain hatchery stocks. Athabasca rainbows were regarded as inferior to faster-growing hatchery stocks, and in many cases the latter were stocked after the Athabasca stocks were poisoned, or simply dumped in with Athabasca stocks. Today, if the Athabasca strain survives at all, it is very rare. It has not been documented in the park at all in recent years, although rainbows with unusual alleles (genetic variations) have been identified from creeks just east of the park's boundary.

Rotenone and toxaphene were used to eradicate undesirable fish before stocking with alien species. Most invertebrates were also killed by toxaphene at the time of poisoning, and many species did not return. Elevated concentrations of toxaphene persist in surface sediments of poisoned lakes even now, several decades after they were used (Miskimmin and Schindler 1995, Miskimmin et al. 1995).

Railroads and roads change the flow patterns of the major rivers in the parks. Many side channels where fish spawn have been cut off (Banff–Bow Valley Study 1996, Mayhood 1992). Other seasonally flooded meanders have been cut off, leading to changes in fisheries and vegetation (Guimond 2001).

Several hydroelectric dams were built on tributaries to the Bow River in Banff National Park under the War Measures Act. Lake Minnewanka, the largest natural lake in the park, was flooded to more than 25 meters (m), or 82 feet (ft.), beyond its natural depth, and the Spray Reservoir raised the water level in the Spray Lakes by 70 m (230 ft.), creating a reservoir 23 kilometers (km), or about 14 miles (mi.), long. The dam destroyed the bull trout fishery of the Spray Lakes and the cutthroat fishery in the river below. D. S. Rawson, a noted Canadian fisheries biologist, considered the Spray River "the finest cutthroat fishery in western Canada." He further stated, "We would be inclined to conclude that reservoirs are fundamentally poor in productivity, the fluctuating water levels are especially unfavorable for our best game trout which tend to feed in shallow water, and that fish plantings are usually ineffective as a management procedure in such bodies of water" (Rawson 1958, 36). The Spray Reservoir was stocked with *Mysis relicta* (opossum shrimp) in hopes that it might help to restore fish production. Smaller dams and diversions were put in place for water supplies and recreation. More than 40% of the flows of the Bow River and its tributaries in Banff National Park have been dammed or diverted.

The two world wars, which turned both government resources and the attentions of adventurers temporarily to other continents, probably slowed development in the Rockies in the early half of the twentieth century. But development came rapidly after World War II. Visitation to the mountain parks and cross-country car travel increased as roads and automobiles improved. Populations swelled as the baby boom hit and immigration increased. Increased mechanization of labor gave people more leisure time to spend in places such as national parks. Modern air travel made it easier for foreign tourists to visit.

Activities in the parks have been poorly regulated until recently. Hotels, shops, restaurants, conference centers, golf courses, and airfields were constructed with no question as to whether they might harm fish or wildlife. Sewage entered the rivers. Recreational activities of many sorts were allowed in national parks, becoming entrenched as "traditional," even "heritage," activities despite their documented damage to the parks' ecosystems. All this possibly could have been tolerated except that rapid and unregulated development outside park boundaries closed off remaining habitat.

The Development of Alberta's Eastern Slopes

The eastern slopes of the Rockies in Alberta are very broad in most areas (figure 15.1), extending almost 100 miles east of the Continental Divide. There were few roads prior to 1950, and small communities along the railroads existed

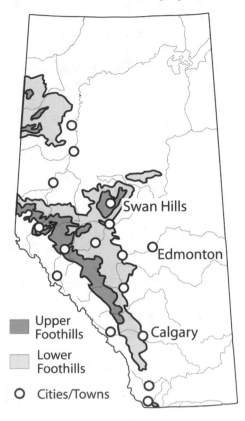

FIGURE 15.1 *Mountains of Western Alberta.* The upper and lower foothills of the Rocky Mountains are indicated by dark and light shading, respectively. Human communities are represented by circles. The uneven southwestern boundary that separates Alberta in the east from British Columbia in the west is the Continental Divide.

on small-scale farming, trapping, logging, and railway service. Dense forests and muskegs made travel difficult. Since 1971, however, a pro-development government has promoted extractive industries and subsidized roads and other infrastructure.

Early Ranching

Land could be leased or purchased very cheaply on the eastern slopes of southern Alberta in the early 1880s. Some early ranches comprised 120,000 hectares (ha), or several hundred thousand acres. By 1882, 1.6 million ha (4 million acres) had been allocated in just seventy-five leases. Many early ranch owners were European gentry, including a large number of "remittance men" exiled by British blue-blood families, with little knowledge of ranching. By 1884, two-thirds of all stocked land in Alberta was controlled by only ten companies (United Western Communications 1991). Typical large holdings extended from the eastern flank of the mountains, where chinooks provided relief from cold and protected valleys provided good winter shelter, to the prairies, where summer grazing took place.

Initially, human and livestock populations were low enough to allow native species to persist, although available habitat shrank. As populations of livestock have increased, riverbanks have eroded, and exotic weeds have spread with imported hay or seed. Native grasses have slowly been replaced by horticultural species. Water quality has declined. Today, most of the streams of southern Alberta are out of compliance with even Alberta's very liberal water quality standards (tables 15.1, 15.2; CAESA 1998). Irrigation uses most of the water along the foothills, leaving little for fish or other in-stream needs. Populations of animals that were once widely distributed in the province, such as grizzly bears, bison, wolves, black-footed ferrets, black-tailed prairie dogs, sage grouse, and bull trout, have declined to endangered levels (COSEWIC 2001).

Although a few large ranches persist today, the landscape is changing rapidly. Lack of water limits further irrigation, either for hay or for grain crops. Large and expanding cities such as Calgary and Lethbridge are exploding with suburban sprawl. Ranches near these cities are sold to developers for quick profits. High-speed highways increase the demand for summer and retirement properties in ranching country more remote from the cities, particularly near the boundaries of national parks.

Oil and Gas Exploration
The discovery of extensive oil and natural gas deposits prompted rapid development in the 1950s. Eastern slopes were quickly riddled with exploration roads and wells. Forests have been cleared for well sites, gas plants, compres-

TABLE 15.1. Percentage Noncompliance of Alberta Streams with Canadian Drinking Water Guidelines for Fecal Coliform Bacteria

	% Noncompliance	No. Samples
High-intensity agriculture	94	32
Moderate-intensity agriculture	100	25
Low-intensity agriculture	90	31

Source: CAESA 1998.

TABLE 15.2. Percentage Noncompliance of Alberta Streams with Canadian Nutrient Guidelines for Protecting Aquatic Life

	Total Nitrogen	Total Phosphorus	No. Samples[1]
High-intensity agriculture	87%	99%	214/220
Moderate-intensity agriculture	65%	88%	343/341
Low-intensity agriculture	32%	89%	163/164

Source: CAESA 1998.

[1]Number at left is total samples for which total nitrogen was reported; number at right is total samples for which total phosphorus was reported.

sor stations, airstrips, helicopter pads, pipeline rights-of-way, and access roads. This activity continues to accelerate. As of 1995, 26,906 oil and natural gas wells had been drilled in the Foothills Natural Region of Alberta, with an average density of 0.28 well per square kilometer (km^2), or 0.73 per square mile ($mi.^2$). The area cleared for well sites alone in the foothills was 377 km^2, or 145 $mi.^2$ (AEP 1996). Today, drilling and related activities occur at a rate four times higher than in the 1990s. According to statistics from the Canadian Association of Petroleum Producers, 13,543 wells were drilled in 2000 alone, and more than 55,000 have been drilled since 1996 (CAPP 2002). There are more than 150,000 km (93,000 mi.) of oil and gas pipelines. Private lands are not exempt because landowners do not own subsurface rights.

Coal Mining
Much of the foothills region of Alberta is underlain by coal. In addition to the small mines that once operated in or near the national parks, there are a number of large mines, some leaving strip scars tens of kilometers long. Although many of these were reclaimed, original aquifers were not reconstructed, and the reclaimed land is usually vegetated with non-native grasses. Coal provides more than 80% of Alberta's electrical power and is exported to other countries.

Forestry
Until the mid-twentieth century, logging was restricted to small cuts around communities. Mills were small, usually operated by a few people. The relatively small and knotty spruce and pine were regarded as far inferior to the nearly knot-free, straight Douglas-fir and lodgepole pine from British Columbia. By the 1980s, however, the fir, spruce, and pine stands of British Columbia and Ontario were approaching exhaustion, and attention turned to the smaller trees

of Alberta. By 1995, logging had occurred in 66% of the 1,297 townships in the foothills area (figure 15.2). Only 91 townships (7%) were free of both oil and gas wells and cutovers (AEP 1996).

Most cutting plans for Alberta were based on data for similar species in eastern Canada. Early clear-cuts in the foothills did not regenerate naturally, and some still show little promise of doing so. Many trees were scarcely six feet tall more than thirty years later. Most cuts are now done at lower elevations, but recoveries and rotation times needed for sustainable forestry are still in question.

Curiously, cutting plans and rotation estimates are made as if there were no other activities in the region. When timber clearing for oil and gas development, road building, community expansion, and other human activities are considered, it becomes clear that forests are disappearing at roughly double the rate assumed

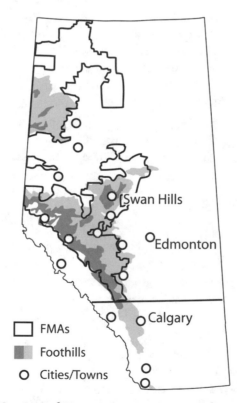

FIGURE 15.2   *Areas of Forest Management Agreements (FMAs) Allocated to Logging Companies in Alberta.* The province is bounded by a heavy line. Upper and lower foothills are indicated by dark and light shading, respectively. No data were available for FMAs south of the horizontal line. From Smith and Lee 2000.

by forest companies to be sustainable (Brad Stelfox, pers. comm.). Climate warming and its effect on fire regimes have also been ignored in managing Alberta's forests. Like the nearby boreal forests, the foothills forests consist of fire-adapted species. The area burned in forest fires each year has increased rapidly since the 1970s as the result of warmer temperatures and less precipitation.

In 1957, a pulp mill was built on the Athabasca River at Hinton, just outside the boundary of Jasper National Park. Early regulations were lax, and monitoring was almost nonexistent. For years, the Athabasca was probably anoxic under winter ice for hundreds of kilometers below the mill. Air pollution caused unpleasant odors to travel as far as the national park. Chlorine bleaching added dioxins and furans to the river. When this was "discovered" in the 1990s, health officials advised against eating fish from hundreds of kilometers of the Athabasca and Peace Rivers.

Linear Disturbances

Development creates a pattern across the foothills. Roads, transmission lines, pipeline rights-of-way, seismic lines, and connected clearings allow easy access by sport utility vehicles, all-terrain vehicles (ATVs), snowmobiles, and other motor vehicles. By the mid-1990s, only 5 of 1,297 townships in the foothills (0.4%) lacked well sites, logging, or significant (greater than 5 km, or 3 mi.) linear disturbances. All 5 townships had some linear disturbance or hiking trails. Surveys for Alberta's Special Places program (AEP 1996) showed that an average square kilometer of land in the foothills had 3.2 km (2.0 mi.) of trails or roads constructed on it. Few areas were more than a few hundred meters from such a path. It is often claimed that such paths are closed after seismic surveys or logging are complete. But this is not the case. Gates, boulders, ditches, and mounds of earth are easily navigated by modern ATVs and snowmobiles. The area's few conservation officers cannot possibly police the thousands of kilometers of trails left in the foothills by industry.

Wildlife models show that many species are affected when the density of linear disturbance exceeds 0.3 km per km^2 (0.5 mi. per mi.^{2}), an order of magnitude lower than existing densities (figure 15.3; AEP 1996). Widespread motorized access interferes with the activities of shy large mammals. Some, such as caribou, wolves, wolverines, and grizzlies with cubs, are alienated from foraging, denning, and breeding areas (Dyer et al. 2001). Wolves use human-made paths as travel arteries, which allow them to exploit woodland caribou, the most endangered mammal in the United States, according to the U.S. Fish and Wildlife Service (S. Boutin, pers. comm.).

Fish populations are not immune from development of backroad corridors. With modern ATVs and snowmobiles, it is possible to tow a boat right to the shore of

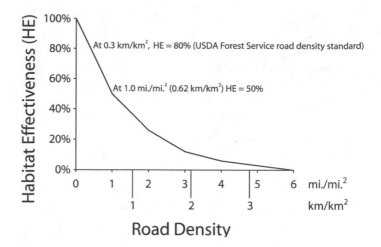

FIGURE 15.3 *Relationship between Road Density and Habitat Effectiveness for Grizzly Bears.* Models for other large, free-ranging species are very similar, showing that large portions of habitat have lost their effectiveness. The density of roads, trails, and seismic lines for the foothills of Alberta averaged 3.2 km/km² (5.1 mi./mi.²) in 1995. Data from AEP 1996.

almost any lake in the region, along with outboard motors, ice augers, sonar equipment for detecting fish and determining water depth, Global Positioning System (GPS) units, and other devices that assist in the efficient exploitation of fish.

Agriculture

Flows from mountain rivers are critical to irrigation in Alberta, which began in the 1890s. Hay and grain production increased rapidly after the Alberta Irrigation Districts Act of 1915. The Bow, St. Mary's, and Oldman Rivers have been dammed, and new dams and diversions are under consideration. The dams disrupt fish migrations. Riparian cottonwood forests die below dams as a result of reduced spring flooding (chapter 6; Rood and Heinze-Milne 1989). Withdrawals from the Bow River have caused fish kills in several years. During most years, large numbers of fish are stranded in irrigation canals, where low levels of oxygen kill them in winter. Fish rescues are organized by the Piegan First Nation and Trout Unlimited to return many of these fish to the river each year.

Large industrial livestock operations, with as many as 30,000 cattle or hogs, are replacing free-ranging cattle. Much of the feed for these operations is imported from other watersheds, along with the nutrients it contains. Waste manure is spread on nearby land, where it enriches both local land and the waters that drain it. Fecal coliform bacteria, *Giardia, Cryptosporidium,* and other pathogens are often abundant, even where human sources are few.

Agriculture is increasingly superimposed on lands that have already been developed for other purposes. The oil industry built the roads and logging companies cleared the land, and the provincial government is now attempting to double agricultural production for Alberta by 2005 by encouraging agricultural development. The Swan Hills, one of few foothills regions with fertile soils, shows several layers of development (figure 15.4).

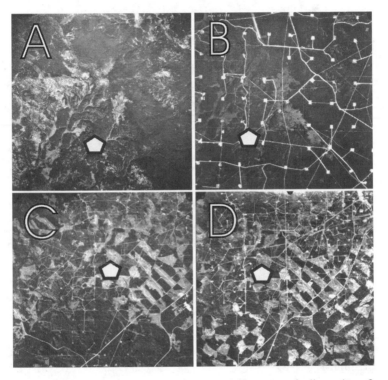

FIGURE 15.4 *Rapid Development in the Swan Hills Region of Alberta.* (See figure 15.1 for location of the Swan Hills.) The pentagon on each image represents the same point, facilitating evaluation of aerial photographs taken at different scales. (a) Photograph taken in 1949 showing the area in a pristine condition, with plentiful pine and spruce forests and wetlands. (b) Photograph taken in 1964 after oil and gas exploration, showing the locations of seismic lines, roads, and pads where oil and gas wells were drilled. (c) Photograph taken in 1981 after further oil and gas exploration as well as clear-cut logging. (d) Photograph taken in 1991 after even more development, including clearing for agriculture. From AEP 1996, 63–67; photographs compiled by Richard Thomas.

A Century of Cumulative Effects

As commercial expansion in national parks is increasingly discouraged, tourist centers are developing at the very boundaries. In the 1970s, Canmore, Alberta, was still a gritty former coal-mining town where small houses could be purchased for a few thousand dollars. This changed rapidly in the 1990s. Canmore's population has grown by 10% per year. Luxury developments and golf courses have been built for the rich. Unfortunately, much of Canmore's development interferes with the movements of wildlife populations that are already restricted by Banff farther up the Bow River. Rocky Mountain House, Nordegg, and Pincher Creek are other "gateway" communities in Alberta poised to explode with tourist development. Canmore and Valemount have become international heli-skiing centers, with many takeoffs and landings per day in peak season. Evidence is beginning to emerge that heli-skiing activity stresses mountain caribou populations.

Ranchettes are spreading to the south and west of Calgary. Once-lonely cattle ranches are being carved into lots of a few acres each. These developments are eating into the foothills territory of southern Alberta. At present, a large development is planned just outside the boundary of tiny Waterton Lakes National Park. Even industrial Hinton, where the downtown pulp mill's "bad breath" has discouraged major tourism so far, appears ready for major development. Several new motels, all part of international chains, have sprung up. These will be successful despite the bad air because accommodations in Jasper are full each summer.

Provincial Protected Areas

In the mid-1990s, the Special Places program identified, with the intent to set aside, the unique areas of all ecosystems in the province. Areas large enough to maintain natural fauna and flora were envisioned. The public was delighted. But preliminary ecological surveys revealed few areas of the province that still had large intact ecosystems. Oil and gas, logging, mining, and other business interests had already shredded much of the landscape of the foothills (figure 15.4; AEP 1996). Preservation would require the buying back of some timber and mineral rights from companies. Many candidate sites for Special Places were rejected by the Alberta government. In other cases, the sizes of nominated areas were cut at the recommendation of local committees.

The government-appointed local Special Places Committee for the Yellowhead Improvement District, where I live, was made up mostly of logging, oil and gas, coal, and other industry representatives. The sites the committee was told to evaluate were almost all tiny forested wetlands, too small and isolated to support large wildlife. As it stands today, protected areas are open to ATVs and snowmobiles as well as oil exploration. The Special Places program is very inadequate for the protection of large mammals and special ecosystems.

What Must Be Done

In less than a century, the national parks of Alberta changed from small islands of civilization in a vast wilderness to small islands of wilderness in a highly commercialized and industrialized region. But the parks themselves are too small, and internal developments too great, for them to be all that is needed to preserve sensitive far-ranging species. The Banff–Bow Valley Study (1996) identified these problems, as did a study by the Panel on the Ecological Integrity of Canada's National Parks (Parks Canada 2000). Both panels recommended improvements to Parks Canada to protect the mountain parks. So far, a few of the recommendations have been implemented, but progress is very slow.

Studies show clearly that for far-ranging animals to survive, changes in land management are also necessary *outside* the parks. Sensitive habitats and travel corridors must be kept intact or managed in ways that consider the needs of wildlife. This is the goal of the Yellowstone to Yukon (Y2Y) initiative, but much harmful development has already occurred (Rasker and Alexander 2000). Strong legislation to protect the habitat of species at risk would help, but the government of Canada has been considering such legislation since 1994, with no resolution in sight.

Look South, Albertans!
Alberta's oil sand reserves in the northeastern part of the province caused an industrial boom in the 1970s and again in the 1990s. It continues today. The province's population is growing rapidly, and Calgary is rapidly becoming the Denver of the North. Edmonton is growing at an unprecedented rate. These populations turn to the mountains and foothills for recreation. Developments are occurring in more remote areas of the foothills and mountains. Clearly, the ranchette development, air pollution, and loss of large wildlife documented elsewhere in this volume will be next, unless strong preventive measures are taken now.

It is time for Albertans to take control of their own resources. Less rapid exploitation of resources and retention of a larger share of the profits would leave something for the life support of future generations of Albertans, as well as for wildlife. "More jobs" is always the siren call that allows industry to get its way, but more jobs always lead to more immigration. This pattern is clear in the United States. Cannot Albertans learn from this experience? We are faced with more crowded highways, schools, and cities, poorer hunting and fishing, more regulated access to national parks and public lands. To me, the touted "Alberta advantage" appears to be more of the mindless, planless development that has created the Denvers and Los Angeleses of the world.

It is time to stop the quarreling between industries and environmental groups over the few remaining pieces of pristine habitat, for they are too small to support sustainable populations of large wildlife. Instead, we should be developing new plans to restore some of the habitat already compromised by clear-cutting, agriculture, mining, and oil and gas development, turning it back into usable wildlife habitat as quickly as we can.

References

AEP (Alberta Environmental Protection). 1996. *Selecting protected areas: The Foothills Natural Region of Alberta.* Edmonton: Alberta Environmental Protection, Heritage Protection and Education Branch.

Banff–Bow Valley Study. 1996. *Banff–Bow Valley: At the crossroads. Summary report of the Banff–Bow Valley Task Force,* ed. R. Page, S. Bayley, J. D. Cook, J. E. Green, and J. R. B. Ritchie. Prepared for the Honourable Sheila Copps, Minister of Canadian Heritage, Ottawa, Ontario.

CAESA (Canada-Alberta Environmentally Sustainable Agriculture) Water Quality Committee. 1998. *Agricultural impacts on water quality in Alberta: An initial assessment.* Edmonton: Alberta Agriculture, Food and Rural Development.

CAPP (Canadian Association of Petroleum Producers). 2002. Statistics regarding recent oil and gas drilling and related activities in Alberta. On-line at <http://www.capp.ca/> (click on "Industry facts and information," "Western Canada," "Alberta," and "Alberta statistics for the past five years").

COSEWIC (Committee on the Status of Endangered Wildlife in Canada). 2001. *Summary of the full list of Canadian species at risk.* Ottawa: Environment Canada, Canadian Wildlife Service, COSEWIC Secretariat. On-line at <http://www.cosewic.gc.ca/pdf/English/Full_List_Species_e.pdf>.

Dyer, S. J., J. P. O'Neill, S. M. Wasel, and S. Boutin. 2001. Avoidance of industrial development by woodland caribou. *Journal of Wildlife Management* 65:531–542.

Gadd, B. 1995. *Handbook of the Canadian Rockies.* Jasper, Alberta: Corax Press.

Guimond, J. K. 2001. Waterbird habitat use of wetland pools in the western boreal forest of Alberta, Canada. Master's thesis, University of Alberta, Edmonton.

Mayhood, D. W. 1992. *A preliminary assessment of the native fish stocks of Jasper National Park.* Prepared for Canadian Parks Service, Jasper National Park, Jasper, Alberta, by Freshwater Research Ltd., Calgary, Alberta.

Miskimmin, B. M., D. C. G. Muir, D. W. Schindler, G. A. Stern, and N. P. Grift. 1995. Chlorobornanes in sediments and fish thirty years after toxaphene treatment of lakes. *Environmental Science and Technology* 29:2490–2495.

Miskimmin, B. M., and D. W. Schindler. 1995. Fossil record of cladocerans and algal responses to fishery management practices. *Freshwater Biology* 34:177–190.

Nelson, J. S., and M. J. Paetz. 1992. *The fishes of Alberta.* Edmonton: University of Alberta Press.

Parks Canada. 2000. *Setting a new direction for Canada's national parks.* Vol. 2 of *Unimpaired for future generations? Conserving ecological integrity with Canada's national parks.* Ottawa, Ontario: Parks Canada, Panel on the Ecological Integrity of Canada's National Parks.

Rasker, R., and B. Alexander. 2000. The changing economy of Yellowstone to Yukon: Good news for wild lands? *Wild Earth* (spring): 99–103.

Rawson, D. S. 1958. Indices to lake productivity and their significance in predicting conditions in reservoirs and lakes with disturbed water levels. In *The investigation of fish–power problems,* ed. P. A. Larkin, 27–42. H. R. MacMillan Lectures in Fisheries. Vancouver: University of British Columbia.

Rood, S. B., and S. Heinze-Milne. 1989. Abrupt downstream forest decline following river damming in southern Alberta. *Canadian Journal of Botany* 67:1744–1749.

Schindler, D. W. 2000. Aquatic problems caused by human activities in Banff National Park. *Ambio* 29:401–407.

Schindler, D. W., and C. Pacas. 1996. Cumulative effects of human activity on aquatic ecosystems in the Bow Valley of Banff National Park. In *Ecological Outlooks Project: A cumulative effects assessment and futures outlook of the Banff Bow Valley,* ed. J. Green, C. Pacas, S. Bayley, and L. Cornwell, chap. 5. Prepared for the Banff–Bow Valley Study. Ottawa, Ontario: Department of Canadian Heritage.

Smith, W., and P. Lee, eds. 2000. *Canada's forests at a crossroads: An assessment in the year 2000.* Global Forest Watch Canada Report. Washington, D.C.: World Resources Institute. Online at <http://www.globalforestwatch.org>.

Stenton, J. E. 1950. Artificial hybridization of eastern brook trout and lake trout. *Canadian Fish Culturist* 6:20–22.

United Western Communications 1991. *The great West before 1900.* Vol. 1 of *Alberta in the twentieth century.* Edmonton, Alberta: United Western Communications, Ltd.

CONCLUSION

Rocky Mountain Futures:
Forecasting a Future We Do Not Want

Jill S. Baron

▲

In 1980, Jack Ives claimed insufficient understanding of the human element to incorporate it into a study of Rocky Mountain ecosystems, although he noted that a true synthesis, which he termed *geoecology,* required links between the human element (geography) and geology, climate, and ecology (Ives 1980). Now, more than 20 years later, our understanding has improved; has it taught us anything?

State of the Rockies

It is clear that the Rocky Mountains are now a profoundly *human* landscape. Our activities have penetrated the entire Rocky Mountain chain, carved up the landscape into progressively smaller fragments, and appropriated nearly all water for societal uses. Lands that are protected from continued industrial or housing development are increasingly subject to recreational overuse. Fire suppression has pushed forests and grasslands well outside their natural range of fire return frequency in most areas, inviting intense, stand-replacing fires. Native grasslands are nearly a historical anecdote, having been replaced by agricultural and municipal landscapes or supplanted by non-native species. Many wetlands have been drained, their valuable flat terrain and waters transformed for housing and agriculture. Riparian areas have been especially damaged by a triple blow of river regulation, overgrazing, and invasive species establishment. Many native plant and animal species require intensive management to persist. And superimposed on these alterations is climate change, atmospheric deposition of nitrogen and other polluting compounds, and increasing immigration.

On the other hand, there are still areas, such as the Flathead River basin, that maintain a full suite of native landscapes: grasslands, riverine corridors, montane and subalpine forests, and alpine zones necessary to permit ecological processes to operate naturally. Active restoration of other areas is allowing the return of at least some natural processes, such as spring flooding and temperature and flow variability, to river corridors.

This book has documented two kinds of human-mediated disturbance to Rocky Mountain ecosystems: direct assaults to the landscapes themselves, such as mining; and alteration of natural processes through either calculated or accidental activity. Both have brought unforeseen repercussions to ecosystems and even to human society. It is obvious now, for instance, that fire suppression is temporary; delaying a regular fire cycle only postpones the inevitable. And although we may not be able to restore abandoned mining lands, there are myriad places where processes or landscapes could be restored should we desire to take on these tasks.

Rocky Mountain Futures

Ecological forecasting is the process of predicting the future state of ecosystems and the services they provide. A forecast depends on knowledge of the current state of the ecosystem and the trajectories of influences on that system: climate, land use, human populations and their actions, technologies, and economic activity (Clark et al. 2001). Can we forecast the future for Rocky Mountain ecosystems?

Indeed, we forecast a future of continued erosion of natural processes and habitats in the Rocky Mountains if decisions continue to be made as they have in the past. The economist A. E. Kahn wrote of the "tyranny of small decisions." Add a mine here, a dam there, housing developments at the grassland-forest interface. Fail to acknowledge the consequences of the strong warming in the northern Rockies on migration corridors, water resources, and the ability of species to adapt. Put out a fire, introduce a species and extirpate another: sooner or later, the piling up of many local decisions culminates in a region transformed.

Failure to consider the broad *ecosystem* consequences of narrow management decisions, such as the decision to stock a lake with non-native fish, or actions motivated only by economic considerations, such as the placement of a condominium development on a floodplain, will give us a shell of the Rocky Mountain region that once was. Because the mountains themselves change little, we can delude ourselves into thinking that the Rocky Mountains are indeed the untouched wilderness we imagine them to be. "For most people, in most times, there has probably been little notion of history: they think that the world has always been pretty much like it is now," observed William H. Calvin, author of a wide-ranging book on evolution and natural history (Calvin 1986, 2). To the ecologically ignorant, in other words, the Rockies look just fine. They do not notice, much less understand the meaning of, the loss of riparian corridors, the missing top predator, the encroachment of non-native grasses, the artificial flow regimes. Unless we educate ourselves about the complexity of natural ecosystems and processes, our trajectory will continue toward simplification of food webs and increased catastrophic disturbances to both natural and human habitats.

A recent report by the Resource Renewal Institute (Siy, Koziol, and Rollins 2001) suggests that this is the path we are on in the Rocky Mountains. The report ranked all fifty U.S. states for their capacity to achieve sustainable development through "green" planning, by evaluating a series of criteria including how well states were governed and whether they were fiscally committed to environmental protection, with pollution prevention programs, renewable energy policies, or climate change action plans. Rocky Mountain states did not fare well in this ranking. Utah had the highest ranking, coming in nineteenth out of fifty states with a high score for its quality of governance and its environmental management framework. New Mexico and Wyoming, however, ranked forty-eighth and forty-ninth, respectively, of all fifty states in terms of overall planning for environmental sustainability. Idaho, Montana, and Colorado ranked twenty-seventh, twenty-ninth, and thirty-sixth, respectively. The only Rocky Mountain state with a pollution prevention program was Colorado, and that program was unfunded. In comparison, the states ranked in the top three—Oregon, New Jersey, and Minnesota—funded open space protection, pollution prevention, and recycling efforts; regularly published a "state of the environment" report; and had long-term land use and environmental plans. None of the Rocky Mountain states had land use plans or long-term environmental plans. It appears that environmental protection will not come from the state level in the Rocky Mountains.

But a local "tyranny of small decisions" can also work in a positive way. Small acts of restoration here and protection there can add up to a regional patchwork of natural processes amid a human landscape. There are examples of grassroots protection and restoration throughout this book, in watershed protection groups, land trusts, planning activities. A future forecast from this scenario holds promise for maintaining Rocky Mountain ecosystems.

What will it take to select this path to the future? First, communities, agencies, and organizations will have to look forward and decide what they want the Rocky Mountain landscape to look like in 50–100 years. This is a longer time perspective than Americans and Canadians are accustomed to. Do we want natural fire regimes, more dynamic river flows that benefit riparian and aquatic species? Do we want intact communities where species are regulated through natural predation and disease?

If the answers to these questions are yes, we must ask in which places natural processes are most likely to be successful and then aggressively acquire and protect these places for the specific purpose of ecosystem maintenance. In this act, we would be joining a growing worldwide movement to protect natural lands that are precious because they are hot spots of biodiversity (Pimm et al. 2001, Myers et al. 2000).

Preservation alone is not sufficient, given the many external influences on Rocky Mountain ecosystems. Inputs from atmospheric deposition, climate change, and atmospheric trace gas chemistry can all be reduced through societal actions, but we must also admit and manage for the inexorable changes they will bring. It comes back to education—not only of professional resource managers but of all who value Rocky Mountain ecosystems. Our technologically advanced and burgeoning human population has become one of the two or three dominant environmental forces on Earth (Vitousek et al. 1997). We can continue to harm global ecosystems and the very support systems on which life depends, or we can begin to adopt more sustainable practices that permit other species to persist at the same time human well-being is maintained (WCED 1988). And what better place to begin than at home—in our case, in the Rocky Mountains?

Within the Rockies, as elsewhere, we must recognize that land, water, biota, and society are parts of an interconnected whole, and manage them accordingly. Again, this will require us to define a goal for Rocky Mountain ecosystems and chart a path that will get us there. The Rocky Mountain ecosystem of today and tomorrow is a mosaic of human habitation embedded within a less inhabited natural landscape. We are faced with complicated societal decisions: where should we restore, where is development appropriate, where are natural landscapes best able to persist?

There is much we still do not know about Rocky Mountain resources—the state of rangelands, the condition of many species, whether migratory rates will be sufficient to keep up with combined climate and societal changes, how large is large enough for species ranges. Many other unknowns were discussed in the preceding chapters, as well as many unplanned experiments taking place from which we must learn and to which we must adapt our management accordingly.

There are many challenges ahead, whatever future we choose as our goal. But we know the effects of our past activities on Rocky Mountain ecosystems—let us allow them to guide our planning for the future.

Acknowledgments

This chapter benefited from discussions with Jim Ellis, Dennis Ojima, Craig D. Allen, Timothy R. Seastedt, William L. Baker, David W. Schindler, and Diana F. Tomback. The chapter title comes from Peter Gleick, "Water in Crisis: Paths to Sustainable Water Use," *Ecological Applications* 8 (1998): 571–579.

References

Calvin, W. H. 1986. *The river that flows uphill: A journey from the Big Bang to the Big Brain.* San Francisco: Sierra Club Books.

Clark, J. S., S. R. Carpenter, M. Barber, S. Collins, A. Dobson, J. A. Foley, D. M. Lodge, M. Pascual, R. Pielke Jr., W. Pizer, C. Pringle, W. V. Reid, K. A. Rose, O. Sala, W. H. Schlesinger, D. H. Wall, and D. Wear. 2001. Ecological forecasts: An emerging imperative. *Science* 293:657–659.

Ives, J. D., ed. 1980. *Geoecology of the Colorado Front Range: A study of alpine and subalpine environments.* Boulder, Colo.: Westview Press.

Myers N., R. A. Mittermeier, C. G. Mittermeier, G. A. B. da Fonseca, and J. Kent. 2000. Biodiversity hotspots for conservation priorities. *Nature* 403:853–858.

Pimm, S. L., M. Ayres, A. Balmford, G. Branch, K. Brandon, T. Brooks, R. Bustamante, R. Costanza, R. Cowling, L. M. Curran, A. Dobson, S. Farber, G. A. B. da Fonseca, C. Gascon, R. Kitching, J. McNeely, T. Lovejoy, R. A. Mittermeier, N. Myers, J. A. Patz, B. Raffle, D. Rapport, P. Raven, C. Roberts, J. P. Rodriguez, A. B. Rylands, C. Tucker, C. Safina, C. Samper, M. L. J. Stiassny, J. Supriatna, D. H. Wall, and D. Wilcove. 2001. Environment: Can we defy nature's end? *Science* 293:2207–2208.

Siy, E., L. Koziol, and D. Rollins 2001. *The state of the states: Assessing the capacity of states to achieve sustainable development through green planning.* San Francisco: Resource Renewal Institute. (Fort Mason Center, Pier One, San Francisco, CA 94123.)

Vitousek, P. M., H. A. Mooney, J. Lubchenko, and J. M. Melillo. 1997. Human domination of Earth's ecosystems. *Science* 277:494–499.

WCED (World Commission on Environment and Development). 1988. *Our common future.* New York: Oxford University Press.

About the Authors

▲

CRAIG D. ALLEN is an ecologist with the U.S. Geological Survey, Bandelier National Monument, with broad interests in landscape ecology, land use change, and the fire ecology of northern New Mexico.

WILLIAM L. BAKER is a professor in the Department of Geography and Recreation at the University of Wyoming in Laramie, specializing in the ecology of southern Rocky Mountain landscapes.

JILL S. BARON is an ecosystem ecologist with the U.S. Geological Survey, Natural Resource Ecology Laboratory, Colorado State University.

WILLIAM D. BOWMAN is director of the Mountain Research Station and a professor in the Department of Environmental, Population, and Organismic Biology, University of Colorado at Boulder.

DAVID R. BUTLER is a geomorphologist at Southwest Texas State University with secondary training in biogeography. He has conducted field research for more than twenty-five years in Glacier National Park, Montana.

DAVID M. CAIRNS is a biogeographer in the Department of Geography at Texas A&M University. He is interested in vegetation response to geomorphology.

THOMAS N. CHASE is affiliated with the Cooperative Institute for Research in Environmental Sciences and the Department of Geography at the University of Colorado at Boulder, where he researches the interactions between climate and land cover change.

BONNIE K. ELLIS is a microbial ecologist at the University of Montana's Flathead Lake Biological Station. She is interested in understanding the physical, biological, and chemical factors that control production in Flathead Lake.

DANIEL B. FAGRE is an ecologist with the U.S. Geological Survey's Northern Rocky Mountain Science Center in Glacier National Park, Montana. He conducts research to understand the effects of global-scale environmental change on mountain ecosystems of the northern Rockies.

BRAD HAWKES has been a fire research officer for the Canadian Forest Service at the Pacific Forestry Centre, Victoria, British Columbia, since 1980.

N. THOMPSON HOBBS is a senior research scientist at the Natural Resource Ecology Laboratory at Colorado State University. He studies the ecology of large herbivores in natural and human-dominated systems.

LINDA A. JOYCE is research project leader for the research project Sustaining Alpine and Forest Ecosystems under Atmospheric and Terrestrial Disturbances, conducted at the USDA Forest Service's Rocky Mountain Research Station, Fort Collins, Colorado.

ROBERT E. KEANE is a research ecologist with the USDA Forest Service's Rocky Mountain Research Station, Fire Sciences Laboratory, Missoula, Montana.

KATHERINE C. KENDALL studies the ecology and population trends of forest carnivore populations as a research ecologist with the U.S. Geological Survey's Northern Rocky Mountain Science Center in Glacier National Park, Montana.

CARL H. KEY is a geographer with the U.S. Geological Survey's Northern Rocky Mountain Science Center in Glacier National Park, Montana. He works on problems ranging from fire ecology to climatic influences on glaciers.

TIMOTHY G. F. KITTEL studies the nature of climate variability and how it influences the structure and function of ecosystems as a scientist with the National Center for Atmospheric Research, Climate and Global Dynamics Division, Terrestrial Sciences Section, Boulder, Colorado, and with the Natural Resource Ecology Laboratory, Colorado State University.

JESSE A. LOGAN is a research entomologist with the Rocky Mountain Research Station in Logan, Utah, with interests in the ecological role of insect disturbances in Rocky Mountain conifer forests.

GEORGE P. MALANSON is a landscape ecologist and modeler at the Department of Geography, University of Iowa, with research interests in mountain geography.

DAVID M. PEPIN is a graduate student in stream ecology at Colorado State University. He studies regulated river ecosystems in the Rocky Mountains.

N. LEROY POFF is an aquatic ecologist and associate professor in the Department of Biology at Colorado State University.

MEL A. REASONER is a science officer with the International Geosphere-Biosphere Programme (IGBP) Mountain Research Initiative in Bern, Switzerland; his research interests focus on paleoenvironmental reconstructions of high-elevation sites in the Rocky Mountains.

J. ANDY ROYLE is a statistician with the U.S. Fish and Wildlife Service with interests in the application of spatial statistical methods to problems in biology, ecology, and natural resources.

HEATHER M. RUETH is a terrestrial ecosystem ecologist at the Ecosystem Center of the Marine Biological Laboratory, Woods Hole, Massachusetts. She is interested in the effects of human activity on ecosystem processes.

KEVIN C. RYAN is project leader for fire effects at the USDA Forest Service Fire Sciences Laboratory in Missoula, Montana.

DAVID W. SCHINDLER is Killam Memorial Professor of Ecology at the University of Alberta, Edmonton. He is the recipient of the 2001 Gerhard Herzberg Canada Gold Medal for Science and Engineering.

TIMOTHY R. SEASTEDT is an ecologist with the University of Colorado at Boulder and director of the Niwot Ridge Long-Term Ecological Research program. He is interested in the role of biotic systems in global change issues and their response to global change.

JACK A. STANFORD is Jesse M. Bierman Professor of Ecology and director of the Flathead Lake Biological Station, University of Montana–Polson.

THOMAS J. STOHLGREN is a research ecologist for the Fort Collins Science Center, U.S. Geological Survey, Fort Collins, Colorado. He specializes in landscape ecology, invasive species, and issues of scaling and spatial modeling.

DAVID M. THEOBALD is a research scientist at the Natural Resource Ecology Laboratory and is assistant professor in the Department of Natural Resource Recreation and Tourism at Colorado State University, where he studies the effects of land use change on biodiversity.

PETER E. THORNTON studies interactions between terrestrial biogeochemical cycles and global climate at the Climate and Global Dynamics Division of the National Center for Atmospheric Research, Boulder, Colorado.

DIANA F. TOMBACK is an ecologist and professor in the Department of Biology, University of Colorado at Denver.

WILLIAM R. TRAVIS teaches environmental geography at the University of Colorado at Boulder and studies land use change in the American West.

THOMAS T. VEBLEN, a professor of geography at the University of Colorado at Boulder, teaches and conducts research in forest dynamics, disturbance ecology, and tree-ring applications to forest ecology.

CATHY WHITLOCK is a professor of geography at the University of Oregon with research interests in the late Quaternary climate, vegetation, and fire history of the western United States.

Index

▲

311